MW01620324

# Enriching the V&A

*A Collection of Collections (1862–1914)*

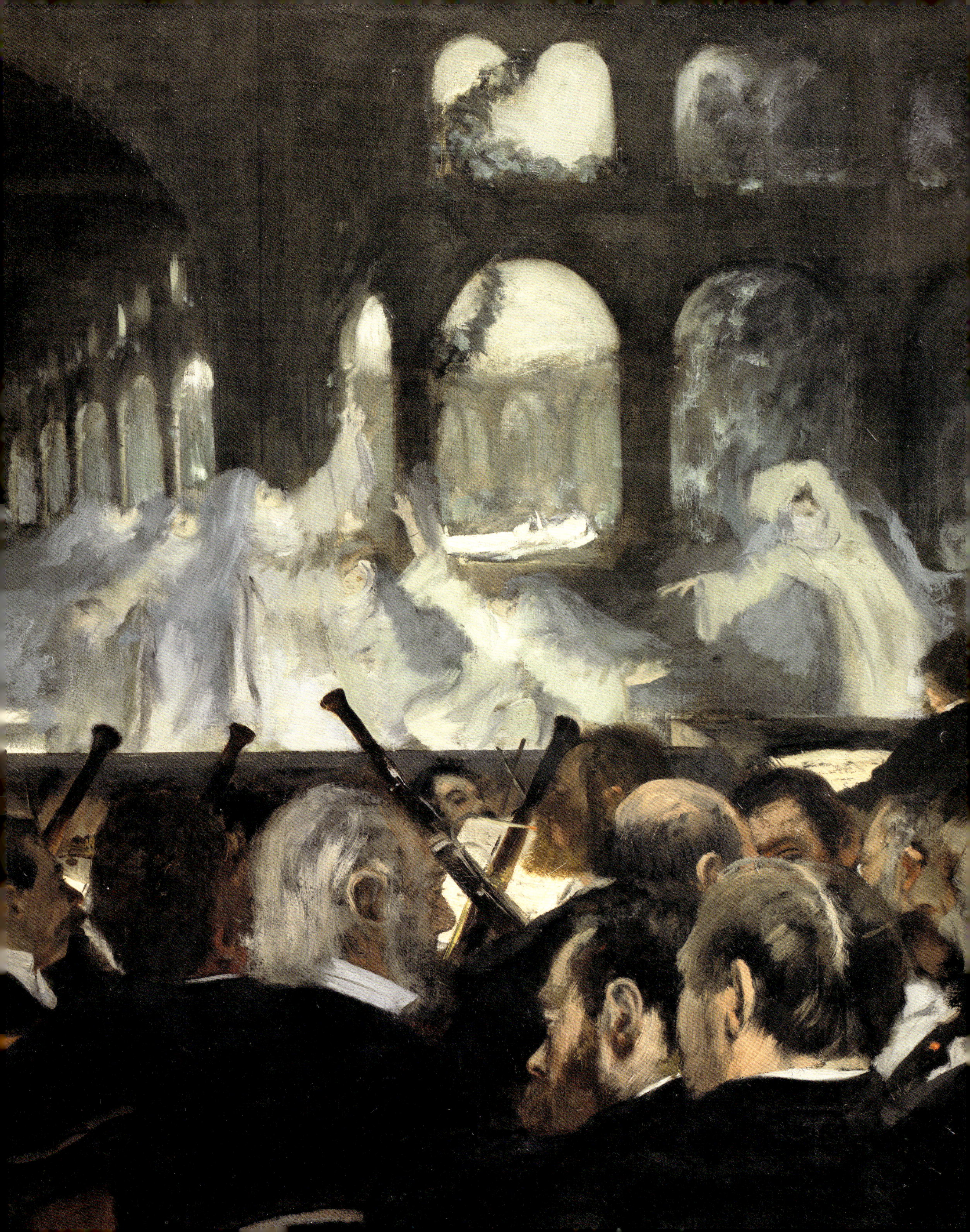

# Enriching the V&A

*A Collection of Collections (1862–1914)*

Julius Bryant

**LUND HUMPHRIES** in association with **V&A PUBLISHING**

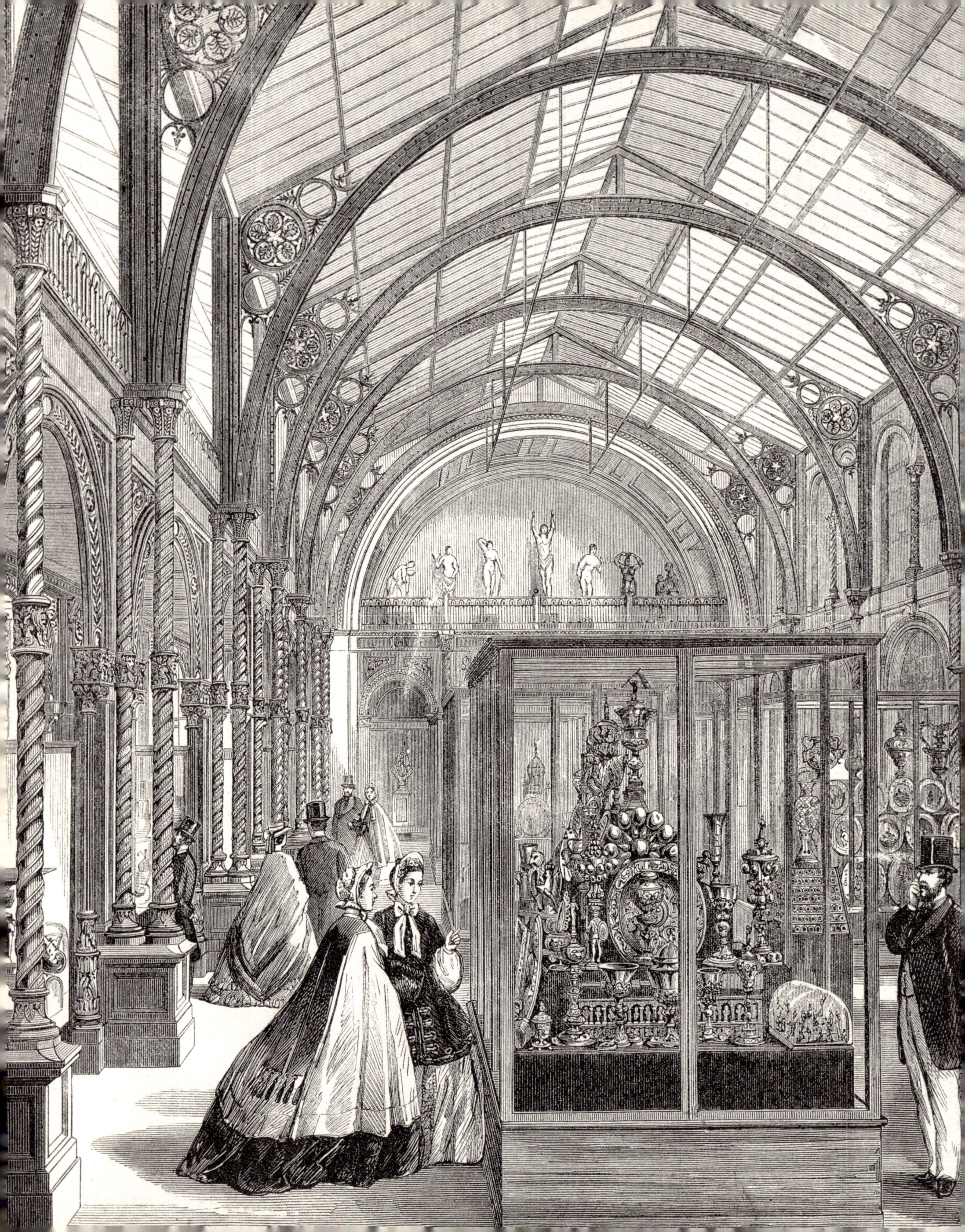

# Contents



FRONTISPIECE: (and fig.104). EDGAR DEGAS, *The Ballet Scene from Meyerbeer's Opera 'Robert le Diable'*, 1876, signed, oil on canvas (detail). Bequeathed by Constantine Alexander Ionides. V&A: CAI.19.

1. ANON., 'The Loan Collection of works of art at South Kensington Museum', *The Illustrated London News*, 6 December 1862, p.613 (detail of fig.6). V&A: National Art Library.

# Foreword

THIS VOLUME IN THE *V&A Nineteenth-Century* series focuses on collectors, as lenders, scholars and donors, whose contributions to the direction and identity of the museum cannot be overestimated. In the museum's early decades, spanned by this study (1862–1914), a tradition evolved of showing loan collections in anticipation of them turning into gifts – a risky practice that could lead to surprise withdrawals. These influential collectors are not as celebrated today as they once were, but in many ways their personalities are still present through their donations. Many remarkable characters await the reader, each with their own tastes and ambitions for art, design and the museum.

Some of the collectors may seem best forgotten, especially those whose actions we rightly deplore today (not least the widespread practice of military looting during periods of imperial aggression). But all the sources from which objects came to the museum need to be understood better and shared if the full life and associative meanings of objects are to be recognised, and if plans are to be made for more appropriate places of safekeeping. The V&A is an active participant in the current debates around the meaning and purpose of decolonisation within cultural institutions, in provenance research and in finding both ethical and workable solutions to restitution claims. Beyond the museum itself, this book is of wider interest as it is also about collecting as a human impulse that everyone shares in so many different ways, one that has been associated with a variety of social values. As such it provides a chance to try to understand the British people's compulsion to collect.

Since 1914, when this study closes, the V&A's focus has moved from collectors' collections in favour of designers, patrons and consumers, as the V&A has reembraced its founding mission to be a resource for creativity and consumption. Despite this strategic change, the museum continues to welcome offers to donate collections, especially through the government's Acceptance in Lieu and Cultural Gifts schemes, and through charitable bodies such as the Art Fund and directly from owners and their heirs. Indeed, in recent years several splendid collections have arrived, as gifts or long-term loans, such as the Rosalinde and Arthur Gilbert Collection, the Royal Photographic Society's collection, the pioneering graphics of The Computer Art Society and the collection of The Wedgwood Museum. The V&A's collections were built through loans and through donations and we will always be grateful to collectors, as lenders and as donors, for their continuing generosity.

**TRISTRAM HUNT, DIRECTOR, V&A**

**2.** HONORÉ DAUMIER, *The Print Collectors*, *c.*1860–64, watercolour. Bequeathed by Constantine Alexander Ionides. V&A: CAI.118.

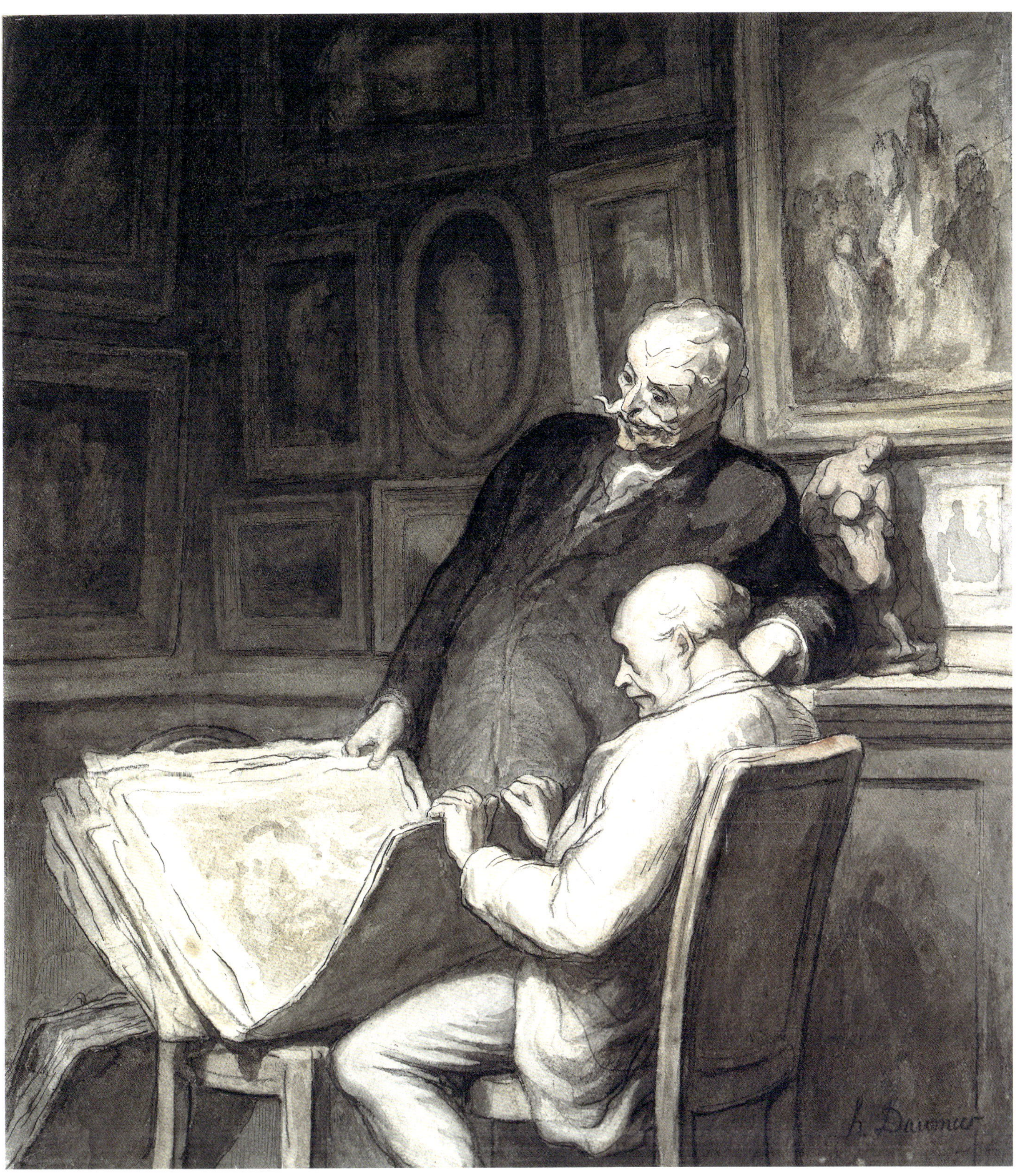
h. Daumier

# Part I: A Museum for Collectors?

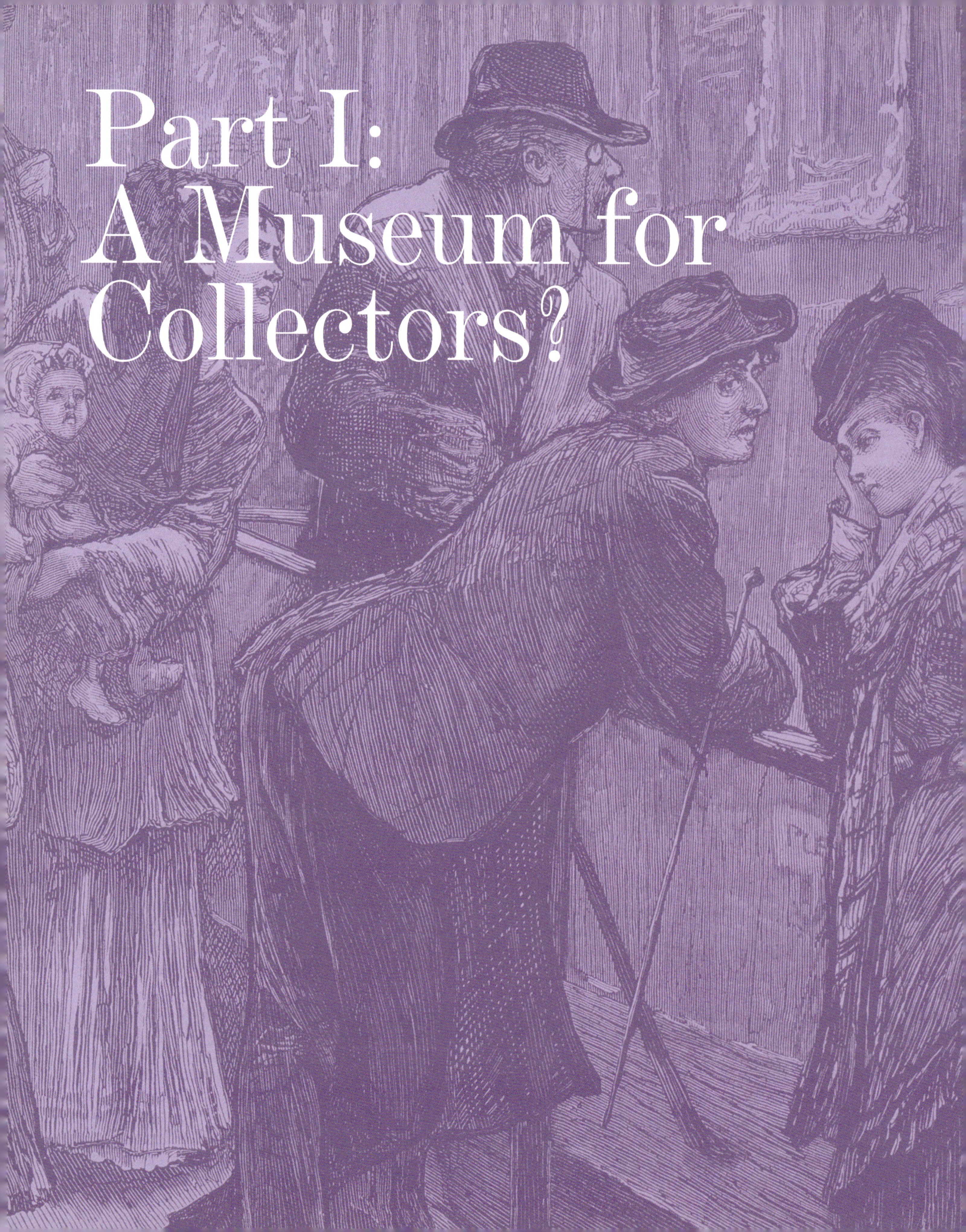

MUSEUMS ARE ABOUT objects and people, about observation and ideas, about finding inspiration and new resources for creativity by looking at things, slowly. The V&A's collections embody thousands of years of human ingenuity and imagination. They have stories to tell about their artists, designers, makers, original owners and first users. Objects also have multiple afterlives and carry evidence and associations about their influence, on later admirers, owners and collectors, and of their changing meanings, especially when private objects become subjects of public displays. These introductory chapters explain how the V&A, while established as a resource to support design reform, soon found a parallel role in society as it flourished into a museum that was also about collecting and collectors. These two agendas seemed to compete at times, causing controversy, but both grew from public concern about the need to raise standards of visual education in Britain, among designers, makers, retailers and consumers. Concern for 'the nation's taste' united this mid-Victorian commitment to refining the art of seeing with a new cult of collecting for the home.

The V&A grew from the teaching collections of the Government School of Design and was founded as an educational museum in 1852 as a direct legacy of the first world's fair, London's Great Exhibition, held in the Crystal Palace in 1851. Initially known as the Museum of Ornamental Manufactures, in 1857 it became part of the new South Kensington Museum, which Queen Victoria renamed in 1899 as the Victoria and Albert Museum. The Victorian and Edwardian museum evolved to address changing priorities. Today, the museum's ambitions for public education through collections are just as relevant, for the V&A champions art, design and creativity in all its forms, for everyone.

# 1 Introduction: A Nation of Collectors

Napoleon Bonaparte thought he could dismiss the British as a mere 'nation of shopkeepers'.[1] But in the wake of wars and revolutions that tore up 19th-century Europe, dispersing historic collections further afield, those voracious traders from across the Channel came to be recognised as something more, as a nation of collectors. Generations earlier, British buying power had been confined to the wealthy elite, seeking souvenirs of their Grand Tours to Rome and beyond. To the Victorians collecting became available to all, from aristocrats to artisans, from masterpieces to manufactured goods, from ancestral palaces to humble homes.

Today, we are all collectors. The instinct is evident from childhood: from when we try to save our most special toys, then move on to pictures of our chosen heroes among sports players and musicians, to 'selfie' snaps taken with celebrities, and to books by favourite authors. Through the years the silent build-up of photographs of friends and family, of useless old clothes that stir sentimental memories, and silly mementoes of great holidays all amount to private collections.

We collect as a way to define ourselves, to find our space and consolidate friendships. In adult life most of us are too busy, or lack the financial means, to continue pursuing this strange compulsion to collect, for which there are many explanations. According to the French sociologist Jean Baudrillard, 'collecting may be seen as a powerful mechanism of compensation during critical phases in a person's sexual development. Invariably it runs counter to active genital sexuality.'[2] One obvious reason for the formation of art collections is social ambition, as the possession of rare objects can give the impression of good taste, erudition and wealth. Historical objects can also carry associations, as souvenirs of places and of previous owners we admire. Whatever their sources and special qualities, objects somehow reflect who we think we are and may still want to become. From weeding our bottom drawers up to reshuffling a mantlepiece display, we are all curators, organising our hidden hoards to provide some sense of order and control in our tiny corners of an irrational universe.

Among the reasons for visiting the V&A, some people come to inform their own collections, perhaps encouraged by recent discoveries by antiques experts and art sleuths in the popular media. Many of the V&A's collections, such as watercolours, photographs, silver and ceramics, are by artists and makers whose works are still available and affordable in the open market, unlike the unique Old Masters in the National Gallery or the priceless antiquities in the British Museum. One does not need to be an active collector to feel at home in the V&A. Everyone who enters also collects in a virtual sense, in the process of choosing which galleries to visit, which objects to study, sketch or photograph to share with friends and to remember to visit next time. Collecting is not only about owning things, but also a way of seeing and understanding the world and ourselves, by selecting what feels, somehow, most relevant to each of us.

The V&A has always sought to reconcile a double identity through its dual roles. This direct legacy of the first world's fair, London's Great Exhibition of the Works of Industry of All Nations,

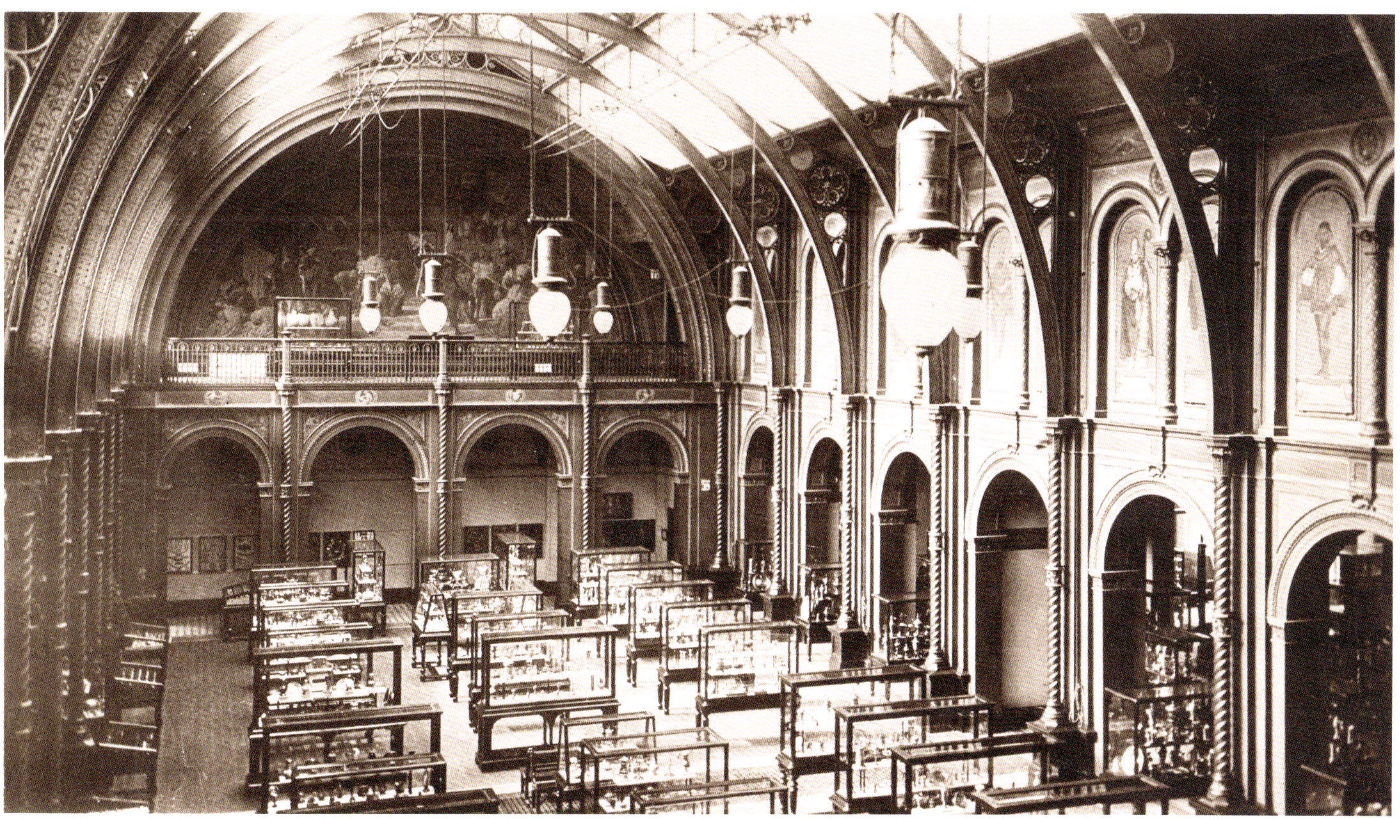

3. KINGSWAY REAL PHOTO SERIES, 'South Court, Eastern Division, Victoria & Albert Museum, South Kensington Museum', *c.*1913, postcard. The caption describes 'the Parliament Hill Treasure, French work of the seventeenth century, dug up in Parliament Hill Fields'. Collection: the author.

began as a government-funded resource for commercial design reform, through showcasing manufacturers and supporting the training of artists and artisans. Despite this reforming zeal, in tune with the industrial and imperial ambitions of Victorian Britain, almost immediately the museum became, as well, a public treasury for beautiful things, to be enjoyed by all classes at their leisure. From its immediate success at reaching out to the general public as well as to designers, the museum attracted a community of collectors. Traditional accounts describe how the Victorian V&A wrestled to reach multiple goals: Prince Albert's intellectual vision to reconcile art and science through education; the utilitarian ambitions of the first director, Henry Cole (1808–1882); the connoisseurship of the curator, John Charles Robinson (1824–1913); the Arts and Crafts social values of the leading critic, John Ruskin; and several more, including the cultivation of collectors. The claims of these agendas and audiences are still with us and continue as a source of the V&A's vitality and ambition.

One reason for the variety of the V&A's holdings is that much of the museum is a collection of collections. Many of these collections began as long-term loans. The museum had first opened in 1852 at Marlborough House (the largest royal loan) opposite St James's Palace. Among the loans and donations from collectors in 1852 were Sèvres porcelain from Queen Victoria, European and Chinese ceramics from Herbert Minton's collection and, from 1856, the Soulages Collection of Renaissance maiolica, on loan pending purchase.[3] For the decorative arts, in which scholarship was still in its infancy, borrowing collections with the prospect of purchase reduced the risk of making mistakes. Borrowing also encouraged a growing group of knowledgeable supporters and could result in donations. Leading dealers such as John Webb were paid, in effect, a rental fee to lend the museum its future purchases, and were happy to show their wares to society even if the deals fell through. Queen Victoria had set an example through making loans and gifts to help launch the museum in 1852.[4] Later lenders ranged from influential aristocrats such as the 5th

Earl Spencer and politicians such as William Ewart Gladstone, to many private collectors who wished to share their discoveries and to those whose homes had simply run out of room.

The variety of lenders and donors reflects the museum's origins and popularity in the age of democratic reform, together with its exceptional working relationship with the monarch, collectors and the antiques trade. By 1879 the museum owned 30,441 objects and had 18,866 more on loan, from 437 lenders, which accounted for about one third of the entire number on display.[5] The sheer amount of loans on view in this period reveals not only the museum's success at cultivating supporters but also a vulnerable dependency, one that grew due to uncertain policies and resources for developing the museum's own collections and staff.

By the mid-20th century several venerable old displays dedicated to single donors' collections had grown less attractive and were gradually dismantled, to be replaced by galleries in which objects could be seen more clearly, reflecting fresh thinking and interpretations for new kinds of visitors. Some donor-collections spanning different materials were shared between curatorial departments, to reappear in a variety of galleries or go into store. The historic collections were redisplayed to emphasise their cultural origins, uses and meanings, together with their materials and techniques. As the V&A re-embraced its founding mission, to inspire and celebrate creativity in art and design, emphasis moved to the best of the contemporary.

Over time an audience of new visitors began to ask of the historical collections: 'Whose stuff was it anyway, and how did it all get here?' This book offers some answers, by exploring the museum's collecting policies and practice between the death of Prince Albert (14 December 1861) and the outbreak of the First World War (August 1914). Through a series of case studies and character sketches, in chronological thematic sections, the V&A's leading Victorian and Edwardian benefactors are reintroduced. By asking what motivated these collector-donors we will see how they influenced the changing aims and identity of the museum in its formative decades. This is a story of collectors who decided to share their enthusiasms, expertise and weaknesses with posterity, rather than send rare objects back into the open art market for dispersal. The contribution of collectors, as expert advisers, lenders and donors, has been vital to the growth of the V&A's collections, and continues today.

No study of collectors and donors can overlook the collections that came through imperial expeditions. As well as collectors and dealers, governments deposited in the museum politically sensitive artefacts acquired through military action in India, Africa and China. To some communities, examples of their heritage in the V&A can be admired as cultural ambassadors, as artefacts in exile, saved from an unstable foreign land no longer under their control. To others, their presence is more challenging, as booty whose restitution to their places of origin is long overdue. Many imperial collectors were looting soldiers, civilian thieves and smugglers, but not all. For most of the second half of the 19th century the museum relied on outside experts as local agents abroad, such as private collectors, dealers, teachers, diplomats, businessmen, artists and writers, in preference to developing and sending in its own curatorial teams. Some of these collectors were pioneers in their fields, advancing scholarship in areas that had yet to attract academic research; some wrote the first published catalogues of the collections they formed and brought to the museum. The process of decolonising the museum (as the complex challenge is now known) requires much more research and understanding of objects' forgotten histories, about people and provenance, no matter how ugly their stories may turn out to be. This book offers a narrative survey, not a comprehensive account. But in reintroducing the formative collectors this study provides references to recent literature and archival sources to facilitate further reading and research. A concise directory of collectors, with the primary research resources for each, is available and expanding on the V&A's website. By placing a selection of private collectors back at the heart of the museum's story we can recognise their quiet influence on what we can actually see today, and some of the issues that raises.

# 2 A Museum of Collections

The Great Exhibition of 1851 presented contemporary consumer products, raw materials, machines and fine art. Nothing was for sale during the show but, in an environment that anticipated the creation of department stores, the first world's fair aroused the general public's appetite for shopping. Carefully arranged displays encouraged critical viewing and, in effect, popular connoisseurship. But it also revealed the poor state of British design and taste, to rectify which the founding of a new 'Museum of Ornamental Manufactures' was one answer. The new museum had its foundations in the teaching collections of the Government School of Design, established in 1837. The partnership between this art school and the museum would grow into a country-wide network of art education whose legacy is the 'Creative Britain' of today. The Great Exhibition presented further lessons. It demonstrated a way to capture, structure and so understand the expanding world through gathering on loan, installing and interpreting objects that could be owned. It presented a new vision of the whole world at peace, united through unrestricted commerce. In an age of revolutions it also revealed how vast crowds could behave, sharing in a polite culture of exhibition viewing and fantasy collecting, secure within a Crystal Palace.

The new museum attracted not only designers and consumers of modern manufactured goods but also collectors, dealers and donors. It did this by showing collections. Queen Victoria's example as a lender was followed by aristocrats and by newly wealthy middle-class collectors. They had witnessed the fate of the former aristocratic collections of France, dispersed through revolution and still floating through the London art market. Ten years after its foundation, in 1862 the museum embraced this other audience and ambition with a vast exhibition of private loans. The 'Special Loan Exhibition', also known as *The Art Wealth of England*, celebrated this nation of collectors (as discussed in chapter 4).

From the 1870s, rival buying power for masterpieces for public collections came from new museums in Europe, founded in emulation of Britain's example, such as Vienna's Museum für Kunst und Industrie (1863), Hamburg's Museum für Kunst und Gewerbe (1866) and Berlin's Kunstgewerbemuseum (1867). In the USA the first museums founded on the South Kensington model include the Metropolitan Museum of Art, New York (first building inaugurated 1880) and the Cincinnati Art Museum (opened 1881).[1] Without Prince Albert to champion its resourcing by government, after he died in December 1861, London's young museum grew to rely on private collectors as lenders and donors.[2] The V&A was not based on a historic royal collection, unlike in Vienna (Belvedere, Picture Gallery inaugurated 1781), Paris (Louvre, 1793), Madrid (Prado, 1819), Munich (Glyptothek, 1830) and Berlin (Altes Museum, 1830). Instead, new collectors (including Queen Victoria) were key to its survival in its vulnerable early decades. Some long loans led to donations in dedicated galleries named after the collectors but many more came and went. However, it soon became clear that many loan displays had little direct relevance to the museum's founding mission, the reform of British art and design.

Another reason for the early reliance on loans and donated collections was the museum's success at expanding its premises, while lacking the resources to fill these new galleries with new purchases. Moving from Marlborough House in 1856–7 to the present location, the Museum of Ornamental Art (as it was renamed) became part of the South Kensington Museum (renamed the Victoria and Albert Museum in 1899). Five years later, in 1862, the museum opened its new North and South Courts as display spaces for loans. Visitors soon found two more major new extensions: the Architectural ('Cast') Courts opened in 1873 and the two-storey National Art Library range was constructed 1879–83, despite the Great Depression in the British economy (1873–96).[3] On the opposite side of Exhibition Road (the backbone of London's new cultural quarter, 'Albertopolis') the museum moved into the former restaurant building from the 1862 International Exhibition, into the Arcades that lined the gardens of the Royal Horticultural Society, and into the Western Galleries, which had been created for a short-lived series of international exhibitions (1871–4).

These new museum galleries soon attracted offers of displays of collections from lenders, who were clearly in need of some free storage space. For example, in 1869 Austen Henry Layard (best known as the excavator of the palaces of the Assyrian kings at Nimrud and Nineveh) placed on loan 'the whole of his valuable collection' of Italian and other paintings, maiolica and glass.[4] The same year he married Enid Guest, the daughter of his cousin Lady Charlotte Schreiber (see chapter 9), and was appointed British Minister in Madrid. The museum returned his loans in 1871. In 1876 when the National Gallery recalled its long-term loan of British paintings, the emptied rooms were swiftly filled with the 5th Earl Spencer's 'family portraits, Dutch masters and copies of well-known Italian masterpieces', as the 'heterogeneous assemblage' was summed up by the *Architect*.[5] Lord Spencer started remodelling his family seat, Althorp, that year. Henry Cole had retired in 1873 and the museum's new director would have welcomed Spencer's support. In 1874 Spencer had been elected chairman of the Royal Commission for the Exhibition of 1851; in 1880 he was appointed Lord President of the Council, the cabinet member responsible for the education system, and hence for overseeing the Department of Science and Art and its museums.

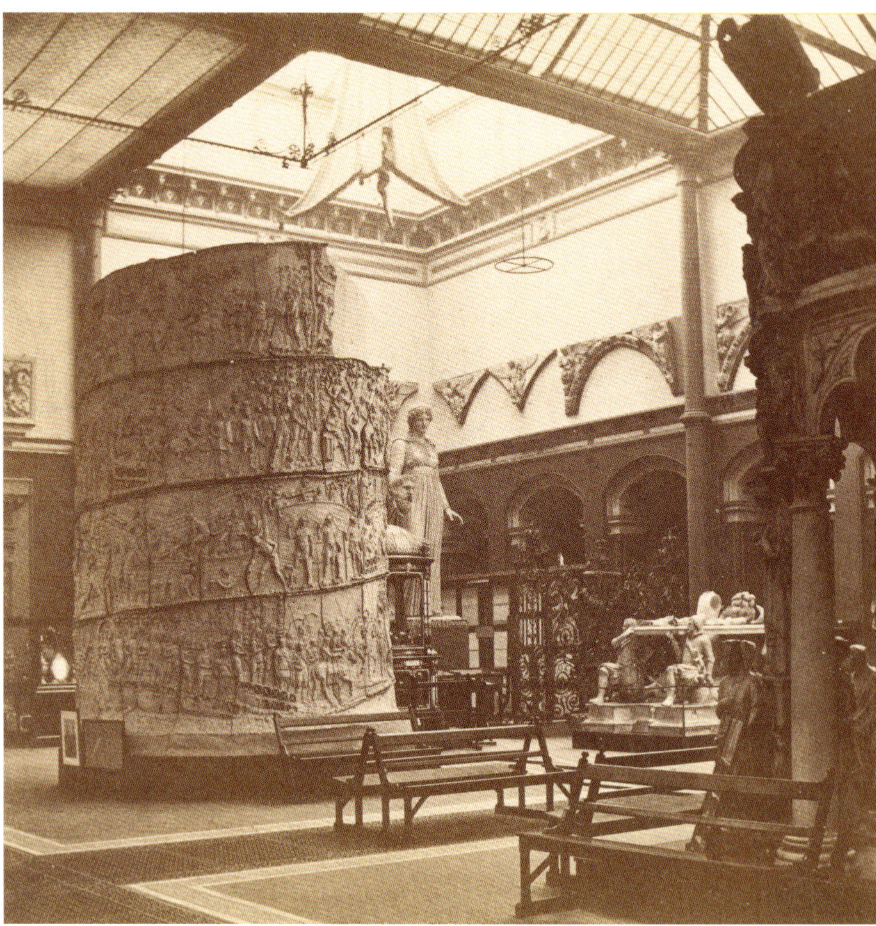

4. J. Davis Burton, 'South Kensington Museum, North Court, showing casts', 1868, No.6 in the *London Series* from a pair of stereoscopic albumen prints. V&A: 60742.

The variety of long-term loan displays did not stop at European art and the decorative arts. In 1877 the archaeologist Heinrich Schliemann placed on loan 4,420 finds that he had excavated at Hisarlik in Turkey, where he had rediscovered the ancient city of Troy. The British Museum had declined to purchase 'The Troy Collection' or to give it a temporary exhibition. The collection proved so popular that it remained on display in South Kensington, filling 25 showcases in the South Court, complete with supporting photographs and drawings, until 1880 when Schliemann was asked to take it all away.[6] In the same years the South Kensington Museum also showed an anthropology collection on long loan in the South Court, from 1878 until 1882. In 1882 an American journalist published his account of it following a personal tour by the lender, Augustus Henry Lane Fox (known by then as Pitt Rivers; see chapter 13), of his 'great collection – perhaps the most important private collection of objects illustrative of anthropology in the world'. However, his next paragraph summarised a recent change in policy over accepting long-term loans: 'Various public men sent their treasures to the museum in its earliest days, when they were more needed than now; but it has been found necessary to select fastidiously from the too numerous articles offered every year as loans . . . Some collections, originally received as loans, it is pretty certain will never be removed.'[7] In 1883 the journal *Truth* carped: 'The Museum is always ready to open its arms to the collections of aristocratic owners who may be in search for *[sic]* a safe and inexpensive resting-place for their treasures, whatever may be the quality of such collections.'[8]

Before moving to South Kensington, the anthropological collection had already been on loan for five years at the Bethnal Green Branch Museum, where the great art collection of Sir Richard Wallace was shown between 1872 and 1875 (see chapter 13). The opening of this new branch museum in 1872 would provide opportunities to make space in South Kensington. The removal from South Kensington to Bethnal Green in 1880 of the 'modern examples of Art manufacture'[9] could be explained as benefitting local craftsmen but it also confirmed to many a change in the parent museum's priorities, from designers, makers and retailers to collectors.

By the end of the 19th century the number of galleries devoted to loans, to purchases and to donated collections gave the impression that the V&A had become a museum primarily about collecting, a role that seemed to some so far from its founding mission – to support design reform – as to prompt controversy. To its critics the museum's acceptance of bulk loans and donations was simply a strategy to woo the wealthy and attract more private collectors. But a more serious agenda had emerged. This was not simply a sign of the triumph of the earnest antiquarians over the fashionable reformers of contemporary design. There were other reasons to give collections and their collectors greater prominence in the museum.

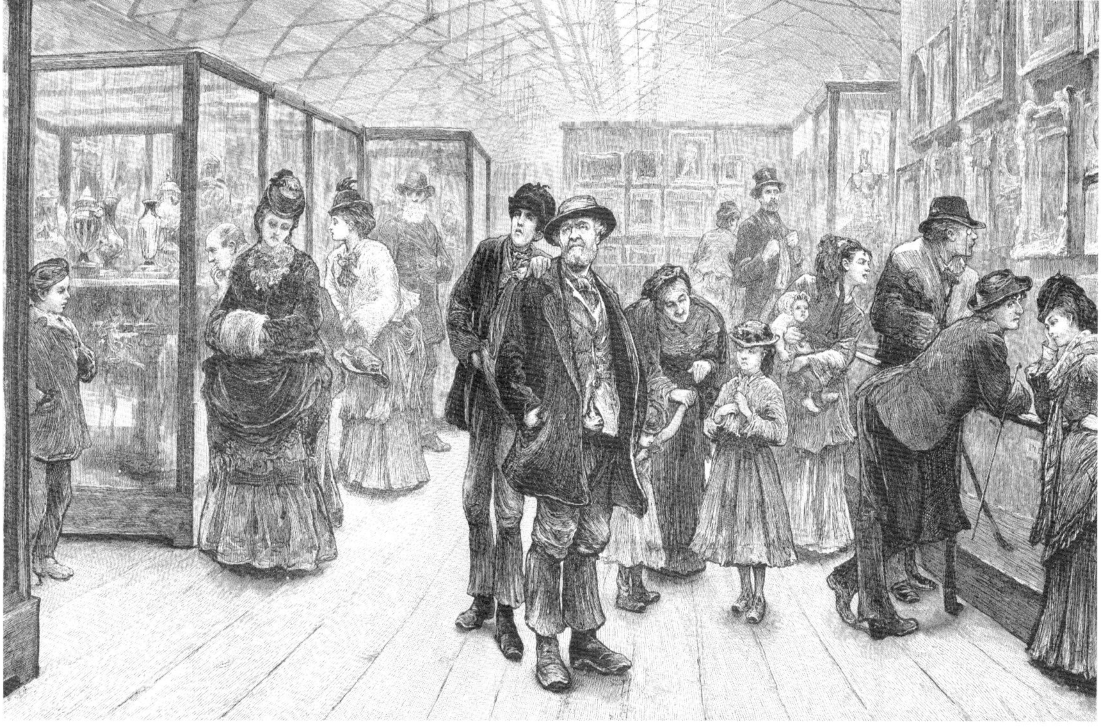

**5.** Anon., 'Art connoisseurs at the East End: A study at Sir Richard Wallace's Loan Collection in the Bethnal Green Museum', *The Graphic*, vol.7, no.177, 19 April 1873. V&A: National Art Library.

# 3 An Englishman's Home is his Art Museum

In Victorian Britain the general public collected like never before. The Victorians discussed collecting as one key to social stability and looked to museums to set an example to all homeowners, no matter how humble. Queen Victoria had presented herself to the British public as a collector and lender to the museum and as a homemaker. For those who could not afford to buy antiques, the new museum culture of collecting was one that could be taken home, for the museum sold reproductions in the form of photographs and electrotypes of metalwork, while manufacturers produced ceramic statuettes of celebrated modern sculptures. The museum's guidebooks carried advertisements from retailers that encouraged further collecting. This social phenomenon was not only symptomatic of the growing urban middle class, with spare wealth thanks to the Industrial Revolution and empire. To the Victorians, collecting was more than simply a pleasure, for it had economic, moral, even religious purpose, as a way to develop the taste of the general public, feed the economy and contribute to the cult of the home and to standards of civil behaviour. In this the museum played a key role, one that could be reconciled with its agenda for design reform. As Henry Cole argued, by displaying collections the museum raised the taste of the public as discerning customers who, in turn, could drive up design standards of new British goods. This public campaign to democratise taste encouraged Victorians to visit museums and exhibitions, to study and to collect for their homes.

In 1855 the museum's curator, J.C. Robinson, wrote in the catalogue to a collection for circulation to regional art schools that the museum serves artists and designers but also 'the collector, whose pursuits it is, for many obvious reasons, clearly a national duty to countenance and encourage'.[1] In Robinson's view, this 'national duty' was not only to admire collections in museums but also to follow the 'pursuits' of a collector, including specialist study, discussion and display at home and through lending to museums. In this way the new generation of Victorian middle-class collectors differed from many of their aristocratic forebears as many collected with a sense of duty, not so much to their family's status but to the education of the public and advancement of scholarship in new fields. The following year, in the introduction to the catalogue of the Soulages Collection, Robinson and Cole observed that fewer historical objects were available to buy and that prices were rising due to 'the establishment of public museums . . . rendering the taste for collecting almost universal amongst educated persons'.[2] A substantial amount of literature from the era promoted this new kind of popular connoisseurship, as a mode of behaviour that leads from attentive viewing and research to the display of carefully selected possessions. Much of it was focused on enhancing the everyday home as a place of beauty and self-definition.[3] Charles Locke Eastlake (nephew of Sir Charles Eastlake, the painter and first director of the National Gallery) in his best-selling work *Hints on Household Taste* (1868) described how 'an Indian ginger-jar, a Flemish beer-jug, a Japanese fan, may each become in turn a valuable lesson in decorative form and colour . . . group them together as much as possible . . . A little museum may thus be formed.'[4]

Anyone could be a connoisseur with their own collection. As Robert Kerr observed in *The Gentleman's House* (1864): 'We live in the era of *Omnium-Gatherum*; all the world's a museum, and men and women are its students . . . Our age . . . has a very notable style of its own, and a very novel one; – the style of this miscellaneous connoisseurship of ours . . . of instinct superseded by learning.'[5] Kerr's verdict was not limited to the homes of the wealthy. The idea of the 'front room' as a special place, where the best of everything could be kept safe, polished and dusted ('ready for when the vicar comes to tea', as the saying goes), survived in communities well into the late 20th century. In working-class homes without a front room to spare, the mantelpiece and some shelves above could suffice as the prime show space for family treasures. There were wider social benefits to this 'national duty' beyond nationwide good taste. According to W.J. Loftie in *A Plea for Art in the House* (1876), 'a wise father' encourages collecting, for 'a little reflection may perhaps convince us, not only that it may be a moral but even a religious duty'.[6] Loftie warned against treating a home as an antiquarian's museum, lined with crowded shelves of Greek vases and dull German stoneware. To him, 'if we look on the home here as the prototype of the home hereafter, we may see reasons for making it as a sacred thing, beautiful and pleasant'.[7]

Leading artists and critics soon lost faith in the art school, new national curriculum and the Department of Science and Art that had promised the renaissance of British design. But the museum's collections, displays and research rooms still commanded respect. Eastlake concluded the penultimate chapter of his *Hints on Household Taste* by describing collections on display at the South Kensington Museum:

> *However much opinions may differ as to the system of instruction in design hitherto adopted in that Department, there can be no doubt that the truly magnificent collection of objects assembled there, and the facility afforded to students who may desire to inspect and study them, reflect the highest credit upon the authorities entrusted with its care. By such means, the art-workman, his employer, and the public whose encouragement and patronage are necessary to both, may learn that which alone can rescue English manufactures from its recent degradation, viz.: – the formation of a sound taste.*[8]

The campaign to reform taste in Britain had begun with a commercial agenda, to improve product design and hence sales, but the ambition also found a moral focus, in refining the values of the homemaker. As an American journalist, M.D. Conway, told readers of the magazine *Harper's* in 1875, after visiting South Kensington's museum and art schools: 'England, land of beautiful homes . . . will no longer have the home to be homely. Her call has gone around the world, and temples and palaces deliver up their treasures that they may gather in London, there to teach the millions how they may beautify the latter-day temple, which is the Home.'[9]

# 4 *The Art Wealth of England* 'Special Loan Exhibition'

The improvement of public taste had been one of the goals of the Great Exhibition in 1851, where international masterpieces of modern sculpture lined the main avenue of the Crystal Palace. In Paris in 1855 France had raised the stakes by including 5,000 paintings (3,634 by French artists) in its reply, the Exposition Universelle. London's second international exhibition opened in South Kensington in 1862 with the biggest show of art ever assembled, of 6,529 oil paintings, watercolours, sculptures and engravings by 2,305 artists in its own new building.[1] At the same time, on the opposite side of Exhibition Road, the South Kensington Museum held its first blockbuster: the 'Special Loan Exhibition'.

In his annual report for 1862 Henry Cole paid tribute to Prince Albert, whose sudden death in December 1861 could have meant the end of 'Albertopolis' in South Kensington as London's first cultural quarter. Cole underlined the continuity between the prince's vision and the year's main achievement. He reported: 'The year has been chiefly remarkable for a special exhibition of objects of art on loan, containing for the most part almost all the objects of medieval art which were exhibited at the Society of Arts in 1859 [*sic*, 1850], the collection of which was so greatly promoted by the exertions of H.R.H. the Prince Consort, the President of the Society.'[2]

The 'Special Loan Exhibition' was soon renamed *The Art Wealth of England* after the title of a commemorative album of photographs by Charles Thurston Thompson, published by the art dealers Colnaghi.[3] The exhibition presented between 9,000 and 10,000 examples of medieval, Renaissance and later decorative arts, in over 40 different categories, ranging from jewellery to armour, lent by 553 British private collectors and art dealers. Their treasures filled two vast courts off a central avenue, all encircled by an arcade, in wrought and cast iron, painted and gilded, beneath a glass roof. Despite simply – but ingeniously – infilling a new courtyard, this great space, engineered in emulation of medieval cathedrals, brought back memories of the Crystal Palace as visitors strolled through row upon row of tall showcases filled to the brim beneath the glittering décor. The exhibition's spectacular glass and iron setting established a 'house style' for the new generation of decorative arts museums that would be founded in emulation of South Kensington, from Boston to Berlin, from Budapest to Bombay.

The show was a huge success: the total number of visitors to the South Kensington Museum at large doubled from 604,550 in 1861 to 1,241,369 in 1862.[4] It set an example to collectors and connoisseurs in new fields of scholarship as future lenders and potential donors and brought over 70 of them together as the exhibition's advisers. To such specialists it revealed how far knowledge of the medieval and Renaissance decorative arts had come since the exhibition of 'Antient and Mediaeval Art' organised by The Society of Arts at its own building in 1850 and the *Art Treasures* exhibition held in Manchester in 1857. It also provided the museum with a shopping list. An annotated copy of the exhibition catalogue in the National Art Library reveals how many loans later entered the museum's

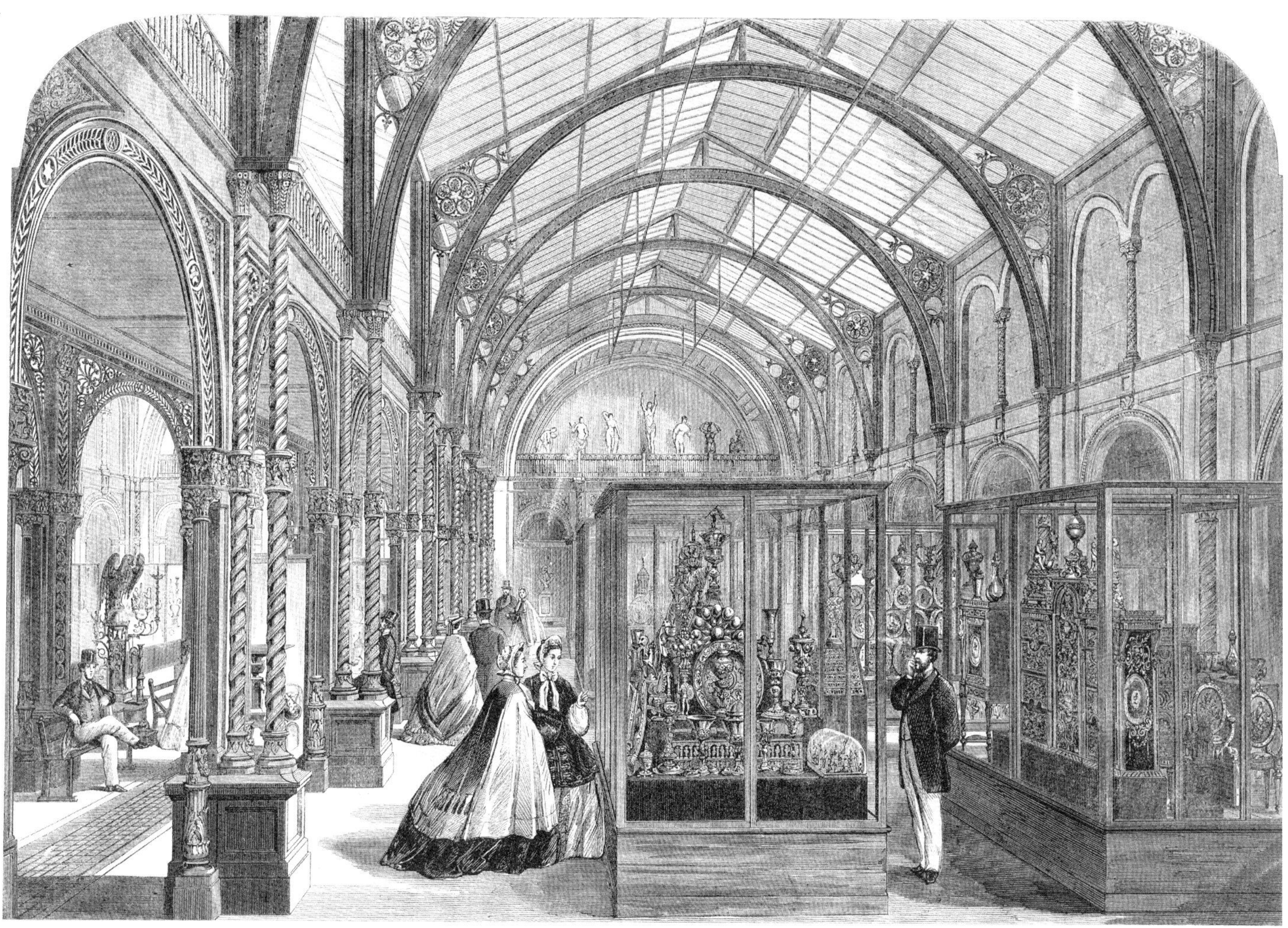

6. Anon., 'The Loan Collection of works of art at South Kensington Museum', *The Illustrated London News*, 6 December 1862, p.613. V&A: National Art Library.

permanent collections. Robinson later recalled 'The catalogue will remain as a permanent record of the art wealth of England, in its especial categories, and of its time, of even greater authority than the analogous work of Dr Waagen's in regard to the pictorial treasures of this country.'[5] He did not claim sole credit for the entire catalogue and exhibition. By the time it appeared in full, in 1863, Robinson had contributed 12 of the 40 sections.[6] Augustus Wollaston Franks (Keeper of British and Medieval Antiquities at the British Museum) later recalled, 'For the Loan Exhibition of 1862 I made gratis the catalogue of several sections extending to over 100 pages.'[7] Robinson also gave credit for the exhibition to a committee of '70 members, comprising nearly all the most eminent connoisseurs and amateurs in the country' and to the committee's secretary, 'Mr R.H.S. Smith, Assistant Keeper of the Art Collection'.

Many of the lenders to the exhibition belonged to the Collector's Club or Fine Arts Club that Robinson and Cole had established in 1857 with the sculptor Baron Carlo Marochetti and the diplomat Vittorio Emanuele Taparelli, Marchese d'Azeglio, to advance scholarship in the decorative arts.[8] The first 96 members included Richard Redgrave (Robinson's senior as Inspector-General for Art at South Kensington), A.W. Franks, Sir Charles Eastlake (director of the National Gallery), John Ruskin, Austen Henry Layard and the scholar-collector Charles Drury Edward Fortnum.[9] Dealers were excluded from membership but attended as guests; women could join but by 1867, among the 201 members, there were only seven.

In his own annual report for 1862, as Superintendent of the Art Collections, Robinson compared the museum's exhibition with the international one across the street by stressing its significance for future loans: 'it may literally be said to have attracted from first to last scarcely less attention than the International Exhibition itself . . . the great success of the effort has doubtless placed the established system of receiving works of art on loan henceforward on a much wider and more comprehensive basis'.[10] He reported how this 'system' of loans was bearing fruit for the permanent collection already, for 'several specimens exhibited in the Loan Collection . . . have been ceded to the Museum by their proprietors'. Major loans to the International Exhibition were also transferring to the museum as gifts, including Gobelins and Beauvais tapestries presented by 'the Emperor of the French . . . His Majesty the Emperor of Russia has also presented to the Museum the two large and remarkable porcelain vases executed specially for the Exhibition at the Imperial Porcelain Manufactory at St Petersburg.' Actual purchases were possible, for Robinson's report describes a special grant of £5,000 from the Treasury 'for the acquisition of works of contemporary art from the International Exhibition', as in 1851, when objects were selected at the close of the Crystal Palace. Choices in 1862 included 'several of the principal works exhibited by . . . Minton . . . Copeland . . . Sèvres . . . Barbedienne . . . Salviati' together with a bronze and carved ivory vase by Baron Henri de Triqueti and an example of the painted furniture designed by William Burges.

Robinson also reported on the acquisition of 'several highly important specimens of medieval art, originally from the Soltykoff collection' for which the museum had paid in total £7, 065 at auction in Paris in April 1861.[11] However, this was funded by an exceptional Treasury grant. An ominous note about future funding issues sounds when he reveals the fate of income earned by the Special Loan Exhibition: 'after payment of every expense connected with it, a considerable pecuniary surplus from admission fees, sale of catalogues, &c. has been paid into the Treasury'.

1862 was a landmark in another way, as the same year Robinson published his catalogue of the museum's sculpture, following a campaign of major purchases that had concluded the year before. The 190-page volume, *Italian Sculpture of the Middle Ages and Period of the Revival of Art* (i.e. the Renaissance), illustrated with photographs, marked the museum's arrival as a centre of new scholarship and claimed, in effect, the field of post-classical sculpture for South Kensington, as the sequel to the British Museum's earlier holdings. It also set a standard of informed connoisseurship, combining both visual expertise and documentary research, for the museum to maintain.

Richard Redgrave described in his own annual report for 1862 the arrival of new long-term loans, 'in conformity with the practice adopted in all sections of the South Kensington Museum, of receiving works on loan to exhibit with those placed permanently in the Museum'.[12] However, in this regard the museum soon became a victim of its own success. Increasingly South Kensington spoke more to private collectors (and to would-be collectors) than to designers and makers of new consumer products. By 1863 difficulties between the first director and his curator came to a head when Robinson challenged Cole's expertise and authority; Cole countered by demoting Robinson into an advisory position (see chapter 10). In 1870 Robinson's replacement as curator, George Wallis, reluctantly reported that, since 1862 'the systematic arrangement of some portions of the courts, which prevailed to a considerable extent a year ago, has had to be broken up in order to find space for objects offered on loan'.[13] Wallis felt powerless against the tides of loans. After the *Art Wealth* exhibition closed, the new South Court served as the museum's loans gallery for the next 45 years.

# 5 Collecting Collectors and Advisers

Much of the Victorian V&A's collecting was led by directors with the help of outside advisers, rather than by in-house curators. The absence of a coherent curatorial department for the Victorian museum is a strange omission among all of Cole's innumerable achievements as the founding director. One reason must have been the challenges he faced in managing his curator, and then, after sacking Robinson, of finding different ways to look after the collections and lenders. Cole's decision not to establish a curatorial structure is one of several explanations for the growing dependence on collectors and advisers.

Another reason for insufficient in-house expertise was the sheer range of the collections, which expanded far beyond their initial focus. In June 1863 the government body overseeing the Department of Science and Art, the Committee of the Privy Council on Education, expressed its concerns at the lack of any strategic decision over collecting (the Committee must have been briefed by Cole, following his falling out with Robinson that year). It noted that in 1845 the Government School of Design (forerunner of the V&A as collecting body) had been authorised to form collections 'not only of architectural casts, specimens of antique sculptures, and prints of ornament . . . but collections more especially of examples of decorative work, in order to exhibit to the students of the school, to inquiring manufacturers, artizans and the public in general'. In 1863 the Committee observed 'the most useful and important section of art, namely that of medieval Italy, is well represented' but 'other sections are incomplete' and thus 'the time has come when . . . definite instructions should be given to regulate the increase and completion of the collections'.[1] The Committee directed that 'future purchases be confined to objects wherein fine art is applied to some purpose of utility, and that works of fine art not so applied should only be admitted as exceptions, and so far as they may tend directly to improve art applied to objects of utility'.

This recommendation is often quoted by historians of the museum who blame collectors for the V&A losing its way. However, the museum's first formal collecting policy concludes with a more all-encompassing ambition: 'the aim of the Museum is to make the historical and geographical series of all decorative art complete, and fully to illustrate human taste and ingenuity'. This summary of the Committee meeting's minutes was included in the Art Museum's annual report, signed by Henry Cole, who doubtless had more than a hand in drafting it. Some of his successors may have felt that an ambitious collecting policy of such breadth gave them still greater opportunities, and little defence against the temptations of persuasive lenders of seductive collections.

Cole enjoyed collecting masterpieces himself and was confident that he could rely on scholar-dealers, such as John Webb, William Blundell Spence and Murray Marks, for new acquisitions and expert advice. Webb lent and sold many objects to the museum between 1852 and 1861 and left £10,000 to support future acquisitions.[2] Like other dealers, Webb was happy to place potential purchases on loan on display in the museum, both in its first home in Marlborough House from 1852 and in South Kensington from 1857. To test public and trade opinion Cole had purchases put out on general display with their prices on the museum labels. The most conspicuous example of a potential purchase on loan from a dealer was the monumental architectural rood screen from St John's Cathedral at 's-Hertogenbosch in the Netherlands. After it was dismantled Murray Marks purchased it from a stonemason's yard in 1869 and offered to lend it to the museum, on an annual rental basis of 5 per cent of the proposed purchase price. As a loan, it was built into the new Architectural ('Cast') Courts and was finally purchased in 1871, on the advice of the architect Matthew Digby Wyatt.[3]

Dealers were also collectors, in a sense, as many kept their best finds back for themselves or for special future clients. Some collectors were also *marchand-amateurs*, keeping the museum in mind while shopping, selling on items to the museum at cost price and selling off their own old buys to upgrade their collections. Cole also looked to the teachers at the School of Design to advise on potential new acquisitions through the Inspector-General for Art, Richard Redgrave. But in the long term Cole's reliance on consultants and other advisers rather than on investing in developing his own team proved to be a false economy.

After his falling-out with Cole, initially Robinson was retained as an adviser, to recommend new acquisitions to Redgrave. In December 1867 his advisory role was deleted when the Department of Science and Art resolved to set up 'a body of referees', to be selected from 'the most competent persons, to be employed as occasion arises, the Department paying them a consulting fee when they are asked to advise'.[4] Robinson was still around, as an art referee on standby, but to the few curators in South Kensington it must have felt like a takeover by the British Museum and the Royal Academy. The selection of referees included five of the British Museum's most senior staff: Samuel Birch (Egyptology), Edward Bond (Manuscripts), A.W. Franks (Medieval Antiquities), Charles Newton (Greek and Roman Antiquities) and Reginald Stuart Poole (Coins and Medals). There were six painters from the Royal Academy (Sir Francis Grant, Solomon Hart, John Callcott Horsley, Frederic Leighton, Daniel Maclise and Eyre Crowe) and three leading figures now working for the new Crystal Palace Company at Sydenham: Matthew Digby Wyatt, Owen Jones and James Fergusson. Later recruits as collections referees included George Birdwood, John Everett Millais, Samuel Redgrave (brother of Richard), Juan Facundo Riaño (see chapter 10) and James William Wild.

Fortnum was invited to join, to represent collectors, but declined. He had travelled in Italy with Cole, Robinson and Redgrave in search of new acquisitions, had lent to *The Art Wealth of England* exhibition in 1862, was sent on buying trips across Europe and the Middle East and would also write two catalogues of the museum's collection, on *Maiolica* (1873) and on *Bronzes of European Origin* (1876). However, Fortnum grew disillusioned with the South Kensington Museum and wrote to Robinson that the 'creation of a committee of Art Referees was a mere sham . . . packed with friends and backers'.[5] Fortnum gave his own collection to the Ashmolean Museum, Oxford.

This use of ad hoc paid consultants did not find favour with the museum's civil service overseers and so nominations for a more formal committee of expert advisers were made in 1882 and 1884. 1885 saw the first meeting of this new General Committee of Advice, chaired by the president of the Royal Academy, Sir Frederic Leighton. Other members included Sir Frederic William Burton (director of the National Gallery), the architect G.F. Bodley, the sculptor Joseph Edgar Boehm, the painters Edward Poynter (director 1875–81 of the National Art Training School at South Kensington – later renamed the Royal College of Art) and Lawrence Alma-Tadema, the scholars John Hungerford Pollen and William Maskell, the collectors Sir Austen Henry Layard and Alfred Morrison and the designer William Morris. However, like their predecessors, they were rarely consulted, except Morris, who regularly advised on tapestries and carpets.

After his falling-out with Robinson, Cole had created in 1864 an alternative path to in-house

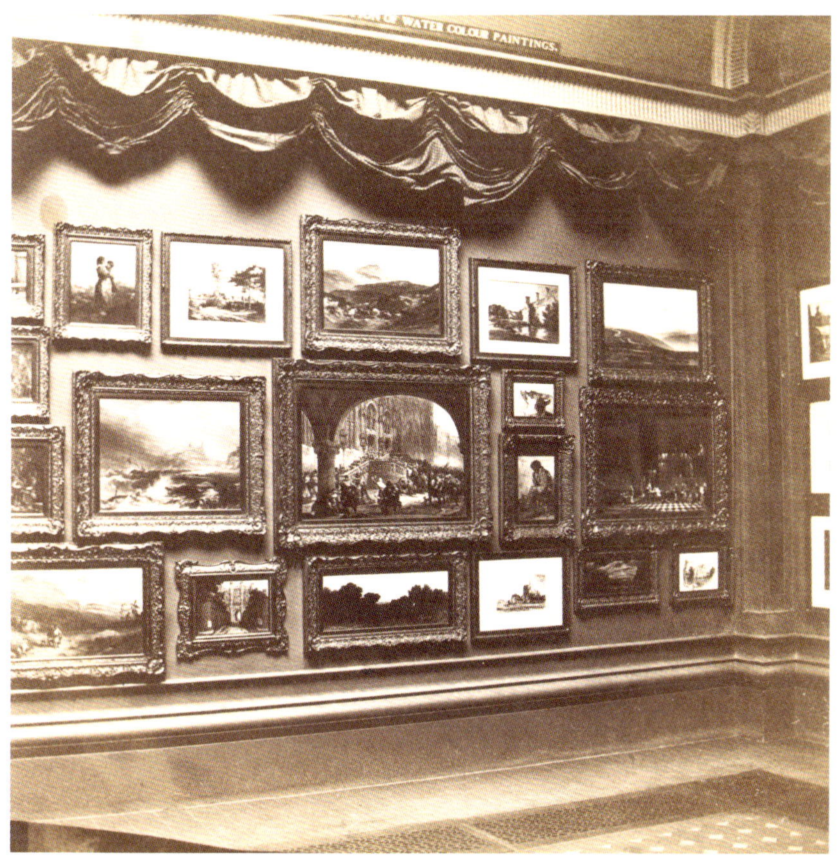


7. J. Davis Burton, 'South Kensington Museum, Ellison Picture Gallery', 1868, from a pair of stereoscopic albumen prints. V&A: 60760.

expertise by appointing Pollen to the new post of General Superintendent of Catalogues. The first task for Pollen was Cole's highly ambitious international research project to document the state of art scholarship, the *Universal Catalogue of Books on Art, Compiled for the Use of the National Art Library and the Schools of Art in the United Kingdom* (1870).[6] Pollen then edited a series of published catalogues, on textiles (1870), lace and embroidery (1871), ivories (1872), musical instruments (1874), watercolours (1876) and glass vessels (1878) as well as Fortnum's two. Pollen himself wrote the catalogues to the collections of architecture and monumental sculpture (1874), ancient and modern furniture and woodwork (1874) and gold and silversmiths' work (1878).[7]

In the catalogue of the collection bequeathed by Alexander Dyce (1874) his prints and drawings were written up by George William Reid, Keeper of Prints and Drawings at the British Museum, the paintings and miniatures by Samuel Redgrave and the 'rings and miscellaneous objects' by Charles C. Black. Commissioned authors brought a degree of objectivity to the catalogues, as when Samuel Redgrave noted that Alexander Dyce's paintings are 'of a very miscellaneous character. The collection was made apparently as objects offered themselves, and without any special design.'[8] Pollen resigned from the museum in 1876 but continued to advise on acquisitions as a freelance Art Referee for another twenty years.[9]

Curatorial collecting was not a priority for George Wallis, Robinson's successor as Superintendent of the Art Collections at the South Kensington Museum. A former headmaster of the schools of design in Manchester and Birmingham, since 1859 he had been 'Agent for the sale of reproductions', responsible for the museum's retail sales of photographs, casts and electrotypes.[10] Responding to the announcement of his appointment in 1863 the *Art Journal* noted that Wallis made 'no pretensions to familiarity with antique works'.[11] He continued to promote the display of reproductions, preferring them to historic originals, recognising their practical advantages as teaching tools for the design reform movement through use in art schools nationwide. As Wallis recalled in 1888, he had no wish to acquire and display original objects to serve as 'a fetish' for 'the conventional dilettanti [*sic*] collector'.[12]

The importance of reproductions to the museum itself cannot be overestimated. As a way to accelerate the growth of the collections, reproductions offered an alternative to bulk borrowing, and provided a way to include the unborrowable. Plaster casts, electrotypes, photographs, 'fictile ivories' and brass rubbings became a major investment for the museum between the 1850s and the 1880s. The campaign of electrotype production had begun on site in 1853, at Gore House in South Kensington where metalwork was copied from the British royal collection, Oxford colleges and museums and castles abroad. Following a popular display of electrotypes by Elkington & Co. at the 1867 Paris Exhibition, and concerns about potential damage to the original objects, Cole drew up a 'convention' and secured the signatures of 15 European princes in support of reproducing works

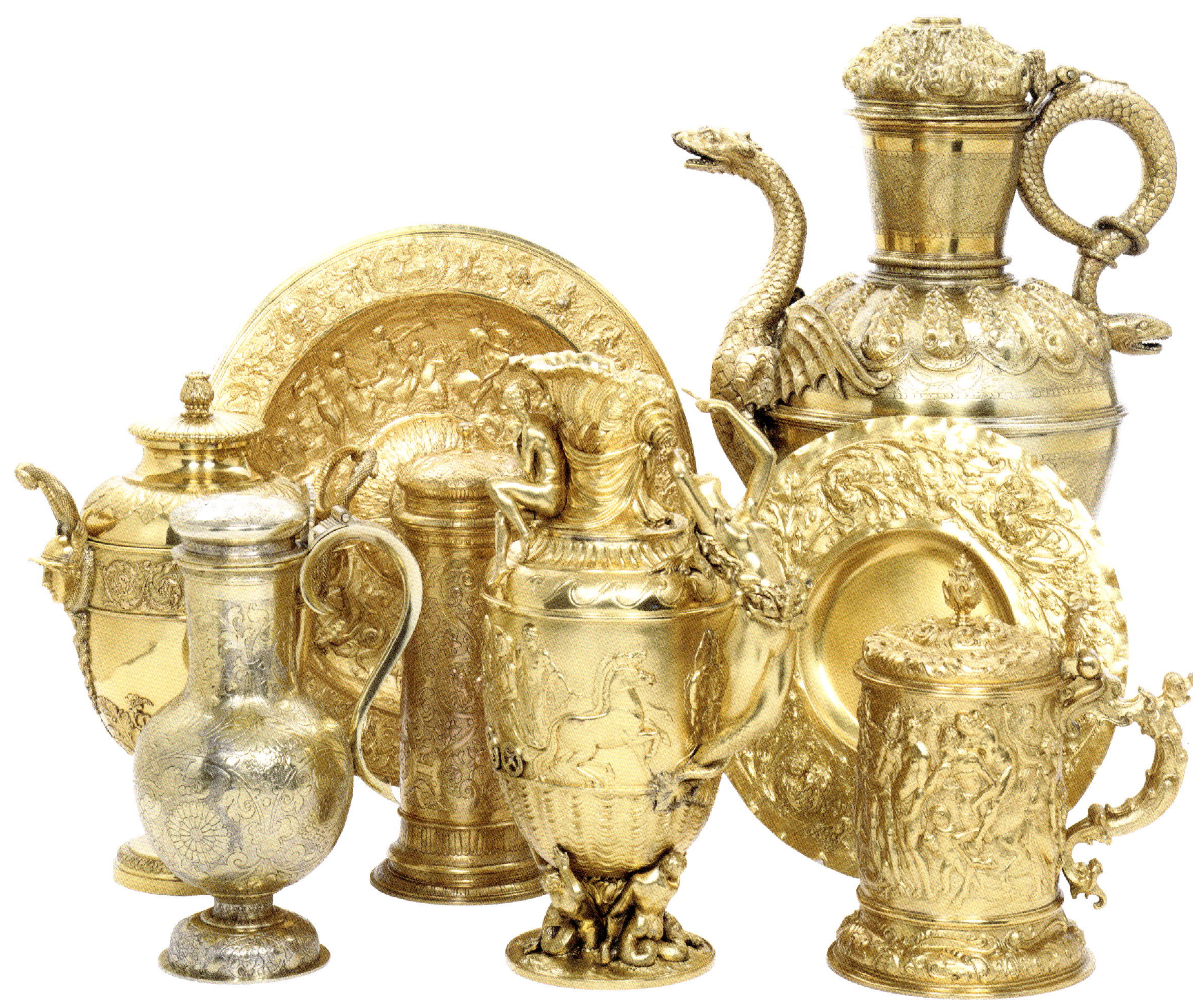

8. A group of electrotype copies manufactured by Elkington & Co., 1854–88, after metalwork in the South Kensington Museum, the Royal Collection, Oxford colleges and elsewhere. V&A: REPRO: 1854B-18; 1861A-2; 1868B-87; 1880C-49; 1884-107; 1884B-108; 1885-107; 1888-104.

of art. The museum's most ambitious campaign was the expedition to Russia in 1880–81 when 237 items were copied, including Elizabethan and Stuart silver in the Kremlin that had been sent as ambassadorial gifts to the Tsars, and so escaped the fate of most fine silver that had been melted down to fund England's Civil War.

Wallis would have felt more at home in the museum's magnificent Architectural ('Cast') Courts, which presented a collection of reproductions that continued to grow. The casts collection holds court today as a rare survivor among museums, and photographs have their own galleries as the national collection. The electrotypes collection was denuded in 1947 when the V&A deaccessioned 879 from the total of nearly 4,000 examples. Fortunately, many still survive and can be spotted on screen, in use as film props.[13]

Wallis finally retired in October 1891, a month before he died, aged 80. He and Pollen were not the only successors to Robinson, for the former curator had developed his promising assistant who shared his commitment to collecting originals. Robert Henry Soden Smith had joined the museum in 1857 to help catalogue the Sheepshanks Collection of paintings (see chapter 6) and was appointed Assistant Keeper of the Art Museum and Library in 1858. From 1867 Soden Smith served as Keeper of the National Art Library (which included prints, drawings and photographs) until his death in 1890. A voracious collector of prints, drawings, photographs and books, Soden Smith was responsible for the library and works on paper when three major collections were bequeathed by Chauncy Hare Townshend (1868), Alexander Dyce (1869) and John Forster (1876) (see chapters 7 and 8). He also advised on acquisitions of ceramics, assisted in cataloguing the Schreiber Collection (see chapter 9) and wrote the catalogue of the museum's jewellery exhibition in 1872. His successor as Keeper of the National Art Library, James Weale, was a leading scholar of Netherlandish art.

Cole's own successor as director when he retired in 1873 was his right-hand administrator, Philip Cunliffe Owen (1828–1894), a brilliant creator of popular exhibitions. From 1871 until 1874 the South Kensington Museum contributed to a series of 'London International Exhibitions' held in the new 'Western Galleries' on the west side of Exhibition Road. The series became more specialist from 1876 with a massive international loan exhibition of scientific apparatus, which led to the Science Museum (see chapter 12). Subsequent shows included the Great International Fisheries Exhibition based on a private collection of pisciculture (1883), the International Health Exhibition (1884) and the International Inventions Exhibition (1885), the latter in the Royal Albert Hall. Cunliffe Owen served on the Executive Council of the inventions exhibition and was fully seconded to help organise the most spectacular, the Colonial and Indian Exhibition (1886). More like a crafts village experience than a museum show, it ran for six months, attracted over five million visitors (today the V&A as a whole aims to attract four million in a year) and led to the purchase of some objects on loan for the South Kensington Museum.[14]

To continue shopping abroad the museum developed a network of enterprising field agents. Groups of items and whole collections were acquired through, for example, Juan F. Riaño, the museum's agent in Spain; Stephen Wootton Bushell, physician at the British legation in Beijing; and the museum's textiles adviser Franz Bock, canon of Aachen Cathedral (and thief) (see chapter 10). Another way was to pay to form a new collection, as when in 1875 Cunliffe Owen invited the Japanese statesman Sano Tsunetami to assemble 'an historical collection of porcelain and pottery from the earliest period until the present day' to show at the Philadelphia Centennial Exposition of 1876.[15] When the collection of Japanese ceramics arrived and went on long-term display in the South Court the catalogue was written by A.W. Franks from the British Museum, as one of South Kensington's Art Referees. New kinds of objects also arrived from Africa, as a consequence of imperial military action, such as the Maqdala regalia and the Asante gold (see chapter 11).

In 1882 William Morris wrote to a fellow museum adviser, the artist Henry Wallis, after finding the museum 'in its usual state of muddle . . . overburdened with . . . all sorts of sickening rubbish; fans; rococo embroideries; the sweepings of the Venice dealers shops and other twaddle . . . The SKM wants thorough reform.'[16] In 1883 an 'Art Collector' writing in the *Morning Post* expressed no confidence in the staff, for 'there does not now appear to be anyone connected with this museum with any knowledge or even taste'.[17] In 1890, in an article on 'Art-Teaching and Technical Schools', the art historian Emilia Dilke compared the museum with its counterpart in Vienna, the Museum für Kunst und Industrie. She noted how 'the Austrian Museum shows, in every department, the influence of definite educational purpose'. By contrast, 'South Kensington is disfigured by the "collecting" mania, and makes one feel as if one were visiting a gigantic bric-a-brac shop.'[18] To Lady Dilke the museum had lost its way, drifting from being an educational resource for design reform to become a muddled museum for collectors.

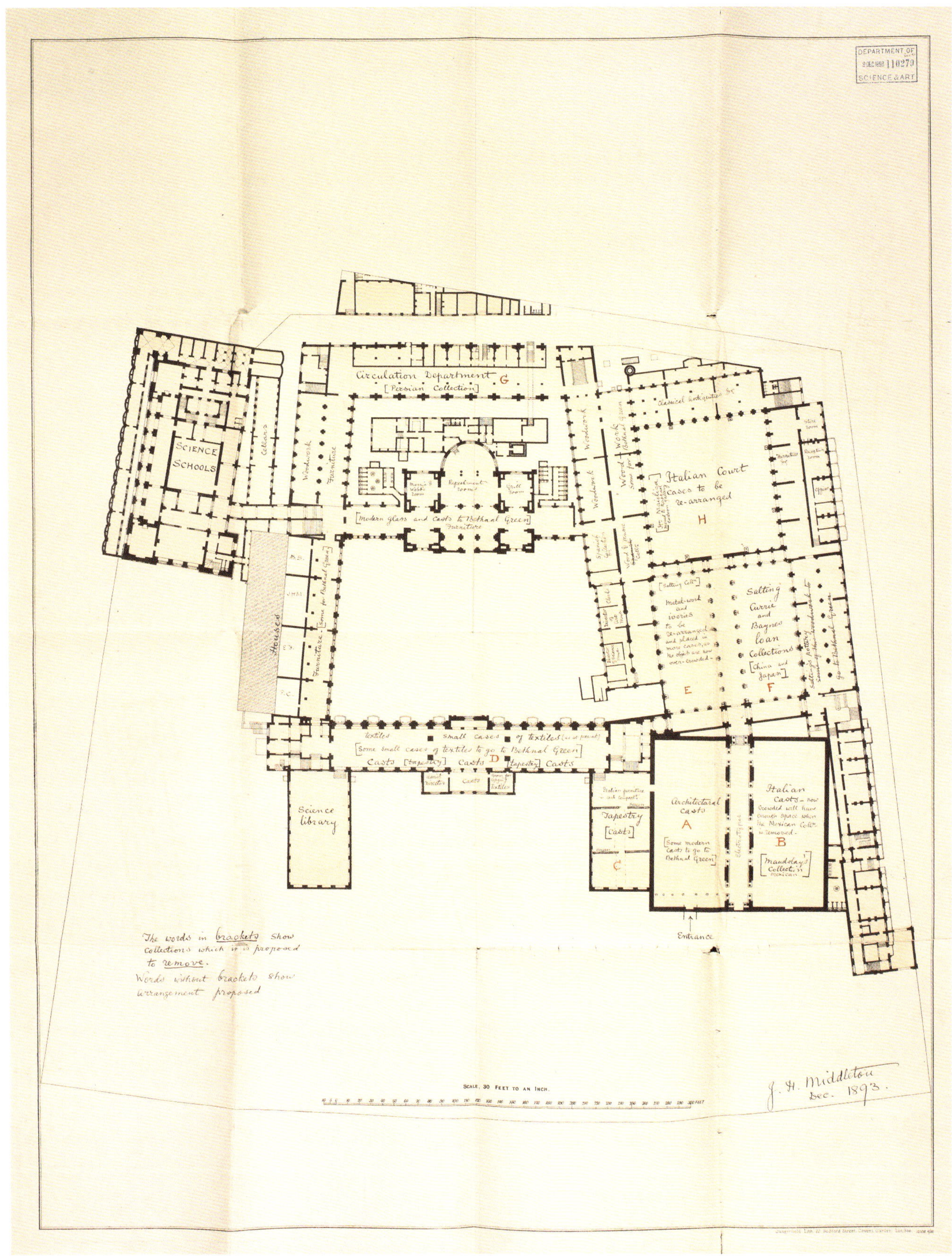
DEPARTMENT OF
110279
SCIENCE & ART
Circulation Department G
[Persian Collection]
Classical Antiquities &c
SCIENCE SCHOOLS
Cellars
Woodwork
Furniture
Italian Court
cases to be re-arranged
H
[Modern glass and casts to Bethnal Green]
Furniture
Houses
[Salting Collⁿ]
Metal-work and ivories to be re-arranged and placed in more cases, as the objects are now over-crowded.
Salting Currie and Baynes loan Collections
[China and Japan]
E
F
textiles small cases of textiles [as at present]
[Some small cases of textiles to go to Bethnal Green]
Casts [tapestry] Casts D [tapestry] Casts
Science library
Tapestry
[casts]
C
Architectural casts
A
[Some modern casts to go to Bethnal Green]
Italian casts – now crowded will have enough space when the Mexican Collⁿ is removed.
B
[Maudslay's Collection Mexican]
Entrance
The words in brackets show collections which it is proposed to remove.
Words without brackets show arrangement proposed
SCALE, 30 FEET TO AN INCH.
J. H. Middleton
Dec. 1893.

Cunliffe Owen retired in 1893. Following public criticism over the acquisition of 'fakes' and of misleading museum labels, to be on surer ground, the first scholar-director was appointed, Dr John Middleton (1846–1896). He had been director of the Fitzwilliam Museum in Cambridge since 1889 and was one of William Morris's closest friends since they first met on a ship to Iceland in 1873 (indeed, Morris must have recommended Middleton for the post).[19] He should have had an easier time, as the retirement of Cunliffe Owen provided the opportunity to create two separate directors for the South Kensington Museum. Middleton served as Museum Director for Art and Major-General Festing as Museum Director for Science, both under the Director of the Science and Art Department. This formal division was a step towards the creation of the Science Museum. Unfortunately, Middleton had become addicted to laudanum since using it as medication when a student at Oxford. After just three years in post, he was found dead in his official residence at the museum. The poet Wilfrid Scawen Blunt noted (17 June 1896): 'jury returned a verdict of misadventure, but it has the appearance of suicide . . . he has been dead to the world and his friends for something like two years'.[20]

The museum's new director, Caspar Purdon Clarke (1846–1911), had trained as an architect in the South Kensington Schools and had served as a buying agent in India, Turkey and Syria for the museum (see chapter 10). In 1883 he had been appointed to the new keepership of the 'India Museum and the Oriental Section generally', after the museum of the former East India Company had moved to South Kensington (see chapter 11). When George Wallis retired in 1891 he had been succeeded as Keeper of the Art Museum by his assistant, Arthur Skinner, who had developed as a scholar since joining the museum in 1879. Purdon Clarke promoted Skinner to be his Assistant Director, overseeing the Art Museum. Skinner had a key influence on the formation of George Salting's collection (see chapter 17). Skinner even challenged Robinson's expertise, when Robinson persuaded Purdon Clarke to accept on loan 73 objects for which he provided draft wall labels. Skinner warned Purdon Clarke (7 August 1901) 'these descriptions were prepared by him, and in my opinion are open to considerable doubt'.[21] But the volume of acquisitions and shortage of scholarship still left Skinner overloaded.

In his first year as director Purdon Clarke announced his major restructuring of the Art Museum: 'the preliminary work of dealing with various classes of objects on entering the museum, formerly performed by the Keeper of the Art Museum, is now distributed amongst the Assistant Keepers'. They were to lead five new specialist sections: '1. Sculpture, Ivories. 2. Woodwork, Musical Instruments, Leatherwork. 3. Metalwork, Jewellery, Medals. 4. Pottery, Glass, Enamels. 5. Textiles, Lace, &c.'[22] Reporting to the Keeper of the Art Museum, these new sections lined up alongside the India Museum, the National Art Library (which still covered prints, drawings and photographs) and the National Gallery of British Art (see chapter 6).

Within a year of Middleton's death in post and Purdon Clarke's arrival a Parliamentary Select Committee on Museums of the Science and Art Department was convened. Over 27 sessions in 1897 and a further 26 in 1898 the committee interviewed the museum's key staff and its overseers; it then published two detailed reports.[23] The Committee finally rejected proposals to give the British Museum overall responsibility, a threat that had hung over South Kensington since Cole retired in 1873. But the Science and Art Department would have to be wound up and in 1899 the Board of Education took direct control of its institutions. The Committee welcomed Purdon Clarke's recent changes and reported on 'the new system of sub-dividing the Museum, the first outcome of which will be the training of official experts, [which] will supersede the need of employing referees . . . the Art referees should not be continued'.[24] The committee found a poor record of acquisitions and reported 'Dr Middleton drew up a list of 50 objects which had been removed. They are either forgeries, "quasi forgeries", or worthless things. These were acquired between 1853 and 1893 and have now been suppressed.'[25] It found 'excessive prices have been paid . . . caused by the absence of experts in the

**9.** Ground plan, South Kensington Museum, 1893, showing the location of loan collections among ongoing rearrangements, annotated and signed by the director, J. H. Middleton.
V&A: Archive, ED 84/154.

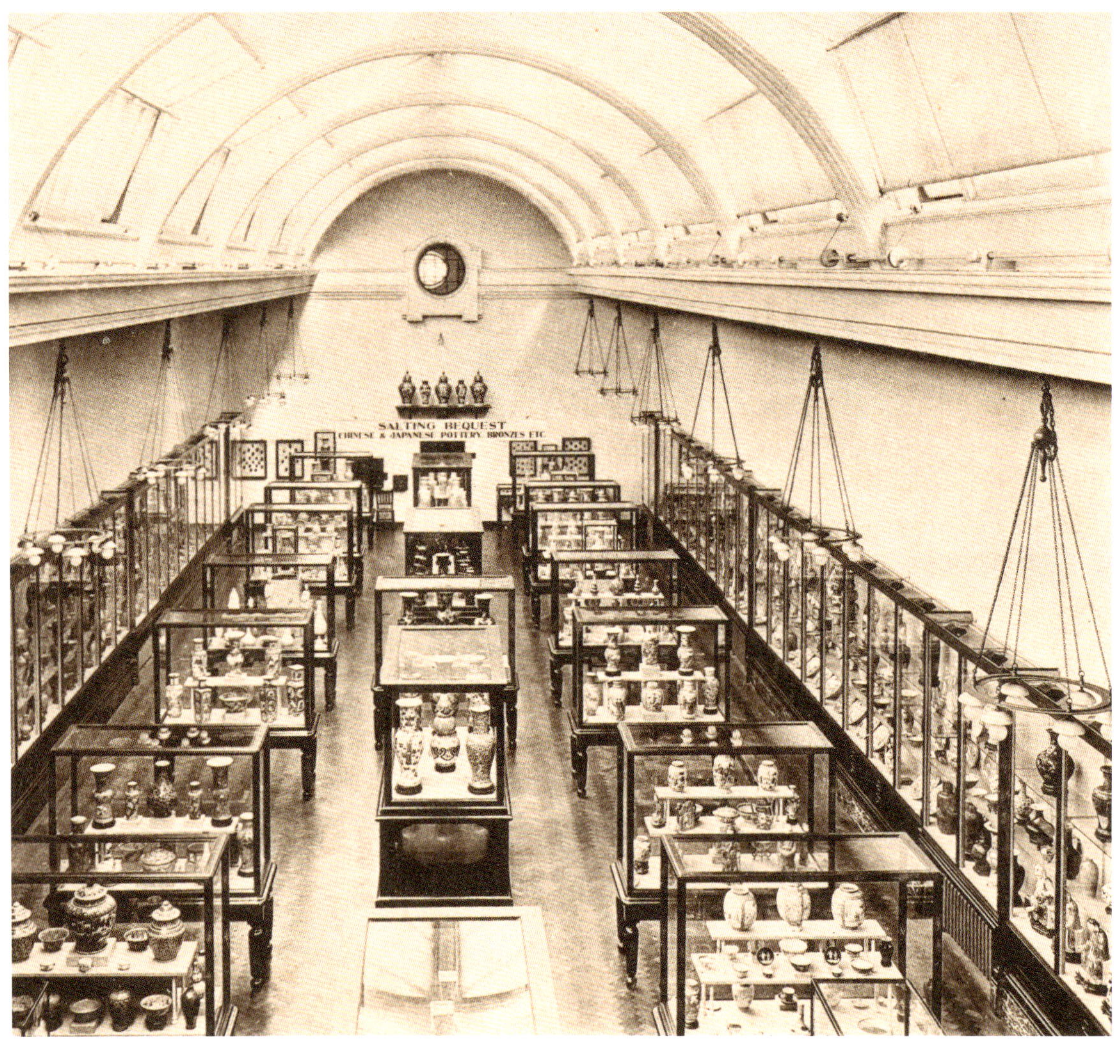


**10.** Victoria and Albert Museum, 'Gallery No.145. The Salting Collection of Chinese and Japanese Pottery', *c.*1912, postcard. Collection: the author.

Museum'.[26] The Select Committee also criticised the museum's acquisition of staff, on finding that one fifth were related to each other.[27]

Despite the changes prompted by the Parliamentary Select Committee the museum still remained dependent on many long-term loans from private collectors, and hence was still vulnerable to surprise withdrawals. In 1898 Stephen Bushell requested the return of his Chinese bronzes after a loan that the museum fully expected to lead to a gift or bequest. Another collector, George Salting, intervened and convinced Bushell to sell and the museum to buy, rather than leave a gap at the heart of the museum's Chinese collections, but substantial funds had to be found. The museum was not so fortunate when two other major loan collections were withdrawn: by J.P. Morgan in 1912, and by his adviser J.H. Fitzhenry, in 1913 (see chapter 18). The consequent gaps and further risks were so extensive as to necessitate the establishment of a new collecting policy and budget.[28] In 1913 the General Committee of Advice was replaced by a new Advisory Council with a much wider remit, to advise the museum's overseers at the Board of Education on policy and 'deficiencies' (see chapter 19).[29] Seventy years later the museum finally achieved equal status to the British Museum when the committee was superseded by the V&A's first Board of Trustees, established by the National Heritage Act (1983). One potential benefit of the Act was to give V&A trustees the authority to review traditional restrictions, as specified in deeds of gift, so enabling greater flexibility over the lending and display of donated collections.

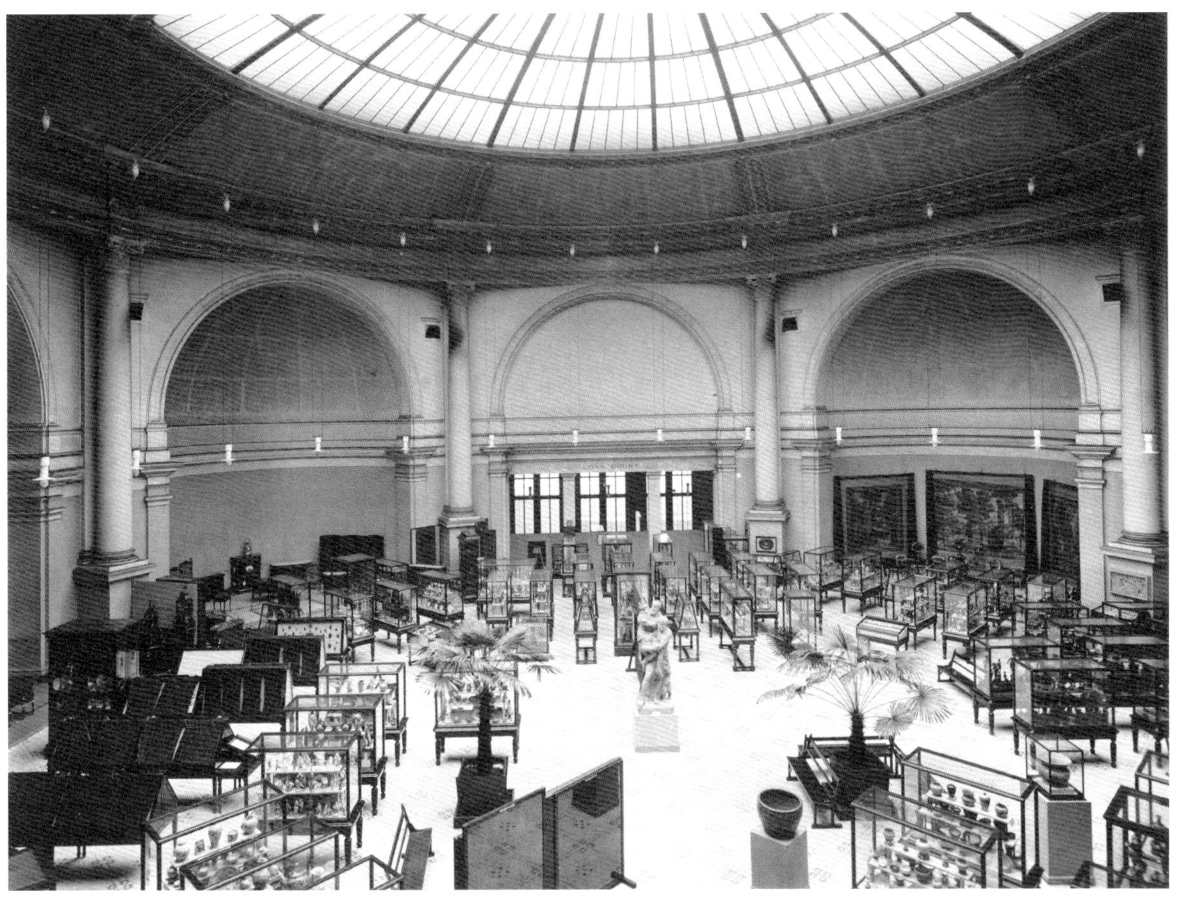

**11.** The 'Loans Court', 1920, photograph. V&A Archive.

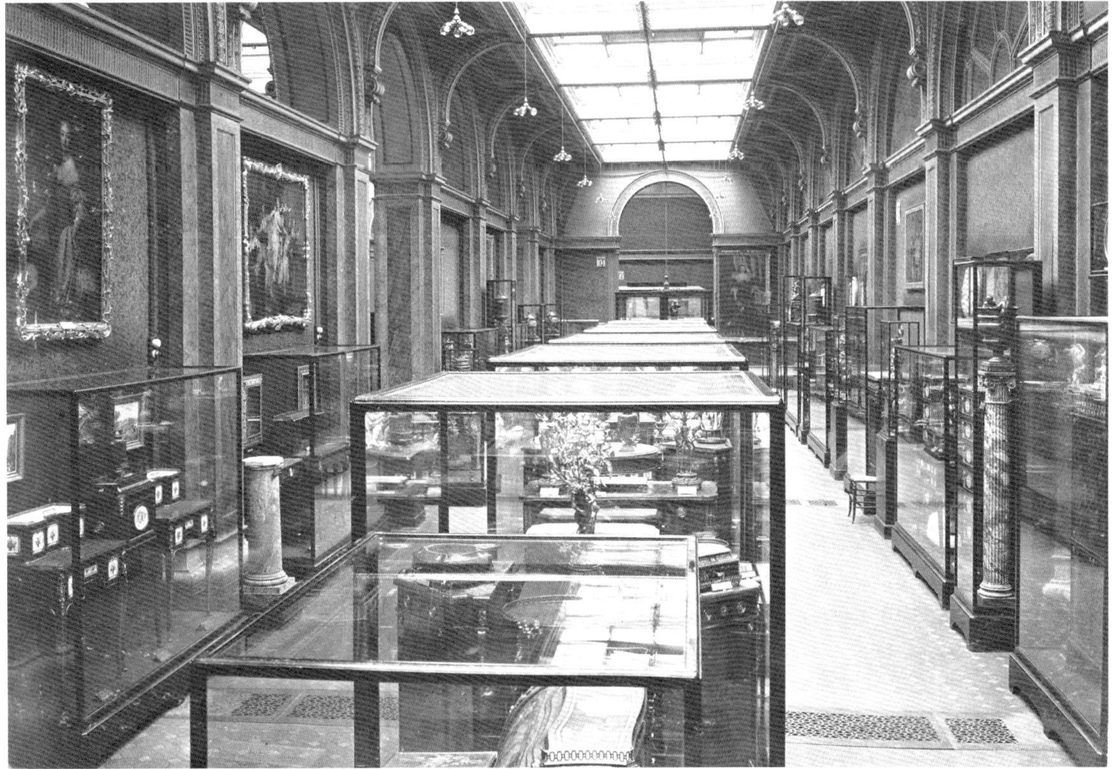

**12.** The Jones Collection on display in the museum, 1910, photograph. V&A Archive.

# Part II: Polymaths of the Graphic Arts

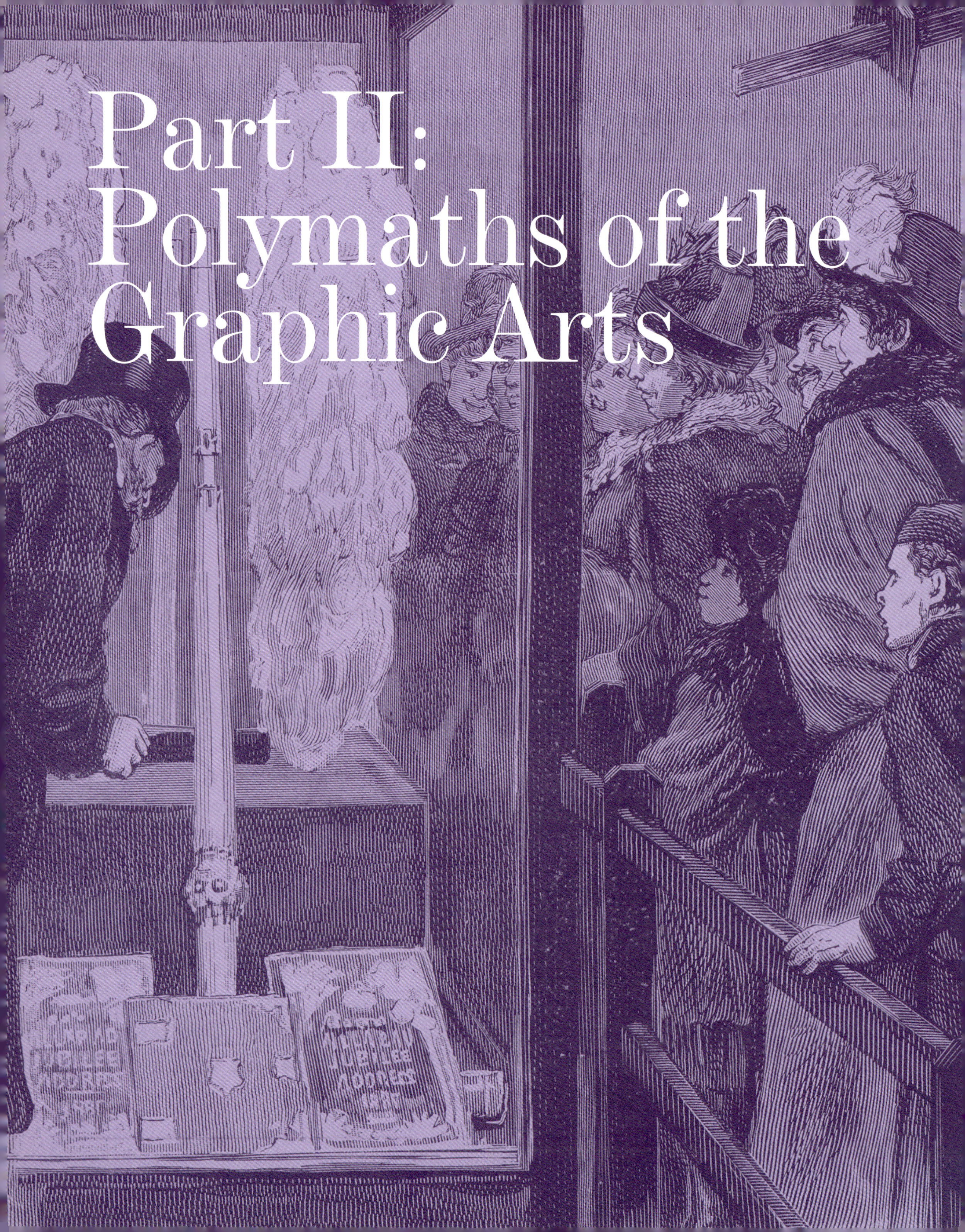

IN **1857**, the Museum of Ornamental Art (as the V&A was then known) moved from its initial home in Marlborough House, beside St James's Palace, to join the new South Kensington Museum, a consortium of 11 museums and collections, eight of which came under the direct control of Henry Cole. There it reopened as the Art Museum alongside a purpose-built gallery of modern British paintings that would become the National Gallery of British Art. A third collection, to be known as the National Art Library, collected not only reference books but also manuscripts, incunabula, master drawings, prints and photographs. Cole's collecting ambitions soon moved towards the graphic arts.

In the following decades, through loans, gifts, bequests and some purchases, the paintings, prints, watercolours, drawings, photographs, manuscripts and books far exceeded in quantity the new acquisitions of exemplary 'modern manufactures' and historical decorative arts. Generous offers from private collectors proved irresistible, with the inevitable result that they began to redefine the South Kensington Museum at large, especially when bequests came with conditions, such as permanent public access. Four foundation donors of graphic arts and libraries are introduced in the following chapters, in chronological order of their gifts: John Sheepshanks, Chauncy Hare Townshend, Alexander Dyce and John Forster.

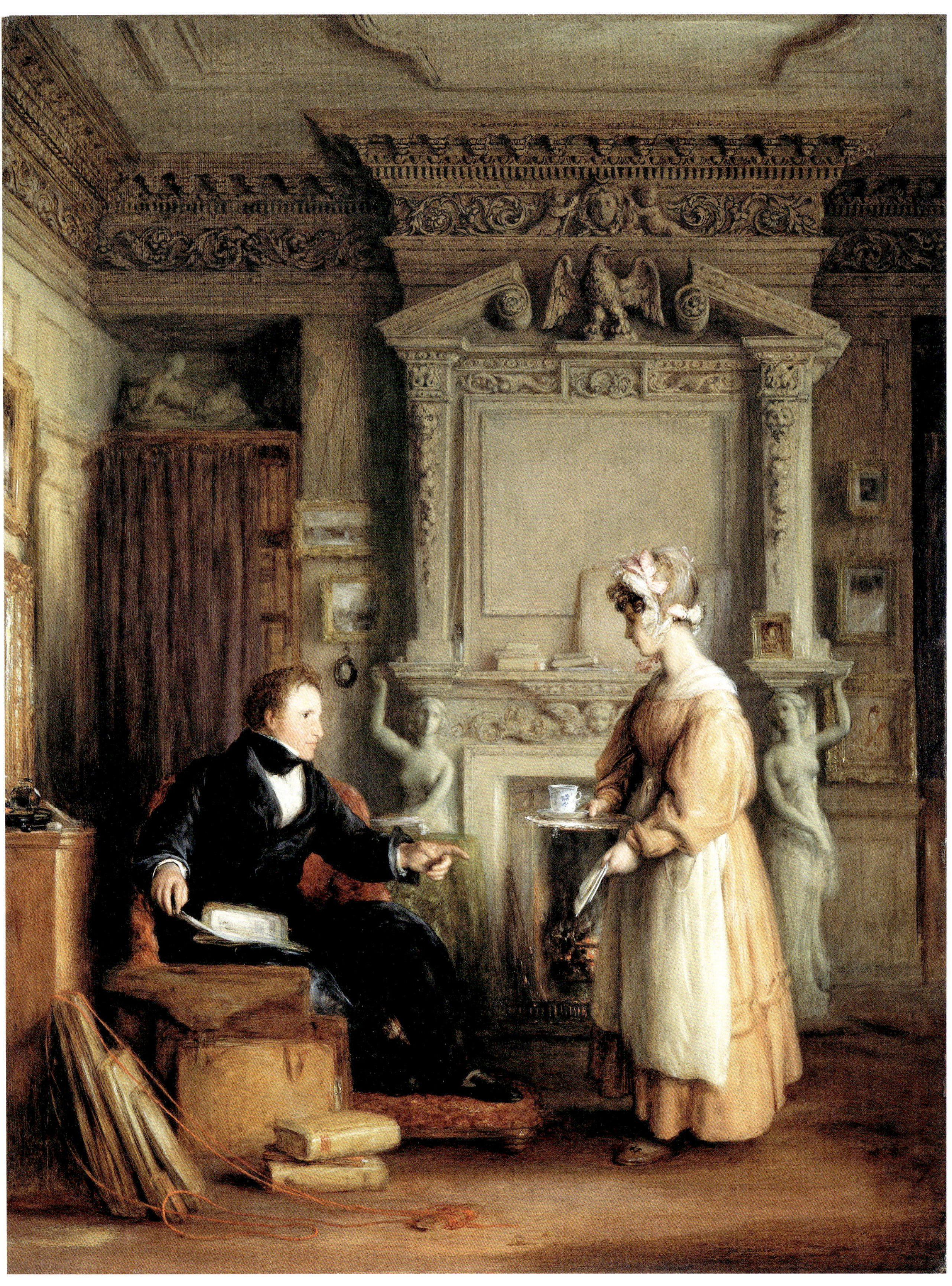

# 6 The National Gallery of British Art: John Sheepshanks

When John Sheepshanks (1787–1863) presented 531 contemporary British oil paintings, watercolours and drawings to the nation in 1857 he envisioned it as rich seed, planted in South Kensington to inspire future donors to help form the National Gallery of British Art. His donation had a much wider influence on the museum. The first group of art works from a living private collector, it carried specific conditions about its accommodation and access hours, together with values that expanded South Kensington's aims, from design reform for manufactured goods to social reform.

In his Deed of Gift, Sheepshanks specified that a 'suitable gallery, to be called "The National Gallery of British Art", shall be at once erected by the British Government' for his collection.[1] This was no act of personal vanity but was rather a way to guarantee its preservation and display. His modesty and sincerity are confirmed by another condition, that his collection be 'deposited in such gallery with any other pictures or works of Art that may be subsequently placed there by other contributors, as it is not my desire that my collection . . . shall be kept apart or bear my name as such'. He required that his collection should be 'used . . . in the Schools of Art' and urged Henry Cole to open the new gallery on Sundays and in the evenings to be accessible to the working man and his family.[2] He chose many paintings illustrative of the popular literature of the day (rather than the allegories and subjects from classical history, the Bible and mythology to be seen at the National Gallery) that were meticulously executed in the tradition of Dutch cabinet pictures of the 17th century. He also favoured irresistible scenes painted by leading modern artists such as Landseer, Constable (fig.17), Turner (fig.14) and Mulready (fig.13) – paintings that a general public could readily enjoy.

Over the next forty years, before the Tate Gallery opened in 1897, the inspiring example of the Sheepshanks Gift led to the arrival, in rapid succession, of multiple collections of both British and Continental art. These include: the Townshend Bequest (1868); the Dyce Collection (1869; see chapter 7); the John Parsons Bequest (1870) of 92 oil paintings and 47 watercolours; the Ellison Gift by Richard Ellison's widow (1860; 1873) of 100 British watercolours 'to promote the foundation of the National Collection of Water Colour Paintings at Kensington' (figs 15 and 16);[3] the bequest (1870) of 222 English watercolours from William Smith (vice-president of the National Portrait Gallery); the Forster Collection (1876); and the Joshua Dixon Bequest (1886; see chapter 13). Isabel Constable's gift (1887–8) of 95 oil paintings and sketches, 297 watercolours and drawings and three sketchbooks from her father's studio became the foundation of the national collection of John Constable's art at the V&A (figs 19, 20, 21, 23).[4] To this was added in 1900 the Henry Vaughan Bequest, which included Constable's 6-foot oil sketches for *The Hay Wain* and *The Leaping Horse* (fig.22), on loan since 1862. Two other major bequests of pictures came in 1900: the Henry Ashbee Bequest, comprising 43 oil paintings and 177 watercolours; and Emily Dalton's bequest of 220 master drawings, including works by Rembrandt, Rubens and Van Dyck, and 205 prints.[5] There were also two public collections of British

**13.** William Mulready, *Interior with a Portrait of John Sheepshanks*, 1832–4, oil on panel. Given by John Sheepshanks. V&A: FA.142.

**14.** J.M.W. TURNER, *St. Michael's Mount, Cornwall*, c.1834, oil on canvas. Exhibited Royal Academy 1834 and bought (or commissioned) by John Sheepshanks, by whom given. V&A: FA.209.

**15.** SAMUEL PALMER, *Going to Sea*, 1858, watercolour. Ellison Gift. V&A: FA.538. Palmer changed the title from 'Going to India: The Blessing' and from 'Return from India', probably in response to reports of the Indian Revolt of 1857–8.

**16.** GEORGE CATTERMOLE, *Cellini and the Robbers*, c.1830–50, watercolour. Ellison Gift. V&A: FA.505. A scene from the memoirs of the Florentine goldsmith, completed 1563, published in English 1822.

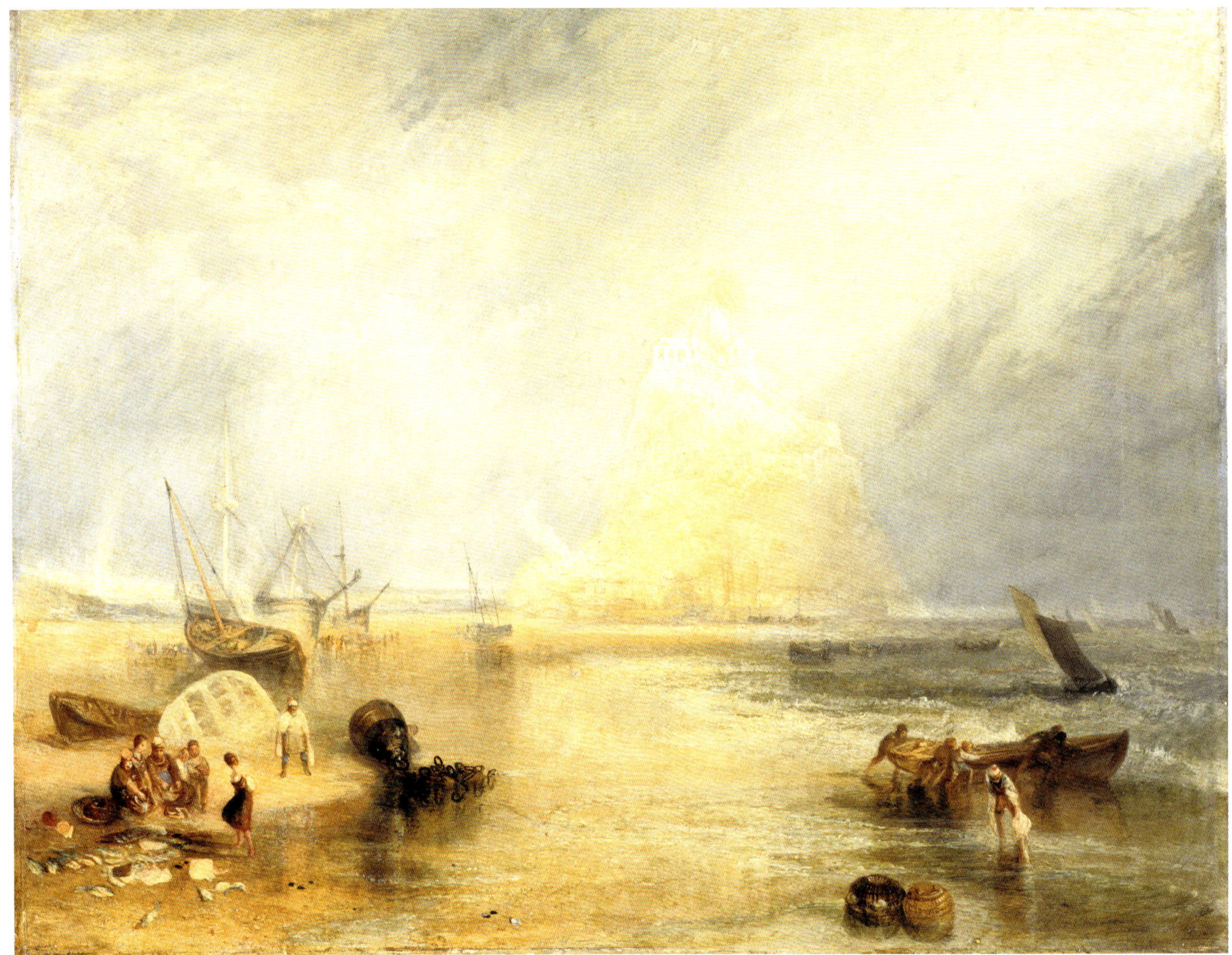

paintings, for from 1860 until 1876 the National Gallery lent to South Kensington the Robert Vernon Collection and the bequest of J.M.W. Turner.[6]

Further masterpieces of British painting arrived in 1901, included in the Ionides Collection (see chapter 15). Several other private collections of paintings came on long loan and left. Although Sheepshanks did not require that the new purpose-built gallery be named after him and be devoted solely to his paintings, many subsequent donors followed his lead in requiring that rooms be found to show their collections, to prevent them being left in store. Some donors were even more specific in requiring that their collections remain together in dedicated galleries to carry their names to posterity – conditions the museum's masters continued to offer and accept in its first half century in order to secure large donations, however impractical for their successors to honour.

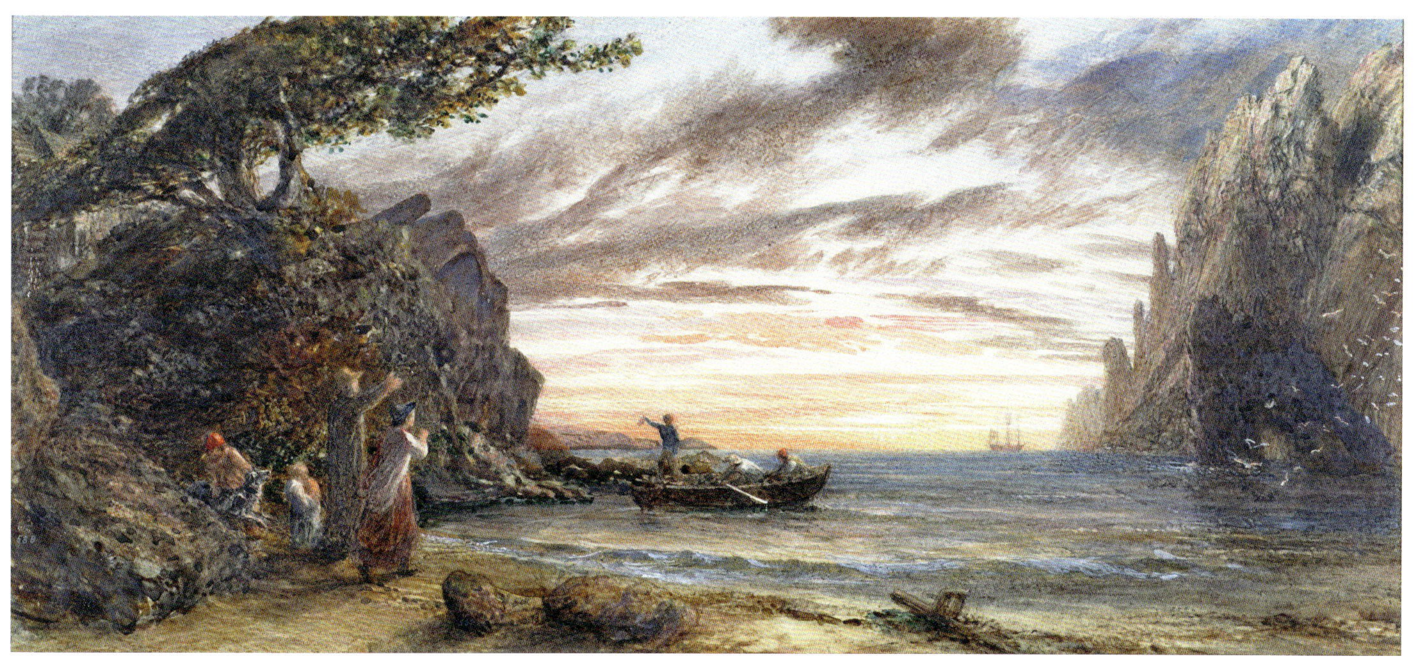

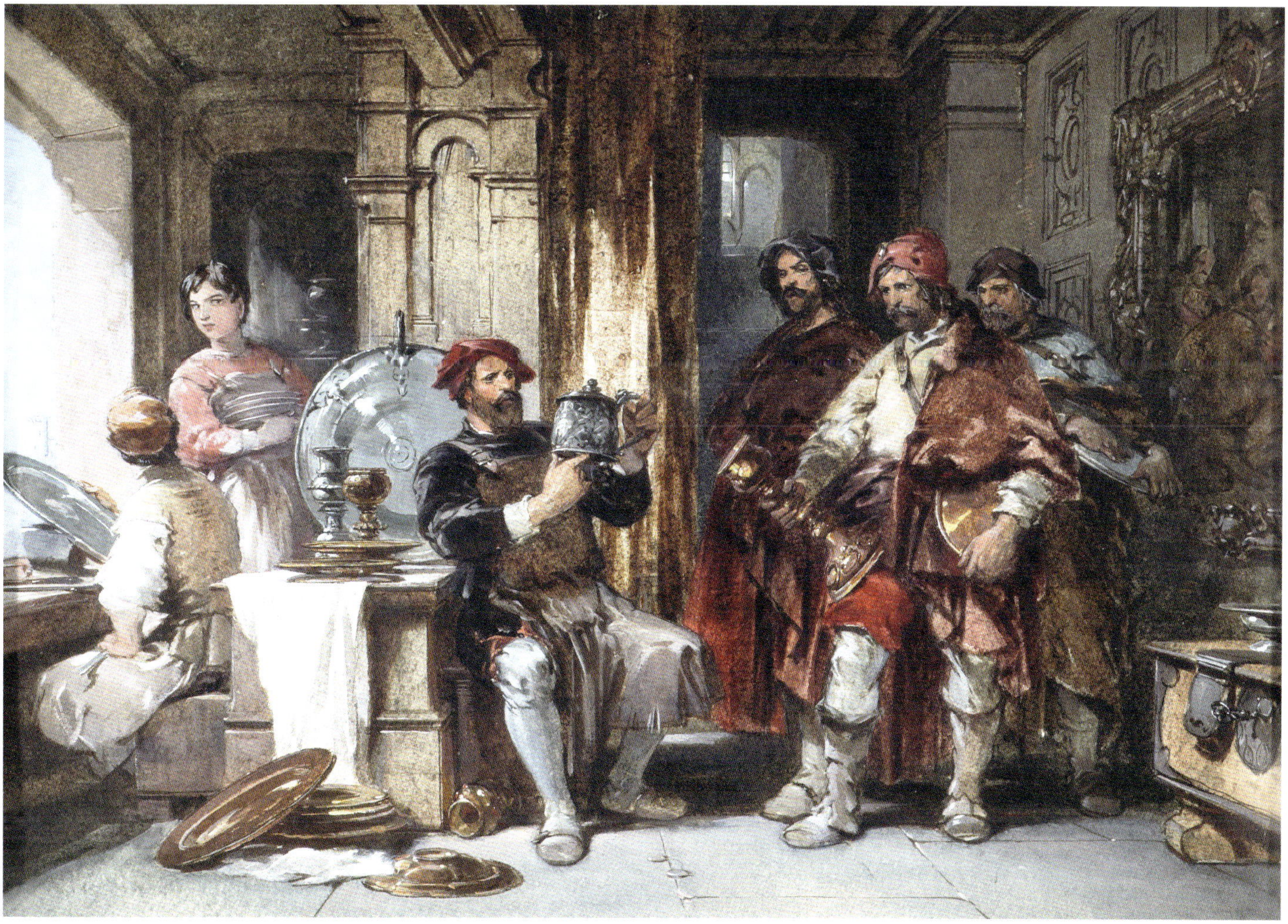

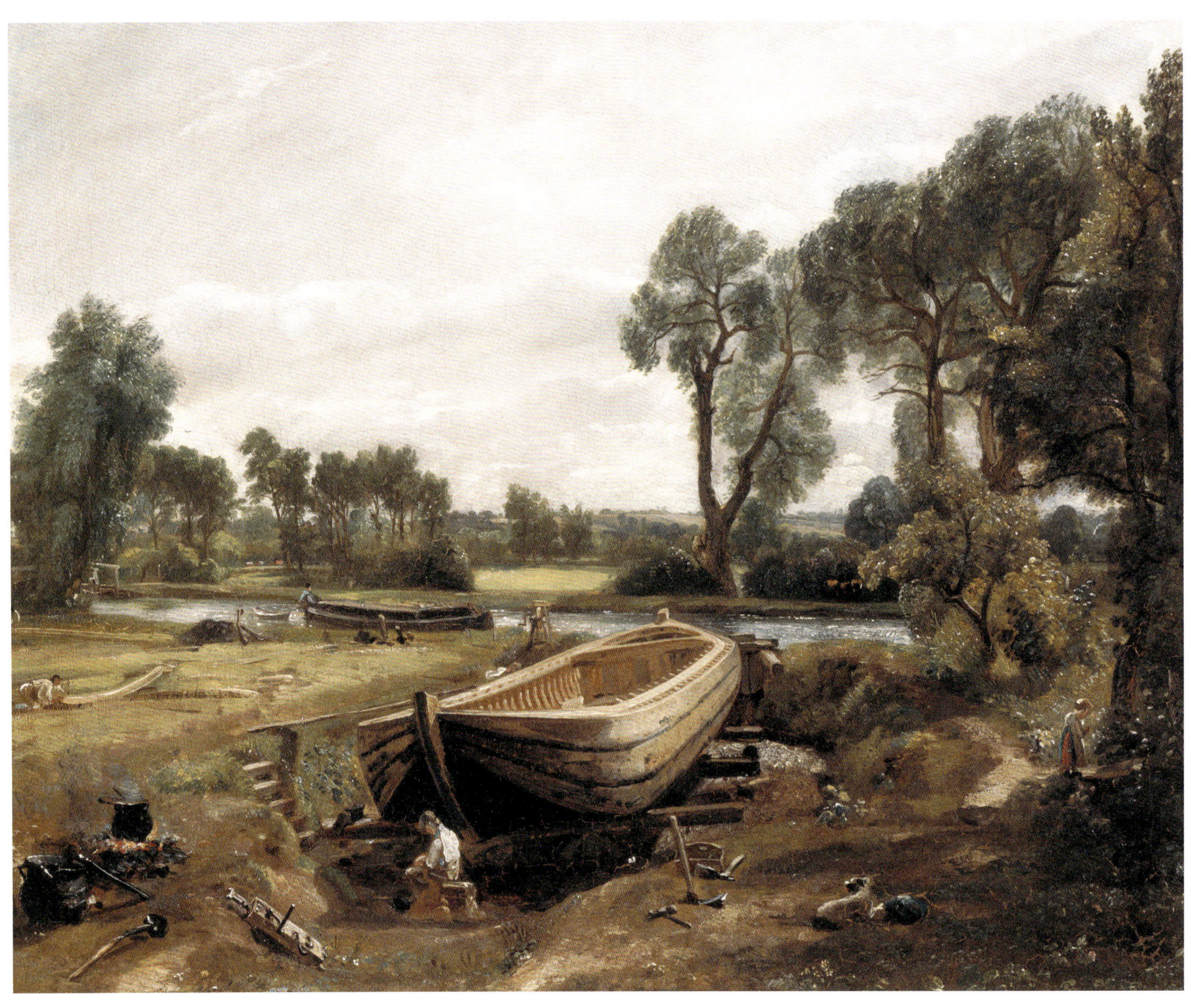

**17.** John Constable, *Boat-Building near Flatford Mill*, 1815, oil on canvas. Given by John Sheepshanks. V&A: FA.37.

**18.** Carl Friedrich Heinrich Werner, *Christian Ludwig Brehm, Ornithologist*, *c.*1850–60, watercolour. Ellison Gift. V&A: FA.549. Brehm's collection of 15,000 bird skins was purchased by Lord Rothschild for his natural history museum at Tring.

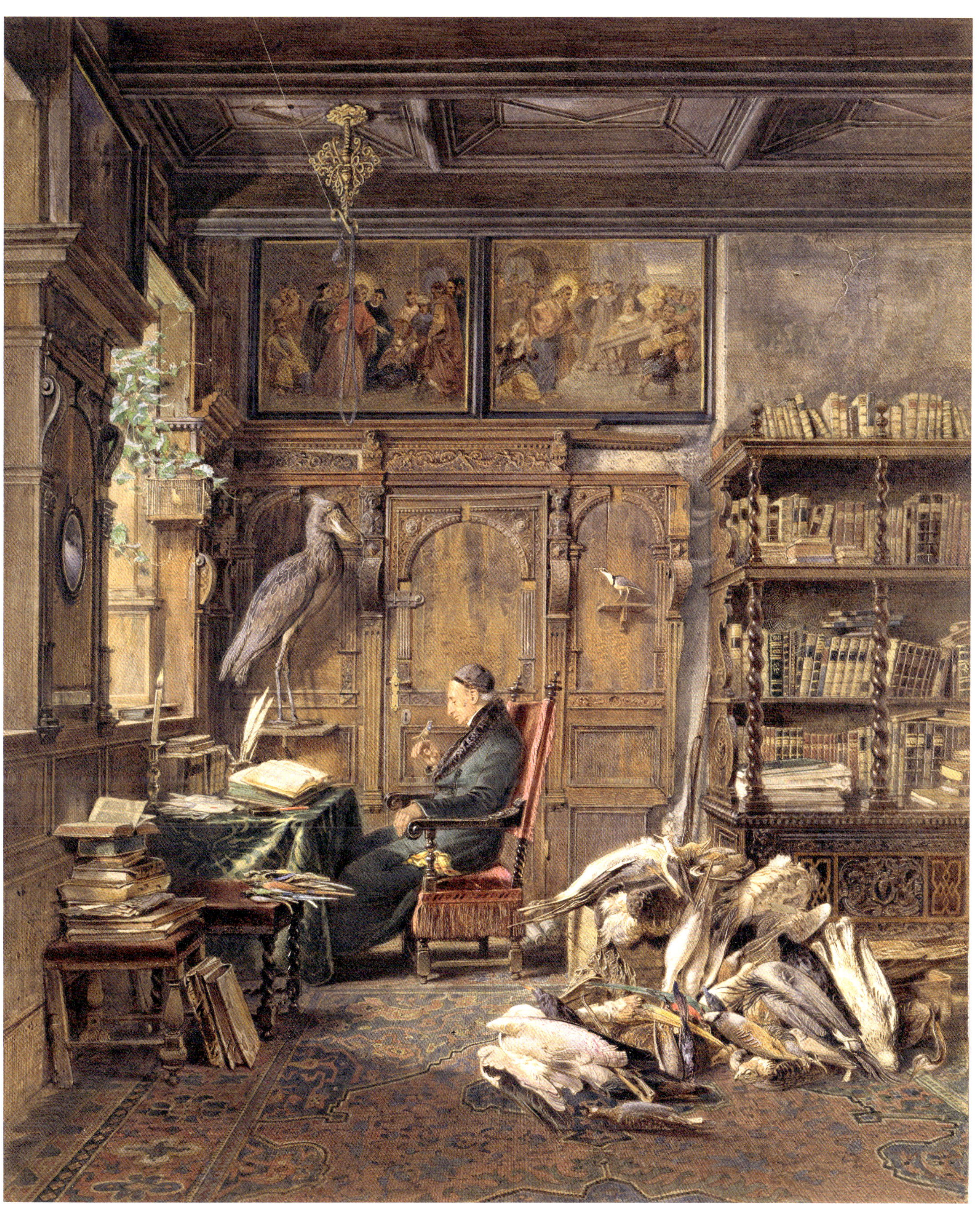

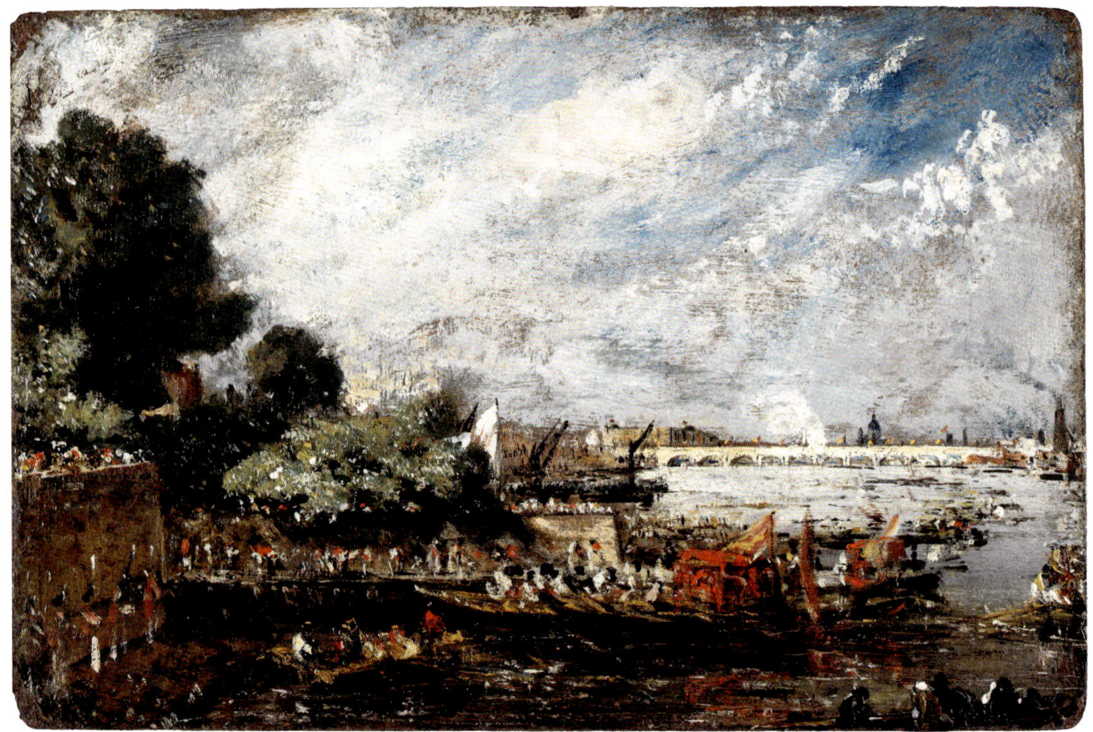

**19.** John Constable, *The Opening of Waterloo Bridge from Whitehall Stairs, June 18th 1817*, *c.*1819, oil on millboard. Given by Isabel Constable. V&A: 322-1888.

**20.** John Constable, *Brighton Beach*, 1824, oil on paper. Given by Isabel Constable. V&A: 335-1888.

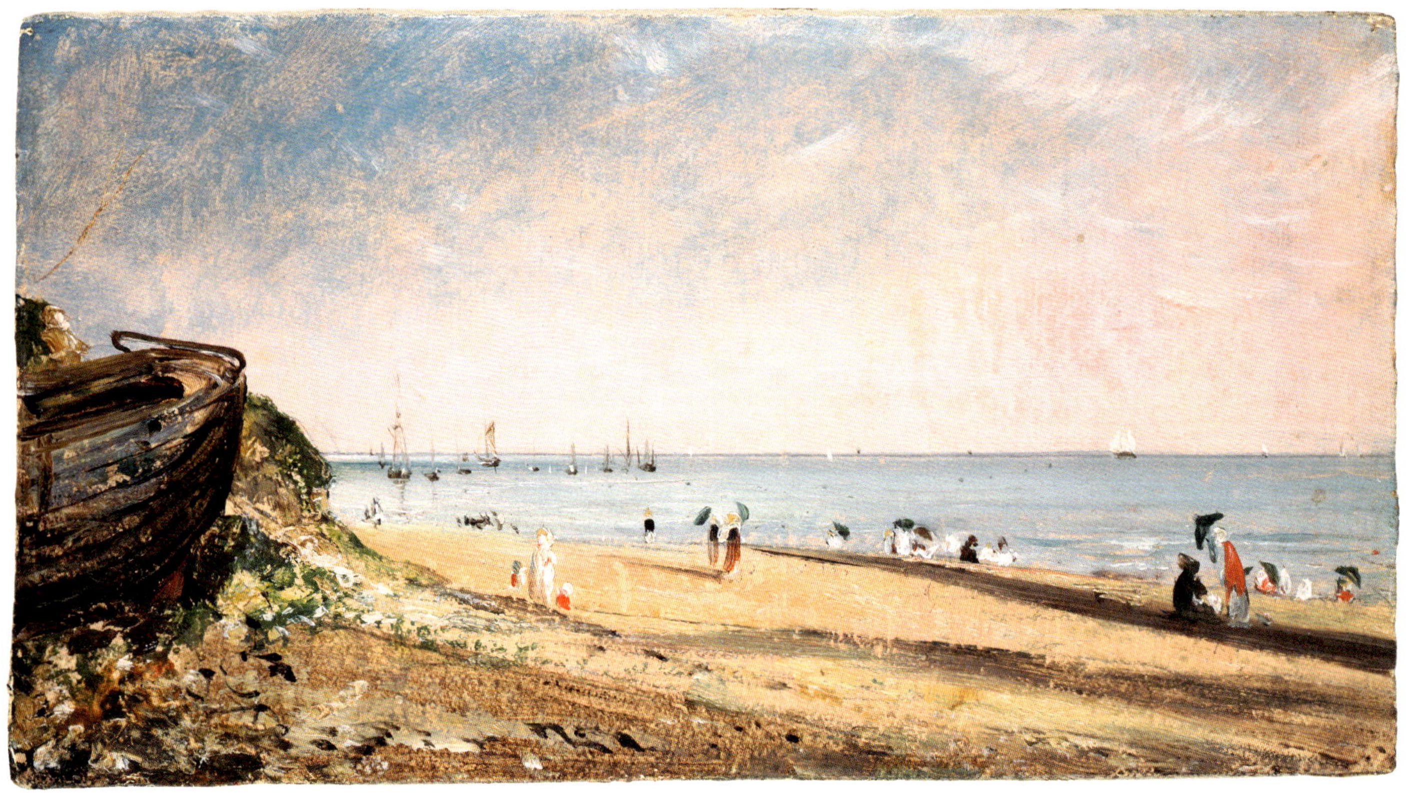

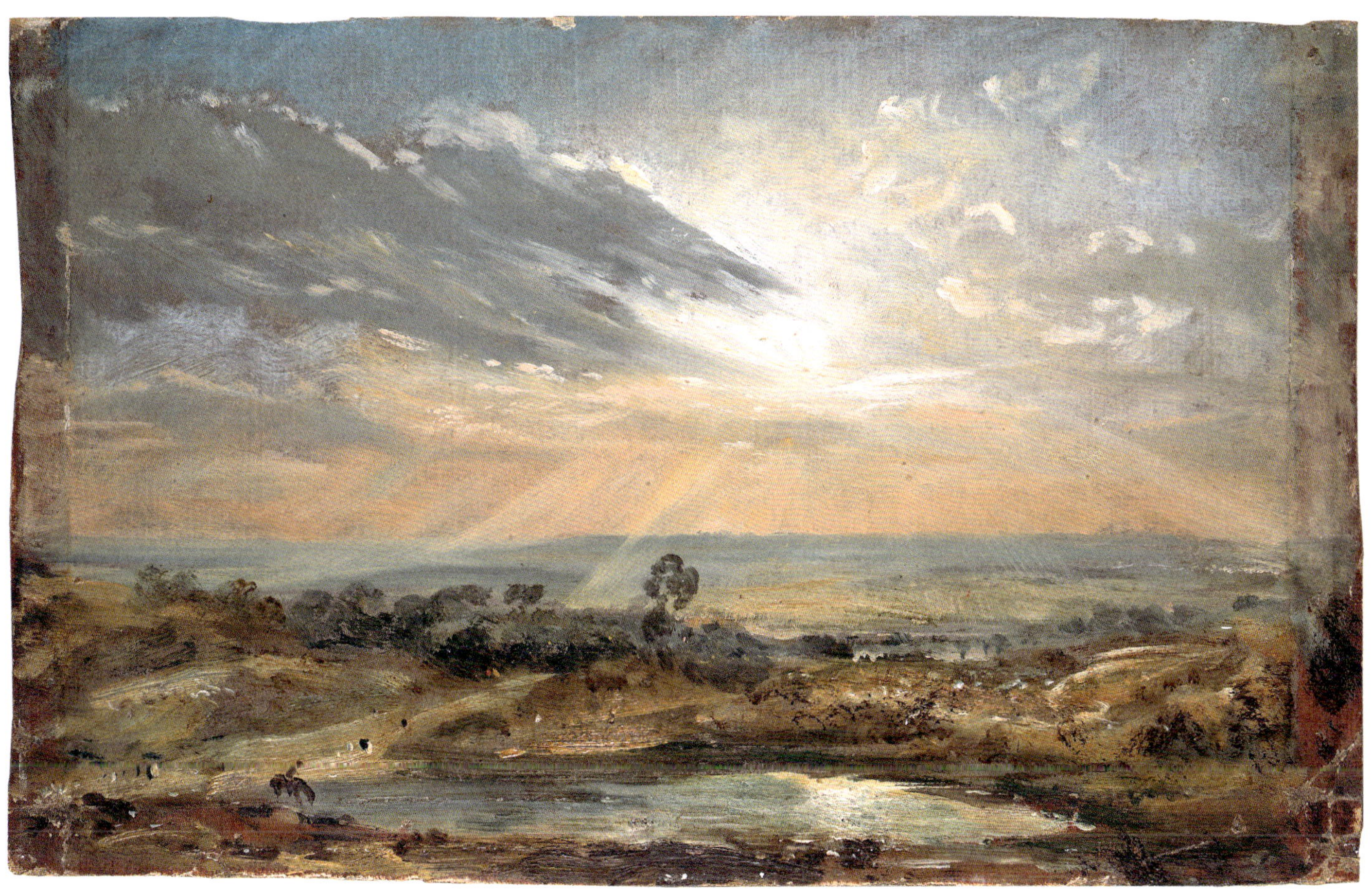

**21.** John Constable, *Branch Hill Pond, Hampstead*, c.1821–2, oil on canvas. Given by Isabel Constable. V&A: 125-1888.

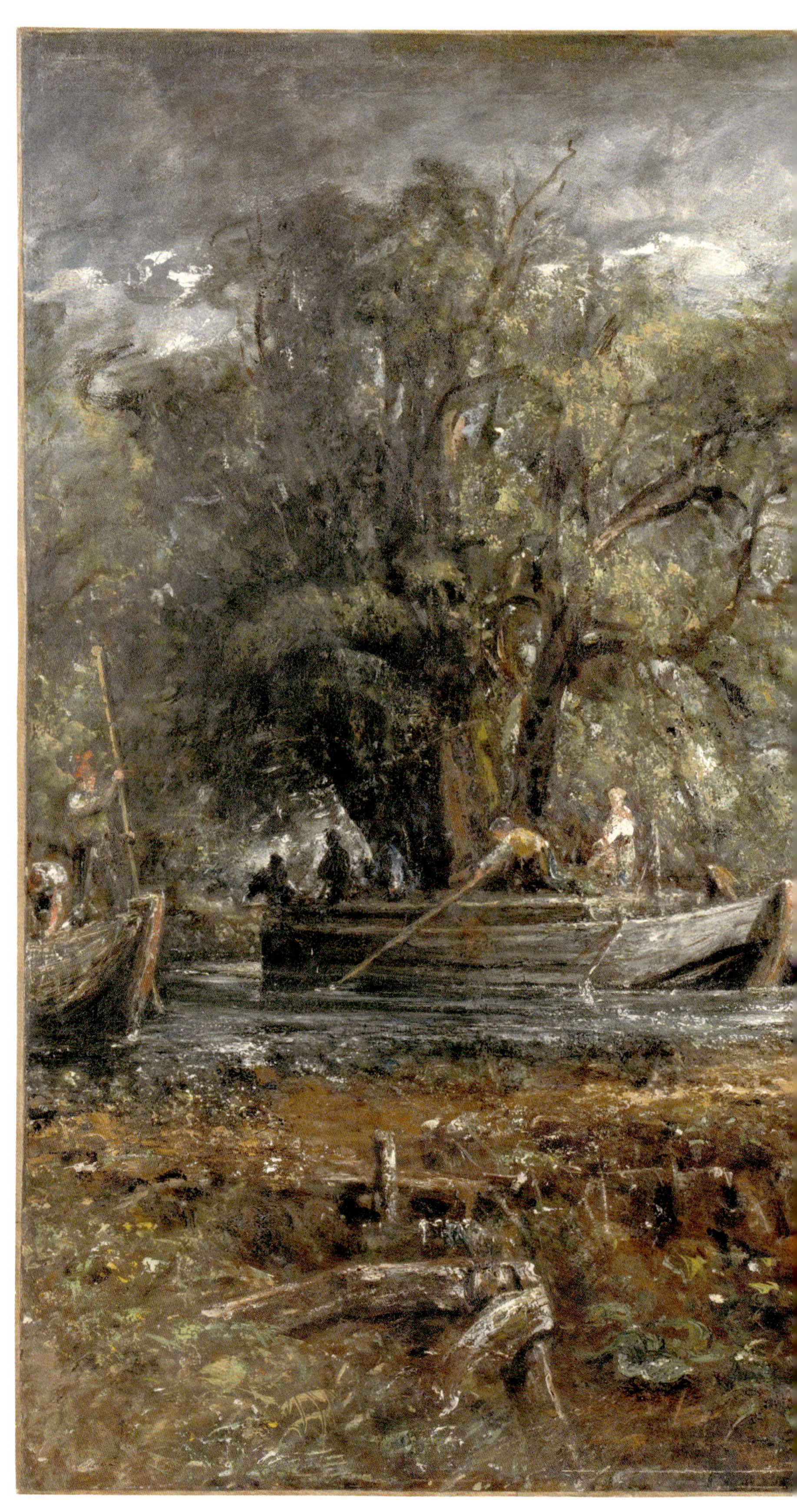

**22.** John Constable, *The Leaping Horse* (full-scale study), *c.*1825, oil on canvas. Bequeathed by Henry Vaughan. V&A: 986-1900.

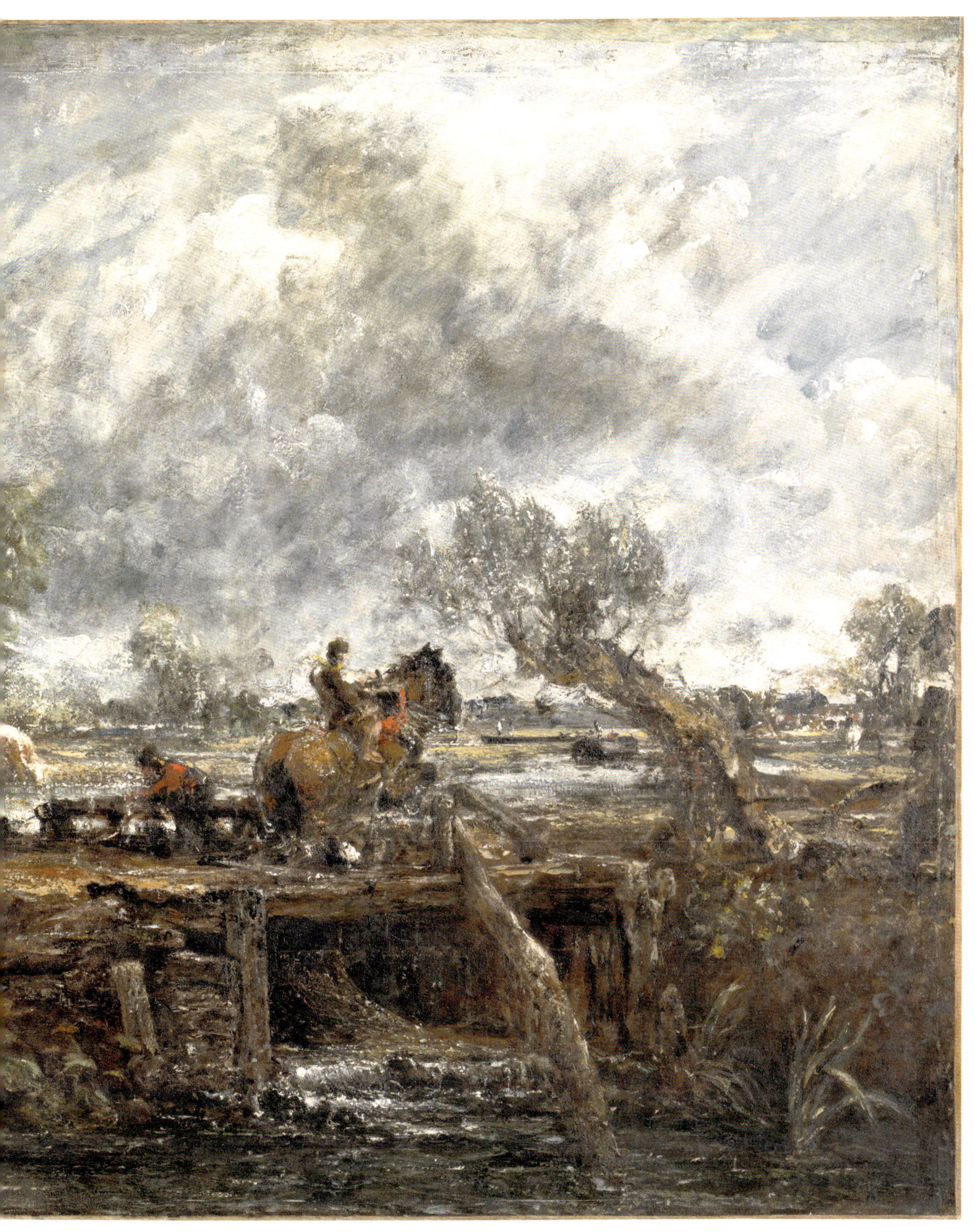

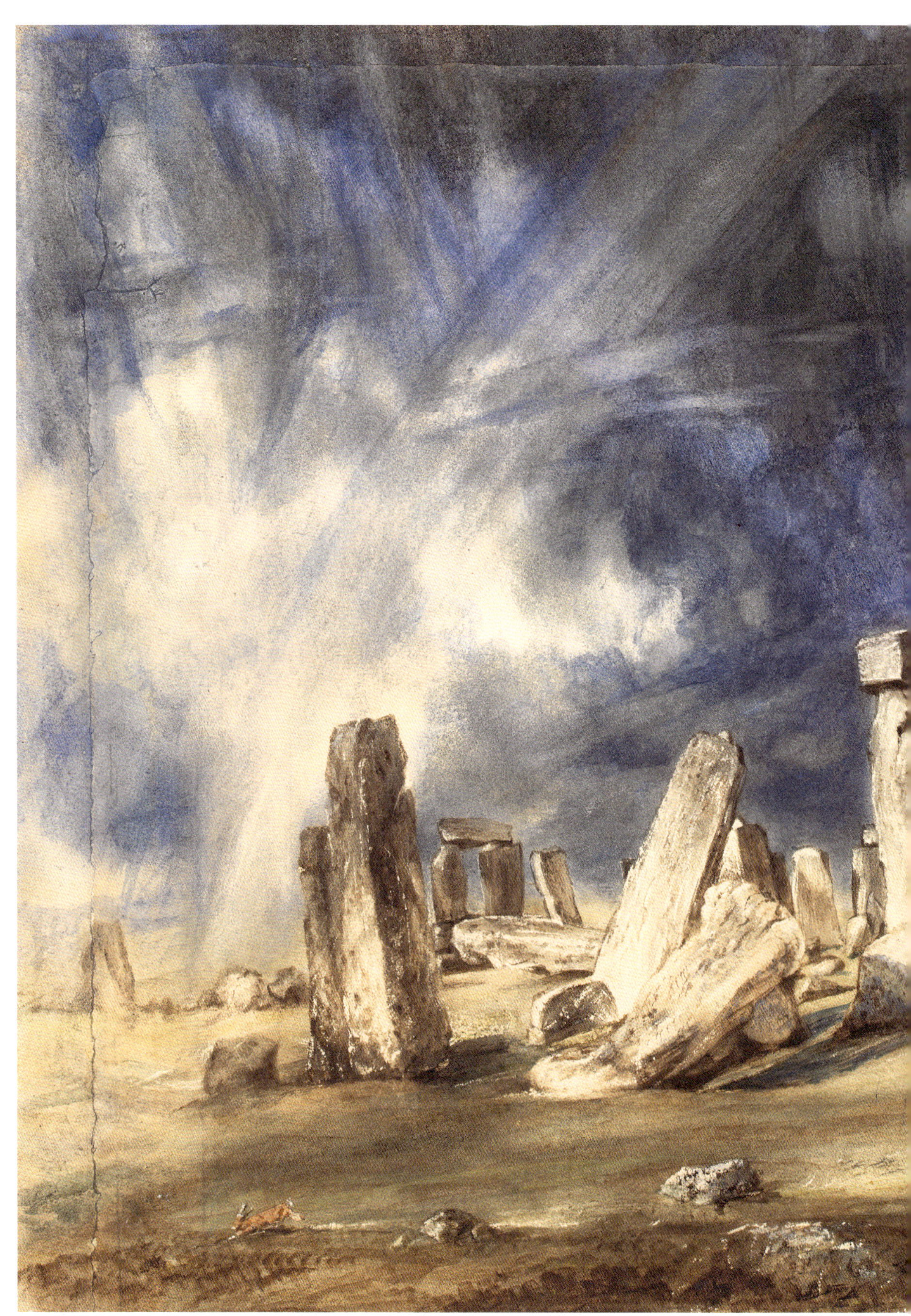

**23.** John Constable, *Stonehenge*, 1835, watercolour. Given by Isabel Constable. V&A: 1629-1888.

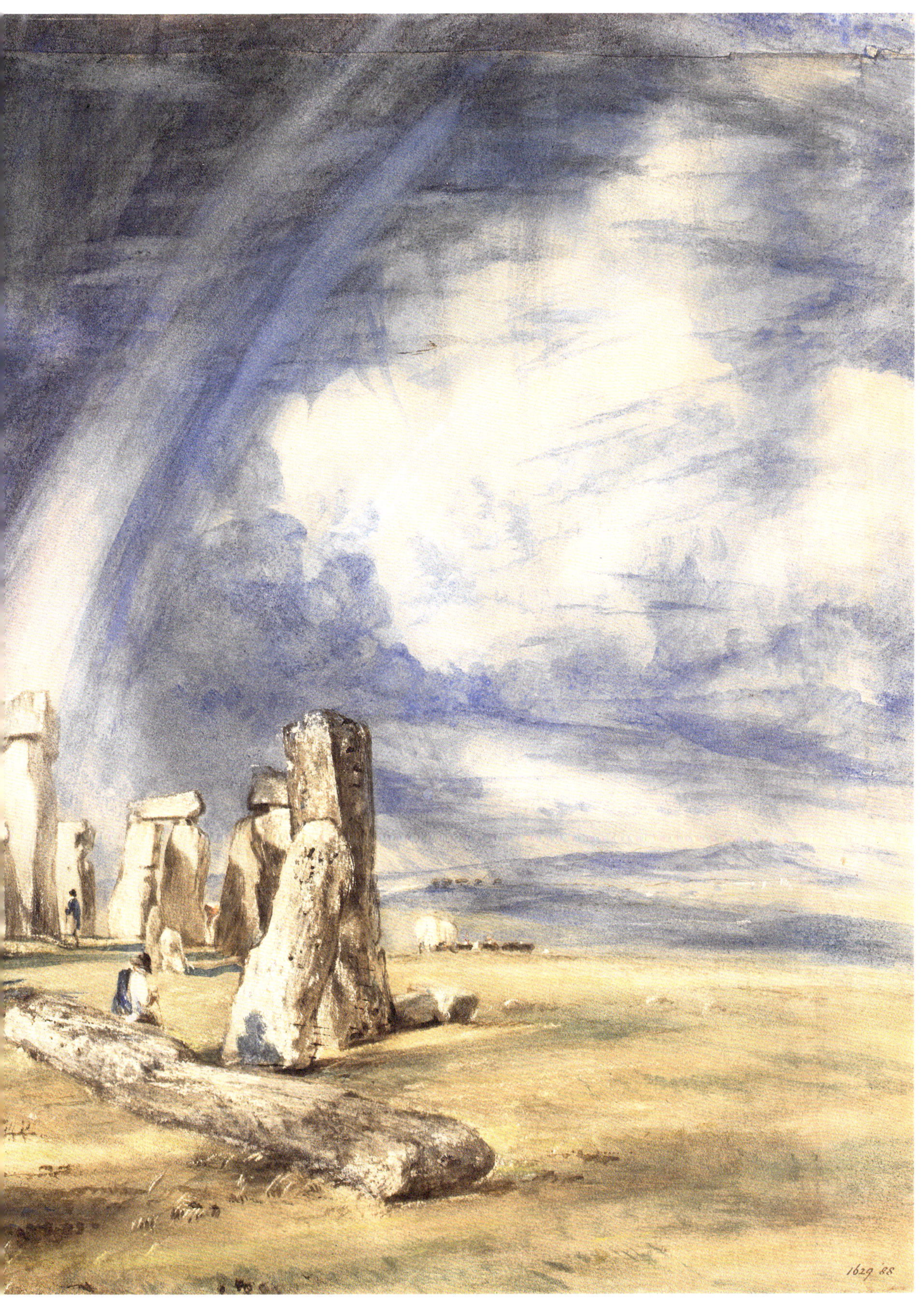

# 7 European Paintings and Drawings: Chauncy Hare Townshend; Alexander Dyce

24. John Boaden, *The Reverend Chauncy Hare Townshend*, c.1828, oil on canvas. Bequeathed by Rev. Chauncy Hare Townshend. V&A: 1411-1869.

Three friends of Charles Dickens – Alexander Dyce, John Forster and Chauncy Hare Townshend – decided to leave their literary libraries and graphic arts collections to the museum. They welcomed the new institution's policy of accessibility to craftsmen, artists and to other workers and their families, rather than favouring the intellectual gentlemen already at home in the Bodleian Library at Oxford University and in the British Museum's reading rooms. First to donate was the poet, mesmerist and chronic hypochondriac, the Reverend Chauncy Hare Townshend (1798–1868). When he visited the museum, as a curator G.F. Duncombe recalled, they 'stopped to examine the jewels in the South Court, and to compare them with those in his own collection . . . it occurred to me that it would be a noble thing for him to leave his collection by will to the South Kensington Museum . . . I made the suggestion to him'.[1]

Dickens agreed to be Townshend's literary executor, dedicated *Great Expectations* (1861) to him and gave him the manuscript. Indeed, Dickens wrote in a letter 'I truly loved him'.[2] They shared a fascination with mesmerism (the science of hypnotism), of which Townshend was the leading British exponent after Dr John Elliotson, at whose home he first met Dickens in 1840. Townshend's publications included two books on the subject: *Facts in Mesmerism* (1840) and *Mesmerism Proved True* (1854). According to the leading American poet William Cullen Bryant, writing to a friend in Paris in 1842, hypnosis was rife in New York, or as he called it: 'animal magnetism, which, since the publication of the Rev. Mr. Townsend's book, has made great progress in America, in New York and elsewhere. It is quite the fashion for people to paw each other into a magnetic sleep.'[3]

To Dickens scholars Townshend is the model for Cousin Feenix in Dickens's *Dombey and Son* (1846–8) and for Melvin Twemlow in *Our Mutual Friend* (1864–5). Wilkie Collins was also among the guests at Townshend's musical evenings in his London home and the house is regarded as the source for Limmeridge House in Collins's *The Woman in White* (first published in serial form by Dickens 1859–60 in his magazine *All the Year Round*, to which Townshend contributed). In the same novel the reclusive aesthete Mr Fairlie, a collector of porcelain, ivories and 'toys and curiosities that sparkled', is modelled on Townshend. Dickens even gave Townshend his crystal ball.

For health reasons Townshend moved to Switzerland, to his villa, 'Mon Loisir', overlooking Lake Geneva near Lausanne, and only visited his London home for two months each summer. There he formed the best private collection of Swiss art outside Switzerland. Now in the V&A, it includes 16 oils by the Swiss painter François Bocion which range from views of Lake Geneva to a portrait of Townshend's King Charles spaniel, Bully (figs 25, 26). Dickens visited Townshend in Switzerland several times and mentions the dog in his correspondence, as 'of a diabolical turn of mind'; once Townshend was 'severely treated by Bully who rules him with a paw of iron'.[4]

Townshend's collection of paintings fills five pages of Gustav Waagen's supplementary volume to his survey, *Treasures of Art in Great Britain* (1857).

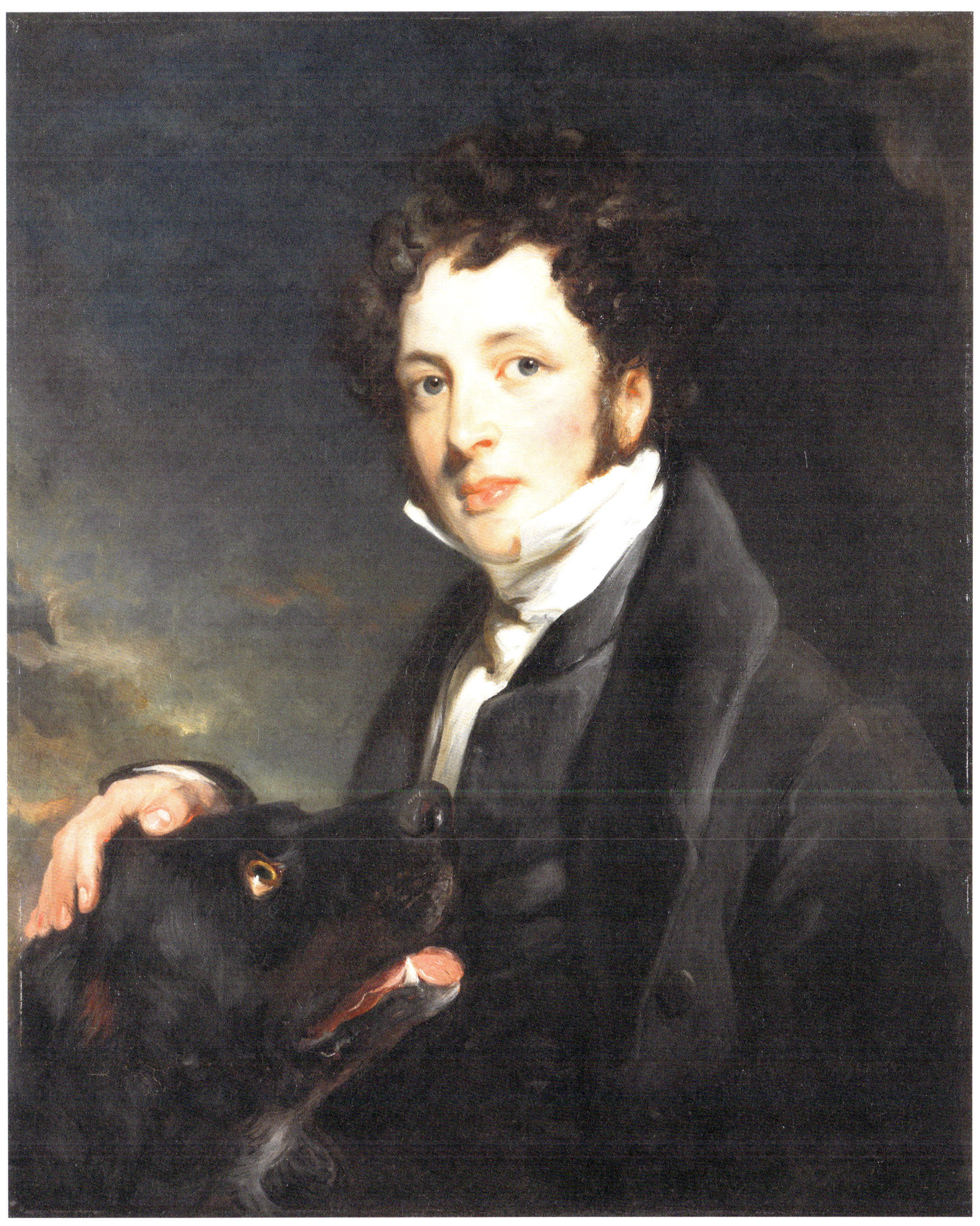

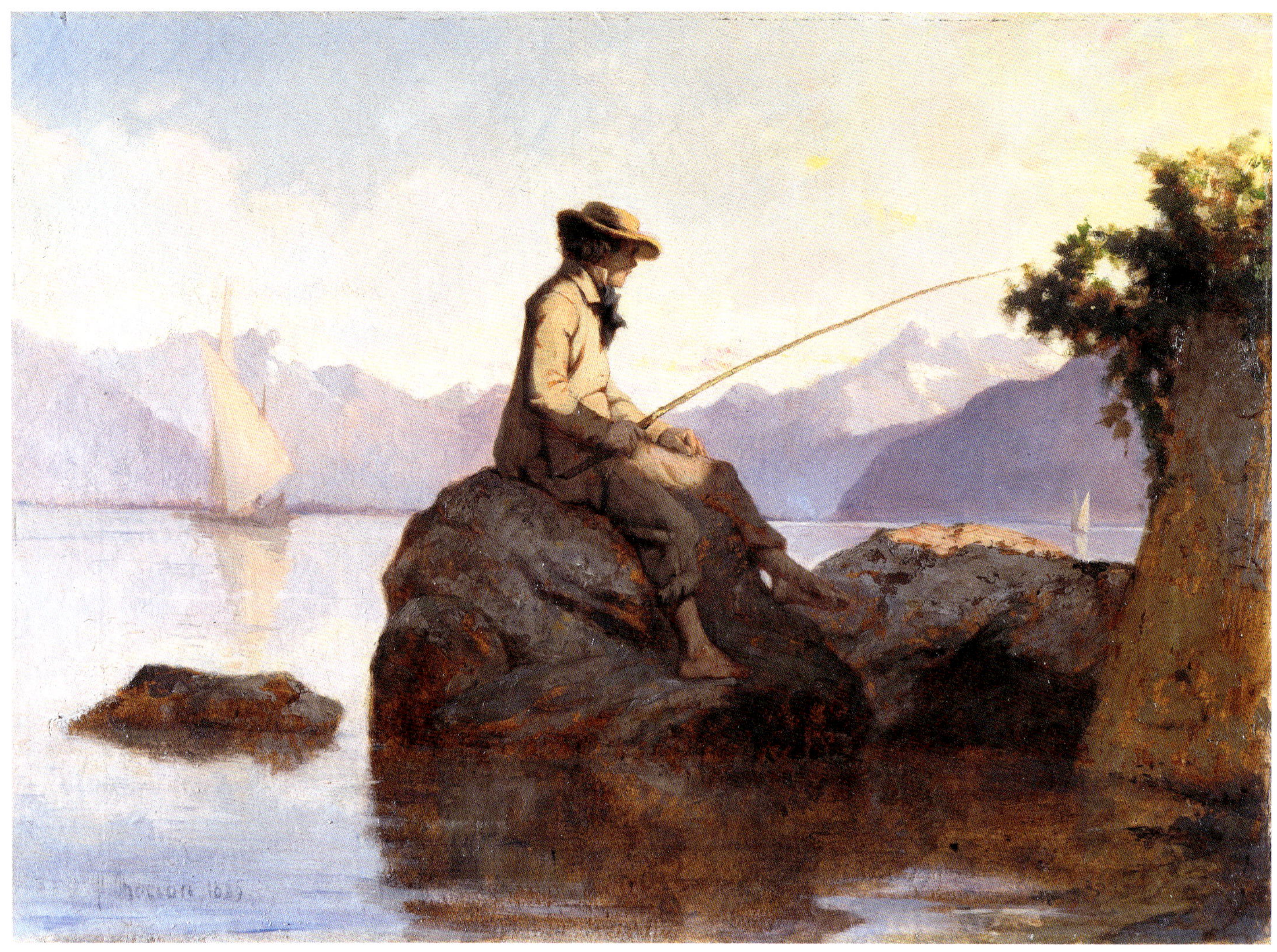

25. François Bocion, *Fishing*, 1855, oil on millboard. Bequeathed by Rev. Chauncy Hare Townshend. V&A: 1595-1869.

The curator of Prussia's royal paintings gallery described 'admirable works by the best painters of Belgium, Holland, Germany and Switzerland, which are comparatively seldom met with in England'.[5] Townshend's bequest includes 186 oil paintings, about 100 of which are by his contemporaries in Continental Europe. Waagen recorded Townshend's painting *The Philosopher,* by the contemporary Belgian Nicaise De Keyser, hanging prominently in his dining room (fig.27), which suggests how the collector may have seen himself. In the same room hung the huge and extraordinarily morbid painting by Francis Danby depicting a poisonous tree and its victims (fig.28). Townshend's collection is also exceptional in Britain for its inclusion of 19th-century Scandinavian landscape paintings, several by artists (such as Knud Andreassen Baade and Georg Emil Libert (fig.29)) who worked in Munich and admired the art of Caspar David Friedrich and of his Norwegian friend Johann Christian Dahl. As painters of the northern Romantic tradition of art they belong to an alternative path, unlike the one described by most histories of Western art running from Florence and Rome to Paris.[6]

This rare British collector of paintings from Continental Europe also ranks with Prince Albert as a pioneer British collector of photographs. Most of Townshend's photography collection was formed in 1855–60 and is exceptional for its survival as a group. Masterpieces of early photography include a series of 20 French seascapes and Fontainebleau forest scenes by Gustave Le Gray (fig.31); landscapes and other subjects by Camille Silvy (fig.32); Roger

Fenton's Crimean War series; and Leonida Caldesi's portrait of the royal family at Osborne.

Townshend died at his London home, 21 Norfolk Street (now Dunraven Street), off Park Lane, facing Hyde Park, in 1868; an inventory of the house was found attached to his will. When the museum was invited to make a selection from his bequest in 1869 it did not digress far into new collecting fields; the principal new area was modern European oil paintings from Scandinavia, Germany and Switzerland. Richard Redgrave (Inspector-General for Art in South Kensington until 1875) chose 189 oil paintings (including works by Tintoretto (fig.33), Canaletto, Bellotto and Fuseli (fig.34)), 177 watercolours, 390 drawings (including the art of British and French caricaturists, from Rowlandson and Gillray to Daumier), 1,815 prints, and 831 illustrated books (including John James Audubon's *The Birds of America*, 1827: (fig.35)). The museum also selected Townshend's pioneering collection of photography as art (unfortunately his stereoscopic photographs and daguerreotypes were not chosen) plus 155 gems and precious stones (most had come from the collection of the banker Henry Philip Hope), 54 cameos and intaglios, and 4,218 Swiss coins.[7] Staff also chose the gold watch and chain of Townshend's father, which had been stolen by the notorious pickpocket George Barrington resulting in his transportation to Australia, where he became a noted writer.[8]

The collection was swiftly installed, for a *Guide to the Art Collections* published in 1869 records the 'Rev. C.H. Townshend's Bequest' among the

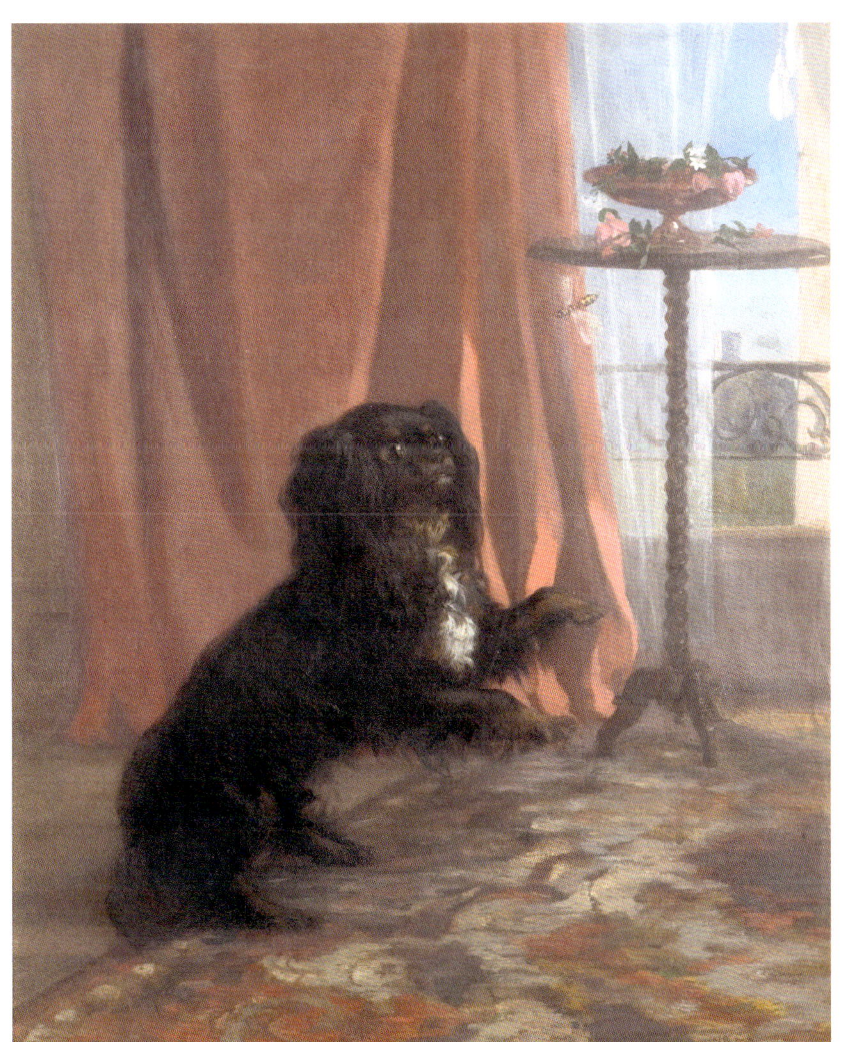

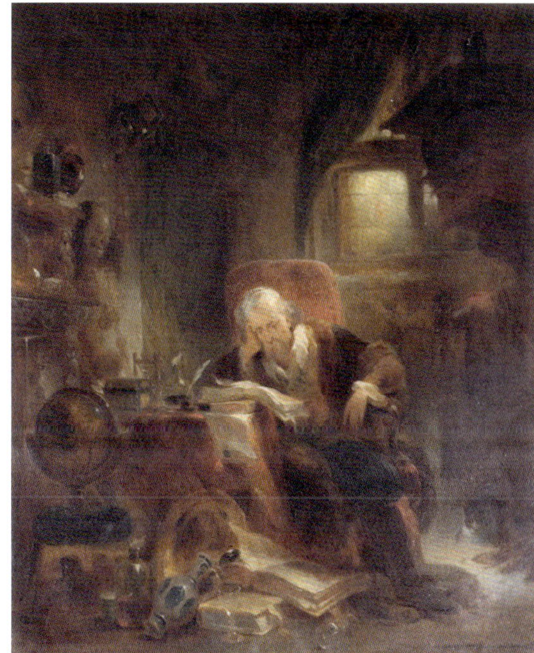

**26.** François Bocion, *The Reverend Townshend's Dog, 'Bully'*, 1855, oil on canvas. Bequeathed by Rev. Chauncy Hare Townshend. V&A: 1621-1869.

**27.** Nicaise De Keyser, *The Philosopher*, c.1850, oil on canvas. Bequeathed by Rev. Chauncy Hare Townshend. V&A: 1557-1869.

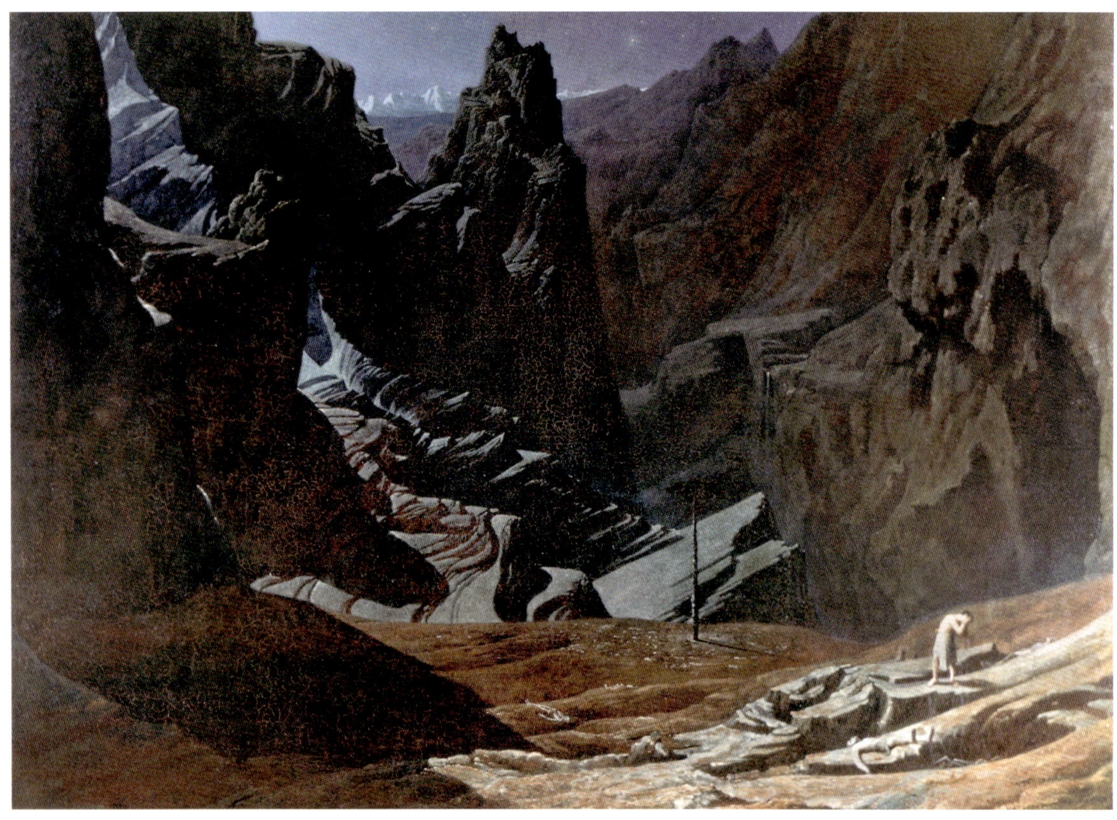

**28.** Francis Danby, *The Upas, or Poison-Tree, in the Island of Java*, *c*.1820, oil on canvas. Bequeathed by Rev. Chauncy Hare Townshend. V&A: 1382-1869.

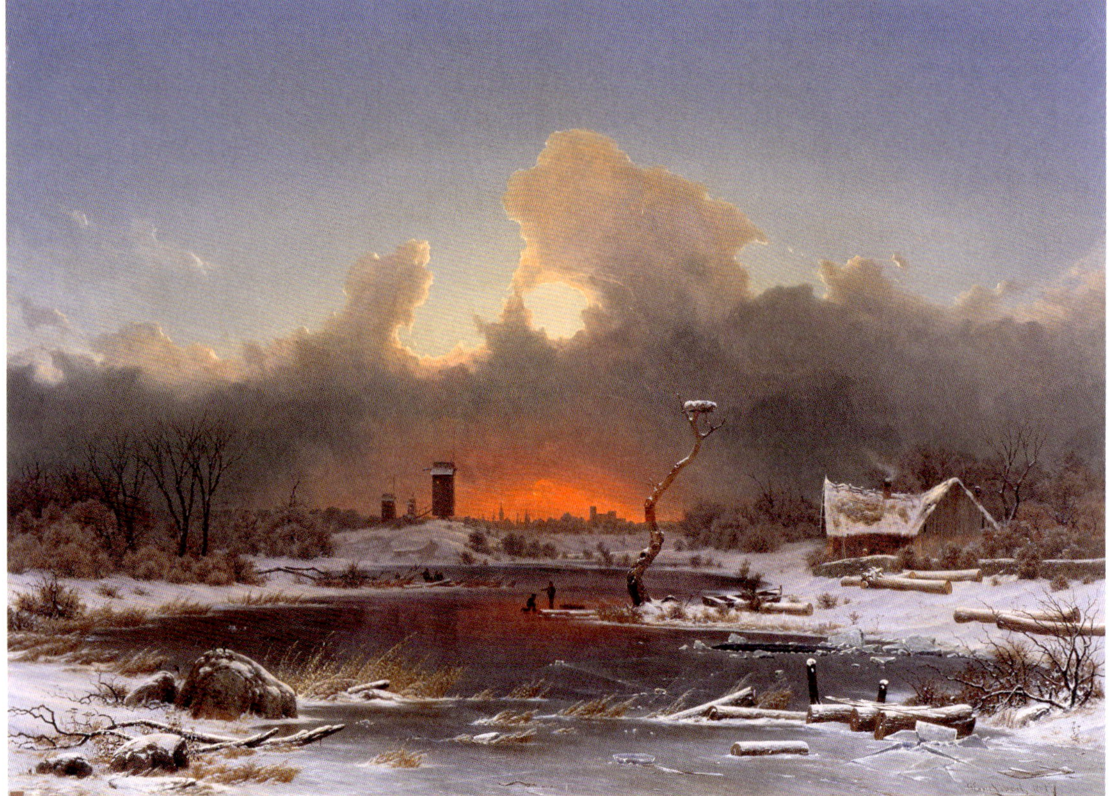

**29.** Georg Emil Libert, *Frost Scene: The Setting Sun*, 1847, oil on canvas. Bequeathed by Rev. Chauncy Hare Townshend. V&A: 1577-1869.

**30.** Joseph Hornung, *The Village Turner*, *c*.1850–60, oil on panel. Bequeathed by Rev. Chauncy Townshend. V&A: 1596-1869.

**31.** Gustave Le Gray, *The Great Wave, Sète*, 1856, albumen print from two collodion-on-glass negatives. Bequeathed by Rev. Chauncy Hare Townshend. V&A: 68004.

**32.** Camille Silvy, *River Scene*, 1858. Bequeathed by Rev. Chauncy Hare Townshend. V&A: 68012.

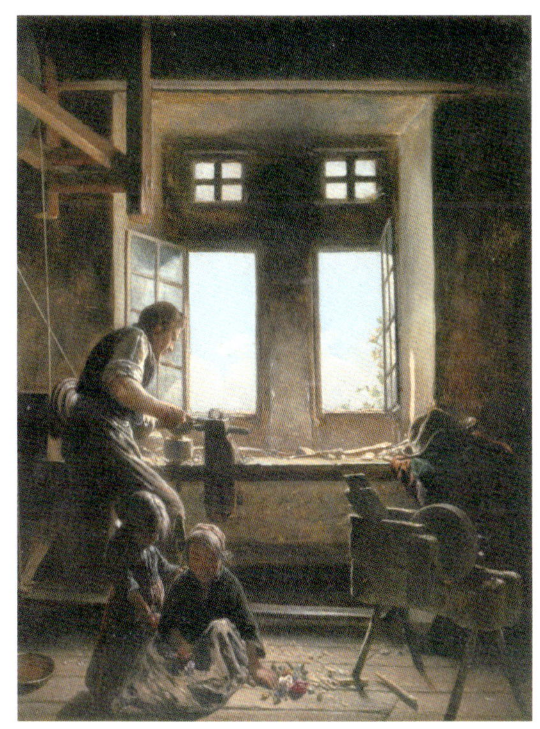

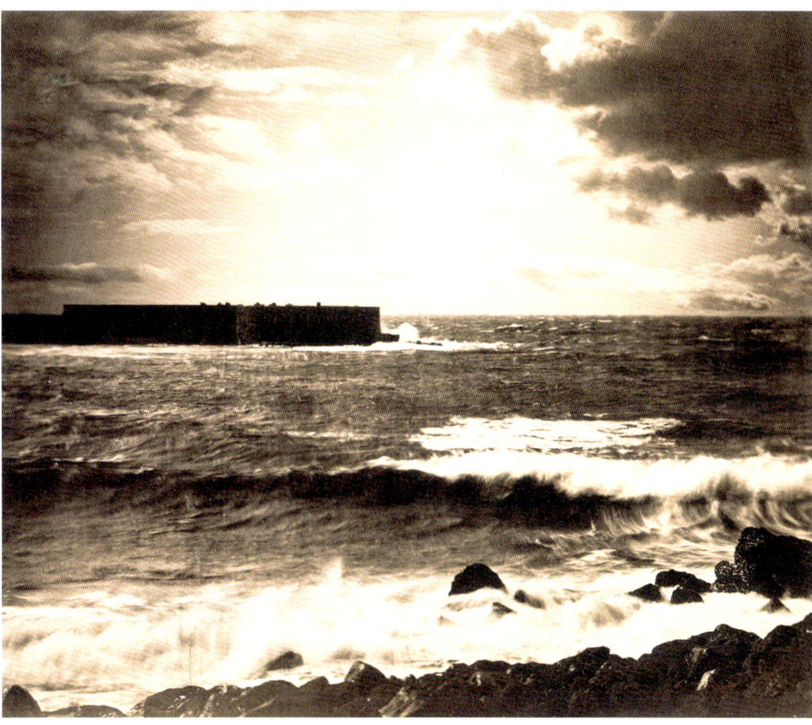

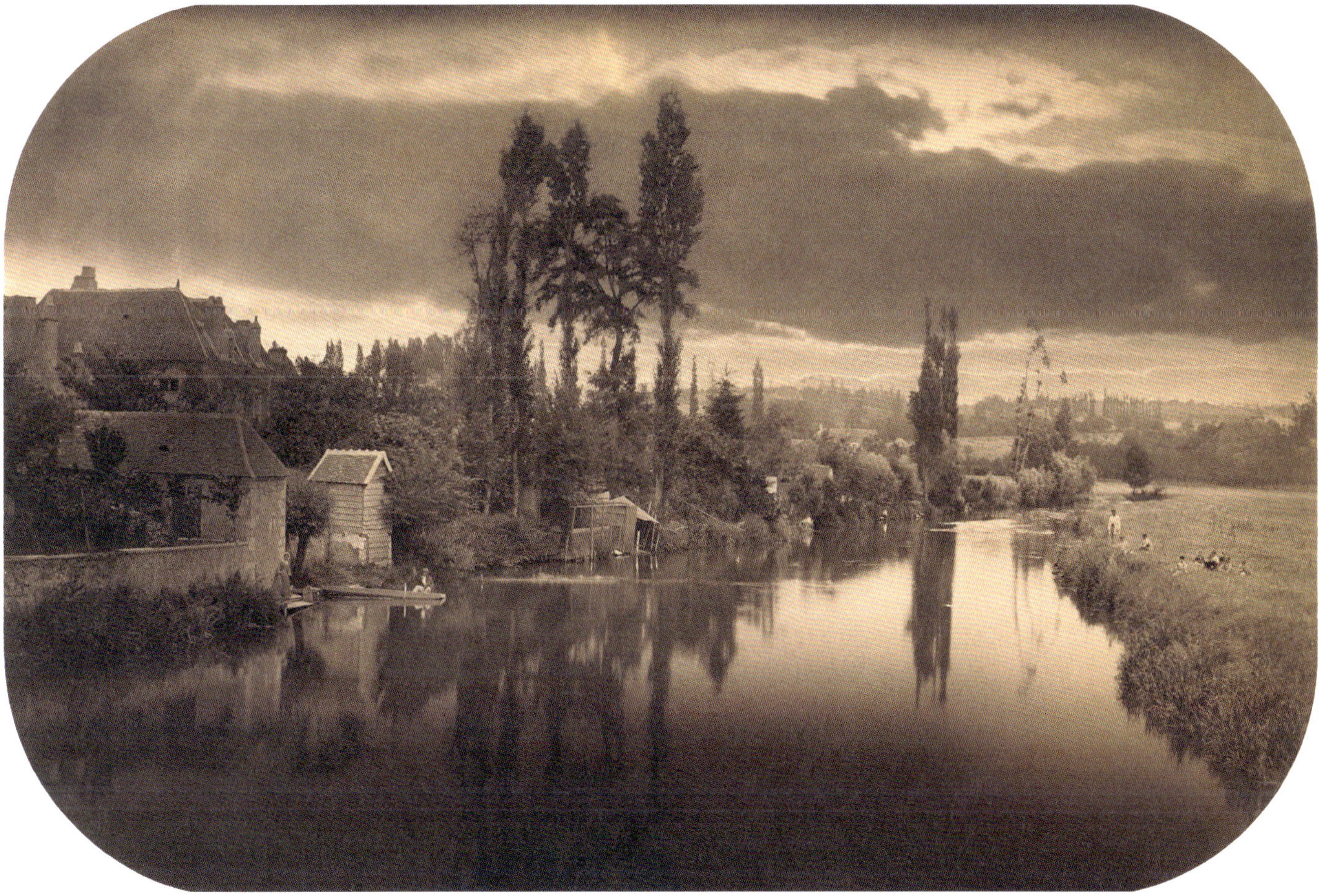

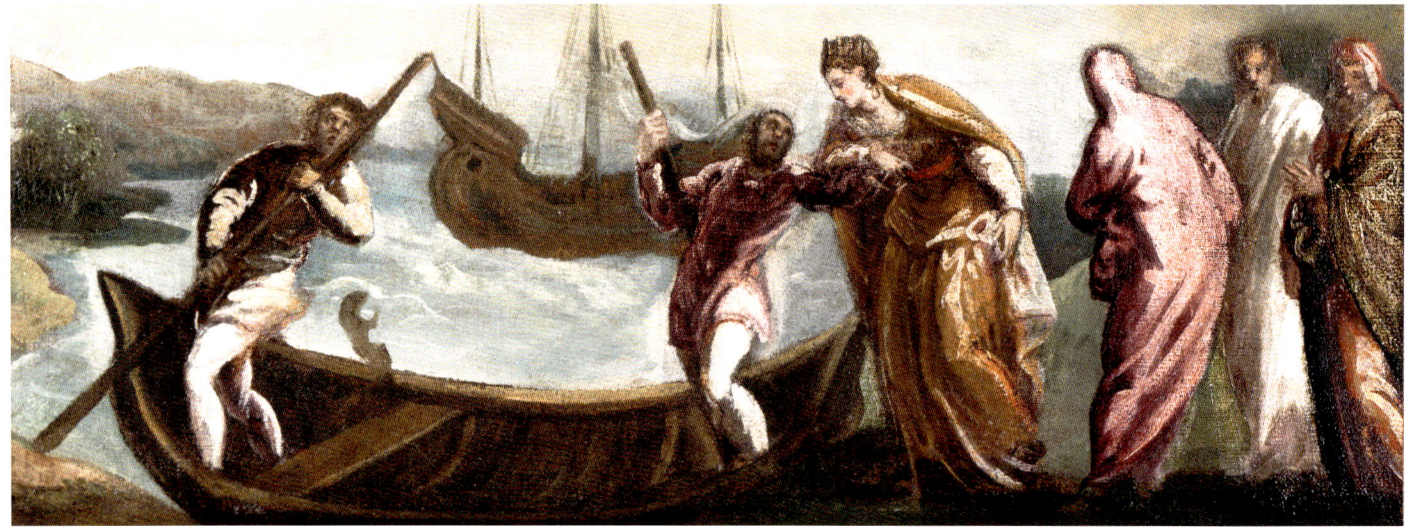

**33.** Jacopo Tintoretto, *The Embarkation of St Helena to the Holy Land*, *c.*1555, oil on canvas. Bequeathed by Rev. Chauncy Hare Townshend. V&A: 1361-1869.

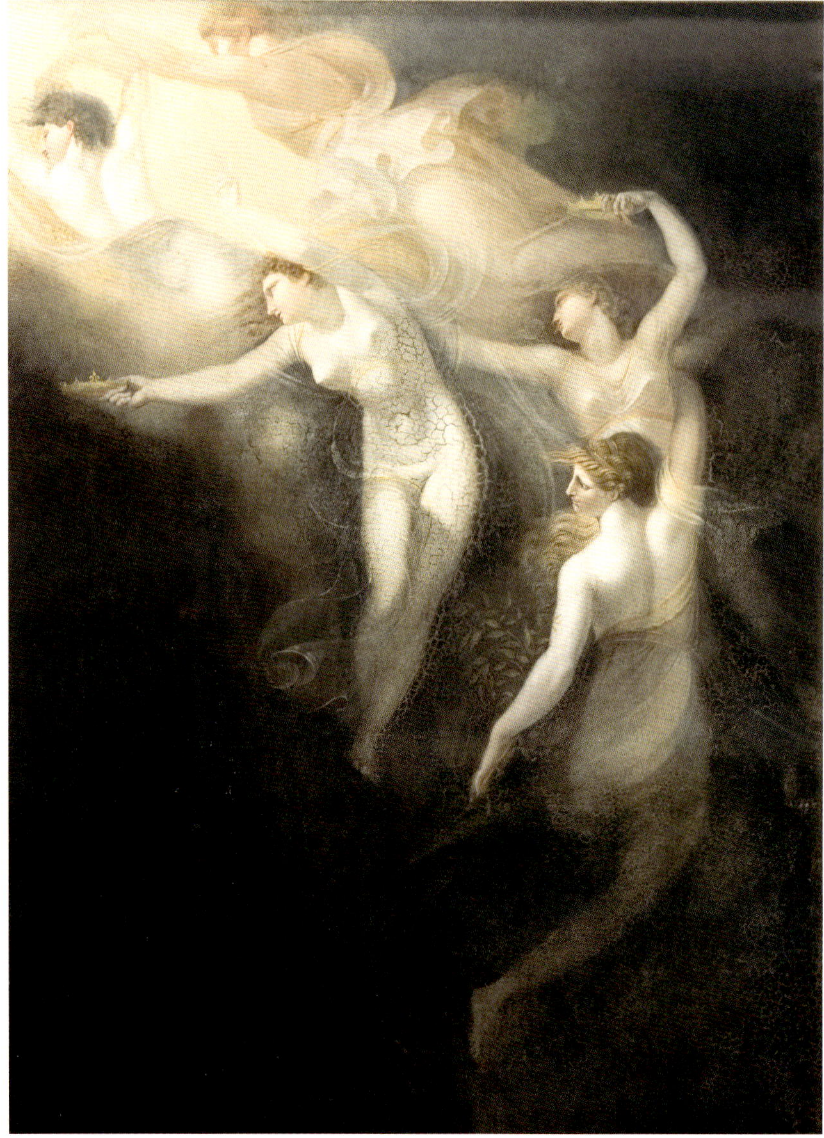

**34.** Henry Fuseli, *The Dream of Queen Katherine*, 1781, fragment, oil on canvas. Bequeathed by Rev. Chauncy Hare Townshend. V&A: 1386-1869.
The inventory of Townshend's home, made in 1863, records this painting on the staircase to the first floor.

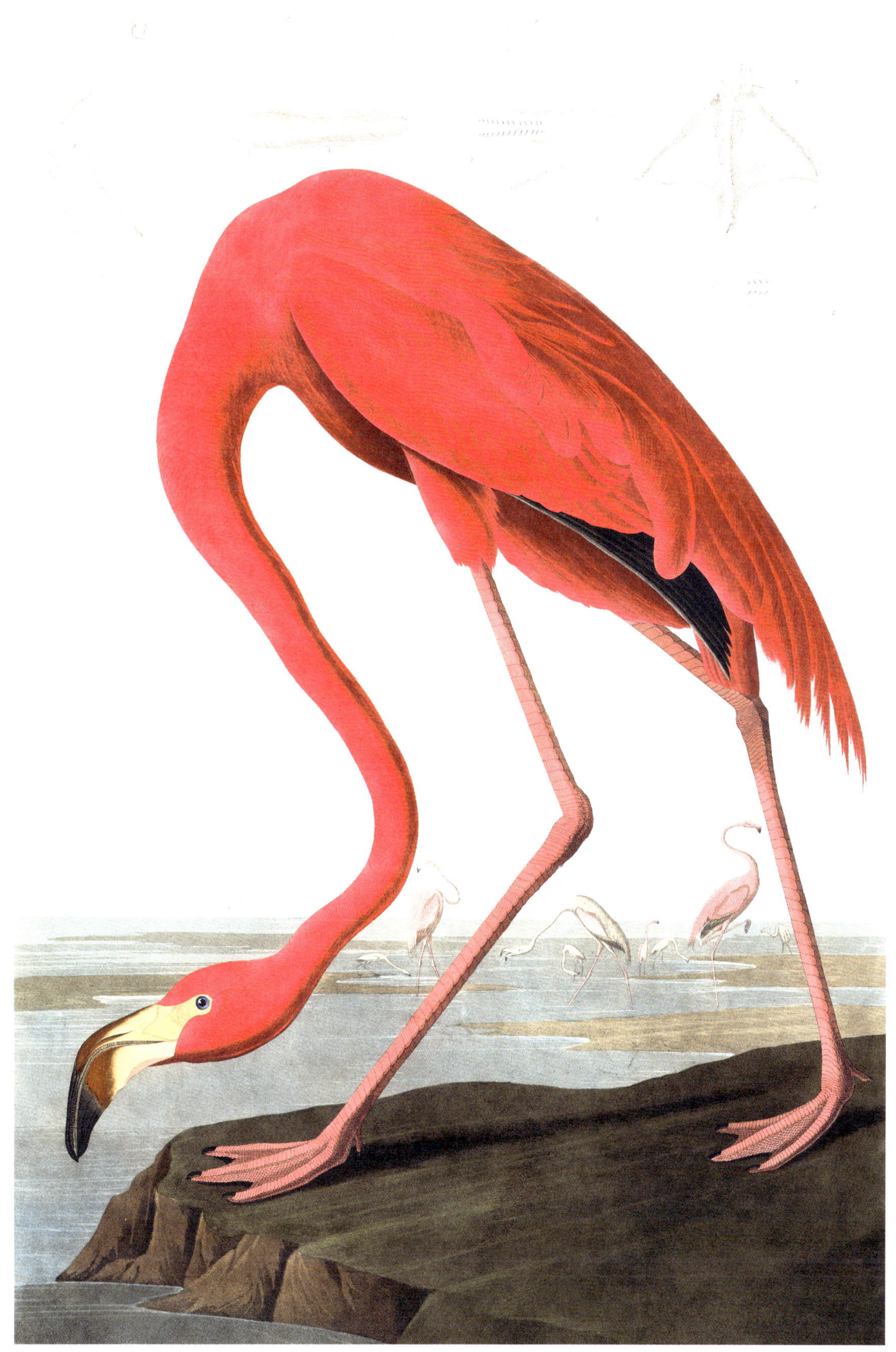

**35.** John James Audubon, *The Birds of America; From original drawings by John James Audubon*, London, 1827–38. Bequeathed by Rev. Chauncy Hare Townshend. V&A: National Art Library. Audubon chose a large format for his book (99 × 66 cm) so that every bird could be shown life size, even if, as for this flamingo, it required a compact pose.

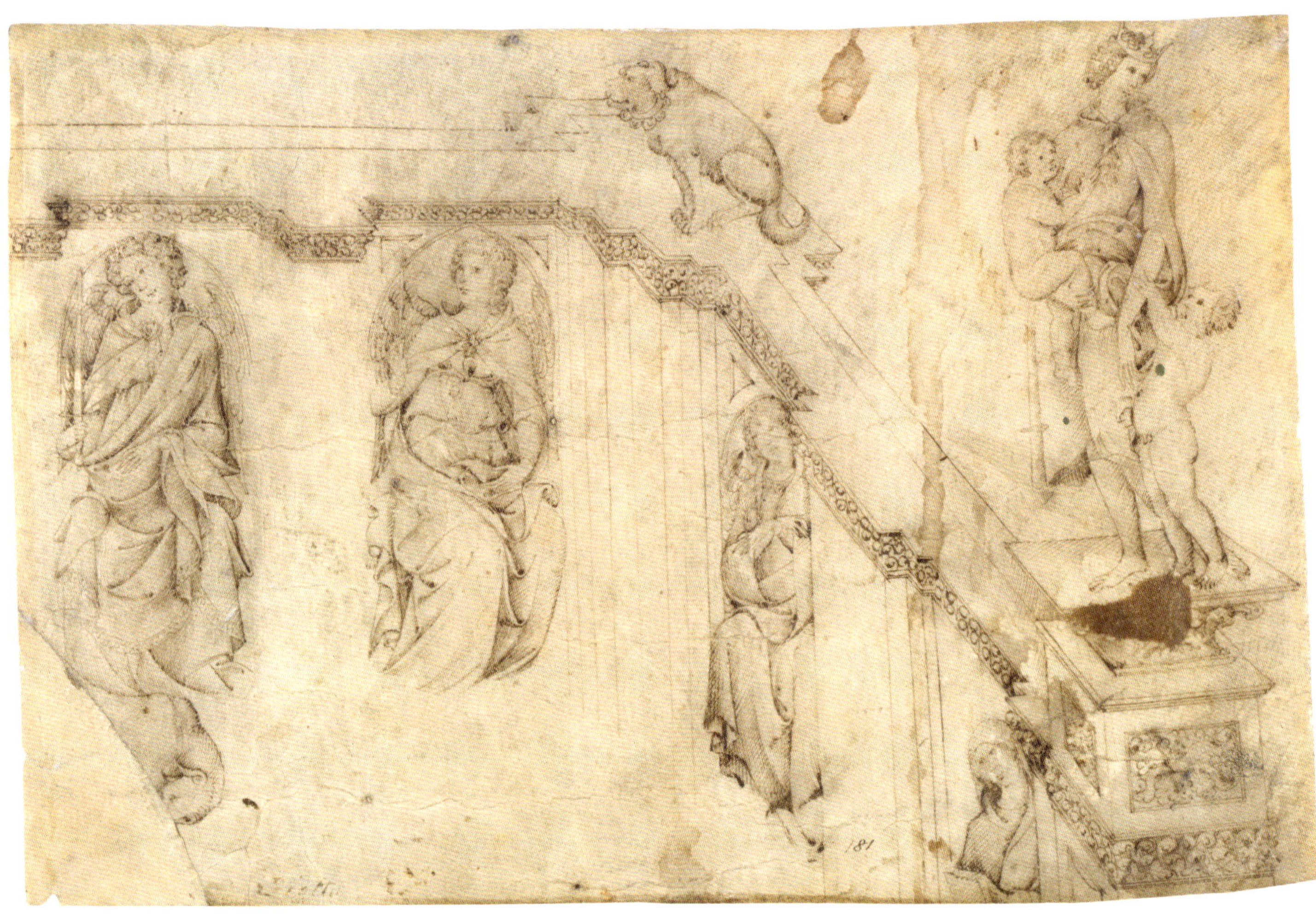

36. Jacopo della Quercia, *Design for the right side of the Fonte Gaia, Siena*, c.1409–15, pen and ink on vellum. Bequeathed by Rev. Alexander Dyce. V&A: DYCE.181.

contents of the Exhibition Galleries. On the west side of Exhibition Road (opposite the building we now know as the Henry Cole Wing) the galleries were also home to Captain Meyrick's collection of arms and armour, Frank Buckland's fish-hatching apparatus, 'Munitions of War lent by the War Department' and other attractions.[9] Townshend's legacy also includes a school in Rochester Street, Westminster (originally providing free evening classes for 400 children over 13), which is still thriving as the Burdett-Coutts and Townshend Foundation Church of England Primary School. At the Wisbech and Fenland Museum, near his family's estates in Cambridgeshire, may be seen the other half of his collection.

The second great early bequest from a friend of Dickens, one that further extended the scope of the young museum's collections and reputation, came from the Reverend Alexander Dyce (1798–1869).[10] This literary scholar was far more prolific and distinguished than Townshend, for he produced editions of Shakespeare, John Webster, Christopher Marlowe, Alexander Pope, Francis Beaumont and John Fletcher. The son of a major in the Madras infantry of the East India Company, Dyce had no wish to follow in his father's footsteps. After graduating from Oxford, he trained to be a barrister at Inner Temple, was ordained as an Anglican priest and then settled in London by 1826 to devote his bachelor life to literature and art. In later years William Hazlitt described him as a 'singularly huge, shambling, awkward, ungainly figure'.[11] At his death in 1869, only months after Townshend, Dyce bequeathed the museum 13,596 printed books, 61 manuscripts, 802 master drawings, 80 oil paintings, 63 portrait miniatures, 1,511 engravings, together with 74 rings and 27 bas-reliefs, plaster casts of gems and other art objects, including a marble portrait by Baccio Bandinelli (fig.37). His cousin William Dyce, director of the Government School of Design (1838–43), was responsible for one of the foundations of the V&A, its teaching collections.

Coming within a year of each other, the Townshend and Dyce bequests took the museum in several directions at once. Among Dyce's 171 Dutch and Flemish master drawings were works by Rembrandt (fig.44) and Rubens; there were also 209 Italian, 373 English, 53 French, 28 German and 5 Spanish master drawings. Dyce's rings complemented the museum's choice of Townshend's gems. Dyce's portrait miniatures laid the foundations for Britain's national collection at the V&A.

A biographical sketch of Dyce in the museum's handbook to his collections concludes: 'It had been Mr Dyce's intention to bequeath his books to the Bodleian; but it was suggested that they ought rather to be placed, with the rest of his collections, where they would be within the reach of a wider world of students'.[12] Following Sheepshanks's example, but taking his terms one step further, Dyce stated in his will that he required 'a proper and sufficient separate room . . . to be built . . . for the purpose of holding my said collection'.[13] A description of the museum (1889) records five public galleries devoted to the Dyce and Forster Collections.[14] Like Sheepshanks, Dyce expressed the wish that, if his conditions could not be met, his collection should transfer to the Fitzwilliam Museum in Cambridge. He differed from Sheepshanks when he required it be kept together as 'The Dyce Collection . . . the books . . . never to be lent or removed, from the Collection'.[15] In 1868 the Plumley Bequest of 63 miniatures and enamels was also to be 'all hung up together in a suitable room . . . as the Plumley Enamels, &c' and was also to be transferred to the Fitzwilliam 'if they fail to comply with these conditions'.[16] The recurrence of these conditions in donors' wills and deeds of gift from this period suggests that they may have been proposed by Henry Cole himself, to encourage donations and, perhaps, to help secure his own legacy.

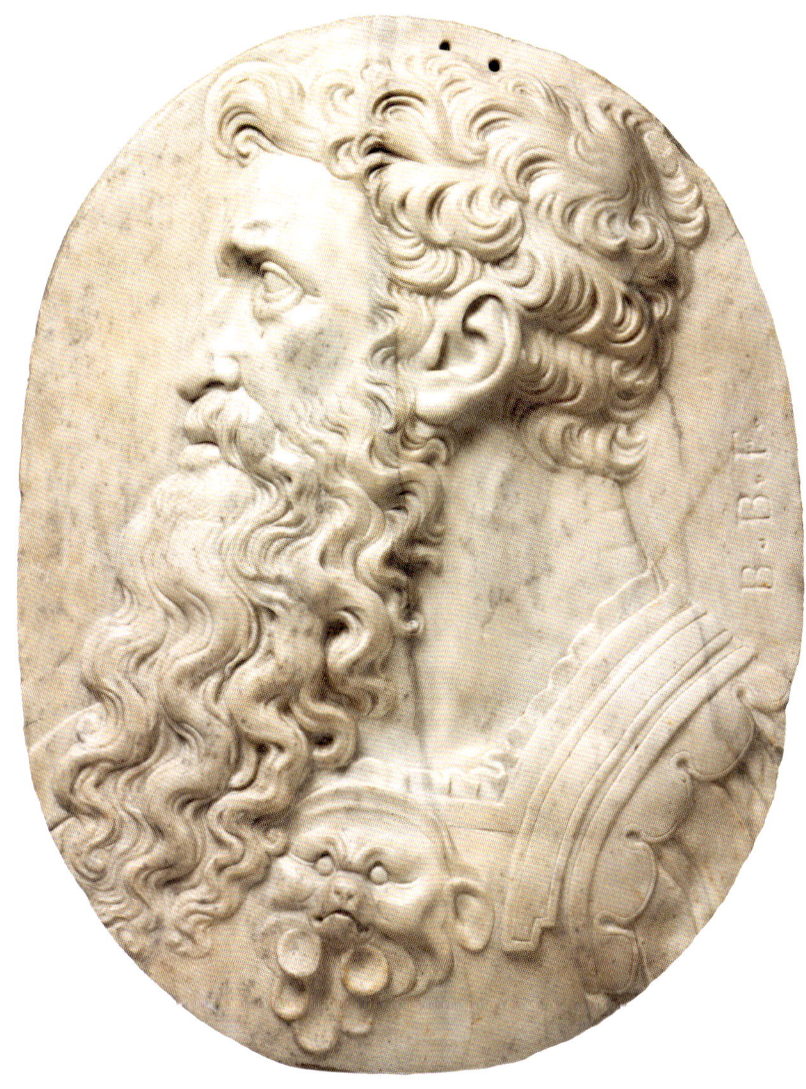


**37.** Baccio Bandinelli, *Head of a bearded man*, c.1550–60, marble. Bequeathed by Rev. Alexander Dyce. V&A: DYCE.3326.

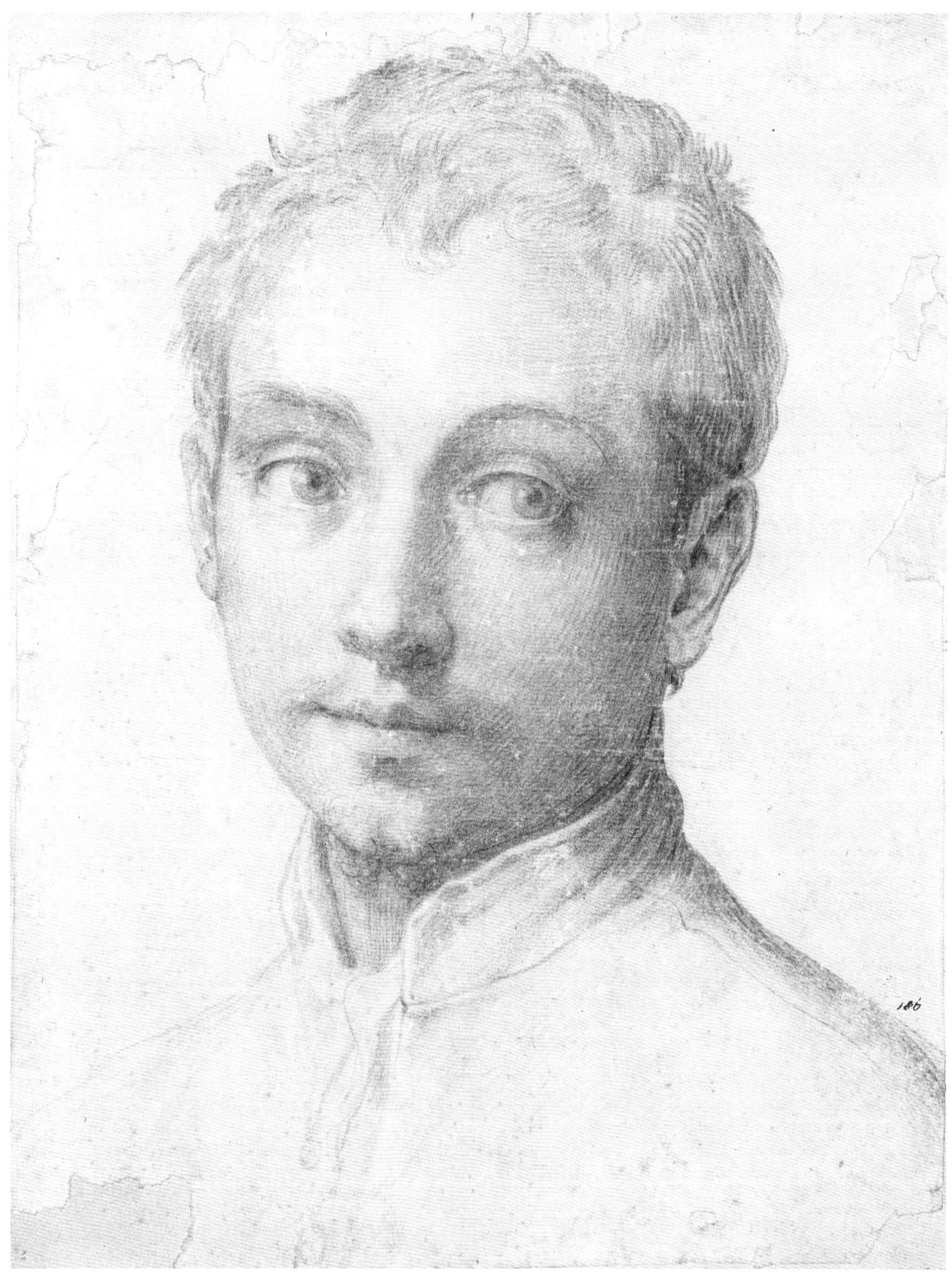

opposite:
**38.** Francesco Salviati, *Portrait of a Youth*, c.1500–20, black chalk on prepared paper. Bequeathed by Rev. Alexander Dyce. V&A: DYCE.186.

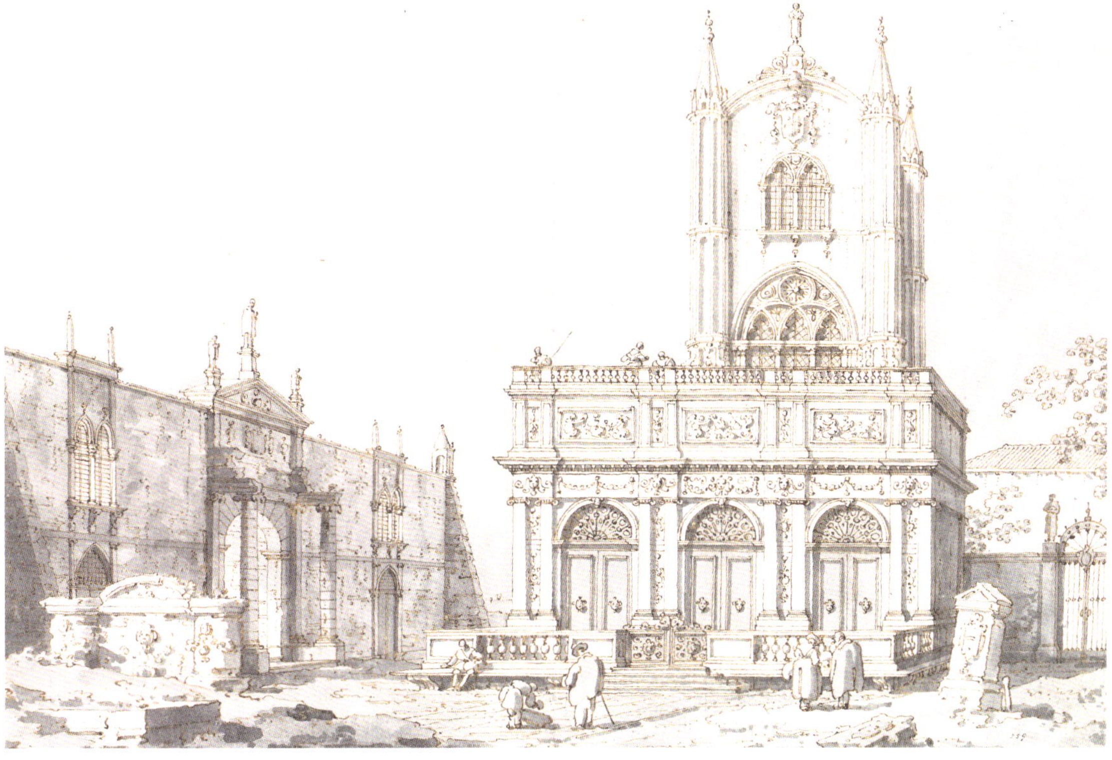

**39.** Giovanni Antonio Canal, known as Canaletto, *View of a Tomb and Chapel*, c.1740–60, pen, washed with neutral tint. Bequeathed by Rev. Alexander Dyce. V&A: DYCE.259.

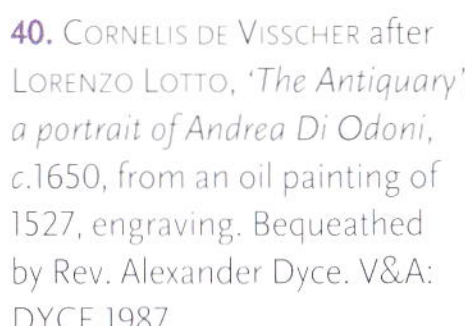

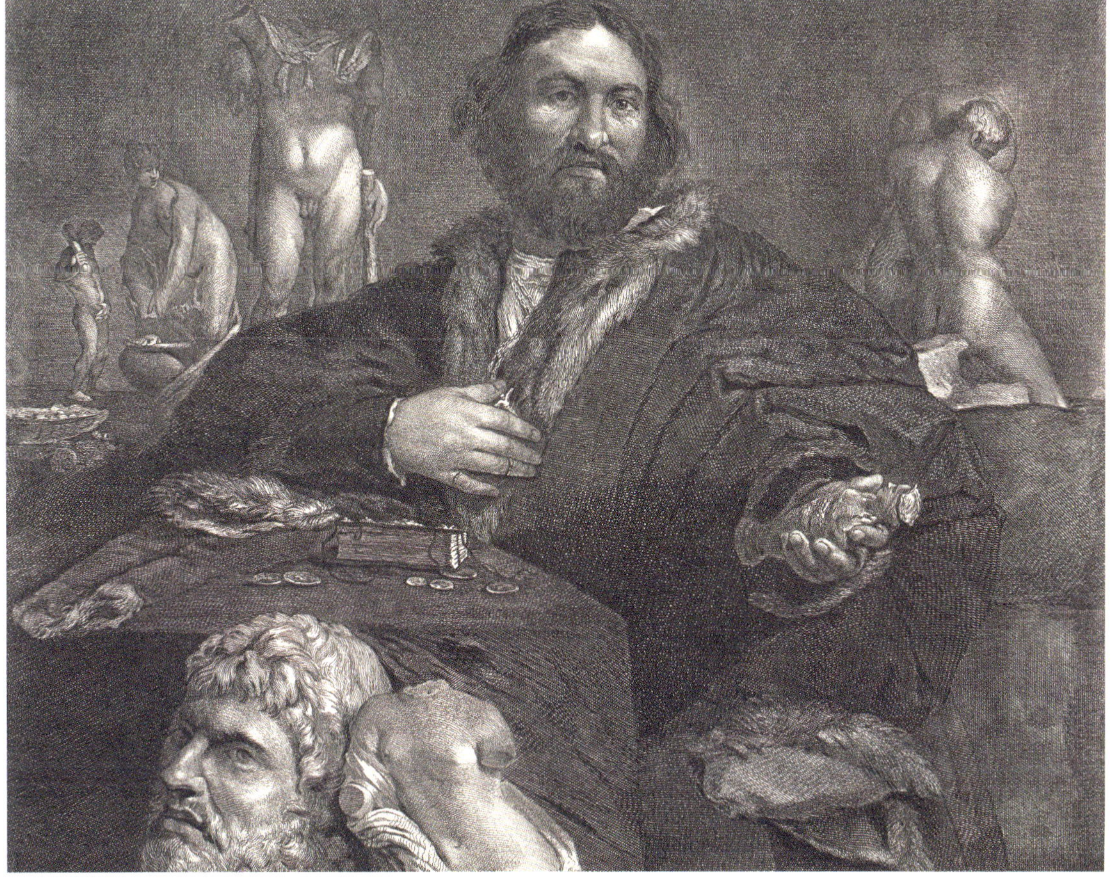

**40.** Cornelis de Visscher after Lorenzo Lotto, *'The Antiquary'*, *a portrait of Andrea Di Odoni*, c.1650, from an oil painting of 1527, engraving. Bequeathed by Rev. Alexander Dyce. V&A: DYCE.1987.

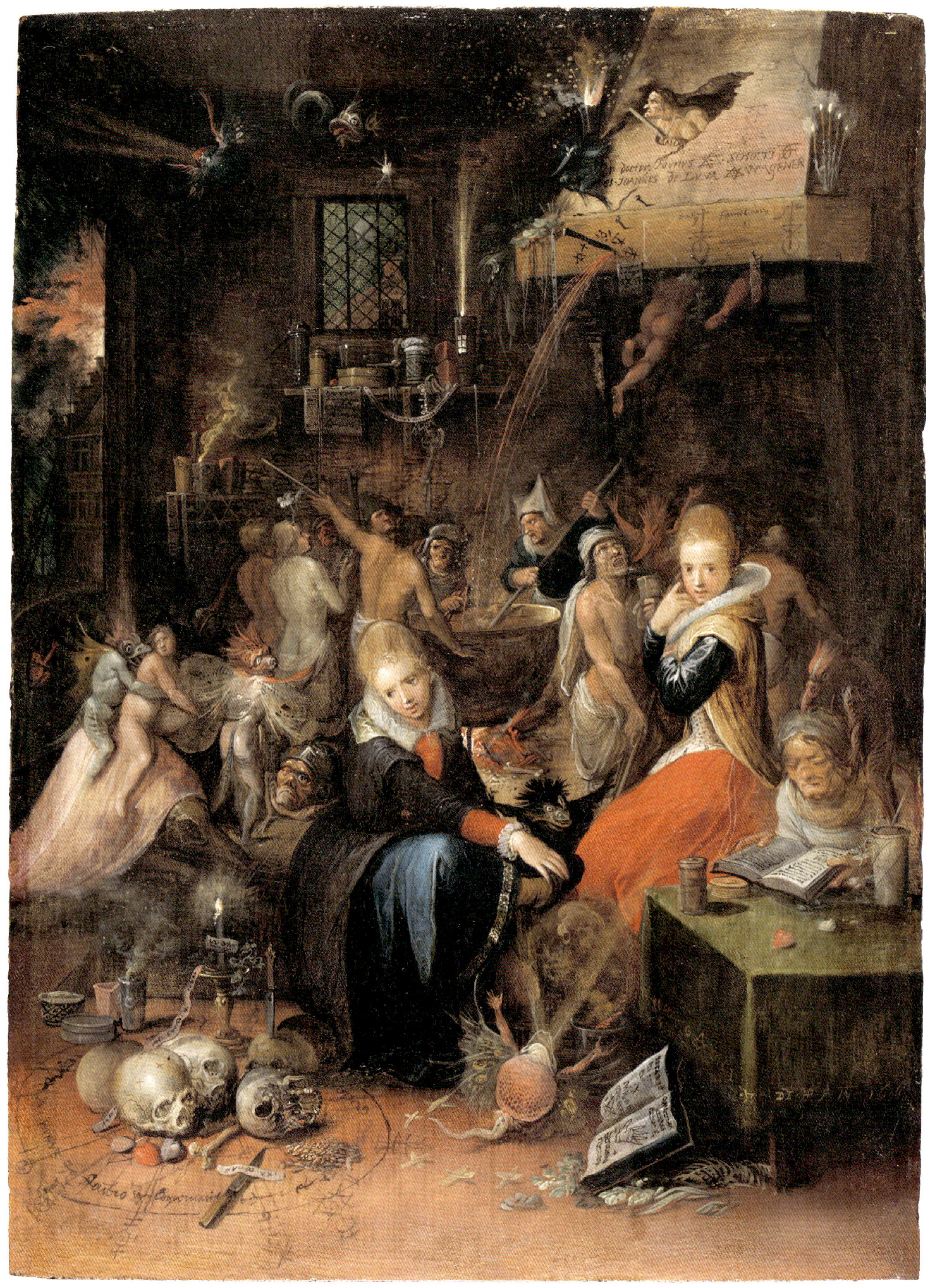
SCHOTTI
JOANNES

OPPOSITE:
**41.** Frans Francken the Younger, *Witches' Sabbath*, 1606, oil on oak panel. Bequeathed by Rev. Alexander Dyce. V&A: DYCE.3.

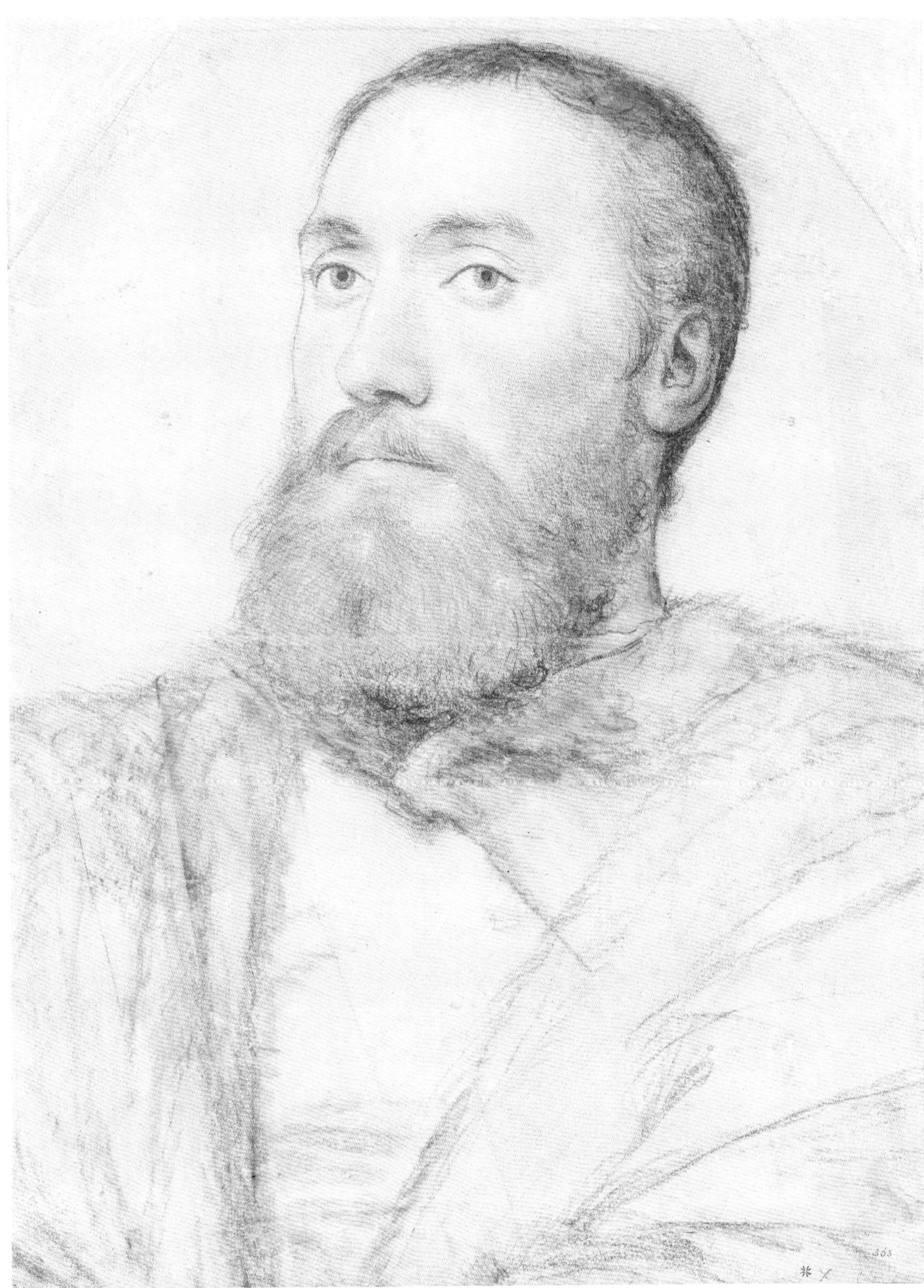

**42.** Hans Holbein the Younger, *Portrait of an Unknown Man, possibly Thomas Seymour*, c.1535–40, black and coloured chalks on prepared paper. Bequeathed by Rev. Alexander Dyce. V&A: DYCE.363.

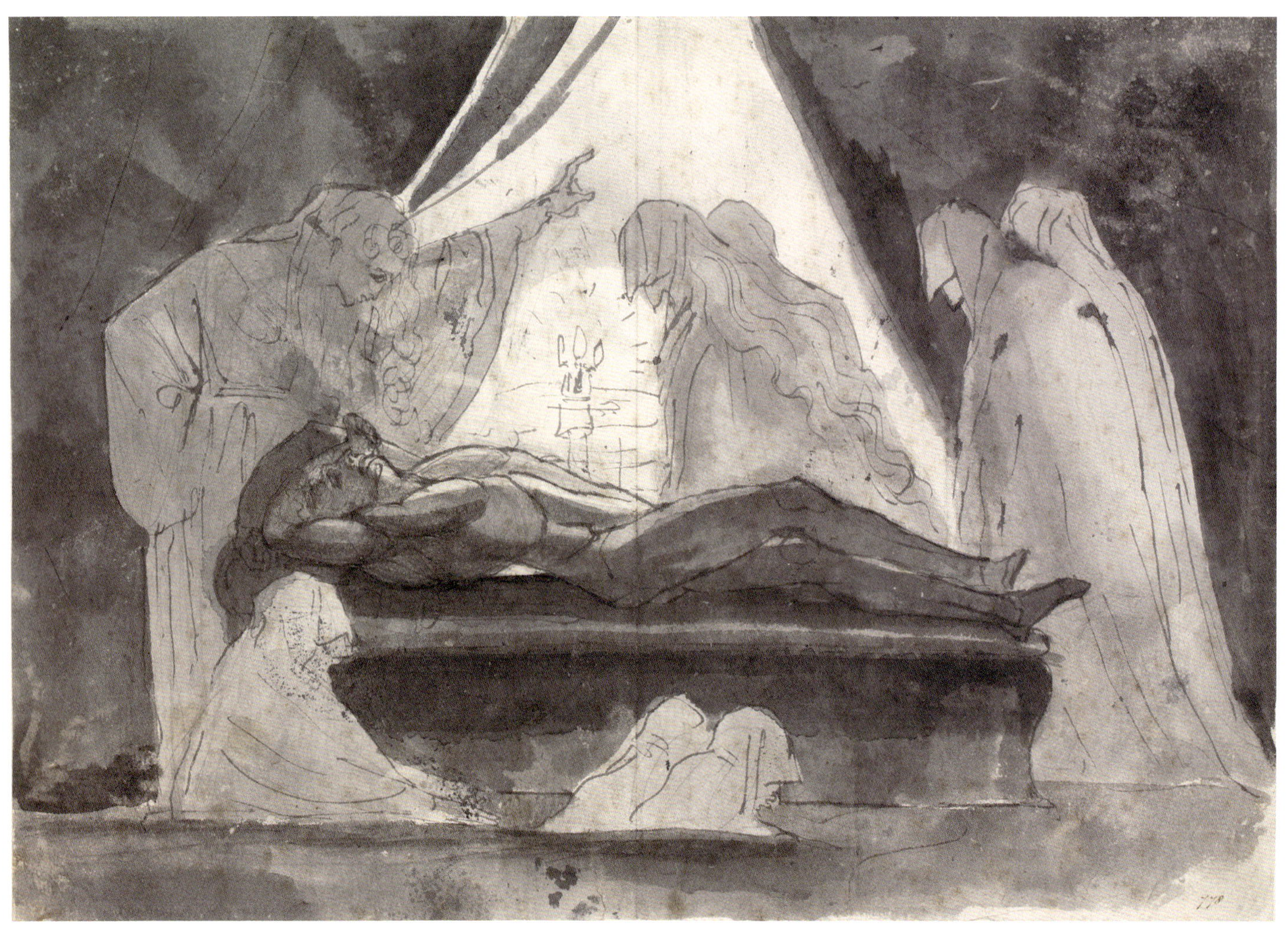

**43.** Henry Fuseli, *Richard III*, *c.*1777, pen and Indian ink, washed. Bequeathed by Rev. Alexander Dyce. V&A: DYCE.778.

OPPOSITE:
**44.** Rembrandt van Rijn, *Study of the actor Willem Ruyter as a countryman, with an alternative study of his head, and a bust-length study of a figure holding a jug*, 1634–8, pen and ink. Bequeathed by Rev. Alexander Dyce. V&A: DYCE.435.

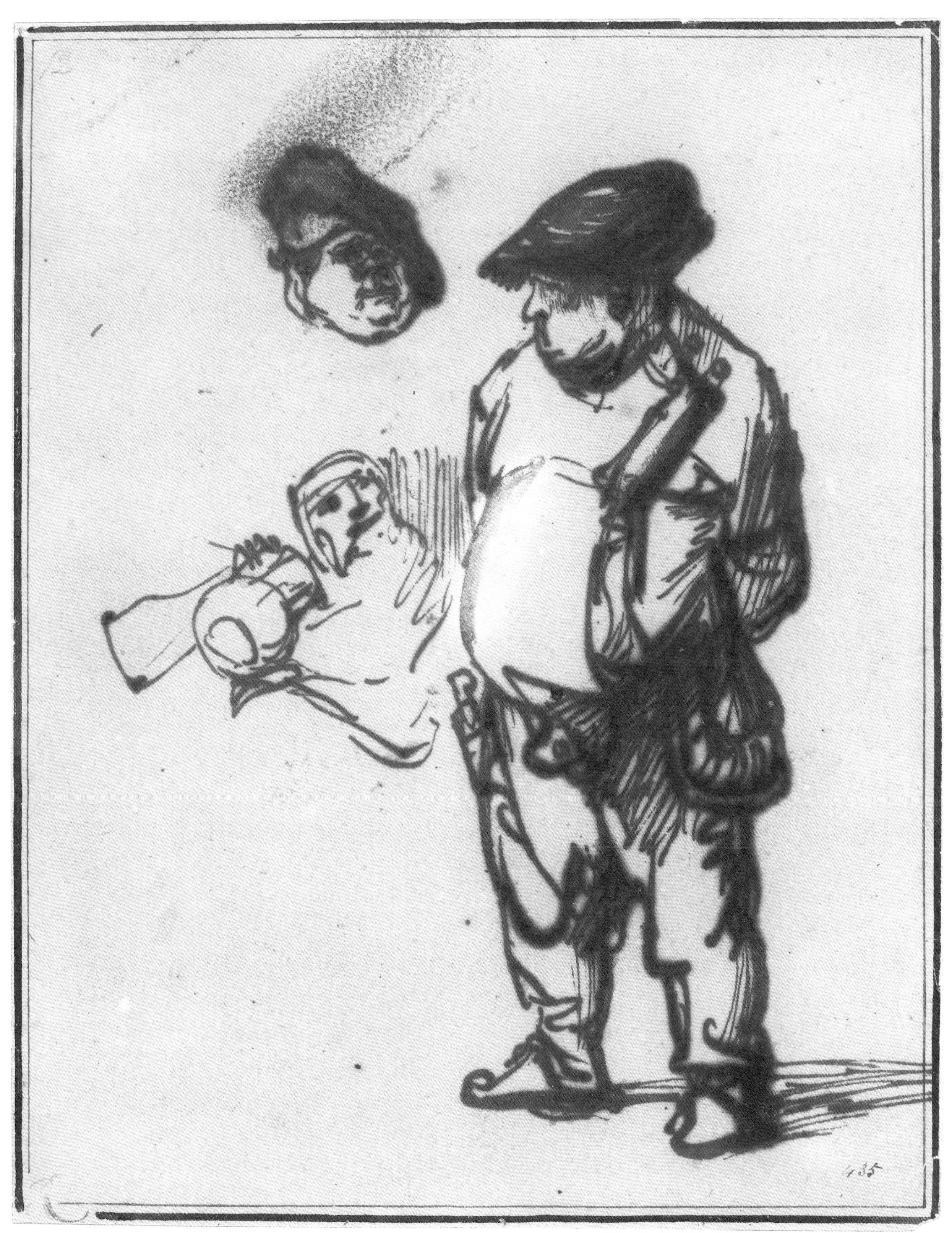

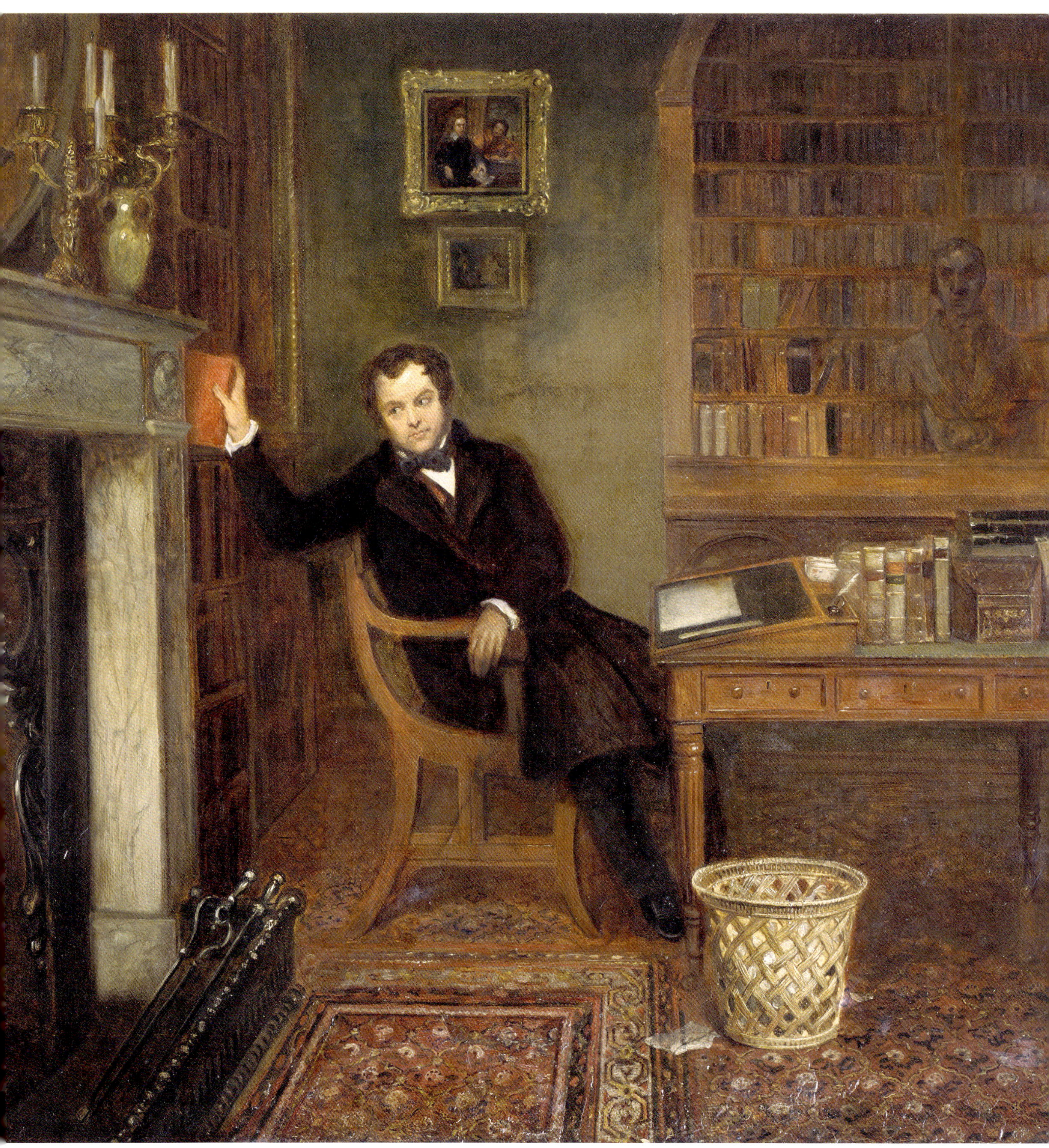

# 8 From Da Vinci to Dickens: John Forster and the National Art Library

THE MOST IMPORTANT single-author archive in Britain, that of Charles Dickens, can be studied in the V&A, thanks to his friend, editor and fellow amateur actor, John Forster (1812–1876). The son of a Newcastle butcher and cattle dealer, Forster studied law at University College, London, trained to be a barrister at the Inner Temple (like Dyce) and then became a drama and literary critic. From 1835 he was literary editor of the weekly journal *The Examiner*, before serving as its editor (1847–55). His legal training and business acumen stood him in good stead as a professional adviser to writers, especially Dickens whom he first met in 1836. From October 1837 until Dickens's death in 1870, according to Forster, 'there was nothing written by him . . . which I did not see before the world did, either in manuscript or proofs'.[1] Forster's best-known biography is his classic three-volume *The Life of Charles Dickens* (1872–4). His archive at the V&A includes Dickens's chapter plans, working notes, volumes of manuscripts including eleven novels[2] and one of his Christmas books, densely overworked with amendments, as well as Dickens's travel books, paintings and illustrations relating to his stories and to their friendships (figs 46, 47).

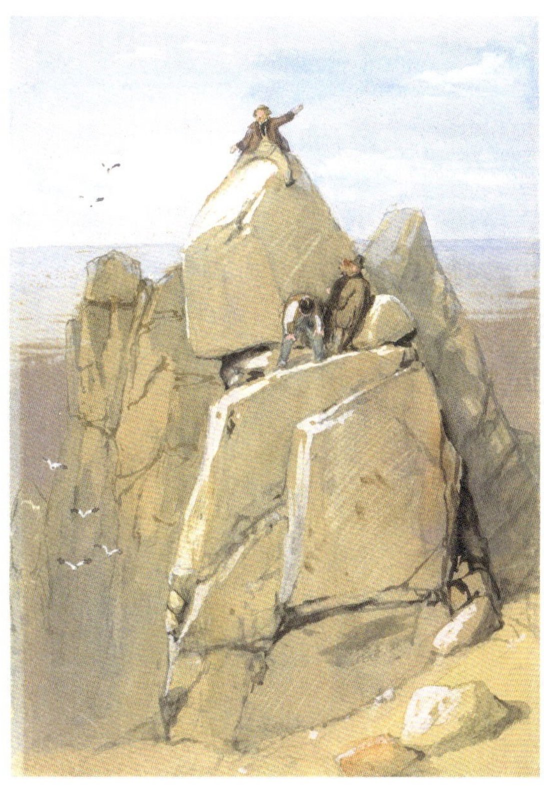

OPPOSITE:
**45.** EDWARD MATTHEW WARD, *John Forster in his Library*, c.1850, oil on canvas (detail). V&A: P.74-1935.

**46.** WILLIAM CLARKSON STANFIELD, *The Logan Rock, Cornwall*, 1842, graphite and watercolour. Bequeathed by John Forster. V&A: F.93. The artist records the day he climbed the rock with Charles Dickens, John Forster and Daniel Maclise.

Friends gathered regularly in Forster's chambers at 58 Lincoln's Inn Fields; when Dickens first read out his novella *The Chimes* there in 1844, prior to publication, Daniel Maclise recorded the reading in one of many sketches in the collection.[3] Dickens took this setting as his source when describing the chambers of Mr Tulkinghorn in *Bleak House* (1853). Henry Cole was also a source for Dickens; the V&A's first director lives on, in caricature, as a pedantic school inspector in *Hard Times* (1854).[4]

There is much more to Forster's bequest in the V&A, beyond Dickens. Palace Gate House, the imposing home he built in South Kensington, still faces the gates to Kensington Palace Gardens. His library of over 18,000 books contained five of Leonardo da Vinci's illustrated notebooks (spanning his years in Milan, c.1487–90, and in Florence, 1505) bound in three volumes as the Codex Forster (fig.48).[5] His collection of autograph letters in 39 volumes includes the correspondence of David

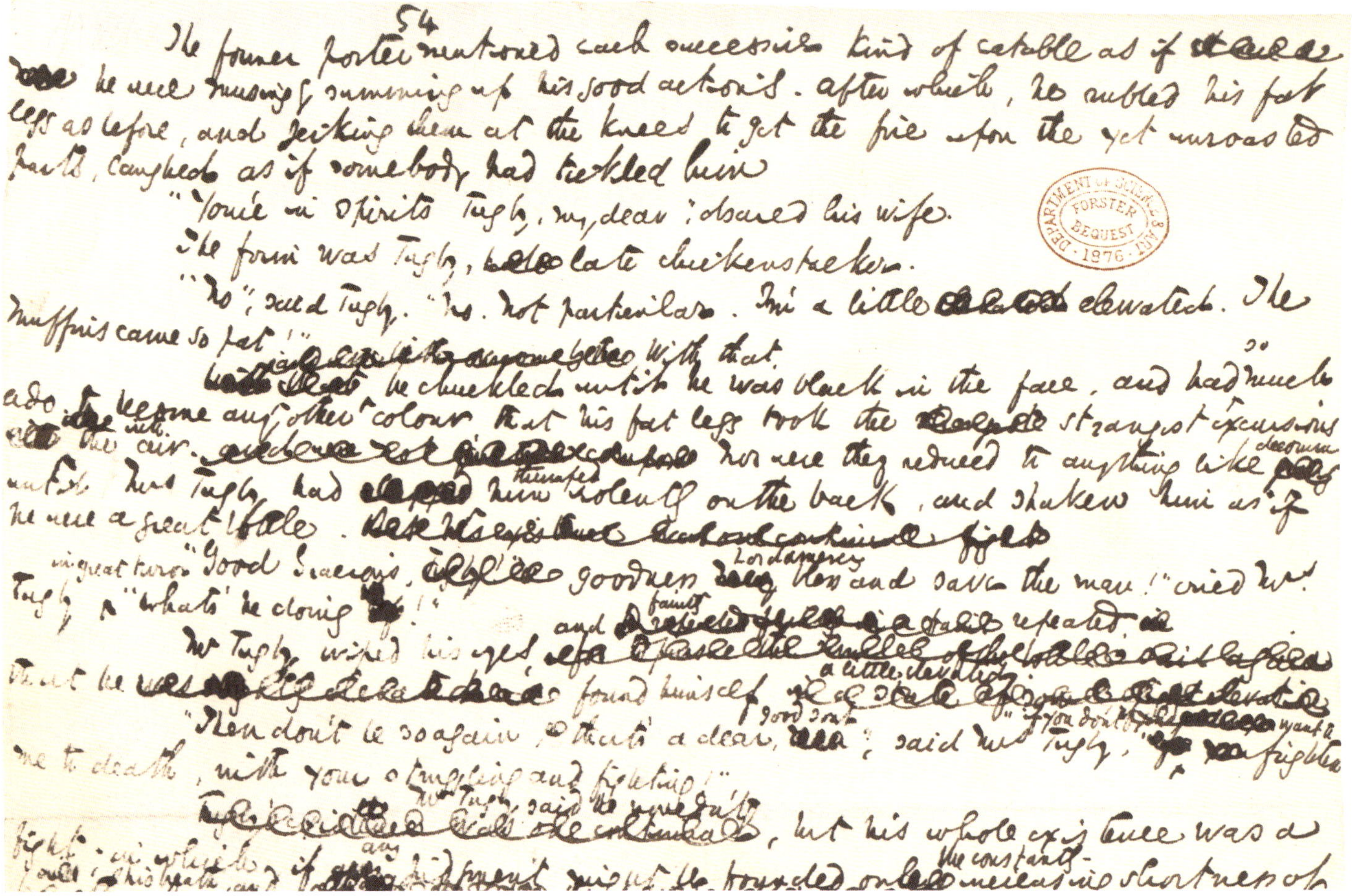

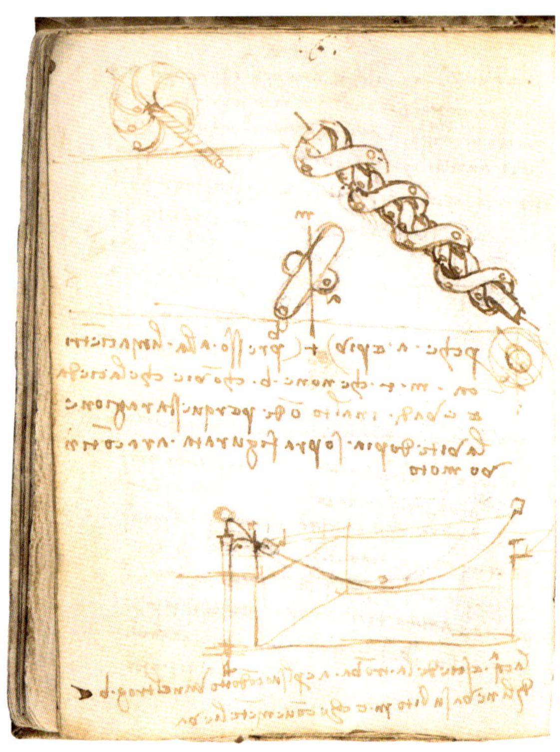

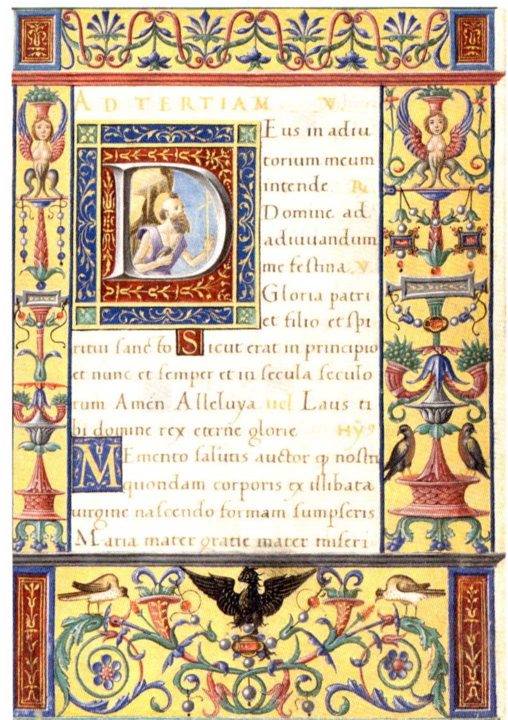

**47.** Charles Dickens, *The Chimes*, 1844, manuscript (detail). Bequeathed by John Forster. V&A: MSL/1876/Forster/158.

**48.** Leonardo da Vinci, notebooks known as Codex Forster, *c.*1487–1505, paper bound in vellum. Bequeathed by John Forster. V&A: MSL/1876/Forster/141/1/II/III. Purchased in Vienna by Lord Lytton who gave them to his friend Forster, unaware of their authenticity. The five notebooks record Leonardo's thoughts on three-dimensional geometry, together with a variety of observations and sketches on topics ranging from anatomy and proportions to hydraulics.

**49.** Pierantonio Sallando (scribe); Bartolomeo Bossi (illuminator), book of hours, known as the Bentivoglio Hours, 1494–1503, manuscript. Given by George Reid. V&A: MSL/1902/1707 (Reid 64).

Garrick. Among his 48 oil paintings are Frith's portrait of Dickens (fig.50), John Everett Millais's portrait of Forster's executor, Lord Lytton, and Gainsborough's double portrait of his daughters (fig.51). The bequest also includes 108 watercolours and drawings, as well as many more sketches by his friend Daniel Maclise.

Forster was a close friend of Dyce and served as his executor. In his will Forster specified the same terms as Dyce required, namely 'a proper and separate room or gallery . . . for the purpose of holding and preserving my said Library and Paintings'. Unlike Dyce, Forster's will did not require that his bequest be shown under the title 'The Forster Collection'. The requirement of both Dyce and Forster for a separate gallery each was the same practical precaution that Sheepshanks had sought. Dyce stated in his will 'I have had regard to the gift of the Sheepshanks collection . . . which I desire generally to follow.' The paintings could be lent but not the books. As with Sheepshanks's gift and Dyce's bequest, if Forster's terms could not be met he wished that the collection be transferred to the Fitzwilliam Museum, which had opened in its new building in 1848.[6] The choice of Cambridge University's museum and gallery as alternative beneficiary probably came from Redgrave as Sheepshanks's adviser. Sheepshanks's influential condition was understandable, for it had been prompted by the National Gallery's inability to provide rooms for Robert Vernon's gift of paintings and for the bequest of J.M.W. Turner. Vernon's gift and Turner's bequest to the nation came to South Kensington on loan in 1860; after they left in 1876 (the year Forster died) the Dyce and Forster bequests moved into the rooms 'formerly occupied by loans from the National Gallery'.[7]

Following Townshend, Dyce and Forster, other bibliophiles' collections strengthened the National Art Library at the V&A. The Piot Collection of 1,243 volumes on 16th- to 19th-century pageantry, festivals and other topics was purchased in 1880. A French collector of Renaissance art, Eugène Piot (1812–1890) was also a noted photographer ('daguerreotypist'), friend of Théophile Gautier and a traveller in Spain, Greece and Egypt. As an art critic and historian, he contributed to the *Gazette des Beaux-Arts* and compiled *Le Cabinet de l'amateur et de l'antiquaire* (1846; 1861–3). He donated part of his collection of prints to the Bibliothèque Nationale and other objects to the Louvre. The sale of his books collection to the South Kensington Museum in 1880 may have been prompted by the need to raise funds for his voyage to Egypt the following year.[8]

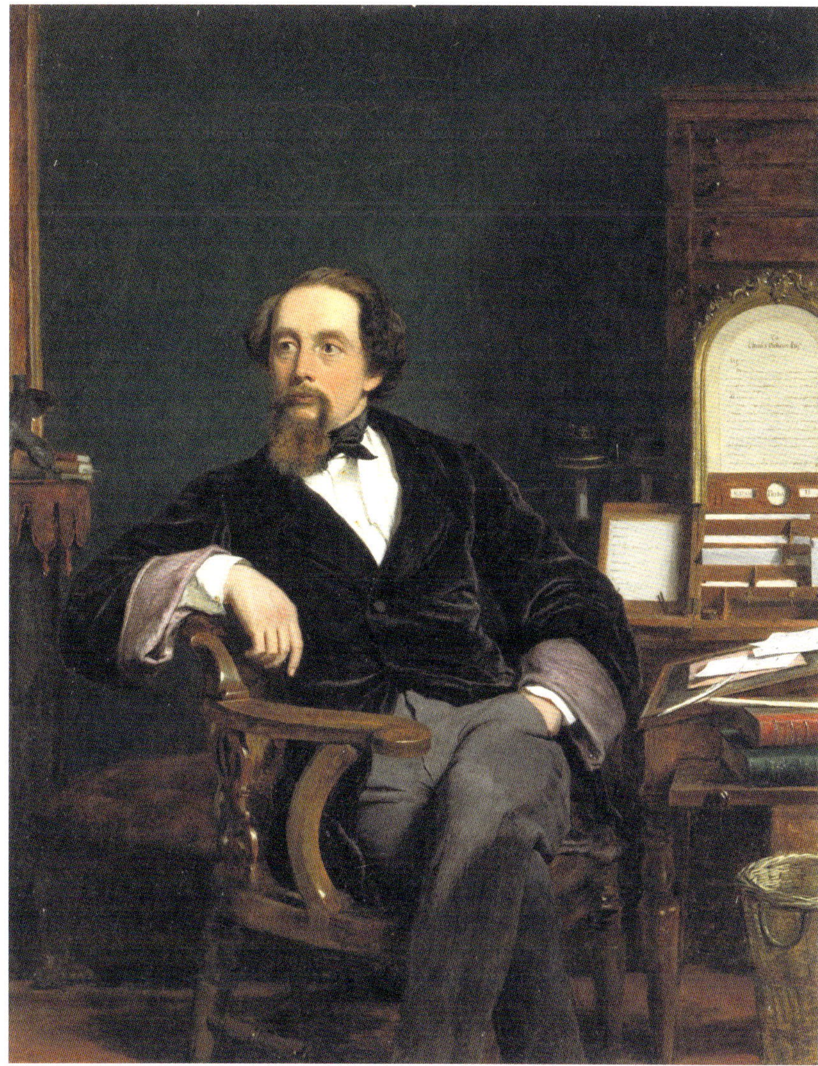

**50.** William Powell Frith, *Charles Dickens*, 1859, oil on canvas. Bequeathed by John Forster. V&A: F.7.

Another collection within the holdings of the National Art Library is that of George Reid (1840–1910) of Dunfermline, a centre of the linen industry. The son of a handloom linen weaver, he worked his way up and became a leading manufacturer of linen damask, retired early and travelled in Europe to form his collection. In 1902 Reid lent for display and then donated to the museum 70 illuminated

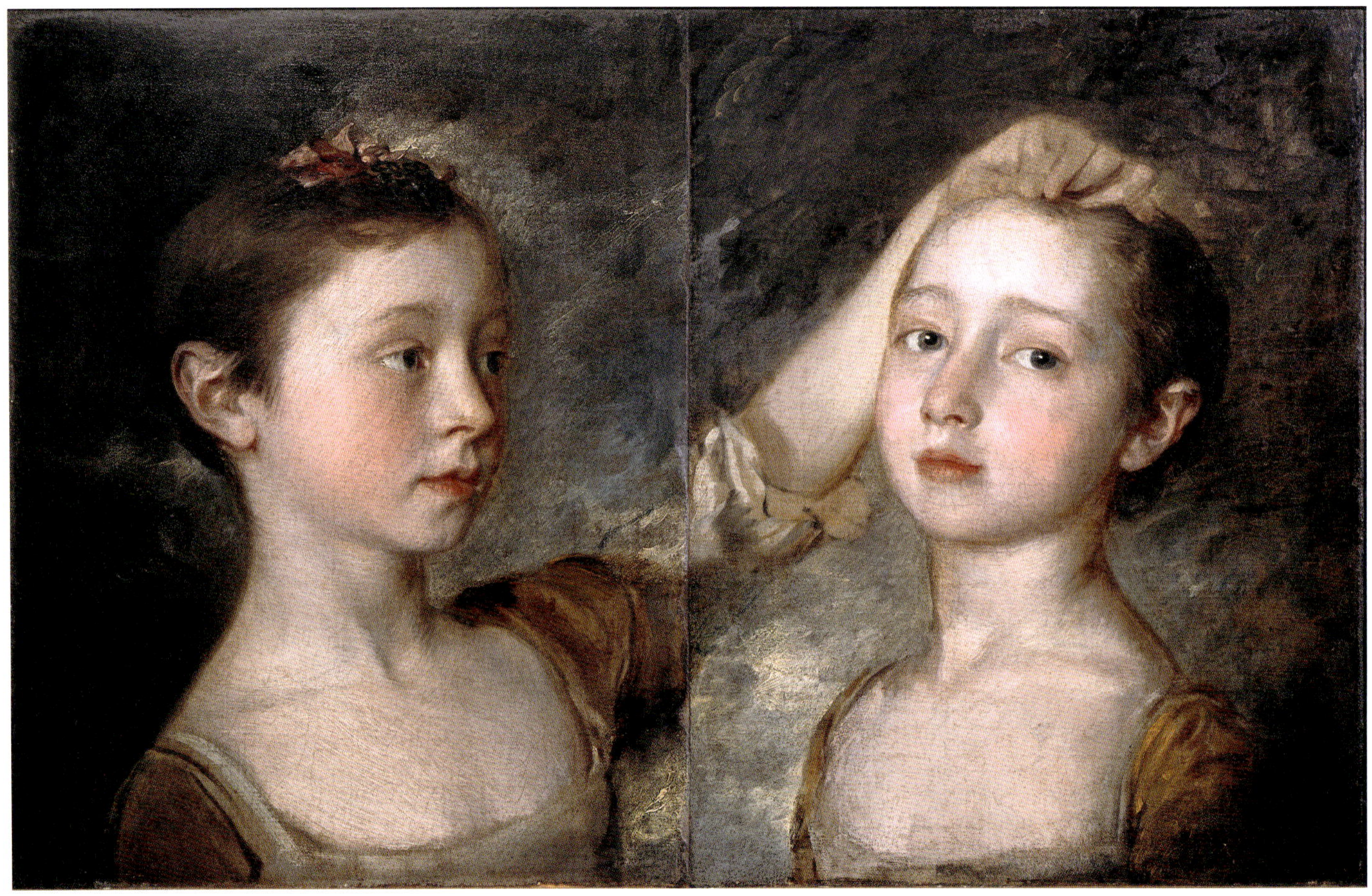

51. Thomas Gainsborough, *Mary and Margaret Gainsborough, the Artist's Daughters*, *c*.1758, oil on canvas (two canvases joined). Bequeathed by John Forster. V&A: F.9.

manuscripts (fig.49); the following year he added 13 more, including a Rheims book of hours (*c*.1280–90) that had belonged to John Ruskin. Most of his donations came from the 14th and 15th centuries. Reid also donated printed books to the museum and manuscripts to the library in his hometown.[9]

Emilia Strong, Lady Dilke (1840–1904), a noted art historian, donated her working library and collection of 650 books, from the 15th to 20th centuries, to the museum in 1904. On Ruskin's advice she had enrolled at the South Kensington Schools in 1859 to train as an artist, before her first marriage to an Oxford don (who was long thought to be a source for Casaubon in George Eliot's *Middlemarch*, 1871). Her pioneering studies of French paintings, furniture, architecture and sculpture are exceptional in their use of documentary sources. In leaving her books to the National Art Library she followed the example of her second husband's father, Sir Charles Wentworth Dilke (1810–1869). A key promoter of the Great Exhibition of 1851, Dilke had donated to the museum in 1867 his collection of publications on the first world's fair, which became the nucleus of this specialist strength of the National Art Library.[10] In 1913 Enid De Cane donated 167 books and pamphlets, 293 photographs, prints and 352 tracings of Italian frescoes from the library of her aunt, Enid, Lady Layard (d.1912), widow of the great archaeologist and collector Sir Austen Henry Layard (1817–1894). Like many books in the library, they are inscribed by their first owner. The National Art Library at the V&A provides reference literature for the history of art, but as a curatorial collection, preserving the diverse intellectual legacy of these, and many other, donors on its shelves, there is so much more to research.[11]

OPPOSITE:
52. Daniel Maclise, *Scene from Ben Jonson's 'Every Man in his Humour' (Act II, Scene I)*, 1847–8, oil on canvas. Bequeathed by John Forster. V&A: F.20. Forster and Charles Dickens acted in an amateur production of this play in 1845. This scene shows Forster as the merchant Kitely in a fit of jealousy (his 'humour') with his pretty wife.

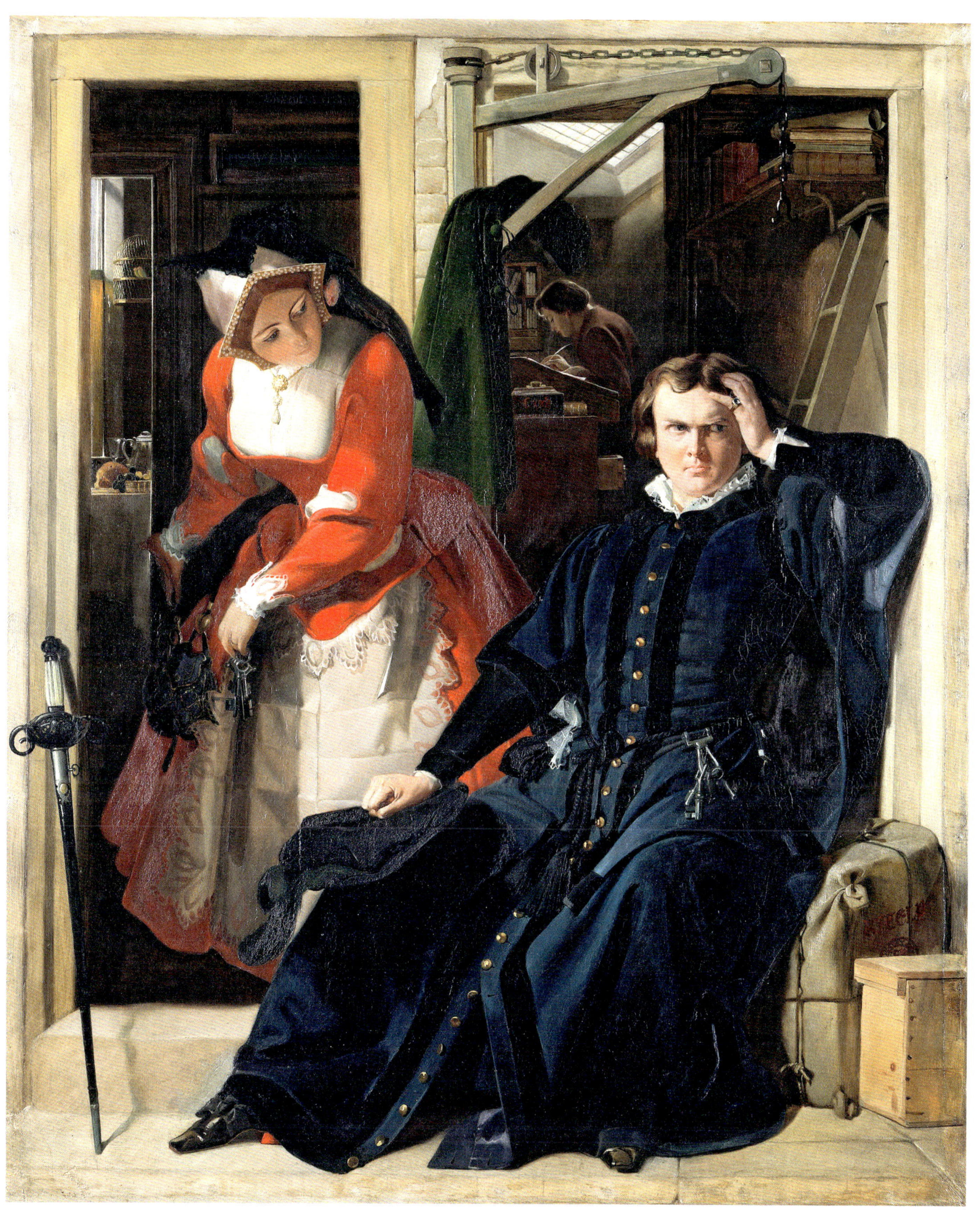

# Part III: Collecting Overseas

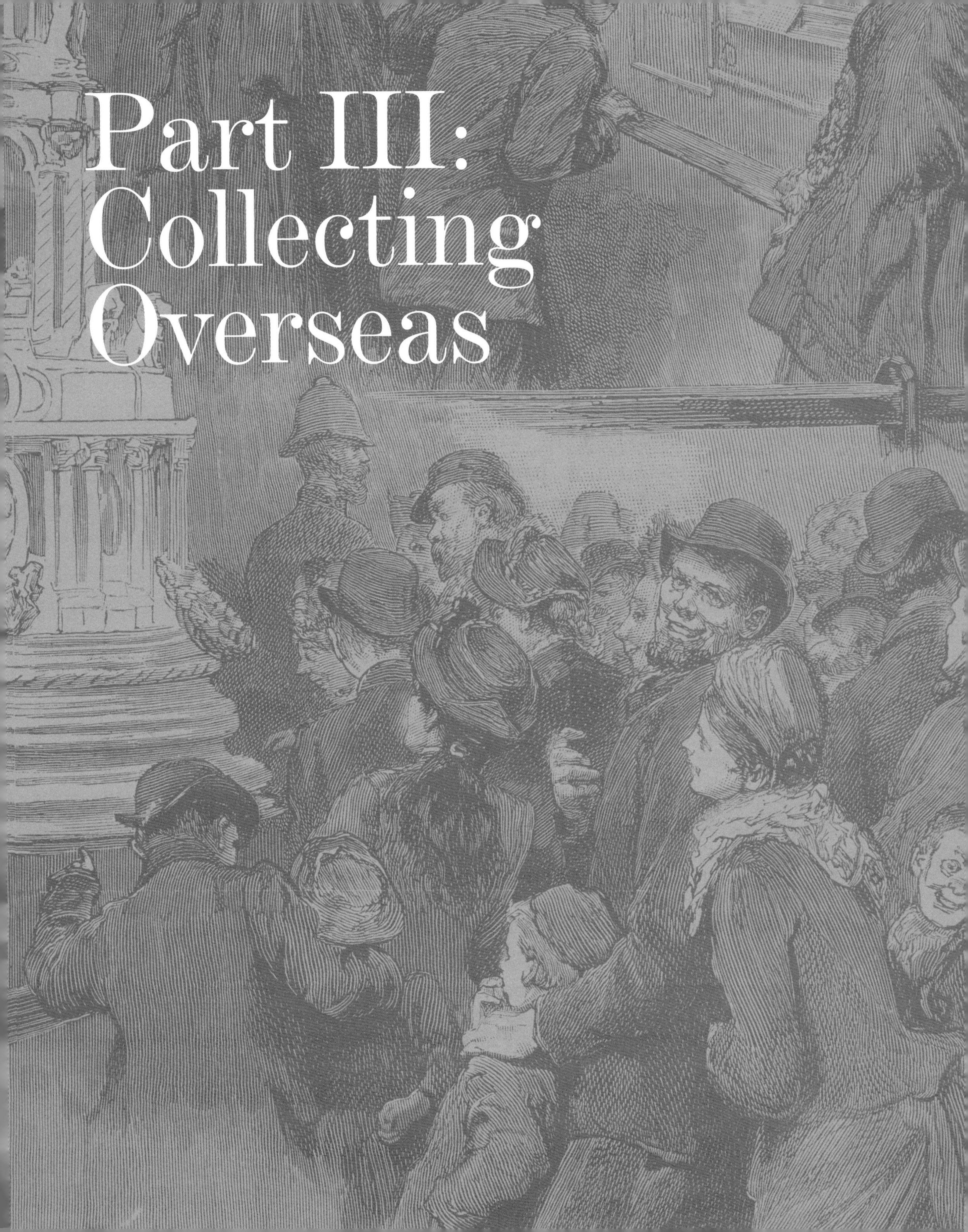

THE 19TH CENTURY was an age of empires when European influence spread across the globe through trade, technology and military force. It was also an era of political turmoil in Europe, when old nations sought to expand, and new nations formed through revolutions. This changing world presented new opportunities for the British to explore the arts of Continental Europe, Africa, the Middle East and Asia and to collect, as private individuals, as commissioned agents for museums, and as armies engaged in imperial expeditions. The spread of empire and trade brought about new international networks of communication that facilitated collecting in ways unknown a century before, when wealthy aristocratic tourists led the way to art and taste. These three chapters provide a brief overview of key collectors, pioneering scholars and of the issues behind new kinds of collections that were brought to the museum from a much wider world.

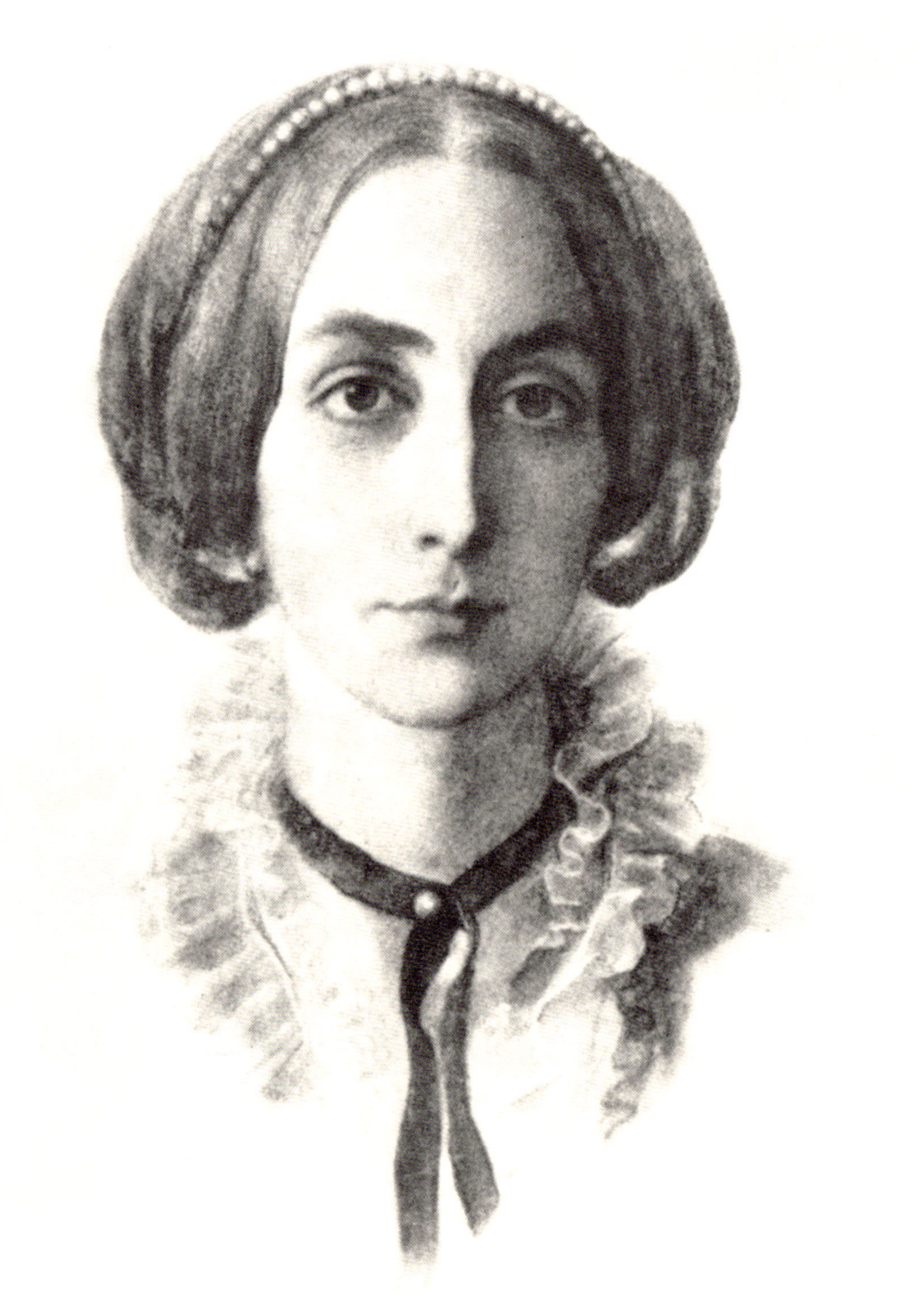

# 9 Lady Schreiber's 'Ceramic Chasse'

OPPOSITE:
**53.** After G.F. Watts, *Lady Charlotte Schreiber*, c.1854, first published in Montague J. Guest, (ed.), *Lady Charlotte Schreiber's Journals* vol. 2 (London, 1911). V&A: National Art Library.

**54.** Sèvres porcelain factory, modelled by Étienne-Maurice Falconet, *La Lanterne Magique*, c.1757, biscuit porcelain. Given by Lady Charlotte Schreiber. V&A: 414:428-1885. This figure group served as a model which was imitated by other porcelain factories in Great Britain.

Shortly after the closure of the Great Exhibition in October 1851 exemplary contemporary ceramics were selected and purchased for the nation. Some were acquired for the Museum of Practical Geology, which had been reopened in new purpose-built premises in Jermyn Street by Prince Albert on 14 May 1851. Examples of contemporary Sèvres and Minton were also purchased for the Government School of Design's teaching collections (to add to their 24 French ceramics) that would be adopted by the South Kensington Museum. Two years later the wider foundations of the museum's holdings of historic ceramics were laid with the purchase of 717 examples from the collection of James Bandinel, of Chinese porcelain, Italian maiolica, Islamic 17th-century wares and English and Continental porcelain.[1] In 1884 the museum gained the world's largest collection of 18th-century English porcelain, earthenware, glass and enamels when Lady Charlotte Schreiber (1812–1895), née Lady Charlotte Bertie, donated 1,800 works of art, including 807 examples of English earthenware and porcelain. The selection was made from a collection of nearly 12,000 examples of English, Continental and Chinese earthenware and porcelain that she had formed over 15 years with her second husband, Charles Schreiber, in whose name the donation was made in 1885, the year after he died.[2]

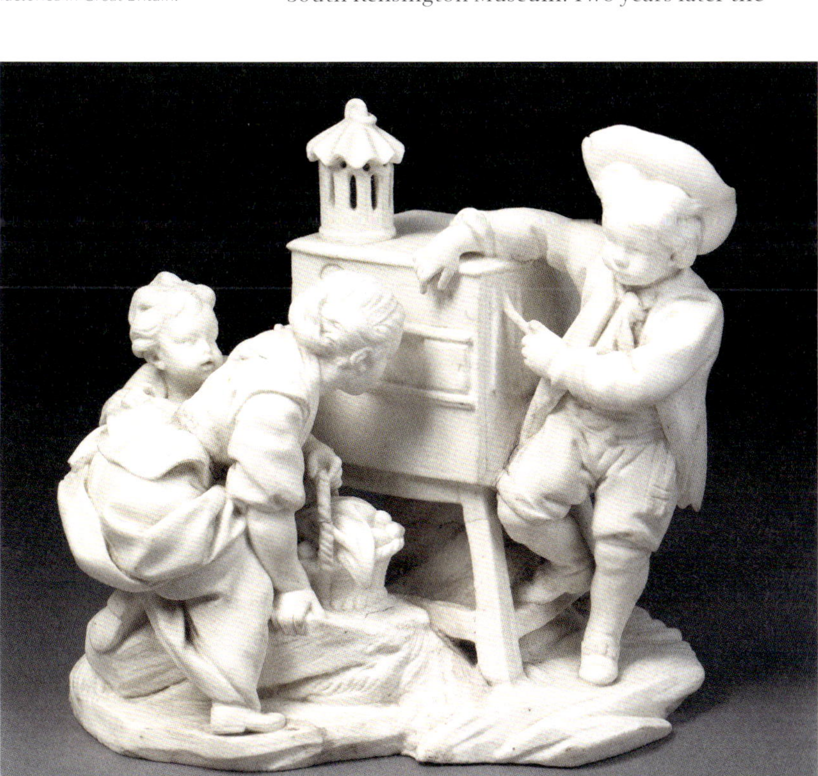

The daughter of Albemarle Bertie, 9th Earl of Lindsey, and his wife Charlotte Layard, Lady Charlotte was also a first cousin of the diplomat, archaeologist and art collector Austen Henry Layard, with whom she formed her first collection, of ancient Assyrian sculptures. In 1833, when she was 21, she chose to marry Josiah John Guest, the owner of a Welsh ironworks, who was her senior by 27 years. Self-taught, she mastered eight languages including Arabic, the Persian language Farsi, Hebrew and Welsh. Her translation from Middle Welsh of the medieval epic *The Mabinogion . . . and other ancient Welsh Manuscripts*, the earliest prose literature in Britain, was published bilingually, in seven volumes (1838–49). It included her account of King Arthur and the Round Table, which inspired Alfred Tennyson's *Idylls of the King* (1859–85). In

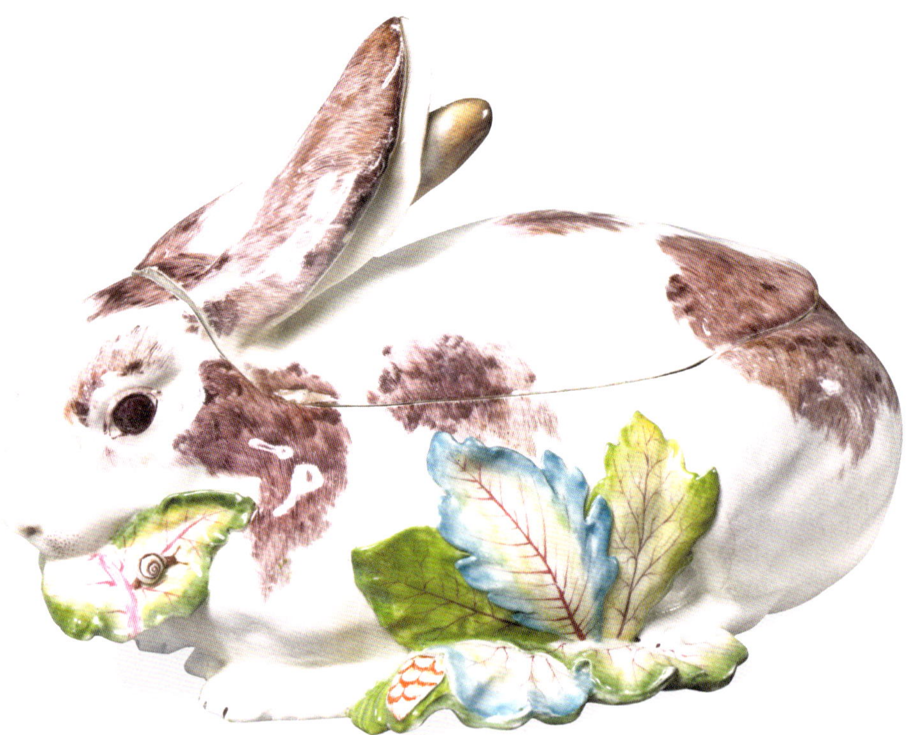

55. Chelsea porcelain factory, tureen and cover in the form of a rabbit, *c*.1755, soft-paste porcelain, painted in enamels. Purchased by Lady Charlotte Schreiber in Rotterdam, May 1876 when she noted in her diary: 'at Van Minden's very cheap; he only asked £5 for it and took £4'; given by Lady Charlotte Schreiber. V&A: 414:328/1,2-1885.

1846 she persuaded her husband to purchase Canford Manor in Dorset. The previous year Layard had begun his excavations of the palaces of the Assyrian kings at Nimrud and Nineveh. He sent ancient Assyrian sculptures to the British Museum and the 'duplicates' to Canford. There a total of 20 Assyrian sculptures and eight casts were installed in a new pavilion extension ('the Nineveh Porch') designed by Charles Barry. Layard became Lady Charlotte's son-in-law when he married Enid, one of her ten children. Seventeen of the ancient Assyrian sculptures today in the Metropolitan Museum of Art, New York came from Canford.[3]

After nearly twenty years of married life, Sir John Guest died in 1852. By then, Dowlais Ironworks Company had become the world's biggest, with 18 furnaces and around 7,000 workers supplying iron to Isambard Kingdom Brunel for the Great Western Railway and for his ship SS *Great Britain*, rail track to America, Germany and to Russia for the Trans-Siberian Railway, as well as cannon balls for the British army. Having long assisted in the administration of the ironworks and in the founding of schools and other welfare initiatives for the families of the workforce she was ready to take on the management of the business itself. From dealing with the accounts, translating correspondence and contracts she now had to negotiate through labour strikes. In 1855 she gave up her role as head of the ironworks when she married Charles Schreiber (1826–1884). A Fellow of Trinity College, Cambridge, he had been employed since 1853 to tutor her eldest son, Ivor, for university entrance (he went up from Harrow to Trinity College, Cambridge). Lady Charlotte was 42, Charles 28 and Ivor 19. She had her portrait drawn by G.F. Watts at this time (fig.53).

With her second husband she found a mutual love of ceramics and twice placed selections from their new purchases on long loan to the South Kensington Museum, before they set off on 'our happy rambles on the Continent'[4] or as she also described them, 'our ceramic chasse'.[5] As her journals and correspondence reveal, between 1867 and 1882 they made 24 expeditions across Continental Europe, regularly spending up to eight hours each day on foot through up to 16 shops, negotiating prices and buying bargains to resell while collecting for themselves, as well as visiting castles, collectors and museum directors. Their evenings were devoted to washing, recording and studying their latest finds. Her collection is exceptional in its supporting documentation and in her scholarship, which may also reflect the example of her cousin, Layard.[6] Indeed, she can be seen as one of a new era of collectors for whom true understanding required more than good taste: for her, connoisseurship required context.

Lady Charlotte kept a daily journal from the age of nine (with some days completed later) until she reached 79. Her detailed record of her shopping tours is a vivid and vital source for understanding not only the world of ceramics, but also the wider international art market in her day. A selection, covering the years 1869 to 1885, was first published in 1911, in two volumes edited by her third son, Montague Guest. He described how 'she hunted high and low, through England and abroad; France, Holland, Germany, Spain, Italy, Turkey, all were ransacked; she left no stone unturned, no difficulty, discomfort, fatigue or hardship of travel daunted her, or turned her from her purpose, and she would come back, after weeks on the Continent, to Langham House, in Portland Place, where she lived, rich with the fruits of her expeditions.'[7]

Her daily descriptions of visits to 'curiosity shops' and to 'Antiquaires', as well as to private collections and museums in European cities include many references to paintings, sculpture and other media and to international players in the

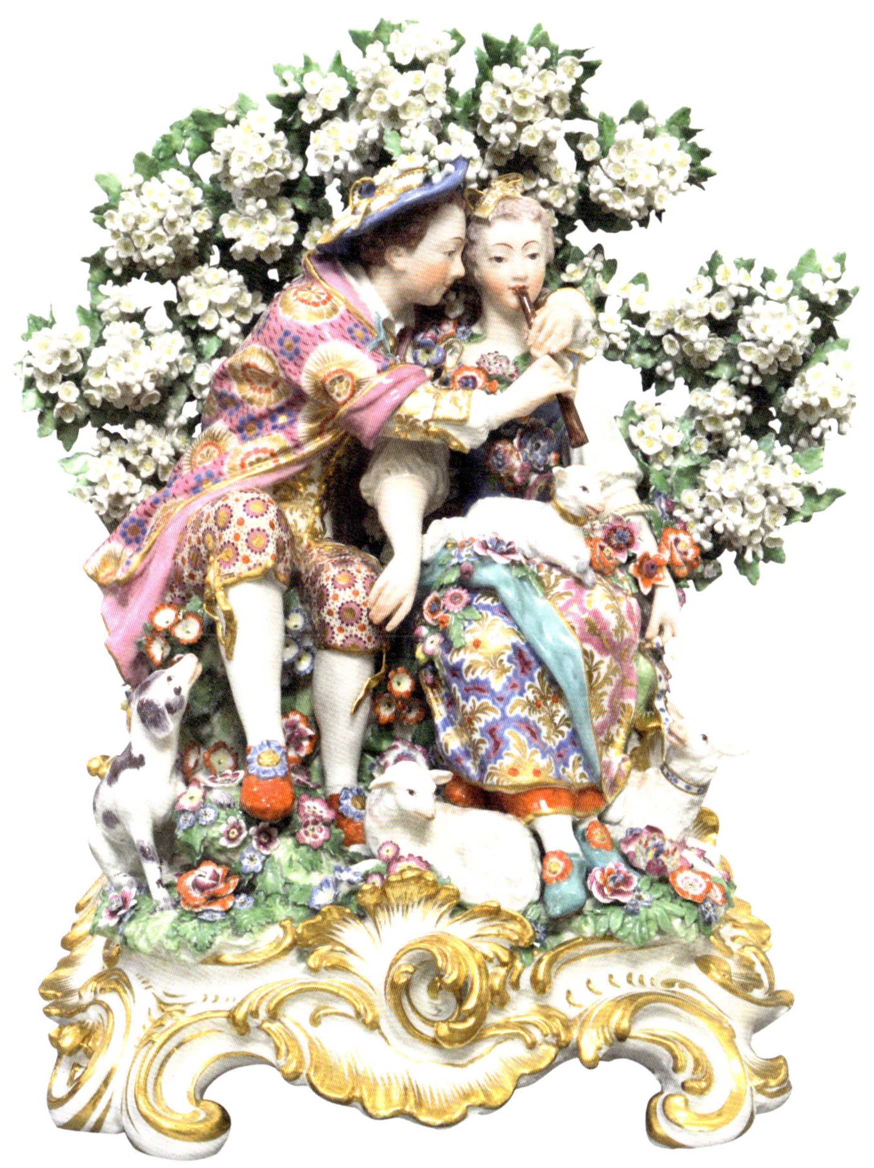

**56.** Chelsea porcelain factory, modelled by Joseph Willems, *The Music Lesson*, c.1765, soft-paste porcelain, painted in enamels and gilded. Given by Lady Charlotte Schreiber. V&A: 414:192-1885.

market, but English porcelain and earthenware were her main quarry. As she left Florence on 3 June 1869, after visiting collections with the leading local dealer William Blundell Spence (who supplied many treasures direct to the South Kensington Museum),[8] she noted in her journal: 'During our short stay we ransacked all the shops we could find for English china.'[9] She delighted in recording her detection of vendors who 'do not scruple to put on marks in a very superficial manner', who painted on more expensive makers' names and logos. She found in a shop in Genoa 'the name "Wedgwood" impressed in the glaze. I confess the English name was rather faint so that the ingenious foreigner might be excused from expecting that it would escape ordinary inspection'.[10] It is remarkable to read just how much English porcelain had found its way into the antique shops of Continental Europe.

Selections of English porcelain were placed on long loan from the Schreibers to the museum in 1866 (for six months), in July 1867 (until February 1869) and in 1869 (224 examples, until 1873). There were practical benefits to lending ceramics to the museum, as Lady Charlotte wrote of some vases she had received as a gift when the giver objected to the loan: 'They would be so much safer there than here – and would remain quite as much mine.'[11] The growing collection was also shown at meetings of the Fine Arts Club, which Charles Schreiber joined in 1858, the year after it was formed by J.C. Robinson, Henry Cole, Carlo Marochetti and others to encourage collectors.[12] Charles Schreiber exhibited selections at meetings from 1863 and many more were shown at receptions at their London home.

In March 1884 Charles Schreiber died in Lisbon, aged 57. Lady Charlotte carried on collecting until December 1885, vowing in August 1884 'for my husband's sake, I must make the collection as good as I can and as worthy to be given to the Nation as possible'.[13] Advised by A.W. Franks of the British Museum and by R.H. Soden Smith, Keeper of the National Art Library (a private collector of ceramics), she made a selection of porcelain which she presented to the South Kensington Museum in 1885 as a memorial to her husband. Ahead of the donation, in 1884 she recorded how she 'went to see G.F. Watts, the famous artist, at his studio, taking with me the chalk drawing he did of me some thirty years ago. He is going to have this and C.S.'s [her late husband] portrait copied that I may send them with the collection to the South Kensington [*sic*].'[14] She then wrote the official catalogue of over 2,000 pieces (with help from Franks, Soden Smith and others) which was published in 1885. The terms of her Deed of Gift specify the title of the collection and that it 'shall be kept together and be exhibited in one room . . . none of the objects . . . shall ever be . . . removed . . . for exhibition at any other place', otherwise the collection was to revert to her family.[15] The Schreiber Collection of English Ceramics filled the Schreiber Room (139) at the V&A, complete with a pair of memorial portraits of the two collectors after the sketches by Watts, that she had 'done in mosaics for the Museum as being more durable than the crayon drawings'.[16]

In the introduction to her catalogue, she modestly described her pioneering field research, which included not only retrieving English ceramics from antique shops across Europe but also taking part in the excavation of kiln sites. Her catalogue was revised by V&A curators in two volumes, the first on porcelain by Bernhard Rackham (1915), the second on earthenware by Rackham, W.B. Honey and Herbert Read (1930). Read also assisted Rackham with the volume on her enamels (1924).[17]

Lady Charlotte Schreiber has been described as 'one of the earliest, most active and successful English collectors of ceramics, and of many other *objets d'art*, including particularly lace, fans and playing cards'.[18] Her English porcelain and earthenware ranges from the factories of Fulham (John Dwight) to Etruria (Wedgwood), from Chelsea and Bow to Derby and Worcester.[19] She also donated her English enamels (London, Birmingham, Staffordshire). To the British Museum she presented her collections of fans (in 1891) and of games (1893) and bequeathed her collection of playing cards (1895). Her legacy also includes publications by the Canford Press, the private press she founded with her sons, named after her country home, where she died aged 82. She also left much of her collection to her children and to her 40 grandchildren.

# 10 Collectors as International Agents

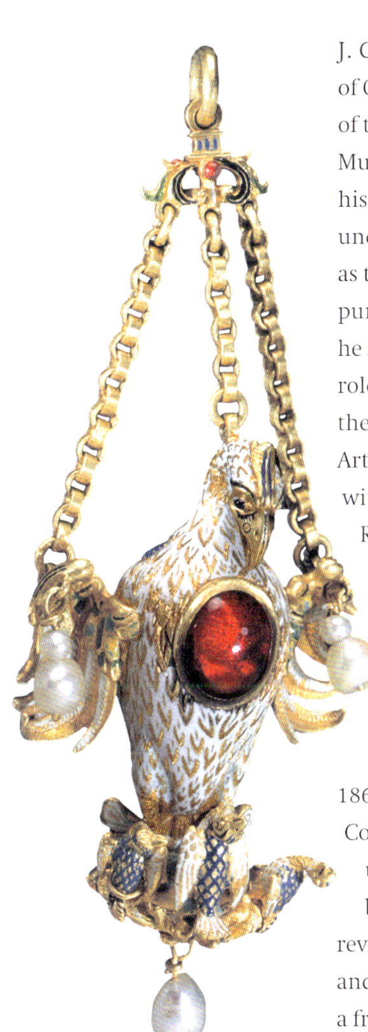

**57.** Unknown maker (Spain), Pendant: *The Pelican in her Piety*, *c.*1550–75, enamelled gold set with a foiled ruby simulant and hung with pearls, the back with black-and-white moresques enamel. From the Treasury of the Basilica of Our Lady of the Pillar, Zaragoza. V&A: 335-1870.

J. C. Robinson, appointed curator of the Museum of Ornamental art in 1854, became Superintendent of the Art Collections of the South Kensington Museum. Following disagreements with Henry Cole, his post was abolished in 1863.[1] His expertise was undeniable, so Cole retained him, part-time, to serve as the museum's travelling agent in search of new purchases. As the museum's Second Art Referee he still reported in to Richard Redgrave, whose roles included responsibility for all acquisitions as the First Art Referee and as Inspector General for Art. In 1863 Cole set out on a shopping expedition with Richard Redgrave and his brother Samuel Redgrave, but after travelling to Hanover, Prague, Vienna, Munich and Paris, Cole came to the conclusion that, in future, foreign dealers should just send sketches of objects on offer with their prices and then be invited to London.[2] Spain, however, remained a gap in the collections and Robinson was sent there in 1863–4, 1865 and 1866. Robinson wrote to Henry Cole from Madrid in 1866, with his usual sense of urgency: 'I am very anxious to get authority to buy . . . now is the time – this country is in semi-revolution, money has disappeared, distress prevails and whatever there is to be sold is in the market [at] a fraction of what would have been formerly asked. This morning I bought a superb cinquecento chalice for little more than the value of the silver.'[3] The following year Henry Cole sacked Robinson for the second time, by deleting his advisory position.

In May 1870 Juan Facundo Riaño y Montera (1828–1901) agreed to serve as the museum's Professional Art Referee in Spain. He had been introduced to Cole in April 1870 when the museum's director was staying with Austen Henry Layard, by then British Minister in Madrid. A collector of Spanish ceramics and glass, Riaño was Professor of Fine Arts at the Escuela Superior de Diplomática in Madrid. His arrangement with South Kensington was prompted not only by the opportunities to collect but also by the museum's campaign to commission plaster casts and photographs of sculpture and architectural decoration from around the world, ahead of the opening of the Architectural ('Cast') Courts in 1873. His duties were defined as: 'to obtain permission to make castings, &c., and to report upon objects for sale suitable for South Kensington Museum; upon cost and progress of reproductions, and upon other art objects referred to him'.[4]

Riaño began with jewellery, in 1870, when the cathedral authorities at the Basilica of Our Lady of the Pillar in Zaragoza sought to raise funds for their building programme. Riaño selected from their treasury a group of jewels, which the South Kensington Museum purchased (fig.57). On behalf of the museum he acquired in Spain manuscripts, textiles, ceramics, glass, and many more items of jewellery. Between 1871 and 1877 he was paid 5 guineas for each of his monthly reports. Riaño was also commissioned to write for the museum two handbooks on Spanish art, published in 1872 and 1879.[5] In 1873 he offered to sell the museum his personal collection of Spanish ceramics and to leave it on loan on display for a year at a rental fee of £110 while a selection was made; 88 items were chosen. In 1892 he offered his collection of lustreware, pottery and glass on loan pending purchase; it was shown at the Bethnal Green Museum for several months before being sold to various buyers, including Glasgow Art Galleries and Museums.

After Cole retired, Robinson returned as an adviser, invited back by the museum's second director, Philip Cunliffe Owen, to serve as a roving agent abroad. In 1879 Robinson sold the museum a collection of 301 Spanish works of art, for the considerable sum of £6,800 (about £872,000 today). Some of Robinson's collection featured in the *Exhibition of Spanish and Portuguese Ornamental Art* in 1881, for which he served on the exhibition committee and wrote the introduction to the catalogue. Not everything had been bought by the museum, as yet. Among the most prominent objects in the exhibition was, as a journalist described, 'a great reredos from the high altar of the cathedral of Ciudad Rodrigo . . . owned by Mr. J.C. Robinson, to whose explorations of Spain and enthusiasm for antiquarian art this fine exhibition is mainly due . . . [it] will not be followed by many similar treasures. The Spaniards have lately learned the value of such things.'[6]

To help justify deleting Robinson's advisory position in 1867 Cole had claimed that he worked as a private dealer when travelling at public expense on museum business. He was also suspected of buying and selling objects to the museum at a profit. Further evidence of this may be in Robinson's offer in 1879 to place on loan to the museum 'a collection of instruments of torture, formerly used by the Inquisition, which he acquired in Spain for Mr Henry Willett, of Brighton'.[7] The offer was declined. Austen Henry Layard felt he saw through him, remarking in 1871 (as a trustee of the National Gallery, when Robinson was being considered as a future director): 'the more I hear of Mr R. the less I like him. He is nothing but a dealer – up to every trick of the trade.'[8]

One of Robinson's main successors as the museum's agent in Italy was Charles Fairfax Murray (1849–1919) who had started at South Kensington as an assistant to Edward Burne-Jones in 1867, painting decorative figures in the Green Dining Room. By the 1880s the international art market had been boosted by rivalry between new museums; among Fairfax Murray's clients as art dealer were several German museum directors, including Julius Lessing, director of Berlin's Kunstgewerbemuseum, Julius Meyer, director of Berlin's Gemäldegalerie and his successor there, Wilhelm von Bode. As an agent for the South Kensington Museum, Fairfax Murray was asked to inspect potential acquisitions, write reports, negotiate and complete purchases. He also found opportunities to form his own collections, with a view to eventual sales. In 1886, for example, he showed the museum's Director of Art, Thomas Armstrong, 13 sheets of watercolours that he had painted, probably to illustrate a publication on his own collection, showing 59 examples of early maiolica (fig.58). Three years later he sent the collection to the museum as a loan, for display and purchase.[9]

Alongside inside knowledge of local art markets and their tricks, a basic requirement for the museum's collectors abroad (and for its curators at home) was the ability to speak languages other than English. For China, the Victorian museum could rely on Stephen Wootton Bushell (1844–1908), a pioneer in the study of Chinese art. When he visited the ruins of Shangdu in inner Mongolia in 1872 with Thomas G. Grosvenor, they were the first Europeans to reach the summer capital of the Yuan dynasty (the model for Coleridge's Xanadu in his poem *Kubla Khan*, published 1816) since Marco Polo in the 13th century. Bushell collected ceramics for the museum in China in 1883, while employed as physician at the British Legation, Beijing (from 1868 until he retired in 1899). He purchased for the museum in total 233 ceramics; in 1874 he offered his own collection of bronzes on loan, 32 of which the museum purchased in 1898. He wrote two museum handbooks, *Oriental Ceramic Art* (1897) and *Chinese Art* (1904; 1906) and catalogued J.P. Morgan's collection of Chinese porcelains, published by the Metropolitan Museum of Art, New York (1907; see chapter 18). Bushell also collected plants and seeds for the Royal Botanic Gardens at Kew and acted as agent in China for the British Museum, to whom he left his own collection of Chinese coins, books and ceramics.[10]

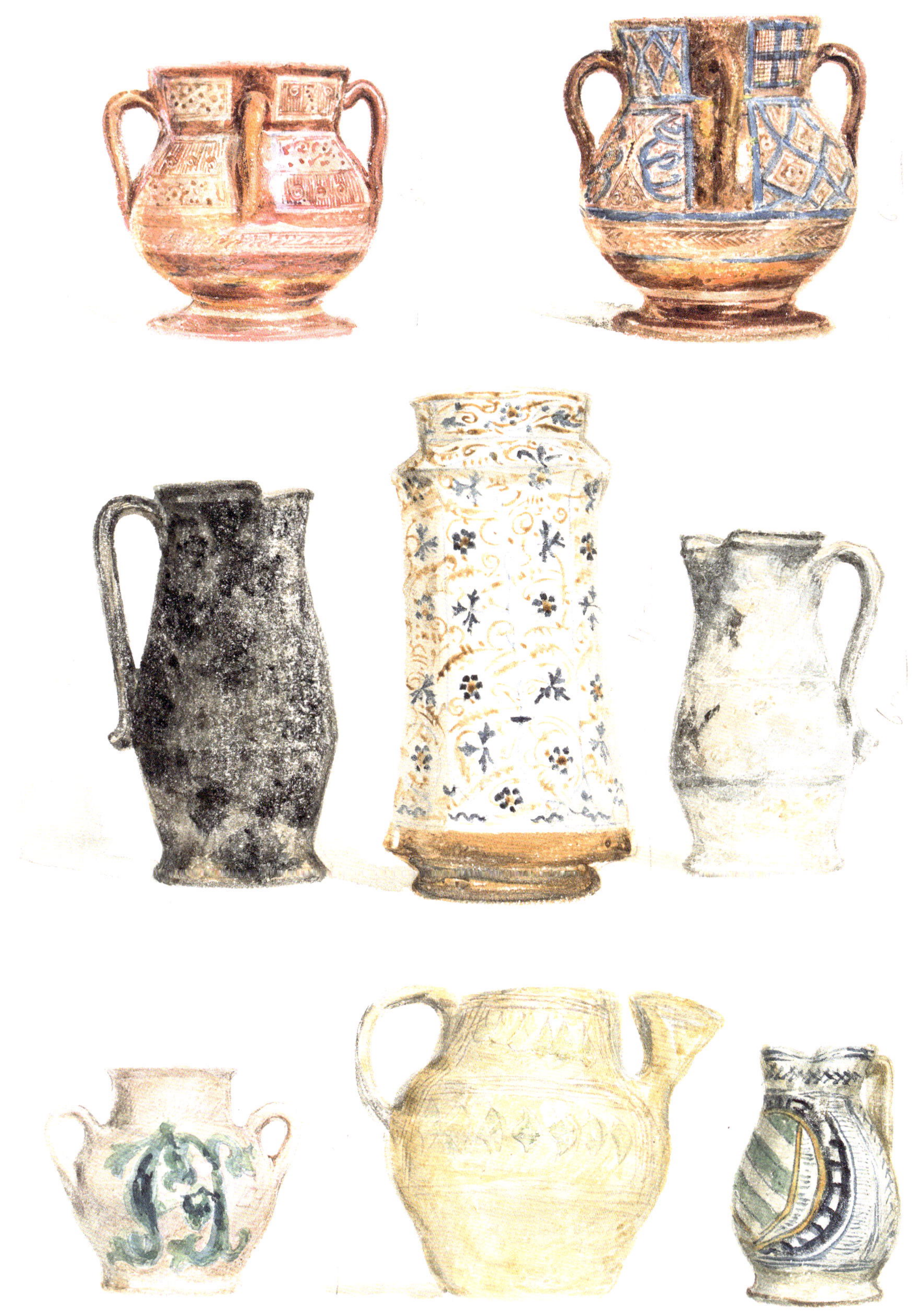

**58.** Charles Fairfax Murray, *Maiolica from the Collection of Charles Fairfax Murray*, c.1886, watercolour. V&A: D.287-1890.

The archaeologist, diplomat and, later, museum director Robert Murdoch Smith (1835–1900) first worked in Asia Minor in 1856–9 as a young officer in the Royal Engineers; there he commanded sappers excavating under the direction of Charles Newton of the British Museum. More than an engineer, Smith discovered the site of the tomb of King Mausolus, as he described in *A History of Discoveries at Halicarnassus, Cnidus, and Branchidae* (1862). From 1863 he superintended part of the Persian section (Tehran to Kohrud) of the telegraph system connecting London to India. In 1865 he was appointed director of the Persian Telegraph Service Indo-European Telegraph Department in Iran.[11]

Smith saw opportunities for collecting beyond his own resources and wrote to Henry Cole in 1873 offering to help 'in the way of purchasing artistic and ornamental objects . . . and generally acting as an agent in Persia of the Department of Science and Art'.[12] In his spare time with a budget from the museum he purchased items in groups between 1875 and 1889. An exhibition of 'Asiatic products', held in 1876 in the museum's South Court, presented nearly 2,000 items, most of which came from Smith, who wrote the accompanying book *Persian Art* (published by the Department of Science and Art, 1876).[13] He was appointed director of the Museum of Science and Art in Edinburgh in 1885.

Smith's contribution established Iranian art at the museum and ensured its admiration by designers, craftsmen, manufacturers and the wider public. But credit should also be given to Jules Richard (1816–1891), a French expatriate resident in Tehran from 1844, from whom Smith purchased in 1875 a collection of several hundred examples of Iranian faience, Chinese pottery, embroideries and brocades that Smith believed were bought in Isfahan. News of the major purchase prompted many offers to Smith of rare objects from private owners in Tehran. An archaeologist and the first known foreign photographer in Iran, Richard worked as a tutor at the Qajar royal college, served as 'Secrétaire Interprète intime du Shah de Perse' and also acted as a buying agent for the museum.[14]

Caspar Purdon Clarke, an architect in the South Kensington team, went to Tehran in 1874 as superintendent of works for the British consular buildings. After returning to London, he went to Damascus in 1876 before travelling in Turkey and Syria to make acquisitions for the museum. In 1880, from a buying trip to India with a budget, he sent back 3,400 objects to the museum; he was appointed keeper of the India Museum in 1883 and director of the South Kensington Museum in 1896.[15] Thanks to Smith and Purdon Clarke the museum's collection of Persian art spanning 12 centuries was largely formed between 1873 and 1893.[16]

In 1882, the year Clarke returned from shopping in India, Stanley Lane-Poole (1854–1931) was sent to Egypt by the museum and acquired 400 objects; on his return he wrote *The Art of the Saracens in Egypt* (1886). The Reverend Greville

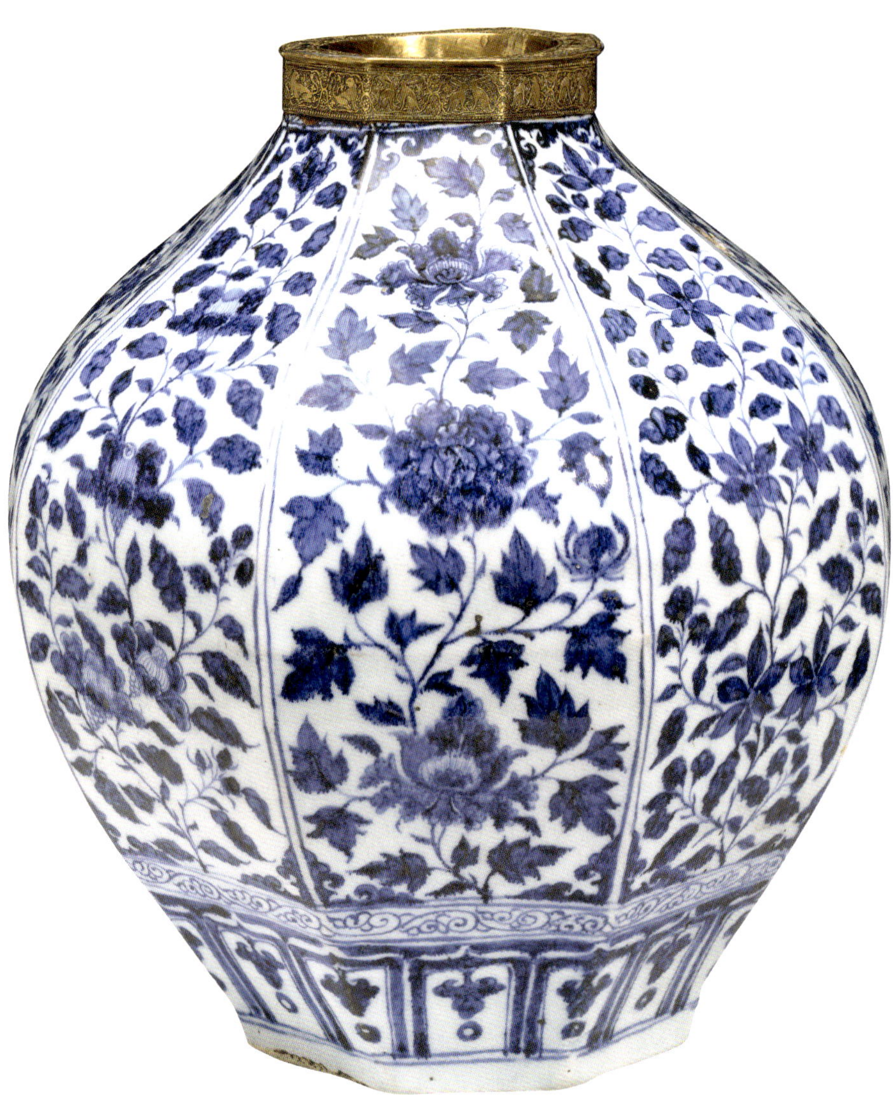

**59.** Unknown maker (China, Jingdezhen), storage jar, 14th century, porcelain painted in underglaze blue, brass mount added in Iran in 19th century. Purchased by Robert Murdoch Smith. V&A: 1599-1876.

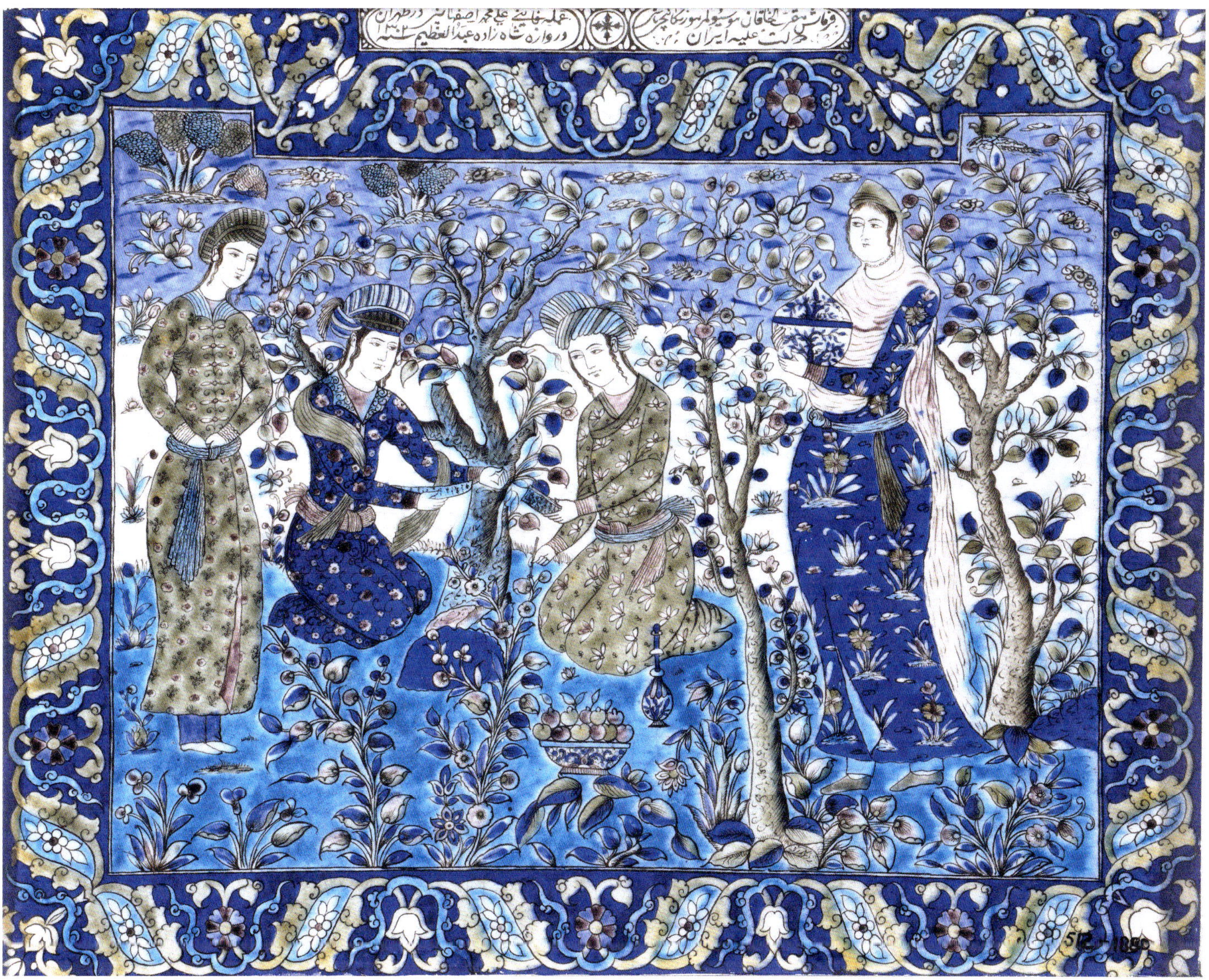

60. Ali Muhammad Isfahani and workshop, tile, 1884–5, fritware, underglaze painted in polychrome. Purchased by Robert Murdoch Smith from the collection of Jules Richard. V&A: 512-1889.

J. Chester (1830–1892) was also commissioned by the museum to buy 'Arabian objects', such as woodwork and mosaics that became available as architectural salvage during the Westernising modernisation of Cairo. More significant were the fragments of Late Antique and early Islamic textiles dug from graves and cut into lots by local dealers, which he sold or donated to the museum. While painfully aware of the looting and destruction of Pharaonic sites, Chester also collected in Egypt for the British Museum, the Fitzwilliam Museum, the Ashmolean Museum and the Bodleian Library.[17]

The museum also enriched its holdings by buying ready-formed collections abroad. In 1869 it had purchased from the Egyptian government the collection of the distinguished architect Husayn Fahmi Pasha al-Mi'mari ('Dr Meymar') that had been shown at the Exposition Universelle in Paris in 1867; this included the monumental minbar (Islamic pulpit) inscribed with the name of Sultan Qa'itbay (fig.61). In 1883 the museum purchased the collection of Gaston de Saint-Maurice, chief equerry of the royal stables in Cairo, comprising around 200 objects. South Kensington's collection of Arab art was formed between 1869 and 1884.[18]

Egyptian textiles were among the collection of over 90 items that the museum purchased in 1860 from Franz Bock (1823–1899), author of the pioneering three-volume study *Geschichte der liturgischen Gewänder des Mittelalters* (Bonn, 1859–71).[19] A pastor in Cologne from around 1857, he was appointed honorary canon of Aachen Cathedral in 1862, the year he sold the museum another collection of woven fabrics that he had placed there on loan.[20] Bock travelled in Europe and the Near East collecting fragments of Byzantine, Asian, medieval and Renaissance silk from many ancient cathedrals and religious foundations, initially as source material for his factory producing silks for ecclesiastical vestments and furnishings. Bock placed his textiles on loan to South Kensington where, he wrote, they 'fill 4 rooms and of themselves form a splendid Museum'.[21] When in 1882 he offered to sell it all to the museum, William Morris (as an Art Referee) supported the acquisition of a selection, but the following year Bock sold his collection to the Manchester Corporation instead. Bock also collected bookbindings, sculpture and metalwork and advised the museum on many other acquisitions. However, Bock is now notorious as 'Scissors Bock' the 'scissor-happy priest' who would cut off and sell fragments from rare textiles he had found in church libraries and treasuries.[22] Best known is the 11th-century German tapestry from St Gereon's Church in Cologne, which Bock cut up and sold, one piece to the V&A and three other pieces to museums in Lyons, Nuremberg and Berlin. It is now considered the oldest Western tapestry to have survived.[23]

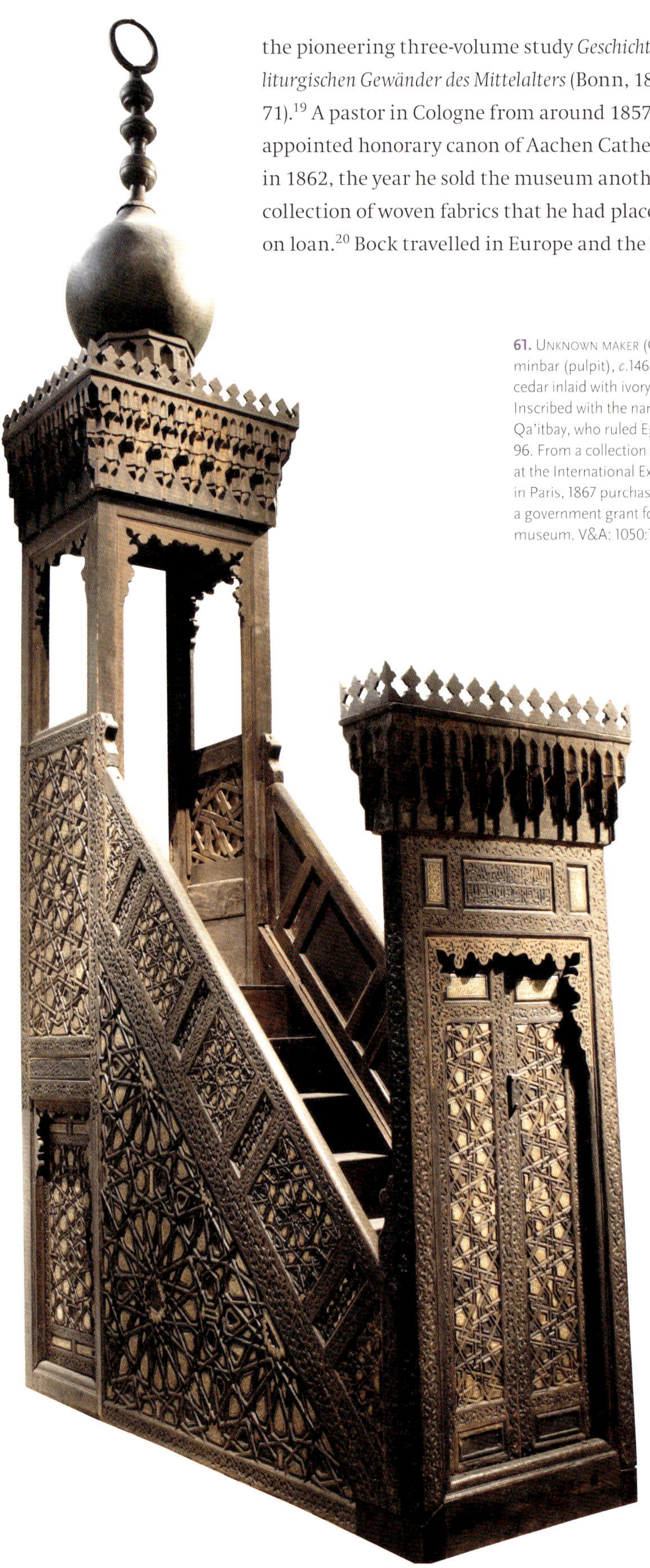

**61.** Unknown maker (Cairo), minbar (pulpit), *c.*1468–96, cedar inlaid with ivory and wood. Inscribed with the name of Sultan Qa'itbay, who ruled Egypt 1468–96. From a collection shown at the International Exhibition in Paris, 1867 purchased with a government grant for the museum. V&A: 1050:1 to 2-1869.

The Pre-Raphaelite painter Henry Wallis (1830–1916) was also a writer and collector. He first approached the museum as a potential lender in 1880. In 1886 he purchased a collection of nearly 300 textiles from Egypt for the museum, many from ancient burials. He also placed hundreds of objects on loan, from Egyptian glass to Italian maiolica, which entered the permanent collection after his death.[24] The professional archaeologist Flinders Petrie (1853–1942) was the source of many textiles from his excavations in Egypt that came to the museum from his employer, the Egypt Exploration Fund or through its sponsors.[25] W.J. Myers (1858–1899), an officer in the King's Rifle Corps, served in Egypt, Sudan and on India's Northwest Frontier. In Cairo he combed the bazaars for Islamic tiles and glass and formed a collection of Egyptian antiquities, which he bequeathed to his old school, Eton College. Myers lent nearly 2,000 objects to the museum; in his will he stipulated that his collections there should be offered to the museum at a reduced price, and many were sold to the V&A by his executors after he was killed in the Boer War.[26] The museum's purchases were divided into three groups and distributed between South Kensington and its fellow museums, under the Department of Science and Art, in Dublin and Edinburgh.

In its first decades South Kensington developed international networks of colonial administrators, diplomats, businessmen and expatriates, who supported the museum as collectors, lenders and donors or as commissioned freelancing field agents. This is how, despite a shortage of funds and of in-house expertise, and the risks of relying on private loans for its long-term displays, the ambitious young museum found ways to collect abroad, buying from the hearts of local markets in an expanding empire of trade, scholarship and conflict.

**62.** Ali Muhammad Isfahani and workshop, Tile panel (tabletop), 1887, painted and glazed fritware. Commissioned by Robert Murdoch Smith. V&A: 559:1 to 9-1888.

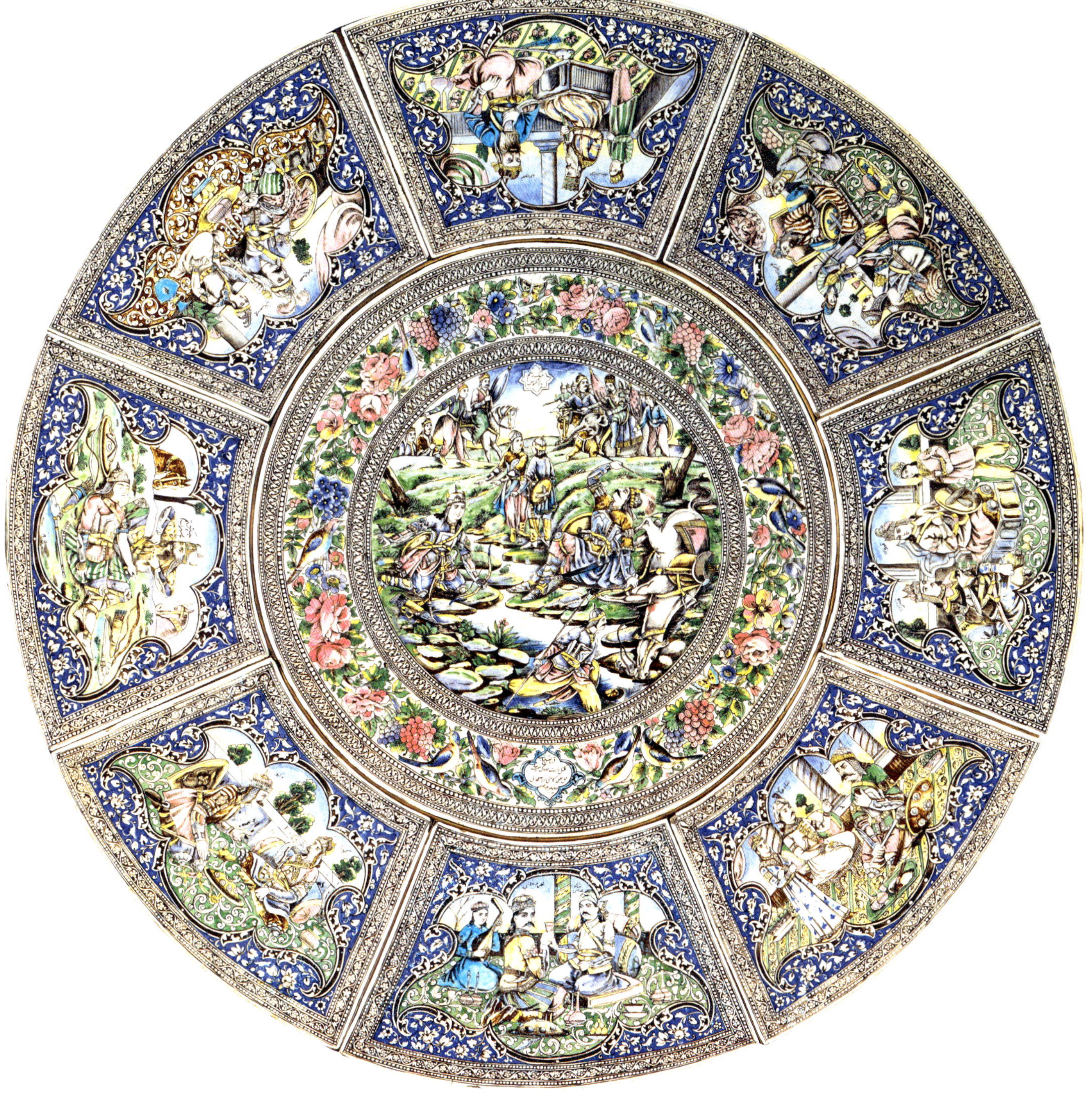

# 11 Imperial Acquisitions

Museums established in the Victorian and Edwardian eras were the products of the age of empires, either overtly through their stated aims and the sources of their collections or less obviously through the sources of their funding. The history of collections formed for the V&A is inseparable from the history of British imperialism, for the museum benefitted from the economic and military power of the British Empire as it competed with other empires. But the V&A has a more specific and strategic connection. As the South Kensington Museum, supporting the design reform movement, it played a key role in international cultural exchange and trade through the empire.

The museum served as a showcase in London for inspiring collections, especially from South Asia. These had been much admired at the Great Exhibition in 1851, where examples were purchased with a government grant to enrich a travelling reference collection for art schools in Britain. When British manufacturers copied and mass-produced patterns to undercut the fashionable imported South Asian textiles, the museum and its network of local Asian agents and artisans helped to find markets for the traditional crafts of India. As an agent of empire, the museum promoted the contemporary arts and crafts of Asia through exhibitions, loans, acquisitions, research and publications.[1] Inspiration also came from beyond the British Empire, especially Japan, which had a greater influence after the museum acquired a collection of Japanese objects in 1875 (see chapter 5).

Objects that came to the V&A as the result of military conquest are of great public concern and are the focus of much current research. Some of the V&A's early acquisitions arrived through routes that would not be acceptable for museums in Britain today, especially if as loot.[2] This chapter briefly introduces some collections from this period that we know owe their origins to military campaigns. Case studies from India, Africa, China and Burma (Myanmar) summarise how objects came to be held by the museum, at a time when British forces considered it standard military practice to seize their enemy's property.

Today, the term 'loot' evokes images of victorious soldiers running rampant through palaces and helping themselves to the most valuable objects, but at this time official procedures were being defined and enforced. Imperial looting was a state-controlled administrative process governed by army regulations. For the British army, new rules sought to institute 'war prize', a naval tradition from the Napoleonic Wars, through which 'plunder' belonged to the Crown and had to be assembled by 'prize agents' for future sale through auction. The Army Prize Fund would help to defray the costs of military action, reward soldiers and benefit the injured and their families.[3] The most significant items of historical interest would be identified for separate treatment. Alongside this attempt to organise and legalise looting, the taking of 'trophies' continued as evidence, and as souvenirs, of victories. However, independent looting and souvenir hunting by soldiers were seen as a breakdown of discipline, classed as offences

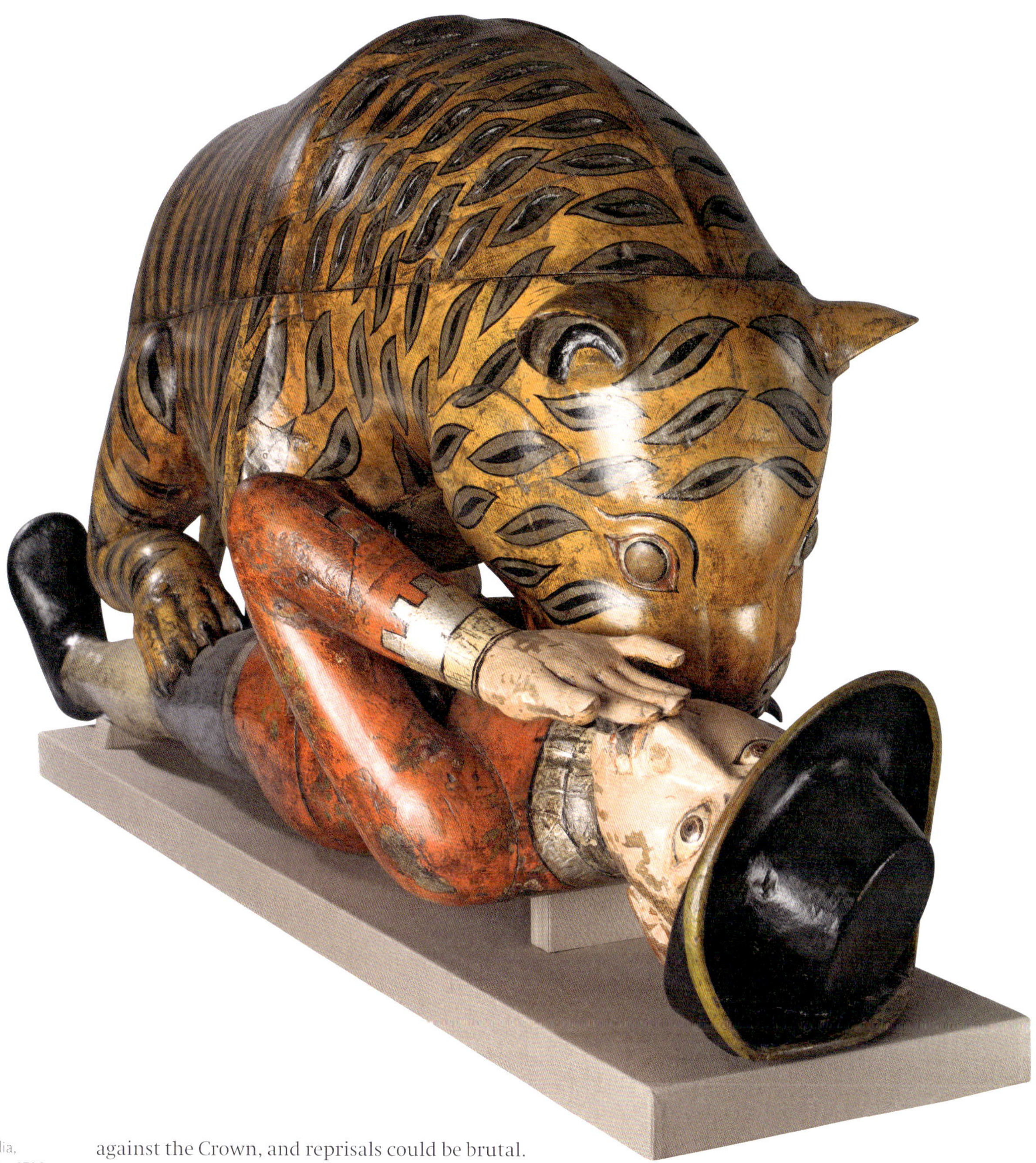

63. Unknown maker (India, Mysore), *'Tippoo's Tiger'*, *c.*1790, painted wooden semi-automaton containing mechanical organ. Made for Tipu Sultan, ruler of Mysore. V&A: 2545 (IS).

against the Crown, and reprisals could be brutal. Even so, official looting by army agents armed only with inventories was no less an act of colonial violence, reliant as it was on military, economic and diplomatic domination. The process has a sinister legacy within Europe in the 20th century.

The largest single acquisition was the India Museum, which had been formed in London since the 18th century, mostly by members of the East India Company, an international enterprise with its own army. In 1858 the new India Office took over the India Museum from the East India Company; it moved to South Kensington in 1874 and merged five years later with the South Kensington Museum.[4] The best-known object in the India Museum was a trophy of conquest, *Tippoo's Tiger* (fig.63), a wooden musical semi-automaton in the form of a tiger devouring a European. It had belonged to Tipu Sultan, the ruler of the kingdom of Mysore. 'The Tiger of Mysore', as he was known to the British, was a powerful military leader who fought the Maratha Empire and four Anglo-Mysore wars but was eventually defeated and died at the Siege of Seringapatam in 1799. Another trophy from the India Museum is the golden throne of Maharaja Ranjit Singh (fig.64), the 'Lion of the Punjab', who expelled the Afghans from the north-west region of the Indian subcontinent and united local rulers to create the Sikh Empire. Ten years after his death the British annexed the Punjab in 1849.

New army regulations could not prevent illegal looting and souvenir hunting by many soldiers, civilians, camp followers and local traders. Part of the problem was the variety of troops involved. In Seringapatam in 1799 Colonel Arthur Wellesley (later Duke of Wellington) commanded soldiers from the regular army, from the East India Company and troops of the Nizam of Hyderabad. Wellesley resorted to restoring order by flogging and hanging troops guilty of personal looting, before his agents could record and value the royal treasury, which took weeks. In Lahore the Sikh state treasury was inventoried by Dr John Login, using information provided by the treasurer, before auction. The most significant objects were not sold for the Army Prize Fund. The throne of Ranjit Singh was retained for the India Museum. Under the Treaty of Lahore (1846) the Koh-i-Nur diamond was delivered from the treasury to Governor General Dalhousie and later presented to Queen Victoria.[5]

One collector who benefitted from sales in India was Colonel Charles Seton Guthrie (1808–1875), an officer in the Bengal Engineers who made notable contributions to the India Museum's collections. Serving in India from 1828 to 1857, at a time when imperial collections were being dispersed, he purchased objects of courtly perfection that had come from the royal collections at Delhi and Lucknow and from the Sikh treasury in Lahore. When Guthrie offered the India Museum 244 examples, 81 were purchased in 1868, including Mughal and other inlaid hardstones. After his death collectors competed at his estate's auction for examples, some of which would later be acquired by the V&A, such as the sword hilt of white nephrite jade set with rubies, diamonds and emeralds (fig.65). Guthrie had kept the star of his collection, an exquisite cup of white nephrite jade abraded to the breathtaking point of translucency (fig.67); the handle is in the form of a ram's head, the foot is shaped as a lotus flower with curling petals. It later belonged to Queen Marie of Yugoslavia but was finally offered for sale in 1962. The inscription in Persian revealed that it was made in 1657 for Shah Jahan (1592–1666), the Mughal emperor of India, the wealthiest person on earth, whose legacy includes the Red Fort at Delhi and the Taj Mahal at Agra.[6]

In 1874 Henry Hardy Cole, son of the museum's director, published a *Catalogue of the Objects of Indian Art Exhibited in the South Kensington Museum*. In the introduction he stressed the importance of the collections beyond design reform, to the wider historical and cultural appreciation of India by the British.[7] When the India Museum's collections transferred in 1879 the imperial character of the South Kensington Museum became more overt. Space was found for the new India Galleries on

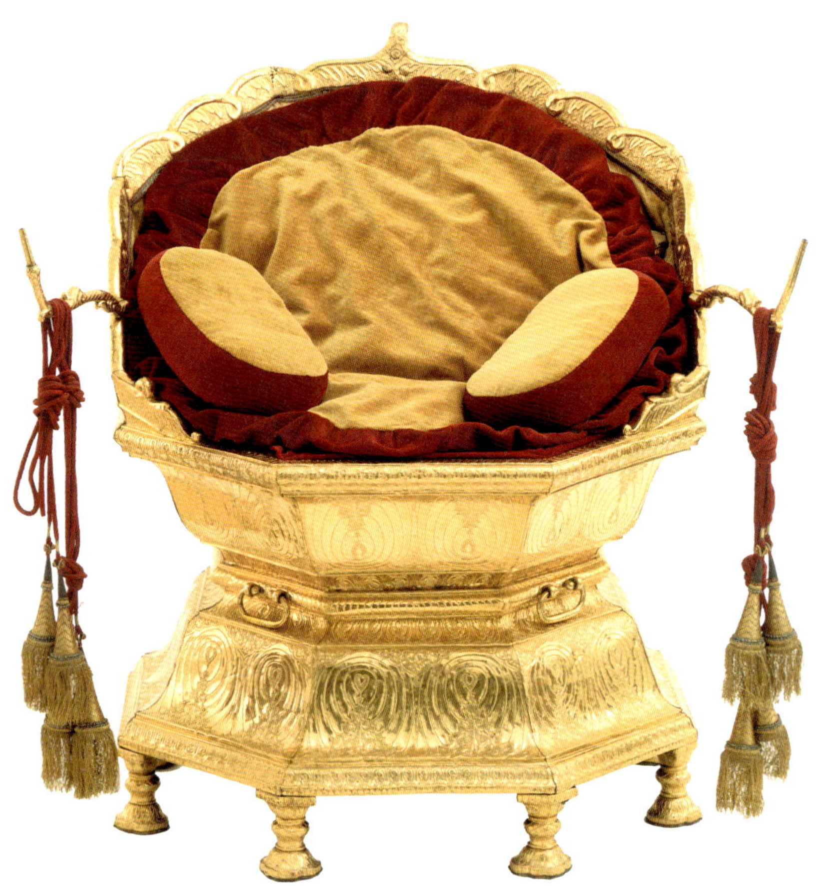

**64.** Hafiz Muhammad Multani, Maharaja Ranjit Singh's throne, probably 1818 or later, sheet gold, cast and chased, on a wooden core. V&A: 2518 (IS).

**65.** Unknown maker (Mughal imperial court workshops, Agra or Delhi), sword hilt *c*.1680–1720, white nephrite jade set with rubies, diamonds and emeralds in gold. From the collection of Colonel Charles Seton Guthrie. V&A: 630-1875.

**66.** Unknown maker (Mughal imperial court workshops, Agra or Delhi), pen box and utensils, *c*.1650–1700, white nephrite jade set with rubies, emeralds and diamonds in gold. From the collection of Colonel Charles Seton Guthrie. V&A: 02549(IS).

**67.** Unknown maker (Mughal imperial court workshops, Agra or Delhi), wine cup of Shah Jahan, 1657, white nephrite jade. From the collection of Colonel Charles Seton Guthrie, purchased with Art Fund support, and the assistance of the Wolfson Foundation, Messrs Spink & Son, and an anonymous benefactor. V&A: IS.12-1962.

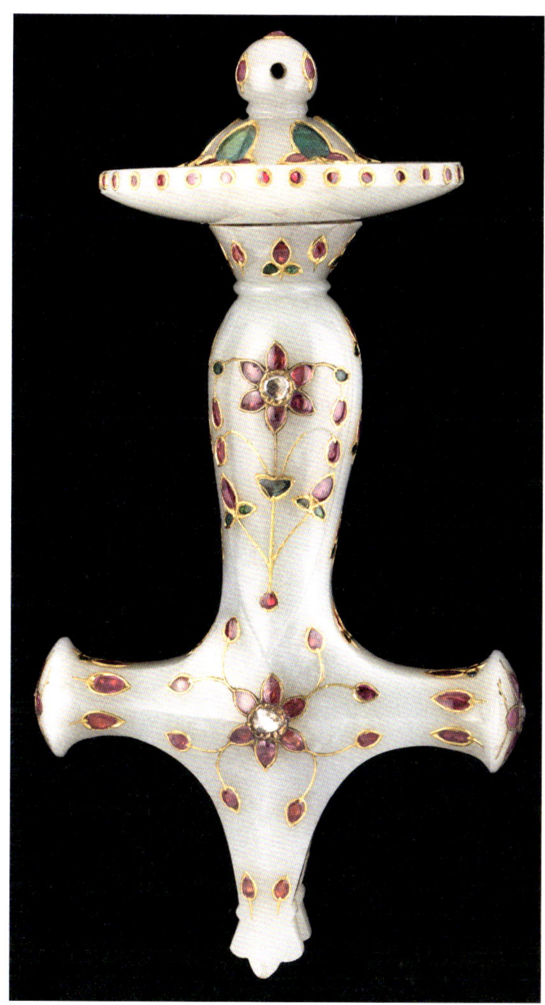

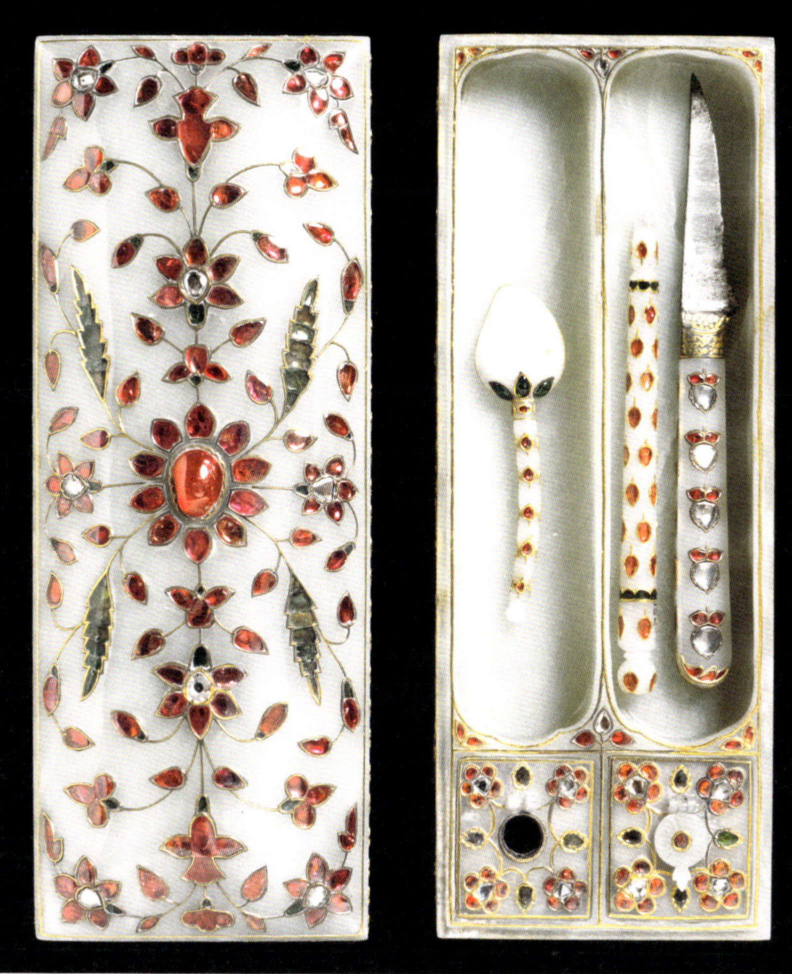

the west side of Exhibition Road where they were visited by Queen Victoria, Empress of India, in 1880. The museum's South Asian holdings expanded further through the collecting endeavours of John Lockwood Kipling, director of the art school and museum in Lahore, and of the museum's first keeper of the Indian collections (and future director of the V&A) Caspar Purdon Clarke.

The best-known group of historical material from Africa comprises objects associated with the British military campaign in 1868 to Maqdala in Abyssinia (Ethiopia). Many were first seen by the British public in the museum's loan exhibition, *Abyssinian Objects from the Emperor Theodore, Lent by the Queen, the Admiralty and Others,* held in 1868. After it closed some items remained on display, as described in a museum guidebook from 1894, alongside Asante gold and objects from South Africa and New

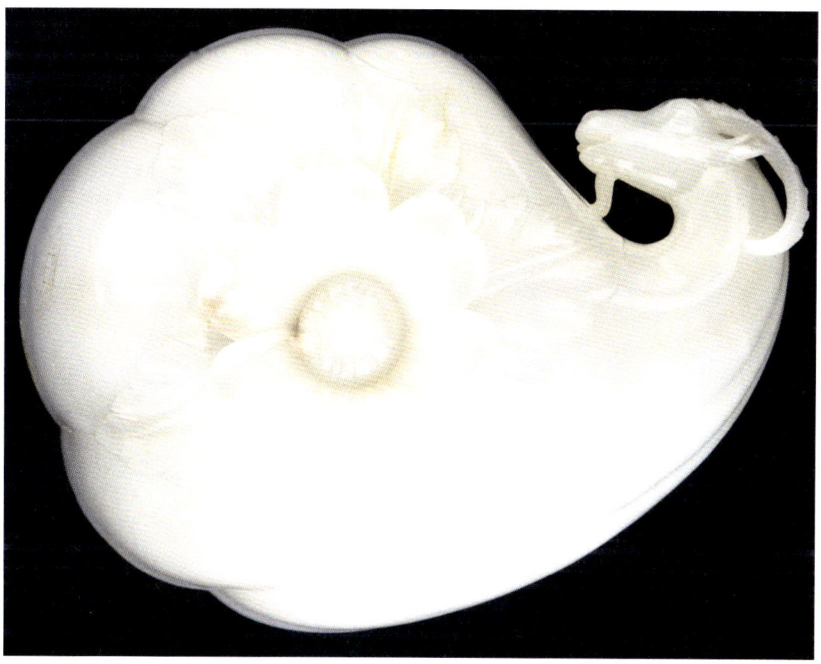

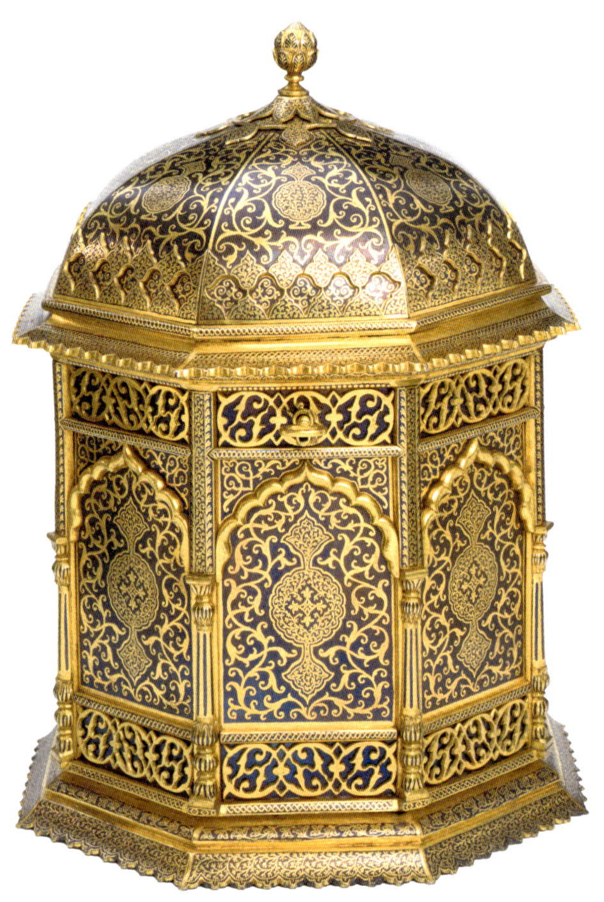

**68.** Unknown maker (Sialkot, Punjab), designed by a student at the Mayo School of Art, Lahore, casket, *c.*1880, steel, blued and inlaid with gold. Acquired by Caspar Purdon Clarke for the South Kensington Museum. V&A: IS. 2411:1-1883.

Guinea.[8] The finest from Abyssinia were recorded in the V&A's inventory of gifts and donations, published in 1901. The inventory is all too brief and simply notes them as: 'The crown of Abyssinia, with robes and personal ornaments of the Queen of that country. (Thirty-three objects). Trophies of the Abyssinian campaign.'[9]

The background to the Maqdala Treasures at the V&A begins with a conflict between empires in Africa.[10] In 1863 Tewodros II, Emperor of Ethiopia (known in Britain at the time as Abyssinia), appealed to Queen Victoria for military support against the Ottoman Turks and Egypt. Frustrated by a lack of satisfactory responses, he imprisoned around 30 people as hostages, including the British Consul, European envoys and missionaries. Britain had no wish to join a Christian crusade against Islam and valued the Ottoman Empire as a counterbalance to the imperial ambitions of Russia. In response to Tewodros's actions, a rescue mission and punitive expedition force was sent under the command of Field Marshal Sir Robert Napier to free the hostages and punish the emperor. The Abyssinian Expedition of 1867–8 of 14,700 soldiers included combat troops from the Indian Army. Among its large entourage came a journalist and artist from the *Illustrated London News* (William Simpson), Henry Morton Stanley from the *New York Herald*, a photographer (Sergeant John Harrold) with seven assistants from the Royal Engineers, and a manuscripts curator from the British Museum (Richard Holmes). The siege of the mountain fortress at Maqdala on 13 April 1868 led to the rescue of hostages released by Emperor Tewodros; he committed suicide rather than face capture. Wild looting ensued before Napier regained control. Troops then assembled items taken from Maqdala and the surrounding area before setting Maqdala ablaze.

Not everything from Maqdala was loot. The earliest items to arrive in England were gifts to the British civil servant who had brought letters from Queen Victoria to Tewodros; they were donated to the museum by the Foreign Office in 1868. Some items were souvenirs purchased by members of the expedition and its followers from local traders and were donated to the museum by their descendants years later. The items confiscated under Napier's direction were auctioned in 1868 for the Army Prize Fund. Other objects had been seized by members of the Royal Naval Brigade that served with the British and Indian troops and were placed on loan to the museum by the Lords of the Admiralty in 1868; these included a crown of gilded silver, a shield and a processional cross. The museum's annual report for 1869 records for that year: 'under the more important donations the Crown of Abyssinia and other objects captured in the Abyssinian campaign of 1868, given by the Right Hon. the Secretary of State for India'.[11] The South Kensington Museum purchased further items from the expedition in 1869 and 1870 and later, between 1905 and 1936, from soldiers' heirs. Today there are 65 objects from Maqdala in the V&A.

Among items from the emperor's treasury were a solid gold sacerdotal crown (a symbolic

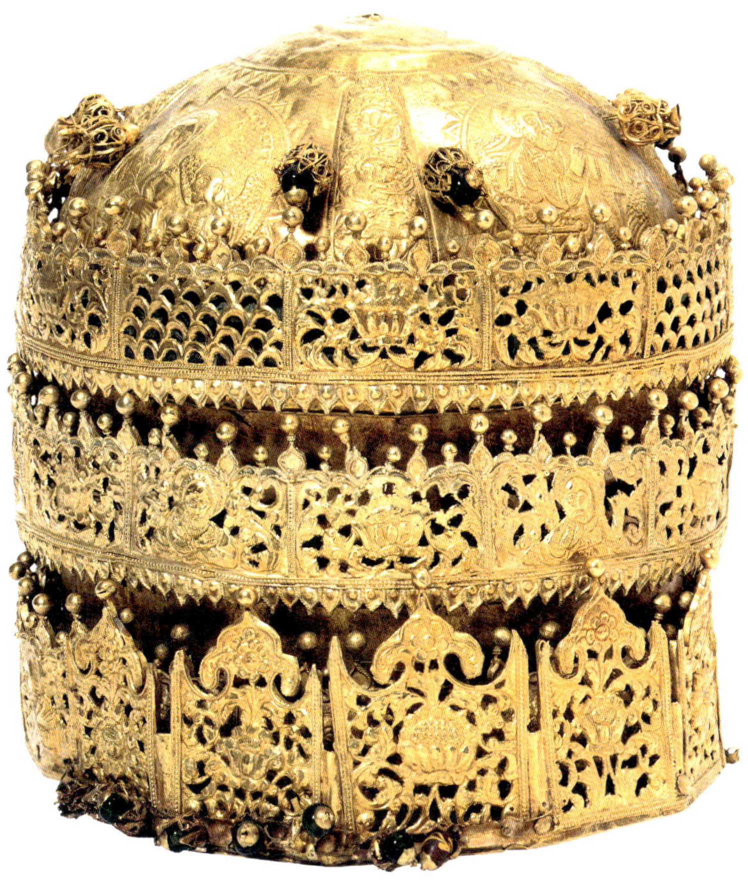

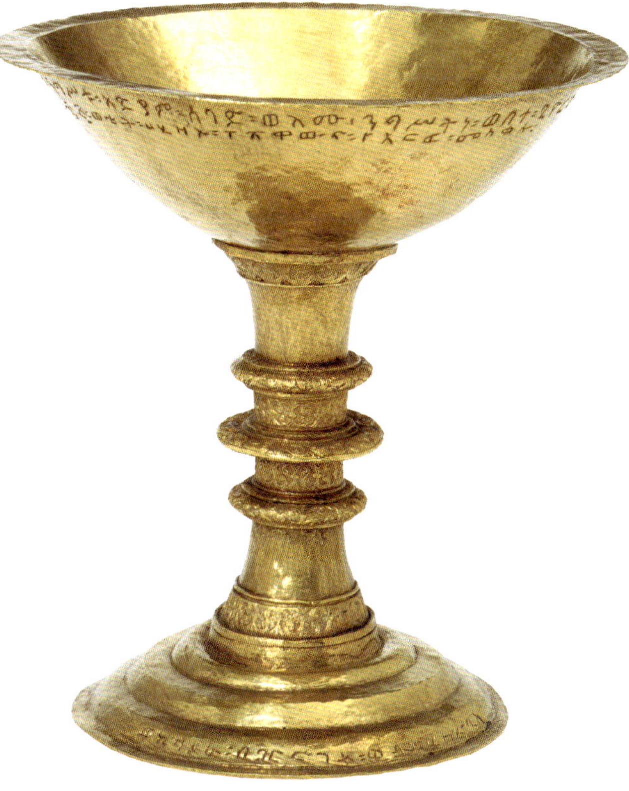

**69.** Unknown maker (Ethiopia, probably Gondar), crown, *c.*1740, gold alloyed with silver and copper with filigree work, glass beads, pigment and gilded copper. V&A: M.27-2005.

**70.** Walda Giyorgis (Ethiopia, Gondar), chalice, 1732–40, gold with hammered, cast and chased decoration, inscribed with dedication in Amharic and name of maker. V&A: M. 26-2005.

crown worn by the head priest in ceremonies and processions; fig.69), a gold chalice (fig.70) and other objects that Tewodros had removed from the Ethiopian Orthodox Church of Our Lady of Qwesqwam, near Gondar, the ancient capital that he ransacked and left in flames in 1866. They had been presented to the church by King Iyyasu II (ruled 1730–55) and his mother Empress Mentewwab. Richard Holmes from the British Museum had secured the crown and chalice from looting troops soon after entering the fortress. Rather than see them sold off for the Army Prize Fund, Holmes hoped they would be allocated to the British Museum, and was given permission to take them back on the understanding that the museum would pay. However, the museum's lack of funds led to a debate in the House of Commons on 30 June 1871 over whether the Government should purchase the crown and chalice for the nation. The Prime Minister, W.E. Gladstone, told Parliament how he

> *deeply regretted that those articles were ever brought from Abyssinia, and could not conceive why they were so brought. They were never at war with the people or the churches of Abyssinia. They were at war with Theodore [Tewodros], who personally had inflicted on them an outrage and a wrong; and he deeply lamented, for the sake of the country, and for the sake of all concerned, that those articles, to us insignificant, though probably to the Abyssinians sacred and imposing symbols . . . were thought fit to be brought away by a British Army.*

Gladstone agreed with the proposal that the crown and chalice be 'held on deposit till they could be returned'.[12]

The following year the crown and chalice were deposited at the South Kensington Museum by HM Treasury. There they joined an elaborately embroidered cotton dress (fig.71), silver-gilt crown, jewellery, and other possessions of Empress Tiruwork Wube (Queen Terunesh) that had been given to the museum by the Secretary of State for India in 1869.[13] The widowed queen had survived the siege but died a month later. Her son was brought to England where he died from pleurisy in 1879. In July 1924, during a diplomatic visit, the silver-gilt crown was sent from the museum to Buckingham Palace where it was presented by King George V to the Crown Prince and Regent of Ethiopia, for Queen Zawditu.[14] In 1983 responsibility for the sacerdotal crown, chalice, a shield and a processional cross passed from HM Treasury and the Ministry of Defence to the Board of Trustees of the V&A, under the terms of the National Heritage Act, 1983. The Act transferred ownership of the objects on deposit from various branches of government to the museum.[15]

After the Maqdala Treasure, the largest group of historic objects from Africa in the V&A is from the Asante Court Regalia (figs 72, 73). Gold casting had been established by the end of the 15th century in West Africa where the Asante, controllers of extensive gold resources, became masters of jewellery and other fine decorative arts made from the locally mined precious mineral. The palace of the Asantehene (ruler) was decorated with fine textiles, ivory and gold and became legendary among early European visitors for its wealth and the quality of its craftsmanship. Following the decline in the slave trade, gold had become the primary economic interest for European powers off the west coast of Africa. By 1872, Britain controlled all the ports along the coast of modern-day Ghana, except for the former slave-trading port El Mina which had long been claimed by the Asante.

Through the Third Anglo-Asante War (1873–4) the British sought to keep their newly expanded influence and control access to the coast. On 4 February 1874 an expeditionary force of 2,500 British troops led by General Sir Garnet Wolseley, along with over 1,000 Indian and West African

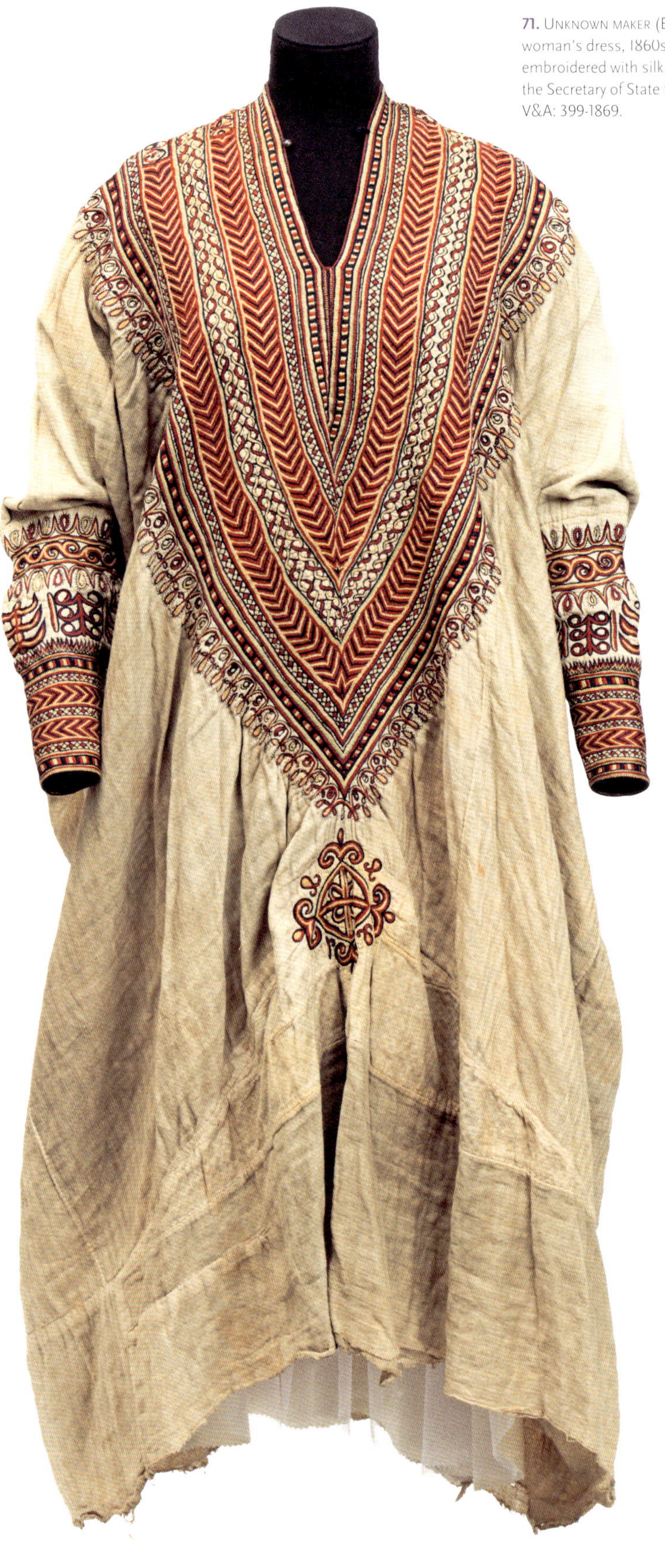

**71.** Unknown maker (Ethiopia), woman's dress, 1860s, cotton embroidered with silk. Given by the Secretary of State for India. V&A: 399-1869.

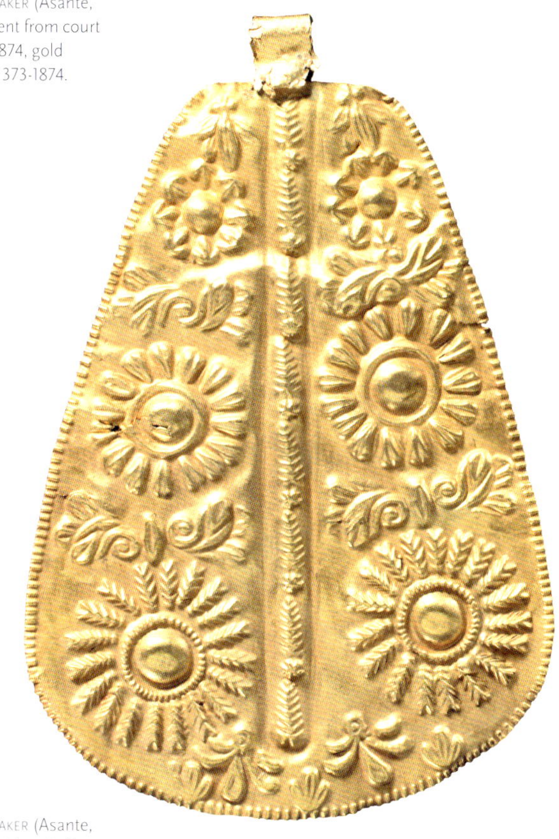

**72.** Unknown maker (Asante, Ghana), ornament from court regalia, before 1874, gold repoussé. V&A: 373-1874.

**73.** Unknown maker (Asante, Ghana), pectoral disc, before 1874, cast gold, in the form of the bud of the fufu plant. V&A: 369-1874.

troops, the latter forcibly conscripted en route, entered the capital, Kumasi. The Asantehene Kofi Karikari fled after being offered terms calculated beyond reach in order to justify, in Britain's eyes, a punitive raid. For reparation funds, Wolseley set the indemnity at 50,000 ounces of gold, banned private looting and directed the removal of royal regalia and other treasures before ordering the burning of the palace. For a punitive raid aimed at regime change, military policy was to remove a defeated ruler's means to govern, by confiscating royal regalia and other historical symbols of office and by destroying official seats of power such as palaces. Once the army had gathered the official spoils, soldiers were given permission to seek souvenirs.

Military procedures led to the auction in London by Garrard & Co., the Crown Jeweller, in April 1874, of much of the gold for the Army Prize Fund. The museum purchased its 13 examples of Asante gold and silverware at the sale; three other items were acquired from individuals a week later and in 1875, 1883 and 1936. The items that had been removed by British forces from Kumasi included silver anklets, gold decoration for swords and state stools, and gold discs (*akrafokonmu*) that had been worn by court officials chosen as *akrafoko* ('soul washers') who ritually purified their ruler's soul to replenish the nation's power.[16] Buyers at Garrard's auction included Sir Richard Wallace, whose collection of Asante gold items can be seen today in the armoury at the Wallace Collection in London.

In the same year as the auction at Garrard & Co. Queen Victoria lent to the South Kensington Museum the 'gold and other objects from Ashanti [*sic*], including the state umbrella of King Koffee Kalkalli', which had been presented to her. They were 'exhibited for some time in the North Court'.[17] Like the expedition, the display was reported in the illustrated press.[18] In July 1874 *The Graphic* illustrated the umbrella still on display in the North Court, sheltering a fashionable young lady, as if safe under the supervision of a cast of Donatello's statue of *St George*, with the heading 'After the Ashantee war' (fig.74). The article described how 'this costly trophy, which is the property of Her

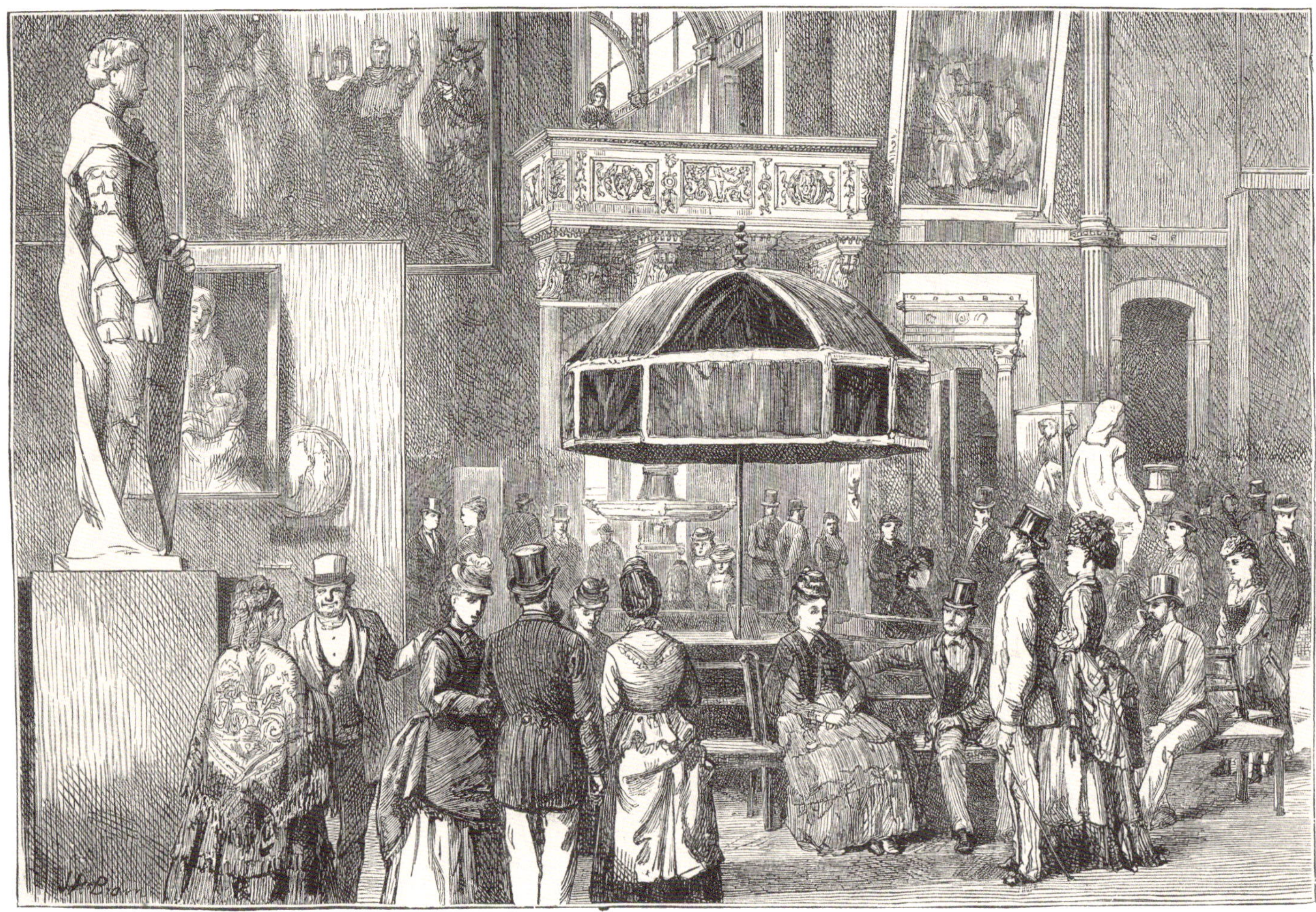

74. Anon., 'London – King Coffee Calcalli's Umbrella at the South Kensington Museum', *The Graphic*, 25 July 1874. V&A: National Art Library.

Majesty the Queen, is now deposited in the South Kensington Museum' and noted 'a great number of these tropical umbrellas are manufactured in Birmingham'.[19]

In a detailed account of the museum published in 1882, the American M.D. Conway admired 'some pieces of work in gold brought back from Abyssinia and from the kingdom of Ashantee [*sic*]'. However, he recognised how the museum's approach to display had changed: beyond admiring examples of art, craft and design from around the world (as fresh sources to inspire British designers and manufacturers) the mood was now one of imperial triumphalism. Conway described how 'these African trophies are unpleasantly suggestive of the worst phase of British policy, or impolicy'.[20] In 1901 Britain established the Gold Coast Colony covering former Asante and neighbouring territories. Twentieth-century acquisitions of Asante material were rare until 14 small goldweights (made of cast copper alloy to weigh gold dust, the common currency of the Asante) from Ghana were bought by the museum in London between 1969 and 1971. Some may date from before Kumasi but many may be later.[21]

The V&A's collection of Chinese art and design includes several items that were identified at the various times of acquisition during the late 19th and early 20th centuries as 'from the emperor of China's summer palace', a provenance that added status to any Chinese work of art but generally lacked any documentary evidence. In the absence of an inventory of the palace, research relies on the quality of each object and on other evidence. The 'summer palace', the Yuanming Yuan, north of Beijing was the second home of the Chinese imperial family whose main residence was the Forbidden City. The country estate comprised over

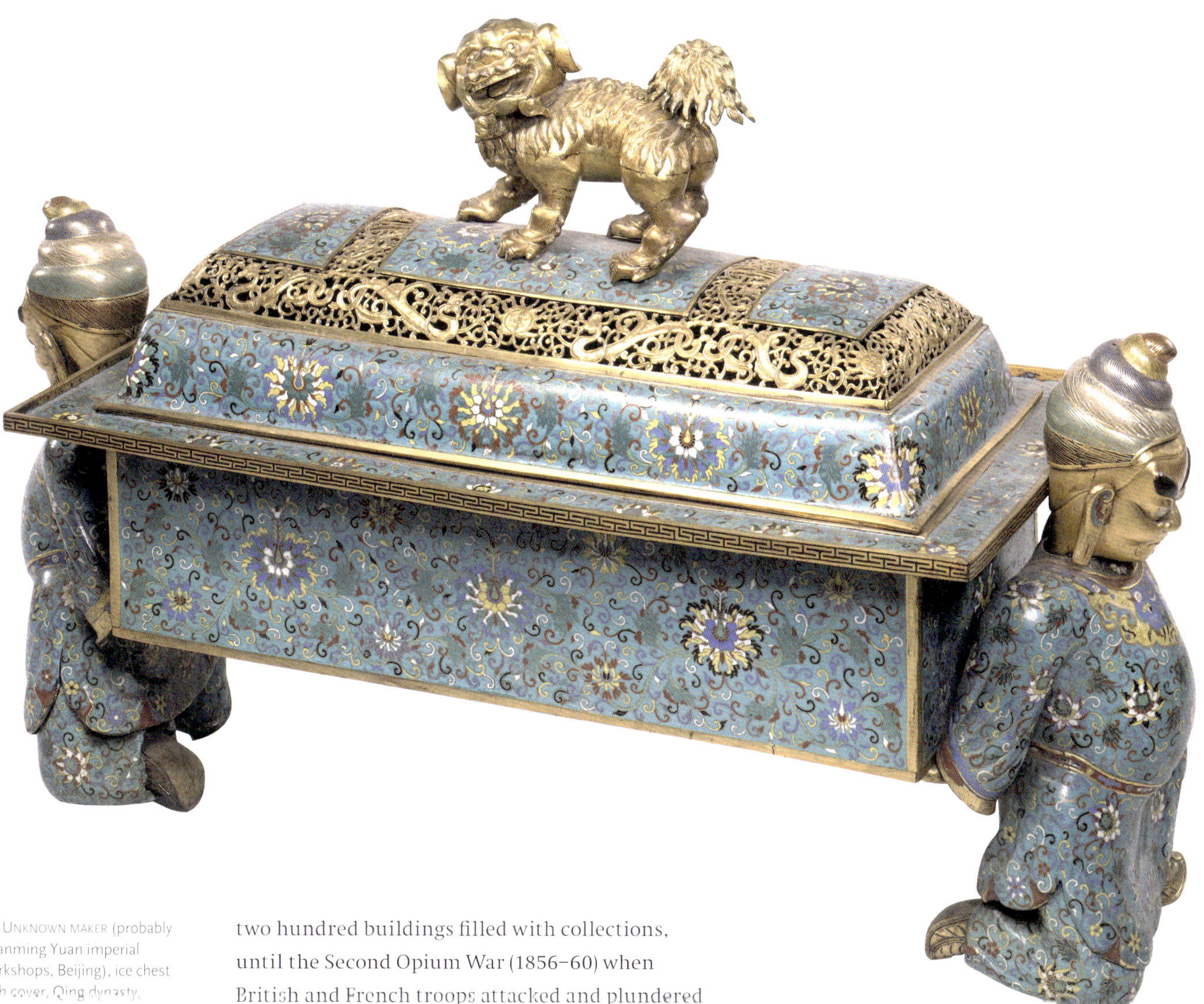

75. Unknown maker (probably Yuanming Yuan imperial workshops, Beijing), ice chest with cover, Qing dynasty, made c.1700–1800, cloisonné enamels on copper with gilding. Purchased in Nuremberg, 1876, as from 'the Summer Palace, Pekin'. V&A: 255-1876.

two hundred buildings filled with collections, until the Second Opium War (1856–60) when British and French troops attacked and plundered it. In retaliation for the taking and torturing of hostages the estate was burnt by troops in October 1860.[22] The two-day auction held outside the ruined summer palace and subsequent division of funds in the field, among French and British troops according to rank, violated army regulations.[23]

A group of ten embroidered cushion covers (fig.77) and textile fragments was acquired by the museum from Viscountess Wolseley after the death of her husband, who had served with the British troops at the Yuanming Yuan in 1860. Further documentary information on their source is unknown but General Garnet Wolseley published his own account of the campaign. He vividly describes the palace's dazzling interiors, complete with 'cushions . . . covered with the finest yellow satin embroidered over with figures of dragons and flowers. Yellow is the Imperial colour, and none but those of royal birth are permitted to wear clothes made of it.'[24] It seems likely that he could not resist acquiring some to bring home. There is little reason to doubt the past ownership of an ice chest (fig.75) from its quality and date of purchase, in Nuremberg in 1876, as from 'the Summer Palace, Pekin'. Another fairly secure provenance is given to an incense burner that belonged to Captain (later General) Charles Gordon who also took part in the destruction of the summer palace in 1860 (fig.78).

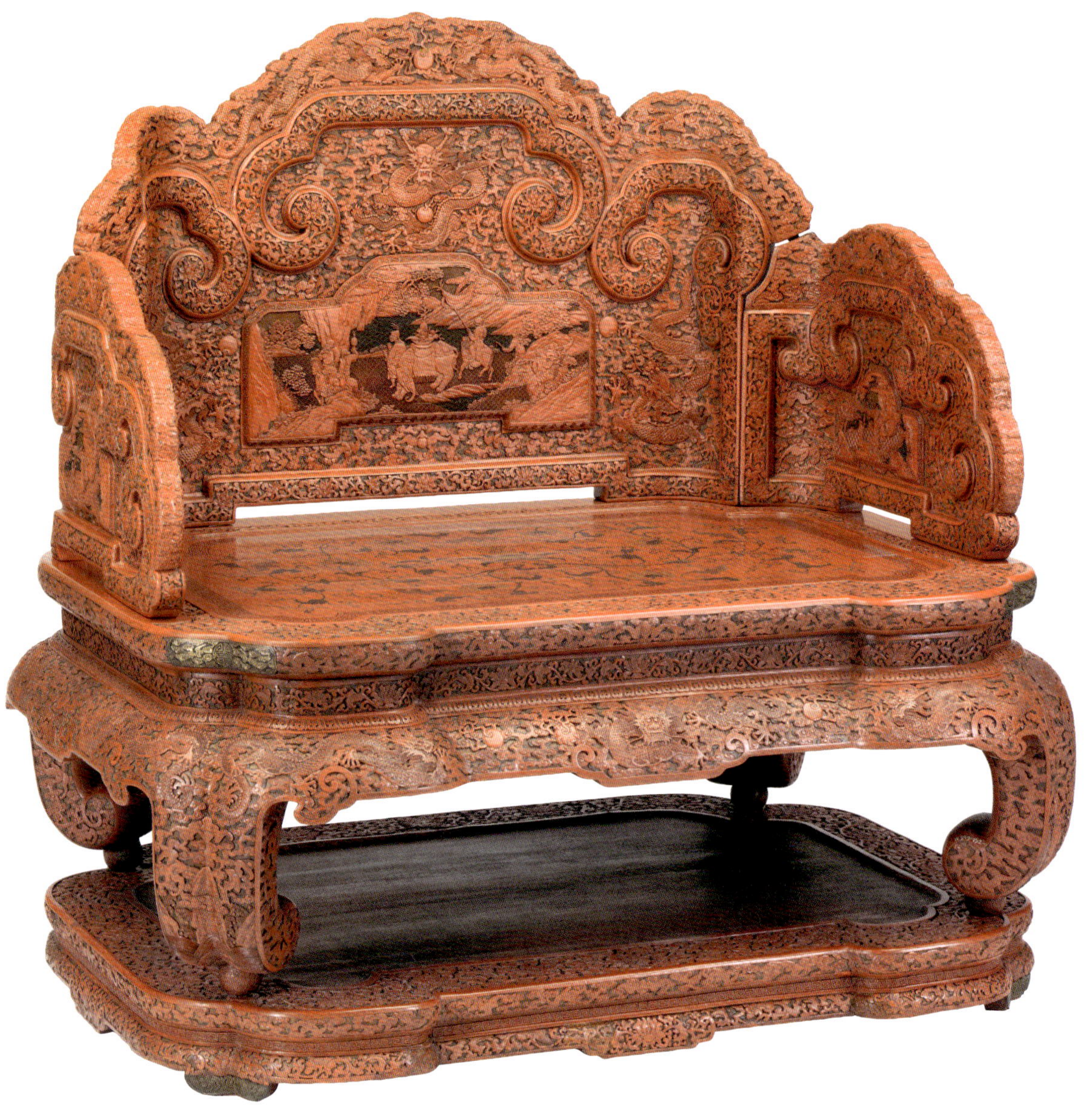

**76.** Unknown maker (probably imperial workshops, Beijing), throne, Qianlong period, made *c.*1775–90, carved lacquer on wooden core. V&A: W.399:1,2-1922.

However, it may not have been seized as loot, for three years later 'Chinese Gordon' helped the Qing government to train the Chinese army to fight rebels, for which he was rewarded with imperial gifts in 1864.

Many of the most 'imperial' objects in the V&A arrived after 1920 and through circuitous routes. A prominent example is the throne (fig.76) probably from Tuanhe Travelling Palace, one of several temporary residences of the Chinese emperors of the Qing dynasty (1644–1911) in their hunting park south of Beijing. It was looted by Russian soldiers in 1900/1901 following the Boxer Rebellion and purchased by the czarist Russian ambassador in China. Following the Russian Revolution (1917) it was brought to London where it was sold by a dealer (Spink & Son) and donated to the V&A in 1922.[25] For objects that entered the museum long before the V&A's current 'due diligence' standards of investigation of prior ownership of all potential acquisitions, provenance is difficult to verify and requires wider research of both European and Chinese-language archives.

As an encyclopaedia of international ornament, the museum also collected electrotype copies whose acquisition may likewise reflect colonial conquest. The first examples of Malay metalwork in the collection were copper-gilt electrotypes of the royal regalia from the Malay state of Perak, copied after the originals were confiscated by the British in 1875 and brought to England for the Colonial and Indian Exhibition held in South Kensington in 1886. They were only returned when a Malay sultan compliant with British commercial interests was on the throne.[26]

The court regalia of King Thibaw (fig.80), who reigned 1878–85 as last monarch of Burma (now Myanmar), was also shown at the Colonial and Indian Exhibition in 1886. It had been seized by British troops in 1885 from the royal palace in Mandalay after King Thibaw's defeat in the Third Anglo-Burmese War. Formally requisitioned as indemnity when Burma lost its sovereignty to the British, the regalia comprised 167 objects. In 1890 it was placed under the custodianship of the museum for safekeeping, and it is recorded in six pages of the museum's inventory, published in 1901. Following a formal request from the Burmese Ambassador in London, it was returned to the Government of Burma in 1964. The same year a gold and jewelled container (fig.80), part of the regalia on display at the V&A, was generously presented by the Government of Burma as a gesture of thanks for the museum's custodianship, which may have saved the regalia from being sold or melted down.[27]

While the V&A has developed collections representing the art and design of India and Asia, the British Museum has traditionally led on Africa, but today the V&A has several thousand objects from the continent of Africa, or associated with the African diaspora, collected across its material-specific departments, including contemporary examples of art and design.[28] The museum also reviews and redisplays the historical collections. In 2018–19, on the 150th anniversary of the siege of Maqdala, the V&A mounted a display following a research project that addressed the various sources of the objects and acknowledged their contested status. This involved dialogue with the Ethiopian

**77.** Unknown maker (probably Yuanming Yuan imperial workshops, Beijing), cushion cover for a shaped chair back, *c*.1760–1820, pattern woven satin and silk. Given by the Dowager Viscountess Wolseley. V&A: T.135-1917.

**78.** Unknown maker (probably Yuanming Yuan imperial workshops, Beijing) incense burner, Qianlong period, made *c*.1736–95, cloisonné enamel on copper with gilding. From the collection of General Charles Gordon. V&A: 13-1894.

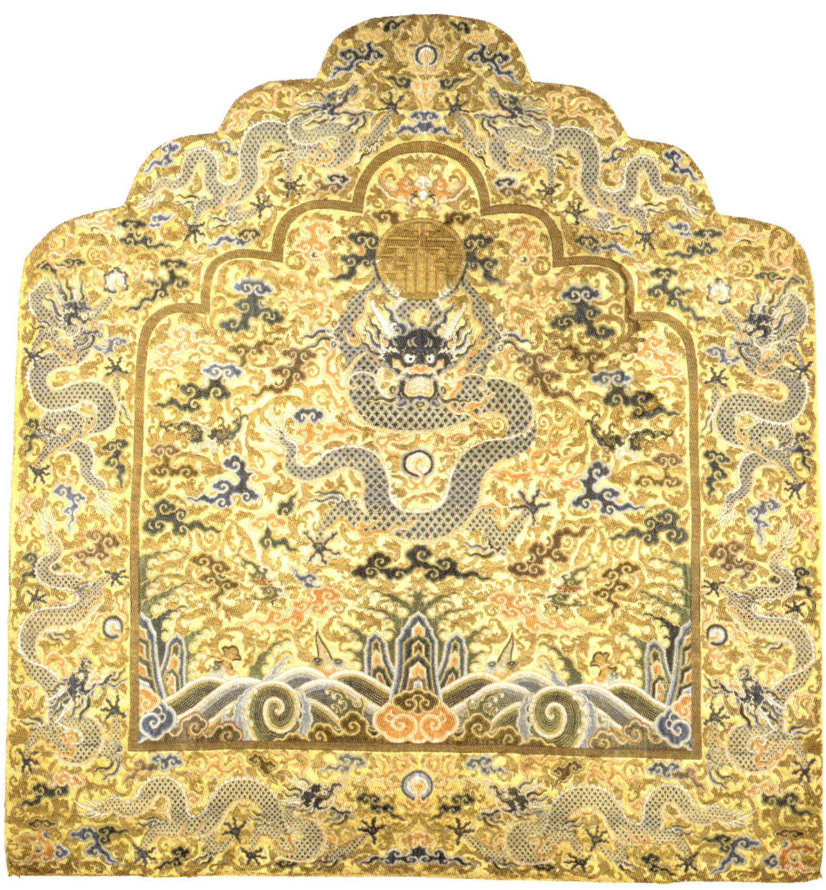

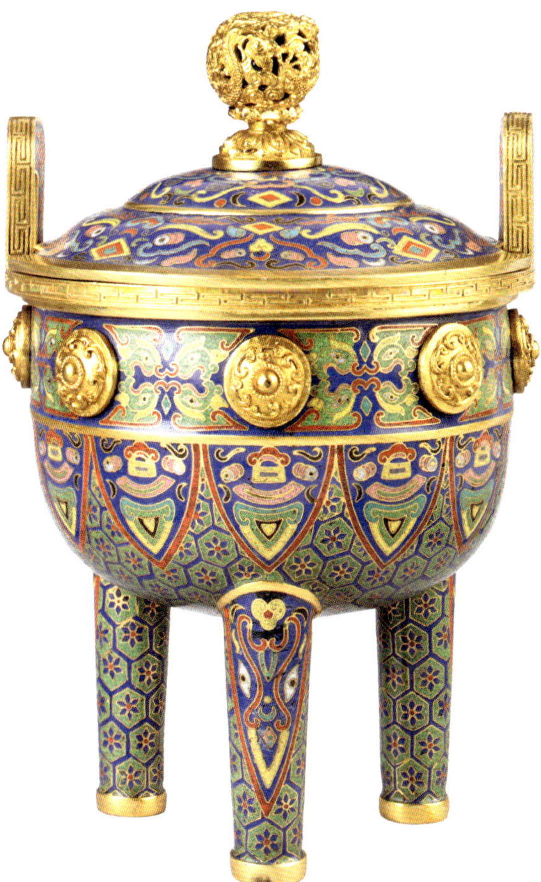

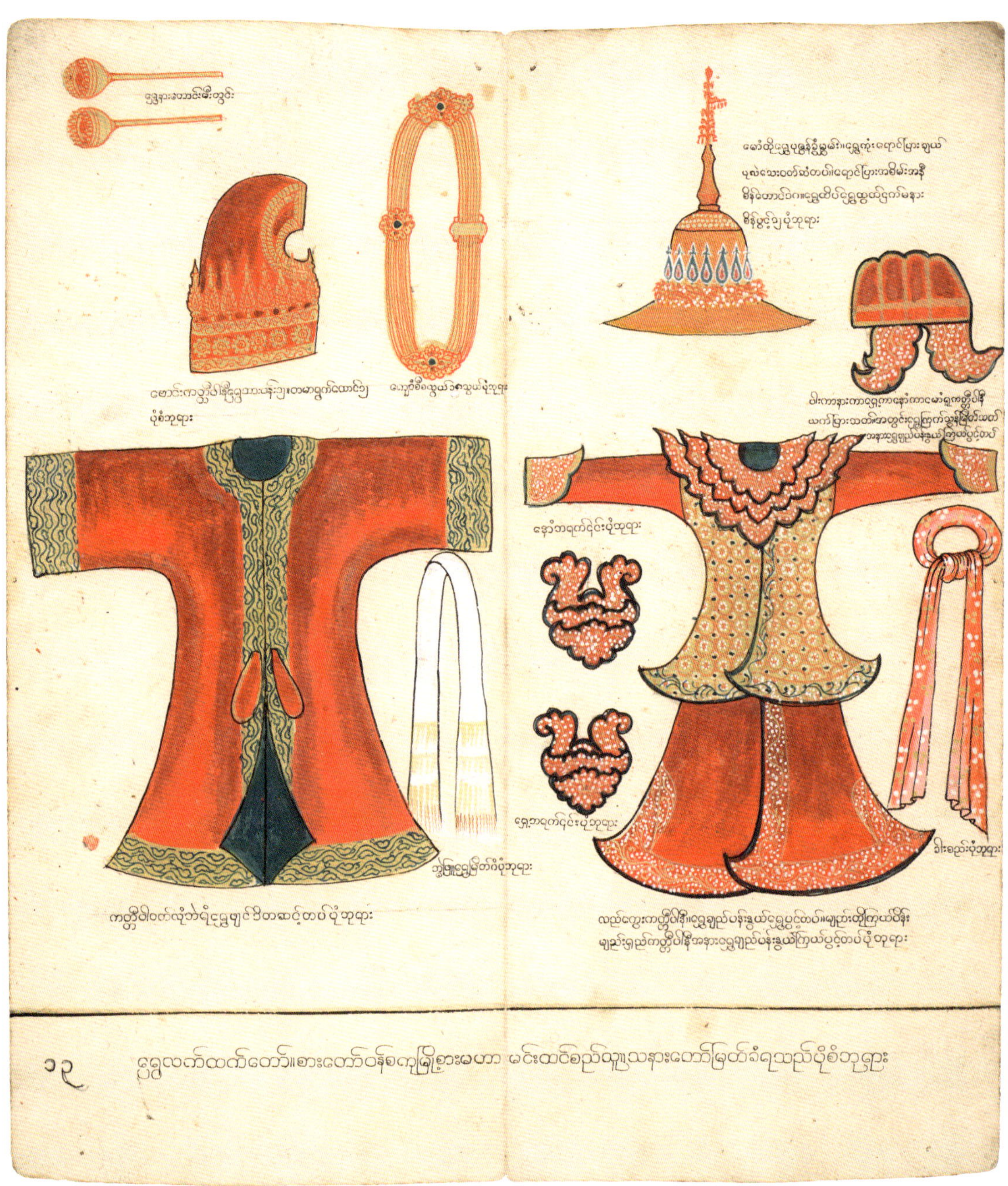

**79.** Unknown maker (Mandalay), manuscript illustrating attire for a court celebration, 1880, watercolour. From the Royal Library of King Thibaw. V&A: I.M.320-1924.

Embassy in London, with leaders of the Ethiopian and Rastafari community in London and members of the Anglo-Ethiopian Society, about the objects' display and interpretation, and about further research into ownership and future locations, such as long-term loans to an institution in Ethiopia.[29] Today, through new research, displays, publications and discussion, especially online, the V&A confronts the uncomfortable histories of collections formed through force and influence. Indeed, the V&A is a field-leader in Britain in publicly addressing issues around colonial looting, repatriation, and international law in liaison with museum authorities in Ghana, Ethiopia and many other nations. While recognising such responsibilities, the V&A continues finding new ways to celebrate and promote public appreciation of the art and design of Asia, Africa and the diaspora.

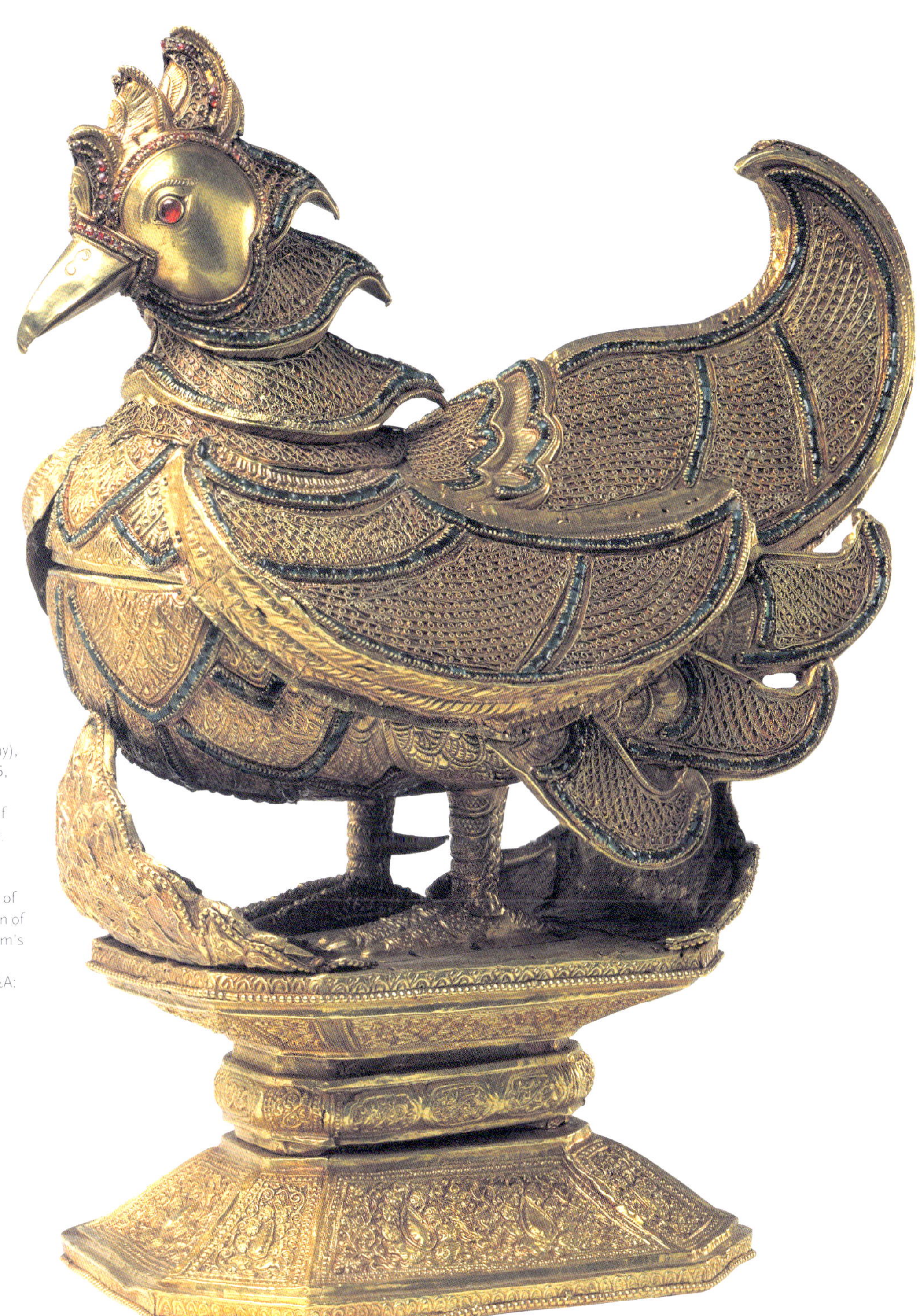

**80.** UNKNOWN MAKER (Mandalay), betel box and stand, *c.*1850–75, filigree work in gold on a gold ground, outlined with bands of rubies and imitation emeralds, with some embossing; eyes of rubies (one now missing). Presented by the Government of Burma in generous recognition of the Victoria and Albert Museum's safekeeping of the Mandalay Regalia, from 1886 to 1964. V&A: IS.246&A-1964.

# Part IV: Collecting for New Museums

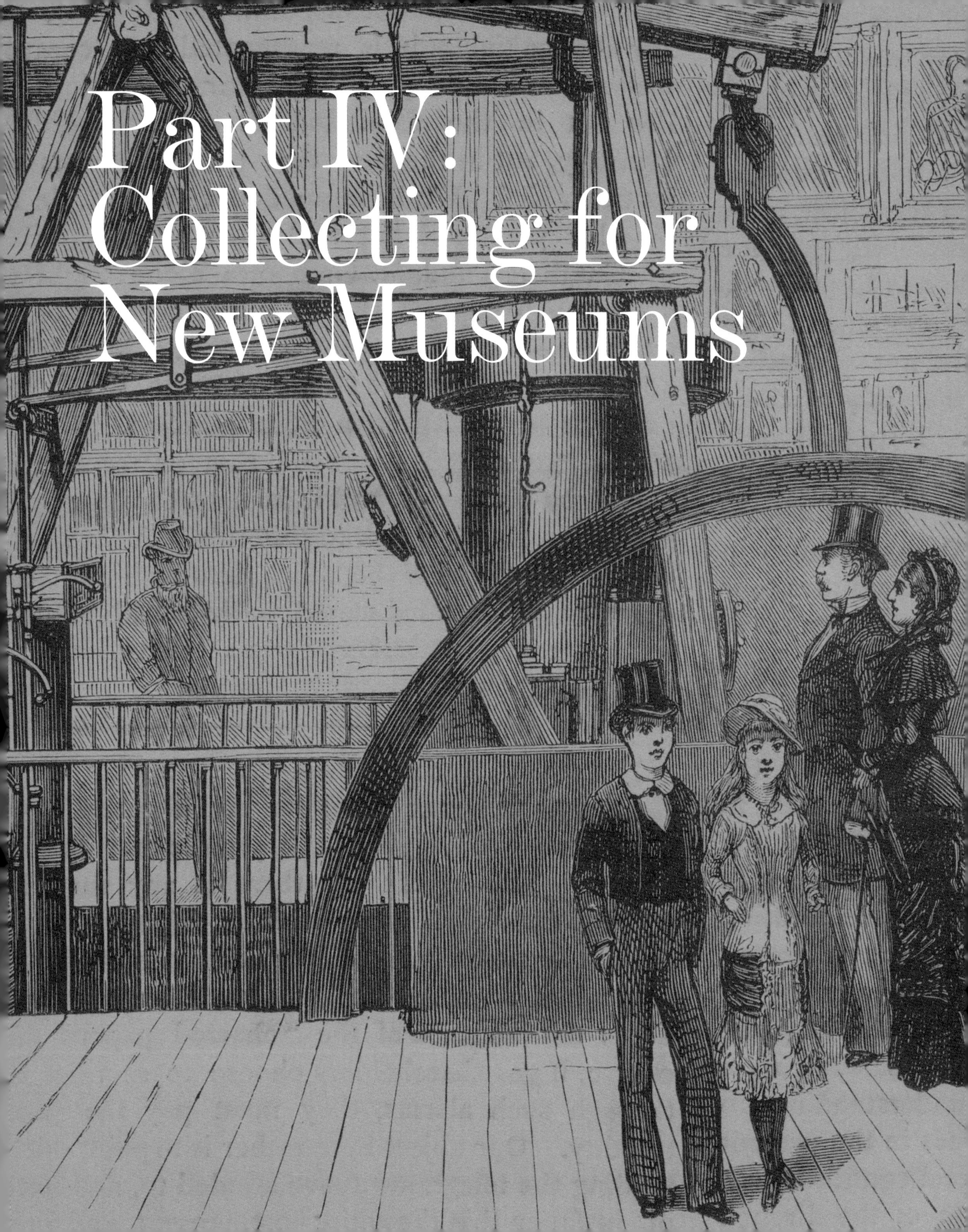

TODAY'S **V&A** IS EXPANDING far beyond South Kensington as a multi-site family of museum venues and online destinations, with new V&As recently opened in Dundee, Shenzhen, Barlaston (the V&A Wedgwood Collection) and V&A East at Stratford, London. This expansion follows ambitions set in its formative years. The South Kensington Museum was a consortium of museums from which others grew, most notably in London the Science Museum. The government's Department of Science and Art, based alongside the South Kensington Museum, managed it as part of a network of institutions. In London, beyond South Kensington, the Department also ran the Museum of Practical Geology in Jermyn Street (founded in 1835 as the Museum of Economic Geology) and the Bethnal Green Branch Museum (founded 1872, now the Young V&A). In Dublin the Department was responsible for the Museum of Irish Industry (founded 1845, now the National Museum of Ireland) and in Edinburgh for the Industrial Museum of Scotland (founded 1854, renamed the Edinburgh Museum of Science and Art in 1864, the Royal Scottish Museum in 1904 and now part of National Museums Scotland). The South Kensington Museum supported regional art schools through circulating its collections and lending from its library. The Department offered grants to encourage purchases of objects by regional museums, as the V&A does still today. This section explains the growth of two institutions from within the original museum, as case studies to illustrate how the arrival of diverse collections, through loans, gifts and bequests, spurred public debate over their purpose and potential.

# 12 Collecting Machines: The Science Museum

In 1883 John Ruskin described 'the miscellaneous collection at Kensington, where Gothic saints and sinners are confounded alike among steam thrashing-machines and dynamite-proof ships of war'.[1] In explaining the rise of the V&A it is easy to overlook the origins of the Science Museum within the Society of Arts, the Great Exhibition of 1851 and in the formation of a museum of art and design. The history of the V&A is often told backwards, taking the present as the starting point as if it all was meant to lead to where we are now. This conventional narrative is driven by a sense of evolution that sheds irrelevant collections before the V&A emerges from its museological chrysalis in all its present-day glory. In reality it was all rather more opportunistic and messier. Prince Albert's vision for the legacy of the Great Exhibition was so broad and ambitious that the origins of the museum are open to multiple interpretations. The Royal Commission for the Great Exhibition of 1851, which Albert chaired, wanted its considerable profits spent on founding an institution that would 'serve to increase the means of Industrial Education and extend the influence of Science and Art upon Productive Industry'.[2] Prince Albert's German adviser, Gottfried Semper, encouraged him to commit to the reunion of science and art, and wrote in 1852 'National education will be perfect, when science shall be pervaded by art and art by science and all human relations by both.'[3] However, Prince Albert was not around to steer the legacy institution through the decisive early years. Had he not died in December 1861, the V&A and South Kensington might be rather different today.[4]

A recurrent clue and reminder from the past of the core significance of science to the museum project can be found in the decoration of the early surviving buildings. The motif that recurs, from above the Victorian main entrance (now facing the garden) to the ceramic reliefs lining the main staircase are not V and A but S and A (VR is used in designs for decoration from 1861 and VA from around 1862). These letters would have reminded Victorians that the museum came under the Department of Science and Art; they can also be read as a symbol for Prince Albert's hopes for the reunion of Science and Art. The Great Exhibition had revealed the extent to which Britain's Industrial Revolution had accelerated production and consumption ahead of any improvements in the art and design of manufactured goods. Prince Albert's vision, inspired by his German education,[5] was to create not just the V&A but a new cultural centre where applied art and applied science could both thrive and stimulate vocational training and recreational education, nationwide. The museum's endeavours to pursue this intellectual project in the 19th century were evident (if not clear) to visitors when they found the collections of both art and science in the South Kensington Museum.

The pediment of the V&A's Victorian entrance building (completed 1868) includes, on the right side, symbols for the fine and applied arts, but from the opposite corner, beside the black silhouette of the Crystal Palace, emerge a railway locomotive, a printing press and a telegraph pole. Below, on the main entrance doors, pairs of portrait relief sculptures welcome visitors with representatives of

Chemistry, Astronomy and Mechanics (Humphry Davy, Isaac Newton, James Watt) opposite Architecture, Sculpture and Painting (Bramante, Michelangelo, Titian). This ideal balance was set when the government's Department of Art and Science was established in 1854 to oversee education and museums across Britain and Ireland.[6]

Once inside the museum, the importance of science was evident to Victorian visitors ascending the main staircase, with its figures symbolic not only of Art, Music and Literature but also of Spectrum Analysis, Geometry, Chemistry and Astronomy. Two stained-glass windows represented Science and Art, the former with portraits of Newton, Leibniz, Copernicus, Galileo, Euclid, Archimedes, Joseph Priestley, William Hyde Wollaston and James Watt.[7] From this staircase visitors could also see (according to a journalist's account first published in 1875) the rear wall of the Science Schools (today the Henry Cole Wing) decorated with 'allegorical figures – Natura, Scientia, etc. – and portraits of scientific men'.[8]

Henry Cole is usually described simply as the first director of the V&A. He was the first Secretary for Art, and Lyon Playfair the first Secretary for Science, at the Department of Science and Art. Each took on a lead school and museum in London: Cole managed the Museum of Ornamental Art and the School of Design (both at Marlborough House) and Playfair the Museum of Practical Geology and the Government School of Mines (forerunner of Imperial College, London). In 1856–7 the Department and its main museum moved to South Kensington and when Playfair resigned in 1858 (to become Professor of Chemistry at Edinburgh University) Cole took on Science as well. Under Cole, the balance swung firmly in favour of art and design at the South Kensington Museum, but he made provision for science. In 1859 Cole appointed Captain John Donnelly as Inspector for Science, to assist him. After Cole retired in 1873 and was succeeded by Cunliffe Owen as museum director, Donnelly was appointed Director for Science in 1874. Like Playfair before him, he was responsible for science schools and classes nationwide and for scientific institutions: the Government School of Mines, the Museum of Practical Geology, the Royal College of Chemistry, the Edinburgh Museum of Science and Art, and the Museum of Irish Industry. Donnelly reunited the two departments when he was appointed Director for Science and Art in 1884, before he retired in 1887.

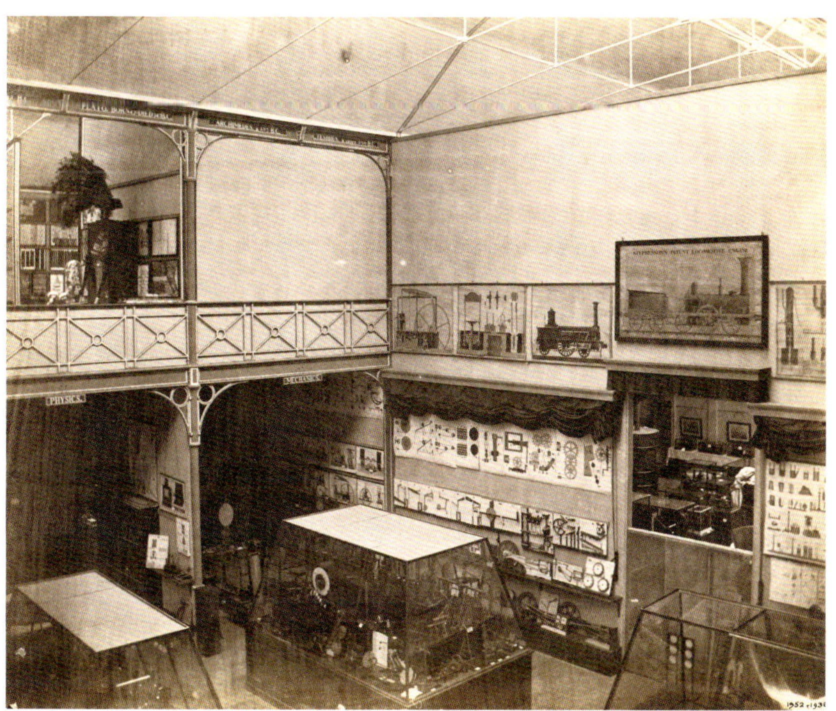

**81.** Isabel Agnes Cowper, South Kensington Museum, Education Collection, Showing Material for Instruction in Science, 1869, albumen print. V&A: 67.060.

In the history of the V&A Henry Cole usually eclipses Playfair, Donnelly and, indeed, Science. Fortunately there was also a collecting curator in the driving seat. In December 1852 Prince Albert invited the engineer Bennet Woodcroft (1803–1879) to create a museum of machines.[9] Woodcroft had been Professor of Descriptive Machinery at University College, London (1847–51) and since 1845 had been a busy contributor to the administration and exhibitions of the Society of Arts. Prince Albert was president when the society originated the Great Exhibition and Woodcroft supported the Prince Consort and Cole in its delivery. Other starting points for the Science Museum were the society's own collection of models of inventions, formed since 1761, some machines from the Great Exhibition of 1851 and the collection of the Patent Office. Woodcroft worked there from 1852 as Superintendent of Specifications and founded what became the Patent Museum of historical machinery. Encouraged by Prince Albert, Woodcroft toured the country to select further exhibits from manufacturers.

When the South Kensington Museum opened in 1857 visitors already familiar with Cole's previous museum – a suite of rooms in Marlborough House, palatially furnished with treasures of art and design – may have been surprised, especially if they began at the Patent Museum. This collection of models of patented inventions, both contemporary and historical, filled the southernmost part of the new building, facing the Cromwell Road – the main route from central London.[10] The industrial machinery included the world's first water-powered textile machine, Richard Arkwright's spinning frame (1767), early steam engines by James Watt, and the engine of Henry Bell's steamship *Comet* (1812). 1862 saw the arrival of steam locomotives: the world's oldest survivor, *Puffing Billy* (1813, built to haul coal trucks at a colliery) and Stephenson's *Rocket* (1829). Here one could also study examples of Woodcroft's specialist field as a designer: screw propellers for steamships. A disappointed visitor described the 'Mechanics Gallery' as 'a charnel-house of a generation of steam engines, whose ghastly skeletons are here exposed to view to remind us of the vanity of mechanical life'.[11] Scientific instruments could also be found in the centre of the building, which was devoted to the Educational Collection of teaching equipment for use in schools, encircled by the Museum of Construction. Stairs led up to the Food Museum and Animal Products Collection in the gallery overhead. Science came before art, for the Art Museum lay beyond, at the north end, leading up into the gallery of modern British paintings donated by John Sheepshanks.

Opportunities to grow became available across Exhibition Road (the main north–south axis of the cultural quarter) after London's second international exhibition was held there in 1862. Its main building was demolished in 1864,[12] but the refreshment rooms remained on its north side, overlooking the gardens of the Royal Horticultural Society, and these became the new Southern Galleries of the museum. In 1863 the Museum of Construction moved across into the western arcades of the gardens. When the Admiralty launched its School of Naval Architecture in South Kensington in 1864 it sent over on loan to the museum its collection of ship models, to which a gallery was devoted. More ship models followed on loan, particularly from Lloyd's Register of British and Foreign Shipping, as the collection expanded to cover marine engineering.[13] Also in 1864 arrived the Buckland Fish Collection, formed by an Inspector of Salmon Fisheries, Frank Buckland (who kindly bequeathed his collection to the museum in 1880). By 1865 the Animal Products Collection was installed in the Southern Galleries.

In May 1876 Queen Victoria opened a 'Special Loan Collection of Scientific Apparatus'. The catalogue of this international loan exhibition, in its third edition, runs to 1,086 pages and has 4,570 entries, many of which describe multiple loans.[14] It was held in the Southern Galleries and in the Western Galleries (north of the Royal Horticultural Society gardens), which had been developed to continue London's international exhibitions (1851; 1862) on a more thematic basis and manageable scale. Scientists campaigned for the retention of the loans and, when the exhibition closed, the Department of Science and Art wrote to lenders

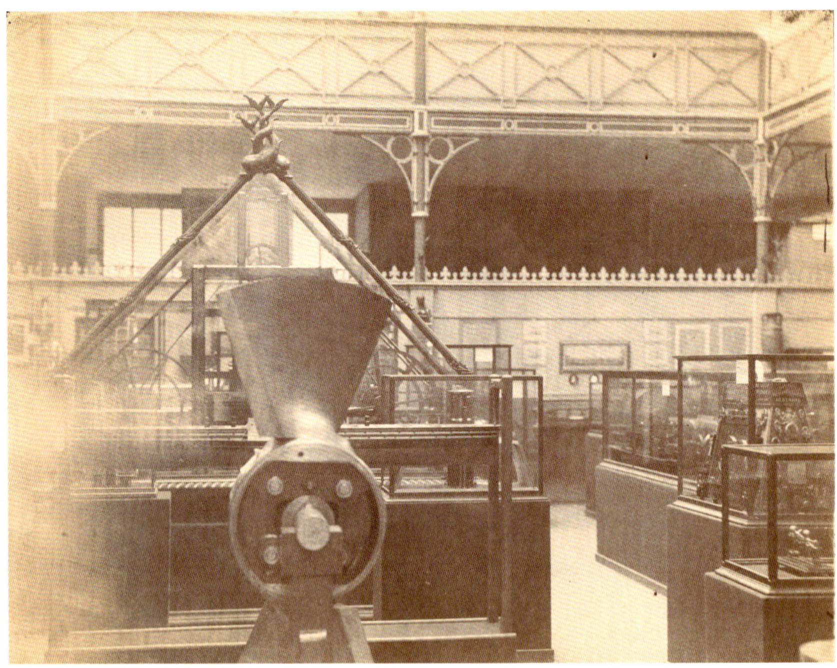

**82.** Charles Thurston Thompson, Interior View of the Patent Museum, South Kensington, *c.*1857–64, albumen print. V&A: 33965.

**83.** After R. Brown, 'Notes at the Patent Museum, South Kensington', *The Graphic*, vol.21, no.27, 3 January 1880, showing Franklin's printing press, the engine of Bell's paddle steamer *Comet*, a pumping engine from Cumberland, Arkwright's spinning machine and Stephenson's *Rocket*. V&A: National Art Library.

# THE GRAPHIC

*AN ILLUSTRATED WEEKLY NEWSPAPER*

No. 527.—Vol. XXI. Reg<sup></sup>

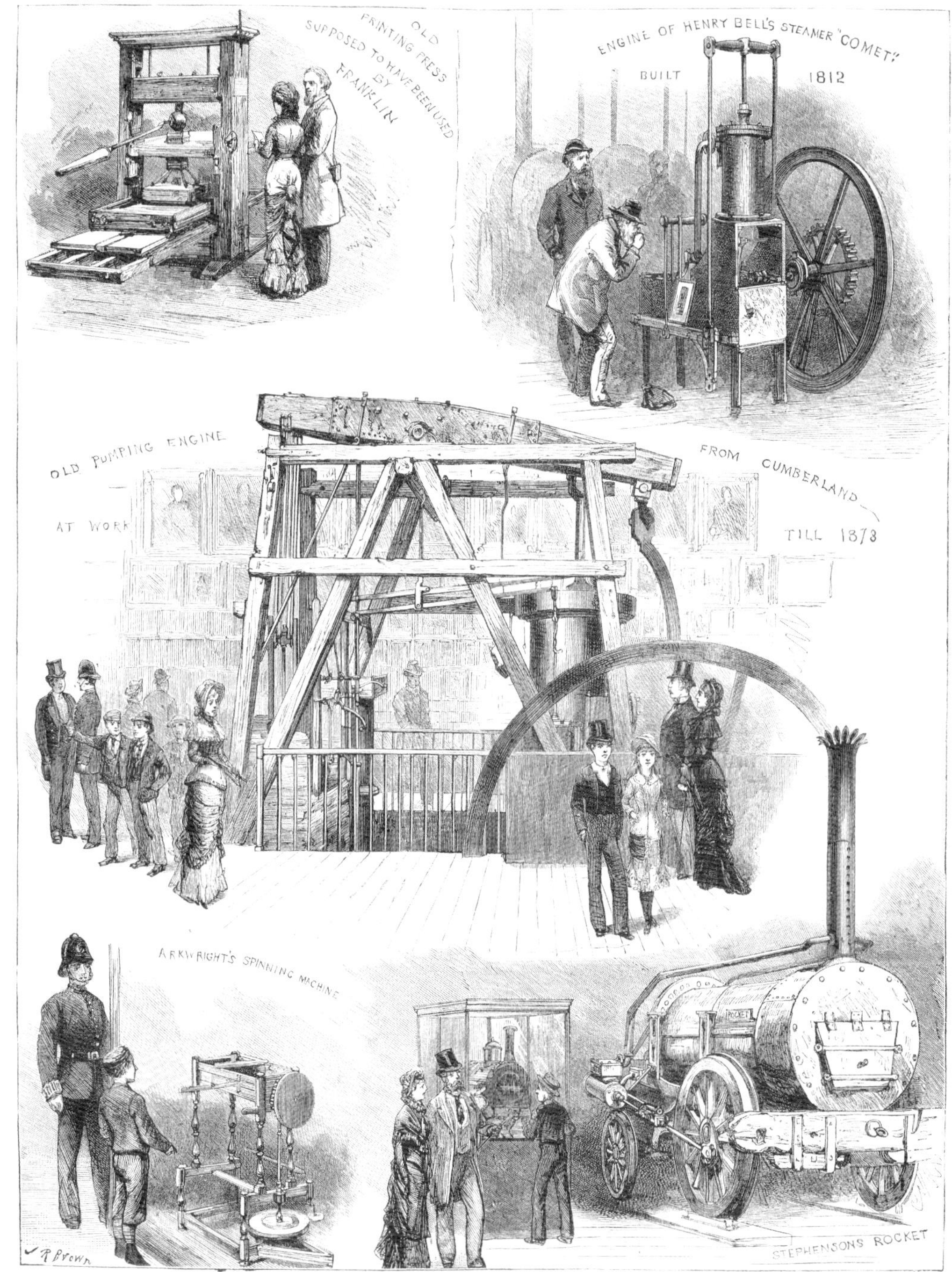


NOTES AT THE PATENT MUSEUM, SOUTH KENSINGTON

asking them not to recall their objects 'pending the establishment of a permanent Science Museum'.[15] Some of the loans were purchased for the South Kensington Museum in anticipation. In 1886, following a thinning out of Woodcroft's collection in favour of telling the evolution of technology, the former Patent Museum joined the steady exodus of science west across Exhibition Road. In 1893 Major-General Festing was appointed the first director of the Science Museum but it remained within the South Kensington Museum administration. Between 1893 and 1895 the Museum of Practical Geology in Jermyn Street transferred its mining and metallurgy models to the South Kensington Museum; its ceramics and glass collections followed in 1901.[16] 1903 saw the arrival of the Woodcroft Bequest of engine models and portraits. Questions were asked: where to put it all?

In 1890 the journal *Nature* had reported a debate in the House of Commons where one member 'affirmed that there were empty rooms in South Kensington Museum which might well be used for the display of exhibits' relating to science.[17] When Aston Webb won the architectural competition in 1891 to build the suite of galleries along Cromwell Road, any decision about the future location of the science collections was postponed, on the assumption that space for science might yet be found in this new building, which doubled the space available for the display of collections.[18] Webb had had no clear brief for the collections that would go on show there. Expectations of having to accommodate historic steam engines may help to explain the scale of Webb's cavernous Edwardian halls. That same year saw a rival bid for the available space on the west side of Exhibition Road, but not for a science museum. The sugar magnate and collector Henry Tate offered £80,000 to build a new gallery there, for the South Kensington Museum had already developed the National Gallery of British Art. Instead, Tate found a more independent location, as a branch of the National Gallery, and in 1897 the Tate Gallery opened on Millbank. In 1898 a House of Commons Select Committee for the Museums of the Science and Art Department recommended that the Science Museum should develop on the west side of Exhibition Road.[19] Nevertheless, in 1899, when Queen Victoria laid the foundation stone of the new building designed by Webb and renamed the South Kensington Museum as the V&A, it was assumed she meant the entire museum, including the science collections. A double-page map in the visitor guide, published in 1908, covers both sides of Exhibition Road under the heading 'Plan of the Victoria and Albert Museum'. It identifies galleries for geology and mineralogy, meteorology, surveying and astronomy, machinery, biology, metallurgy and chemistry, physics and mathematics, and ship models. In the text, thirteen pages are devoted to the Science Museum, sandwiched between descriptions of the Jones Collection and the Indian Section.[20]

Prince Albert's vision was of a united campus of learned institutions that would come together for education, exhibitions and conferences. When Queen Victoria laid the foundation stone in 1867 of 'The Central Hall of Arts and Sciences' she named it 'The Royal Albert Hall of Arts and Sciences'; today it is best known as a concert venue. In the 20th century ambivalence risked turning into polarisation. After the present Science Museum opened in 1928 the legend grew that when families arrived from the underground station and headed north up Exhibition Road, fathers and sons turned left (west) for science and other museums while mothers and daughters turned right for art, at the V&A. The unresolved reunion of art and science in South Kensington continued as buildings changed hands. The Huxley Building, formerly the Science Schools (where H.G. Wells had trained under Professor T.H. Huxley), transferred from Imperial College to the V&A; it opened to the public as the V&A's Henry Cole Wing in 1983. The Royal College of Art vacated the V&A's rear buildings in 1991 but science moved back in when the former artists' studios became the museum's conservation department. Today, for the 21st century, the Exhibition Road Cultural Group promotes a more united vision, after an indirect evolution driven not so much by policies and politicians as by collections and collectors.[21]

# 13 Collections for East London: The first 'Branch Museum'

BY 1864 THE SPREAD of new buildings across the South Kensington site gave the museum the opportunity to remove most of the temporary iron structure it had occupied since 1857.[1] These standard utility sheds had been designed to be dismantled and recycled, so now the time had come for them to be divided into three and offered to the London boroughs to the north, south and east, to form branch museums run from South Kensington. However, the only response came from the East End of London, where plans had already been developing for a museum and education institute to support a rich local tradition of crafts, especially furniture making. On 24 June 1872 the 'Bethnal Green Branch of the South Kensington Museum' celebrated its launch with a royal opening by the Prince and Princess of Wales on behalf of Queen Victoria. One reason for the lack of enthusiastic response from the other outer London boroughs may have been a lack of clarity about what a new museum could expect to receive on loan from South Kensington.

As well as most of the recycled building, collections came to Bethnal Green from South Kensington. In the forecourt stood Minton's colossal *St George Fountain*, the eye-catching majolica landmark from the International Exhibition of 1862.[2] The core collection was two museums that had been housed on a temporary basis in South Kensington since 1857. The Animal Products Collection showed how feathers, hide, hair, bone, sharkskin and other natural waste could be put to good use, while the Food Museum explained how the body functions and how it can be kept healthy with modest means.[3] To these educational displays were added a succession of art collections on loan.

An early description is given by Charles Dickens Jr in *Dickens's Dictionary of London* (1879):

> *It was opened on the 24th June, 1872, by their Royal Highnesses the Prince and Princess of Wales, and was for nearly three years mainly occupied by the magnificent collections of paintings and other works of art belonging to Sir Richard Wallace, Bart., M.P.. On the withdrawal of these collections they were replaced by various contributions on loan, chief among which have been the Indian presents of H.R.H. the Prince of Wales and the paintings forming the Dulwich Gallery.*[4]

The scale and impact of the Wallace Collection at Bethnal Green over three years cannot be overestimated, for Richard Wallace lent hundreds of items including oil paintings, sculpture, furniture, maiolica, porcelain, portrait miniatures, jewellery and snuff boxes, from medieval and Renaissance treasures to French 18th-century furniture and porcelain, from Old Masters to modern art.[5] The published catalogue runs to 125 pages with 2,030 numbered objects. There was a degree of risk and experiment about launching the new museum in this way, in a very different neighbourhood to South Kensington. Nevertheless, five million visitors came before the loan ended in 1875, when Wallace moved into Hertford House, Manchester Square, where the Wallace Collection opened in 1900. When the writer Henry James visited Bethnal Green to see the

# THE GRAPHIC

*AN ILLUSTRATED WEEKLY NEWSPAPER*

No. 952.—Vol. XXXVII. *Registered as a Newspaper* | SATURDAY, FEBRUARY 25, 1888 | WITH EXTRA SUPPLEMENT | Price Sixpence *By Post Sixpence Halfpenny*

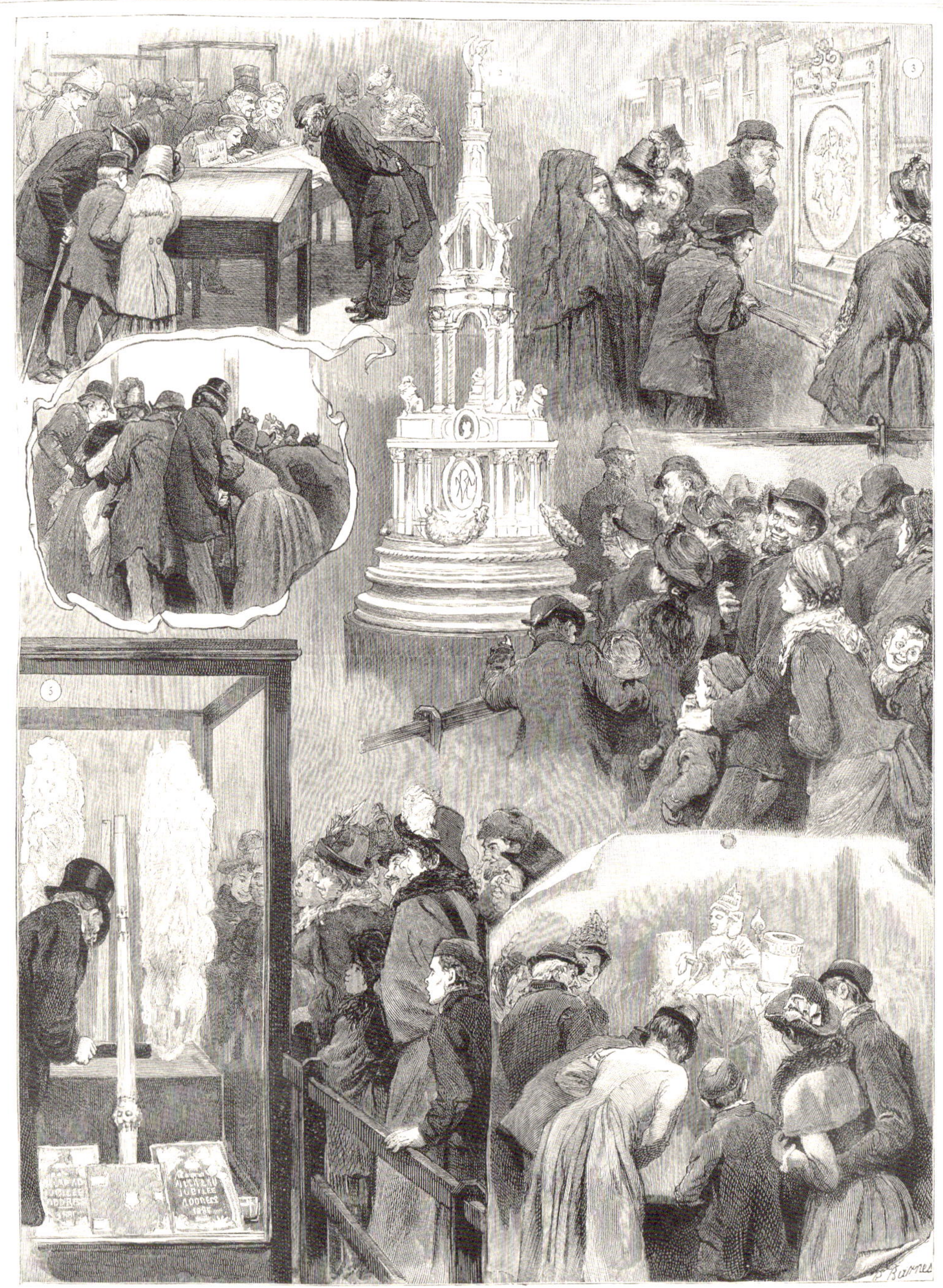

1. Inspecting Jubilee Presents
2. The Jubilee Cake
3. A Mosaic Picture from the Vatican, the Gift of His Holiness the Pope
4. An Object of Interest
5. Two Ostrich Feather Screens, the Gift of the Ostrich Farmers and Women of the Cape
6. Luckshine, the Goddess of Prosperity, the Gift of His Highness the Maharajah of Travancore, K.C.S.I.

EXHIBITION OF HER MAJESTY'S JUBILEE PRESENTS AT THE BETHNAL GREEN MUSEUM

**84.** Anon., 'Exhibition of Her Majesty's Jubilee presents at the Bethnal Green Museum', *The Graphic*, vol.37, no.952, 25 February 1888. V&A: National Art Library.

85. Unknown maker (Japan, Nagoya), vase, 1860–80, cloisonné enamels on copper with gilded copper rim. Bequeathed by Joshua Dixon to the Bethnal Green Museum. V&A: 1273-1886.

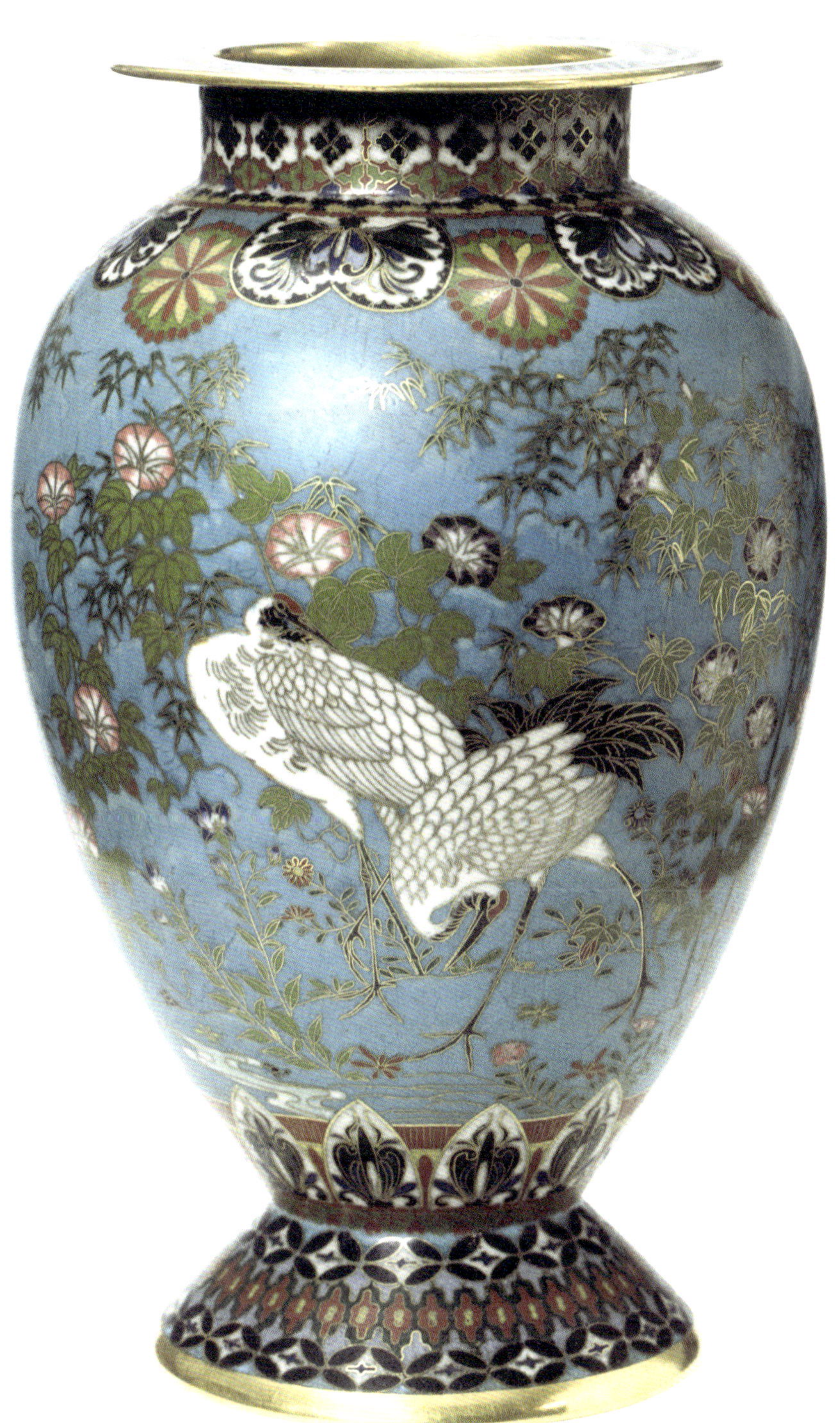

Wallace Collection he recorded 'a graceful legend that the masses, when admitted, exhibit, as one man, a discrimination of which Mr Ruskin himself might be proud, and observe and admire on the very soundest principles'.[6]

In contrast to the splendours of the Wallace Collection, in the basement lay the Anthropological Collection. Its lender, Augustus Henry Lane Fox, explained in his catalogue (1874) his installation according to his reading of Darwin's theory of evolution: 'The collection to which this Catalogue relates occupies the whole of the South Basement of the Museum buildings. The series commences at the East End with the typical human skulls and hair of different races, and then proceeds with specimens of the culture of modern savages and barbarous races.'[7] In 1878 his collection moved to the South Kensington Museum for display (see chapter 2) and continued to grow as he purchased more artefacts from dealers. The museum refused to accept any more loans in 1881; the following year his offer was accepted by the University of Oxford. In 1884 16,936 objects arrived there (and possibly 6,700 more) and were installed as the new Pitt Rivers Museum.[8]

In 1880 the annual report of the Department of Science and Art described how the 'Bethnal Green Branch of the South Kensington Museum' benefitted from 'the temporary transfer from South Kensington of all modern examples in Art manufacture acquired since 1851 . . . working men greatly appreciate this opportunity of studying examples of ornamental Art bearing on their daily work'.[9] The modern collections remained at Bethnal Green for a century. This was much to the chagrin of Henry Cole, who had retired in 1873. Angry that the rejected display included his own award-winning tea service made by Summerly's Art Manufactures he suspected the influence of his old foe J.C. Robinson, who had returned to favour as a consultant. The removal of the modern from South Kensington continued in 1909 when, following controversy over the acceptance of George Donaldson's gift of contemporary French furniture (see chapter 16), it went on long-term display at the Bethnal Green Museum.

From 1876 until 1884 A.W. Franks of the British Museum lent to the Bethnal Green Museum part of his personal collection of Asian ceramics. In 1883 the Marquis of Bute's collection of 200 paintings opened, with a catalogue 82 pages long. When the loan exhibition transferred to Glasgow Art Galleries and Museums in 1884 Joseph Bond placed

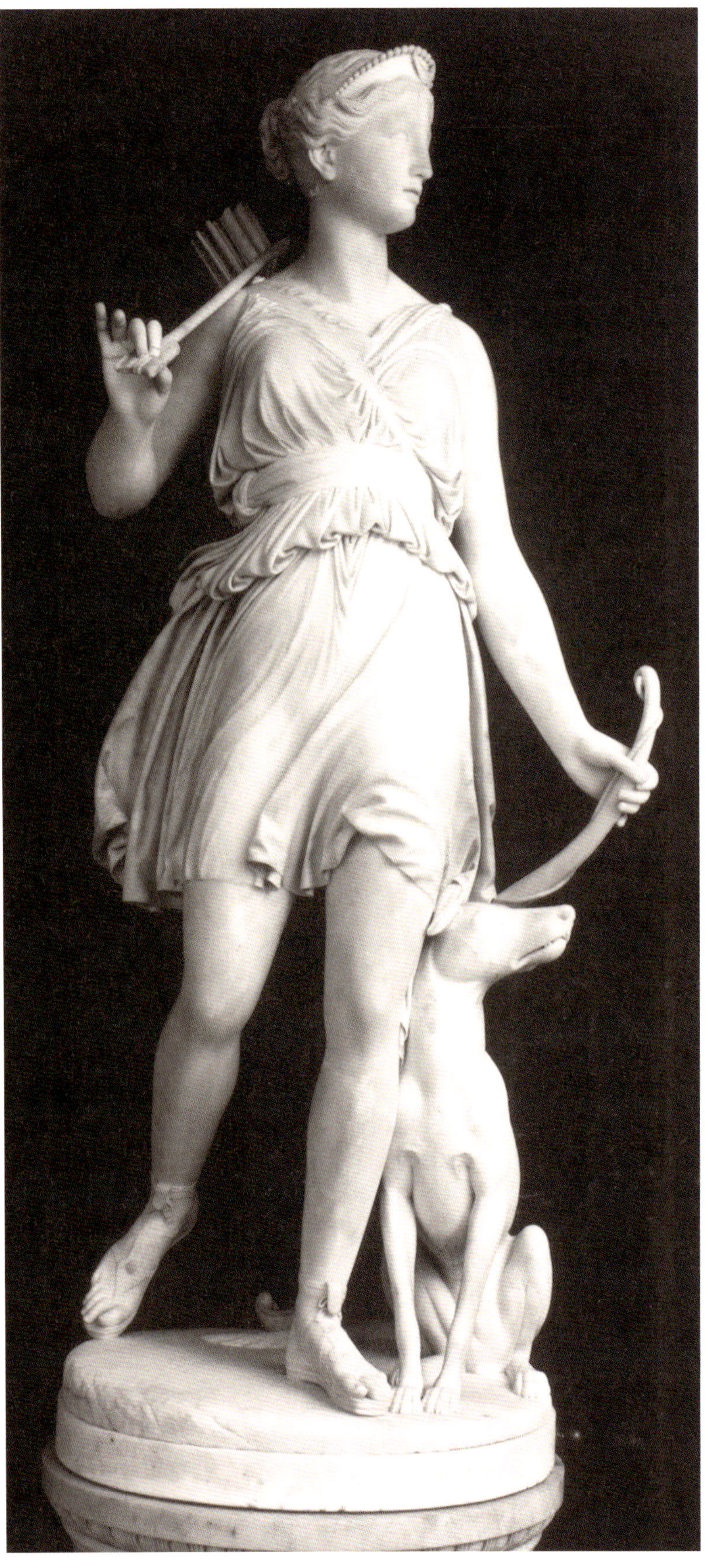

on loan to Bethnal Green his collection of English Georgian silver (fig.87). Bond had previously lent his growing collection of silver and porcelain to the South Kensington Museum, which purchased 106 examples. In 1886 Bond died intestate; four years later, when the Treasury Solicitor finally allocated it to the museum, the Bond Collection moved to South Kensington, to join the earlier purchases.[10]

A guide to the 'Bethnal Green Branch of the South Kensington Museum', published in 1890, proudly records 'the principal Loan Collections exhibited'. In addition to those cited above these include, in 1875: ivory carvings lent by W.E. Gladstone, MP,[11] and pottery and porcelain from the collection of R.H. Soden Smith (of the South Kensington Museum). In 1878 there was a 'Special Loan Collection of Decorative Furniture'; in 1881 paintings from the Duke of Edinburgh and in 1885 loans from the National Portrait Gallery.[12] In 1888 the museum attracted more visitors than its parent institution in South Kensington when Queen Victoria lent her collection of gifts received from throughout the empire to mark her Golden Jubilee in the previous year (fig.84), ranging from a statue of 'Luckshine [Lakshmi], the Goddess of Prosperity, the Gift of His Highness the Maharajah of Travancore, K.C.S.I.' to ostrich-feather screens from 'the Ostrich Farmers and Women of the Cape' (South Africa).[13] Bethnal Green was ahead of South Kensington again in 1896 when a 'Special Loan Exhibition of 17th and 18th century English Furniture and Silks . . . was undertaken with a view of assisting the two great local industries, the manufacture of furniture and silk weaving'.[14] It is now regarded as the earliest major museum exhibition of English furniture.[15]

The branch museum soon attracted its own donations. In 1885 the former cotton merchant Joshua Dixon (1810–1885) bequeathed 'to Bethnal Green Museum' his collection of 295 oil paintings, watercolours, drawings, engravings, enamel paintings, sculptures, bronzes and other works of art (figs 85, 86, 88, 89).[16] The son of a merchant and inventor in the woollen textile industry, Dixon made his fortune as a cotton trader between Liverpool and New Orleans.[17] The guidebook

OPPOSITE:
**86.** Giovanni Maria Benzoni, *Diana Hunting*, 1859, marble, exhibited at the International Exhibition, London, 1862. Bequeathed by Joshua Dixon to the Bethnal Green Museum. V&A: 1268-1886.

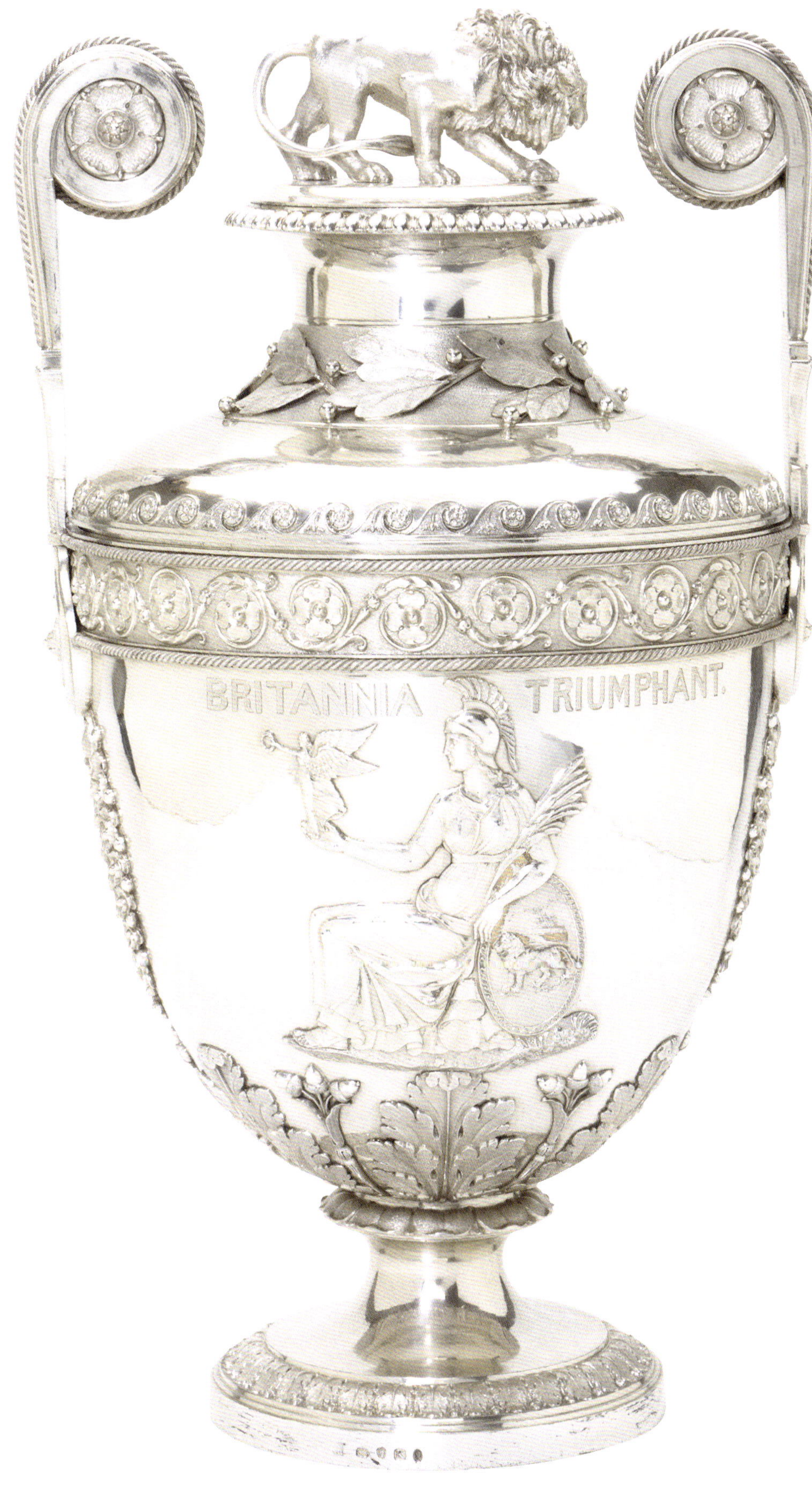


**87.** Designed by John Shaw, modified by John Flaxman, *The Trafalgar Vase*, 1805–6, silver. Given by Joseph Bond. V&A: 803:1,2-1890.

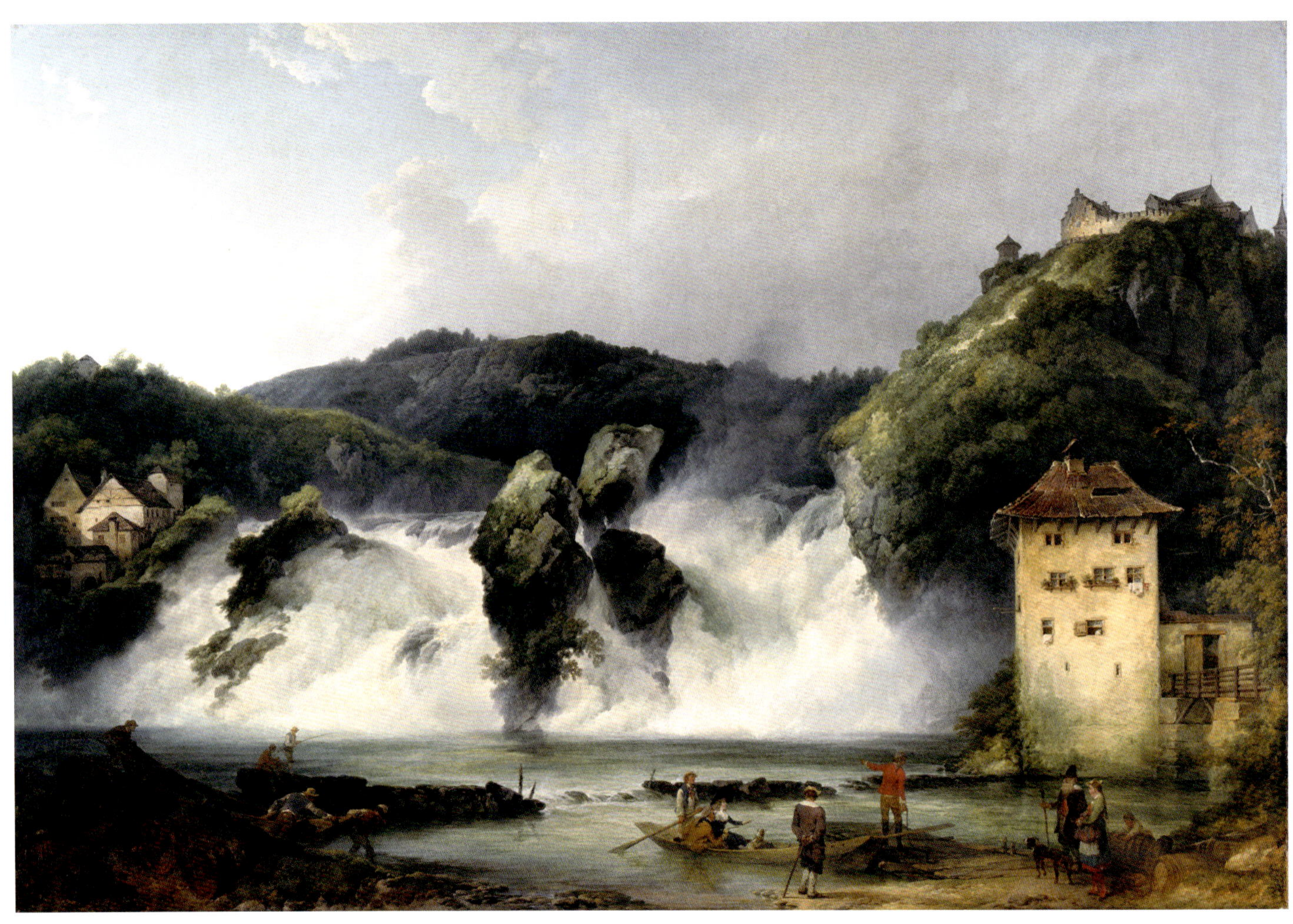

88. Philip James de Loutherbourg, *The Falls of the Rhine at Schaffhausen*, 1788, oil on canvas. Bequeathed by Joshua Dixon to the Bethnal Green Museum. V&A: 1028-1886.

from 1890 describes the Dixon Bequest filling the Central Court, along with 'The Massey Mainwaring Collection of Furniture, Porcelain, Silver Plate, and other Art Objects'. The Food Collection could be found in the north gallery, the Animal Products in the south; the upper galleries showed the 'Collection of National Portraits' and the basement displays included 'The Doubleday Collection of Entomology' and a display of 'Waste Products'. By 1900 a total of 40 collections had come and gone from Bethnal Green. In 1906 a journal deduced the core message brought from South Kensington to Bethnal Green as simply: 'There would be hope for the British workman if he took to collecting.'[18]

The idea of helping the working man of Bethnal Green to become a collector caused some amusement in the press. In 1873 a sketch in *The Graphic* showed 'Art Connoisseurs at the East End: A study at Sir Richard Wallace's Loan Collection in the Bethnal Green Museum' (fig.5).[19] But it echoed a set of values and a moral agenda shared with the South Kensington Museum, based on the cultivation of taste and of the home. Three years after the opening of the Bethnal Green Museum, Octavia Hill published *Homes of the London Poor* (1875) in which she called for a recognition of the need for beauty at home, writing: 'I have tried . . . to develop the love of beauty among my tenants. The poor of London need joy and beauty in their lives.'[20] In 1883 the *Eastern Argus* praised the influence of the Bethnal Green Museum and asked 'What home is there without its water-colours or oil paintings? From the Queen in her state apartments at Windsor Castle, to the labourer in the mean and tidy cottage, the same decoration of the walls is found!'[21] The acquisition of taste and its application to the home, through collecting, even at the humblest level, was seen as a way to social health and stability that museums could encourage. Too often dismissed as a self-indulgent middle-class distraction from South Kensington's prior mission to reform the design of mass-produced goods, collecting was appreciated by Victorian champions of social reform for its wider potential. In the 20th century the Bethnal Green Museum's role varied until it was relaunched in 1974 as the Museum of Childhood.[22] In 2020–22 it was transformed to be a source of inspiration to children, young adults and their educators as the Young V&A.

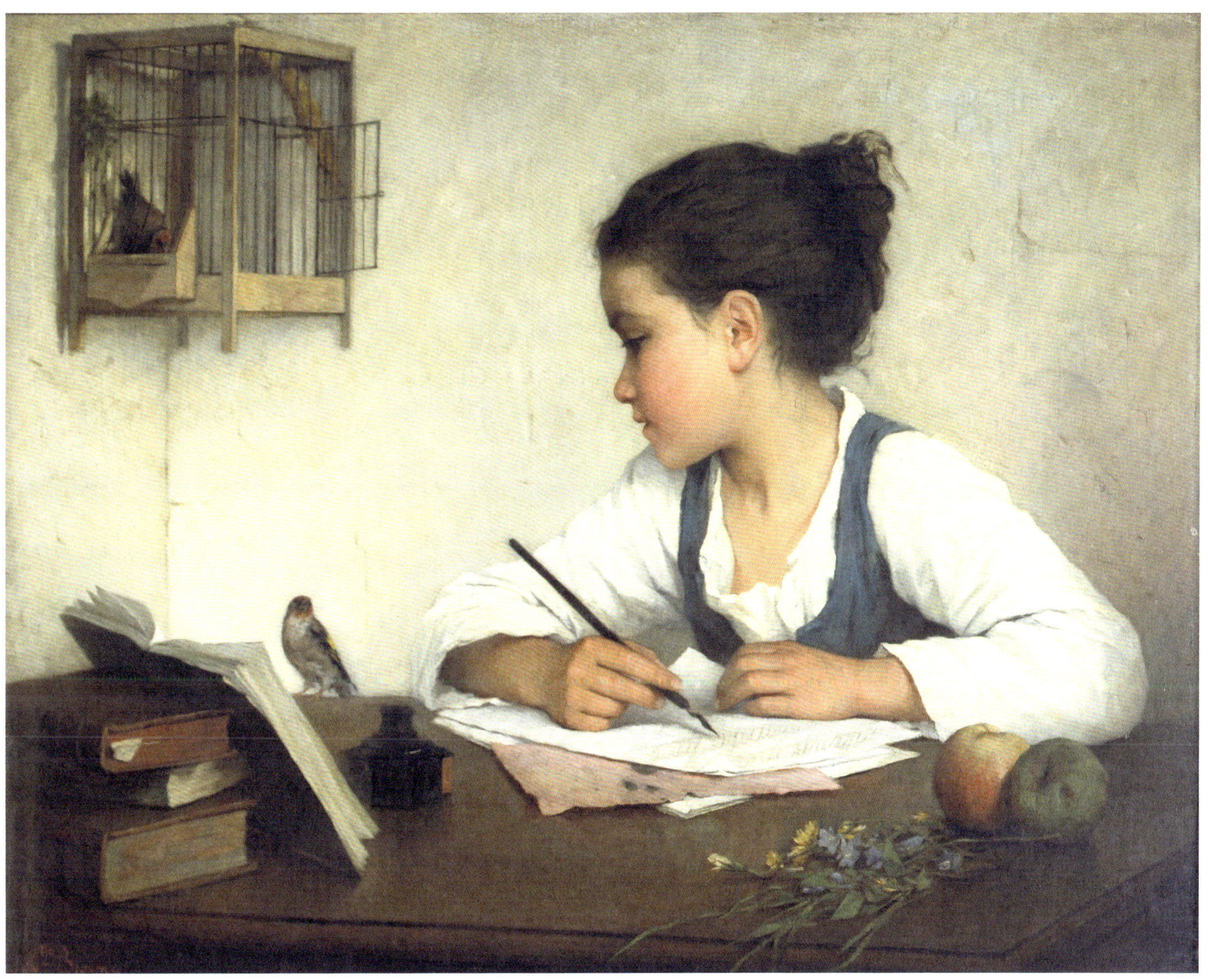

**89.** Henriette Browne, *The Pet Goldfinch*, *c.*1875, oil on canvas. Bequeathed by Joshua Dixon to the Bethnal Green Museum. V&A: 1083-1886.

# Part V: Collectors at Home

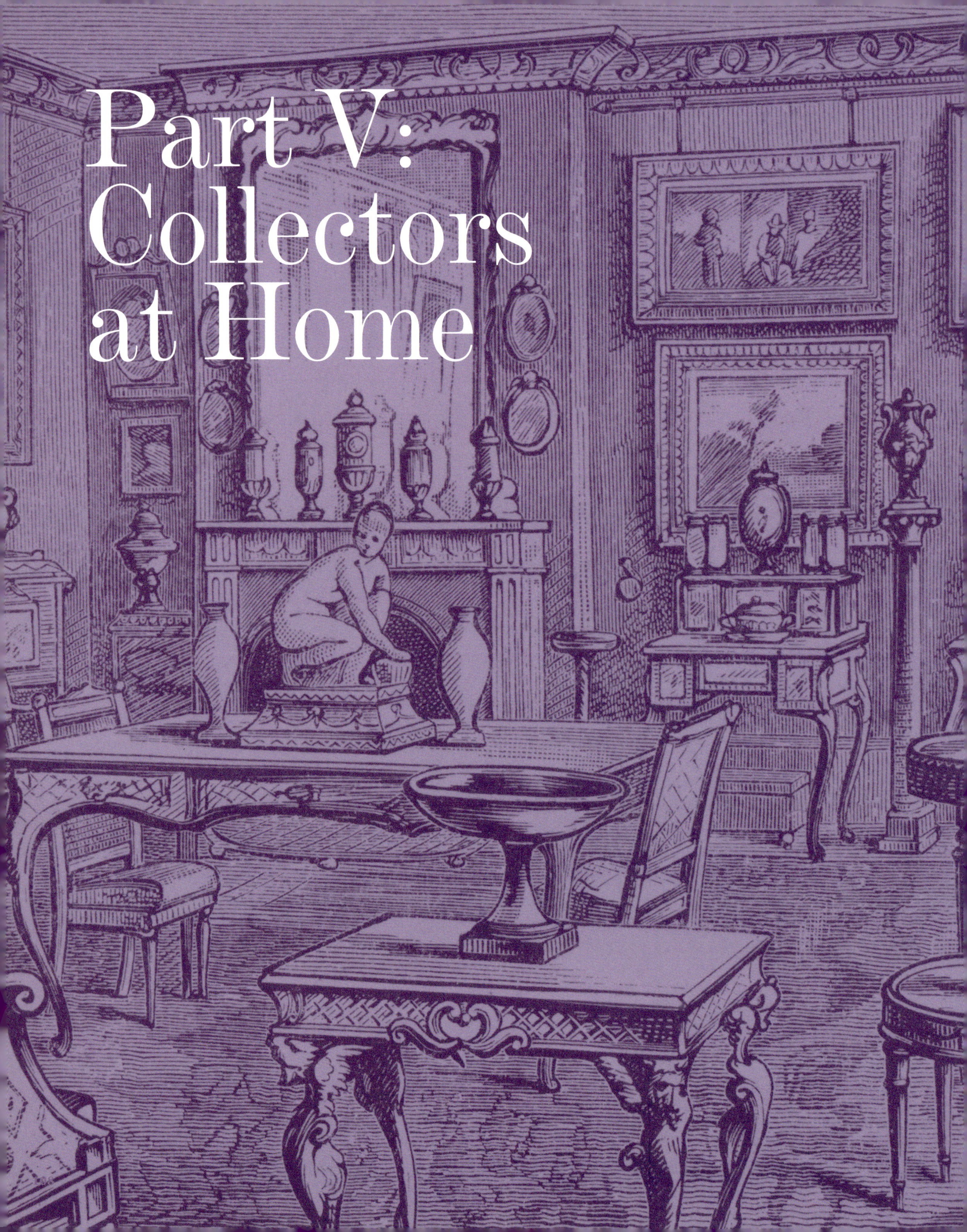

SOME OF THE GREATEST private collections were formed with the museum in mind and were shown to the public, while they continued to grow, as long-term loans. Two Victorian collections stayed at home, where they were well documented as arranged by their owners before they came to the museum; they provide examples of very different approaches to display. Record drawings and photographs reveal that neither favoured the dark romantic mysteries of the traditional antiquarian interiors beloved by eccentric eclectic scholars intent on evoking cabinets of curiosities, princely *studioli* and *Kunstkammern*. Both John Jones and Constantine Alexander Ionides carefully composed their interiors with acquisitions, and for very different effects. Jones's home evoked the late 18th-century ambience of an elegant Parisian townhouse, as an admirer of Marie Antoinette, or more like a museum period room. Ionides, by contrast, created an Aesthetic interior, influenced by the Chelsea home of Dante Gabriel Rossetti and by commercial galleries of the Aesthetic Movement, where contemporary paintings were enhanced by interior decoration and decorative arts. Both Jones and Ionides must have been inspired, in different ways, by their visits to the South Kensington Museum.

# 14 Marie Antoinette in Piccadilly: John Jones

John Jones (1798/9–1882), a tailor and military clothier, made much of his fortune from the Crimean War (1853–6). No record is known of his aims as a collector but in his central London home he created an *ancien régime* ambience, rich in glamorous associations with Marie Antoinette, the last queen of France before the French Revolution. Thanks to the endeavours of the V&A's second director, Philip Cunliffe Owen, in 1882 the museum secured the collection. Jones had set up his London shop and workshops around 1825, at 6 Waterloo Place, before relocating the business to 6–8 Regent Street. The collection grew in his chambers upstairs. In 1865 he moved to a town house, 95 Piccadilly, overlooking Green Park from the corner of Whitehorse Street. Soon after Jones's death in 1882 the densely packed entrance hall, drawing room and dining room were recorded in detailed views (figs 90, 91), which were published the following year in the museum's handbook to the collection. A.W. Hogg's sketch of the dining room (fig.91) includes a bust of Marie Antoinette, as if presiding as hostess.[1] Among the objects illustrated, five were captioned as 'formerly Marie Antoinette's' and in the text several others claim the same romantic provenance (figs 92, 101).[2]

The Jones Collection is not all French and the many British and earlier European paintings suggest a previous phase of collecting and a change in direction,[3] as does the set of Gothic Revival carved and painted bookcases he commissioned for his library between 1858 and 1862. The collection includes 105 oil paintings (figs 94, 96, 97), 137 portrait miniatures and enamels, 135 examples of 'decorative furniture' (figs 99, 101), 109 sculptures, 89 pieces of Sèvres porcelain (fig.95), 52 bronzes and ormolu objects, 16 clocks, 313 prints and around 780 books, including a copy of Shakespeare's First Folio (1623) and a Third Folio (1664) signed on the title page by Wordsworth, Dickens and Robert Browning. In his annual report on the South Kensington Museum Cunliffe Owen described how the bequest 'consists chiefly of very choice examples of French Eighteenth Century Art, a class more keenly sought after by wealthy collectors than any other. . . . Hence it would have been impossible for the Museum to acquire an adequate representation of this class of Art except by gift or bequest. Hitherto the deficiency has in some measure been supplied by loans.'[4]

To collect French 18th-century paintings and decorative arts on this scale was a new departure for the museum. The main precedents were Sir Richard Wallace's Loan Collection, which had been the main attraction at the opening and first three years of the Bethnal Green Museum (1872–5; see chapter 13), and the purchase in 1869 of a room designed for Madame de Sérilly, a maid of honour to Marie Antoinette. The museum's second period room, it was installed by 1872 when it was photographed furnished with a harp, given to the museum in 1863 and said to have belonged to Marie Antoinette.[5] Jones may well have been shown 'Madame de Sérilly's Boudoir' by the museum's director in the last decade of his life and assumed his collection could be installed the same way.

In 1883 Gilbert Redgrave (son of Richard Redgrave, formerly Inspector-General for Art)

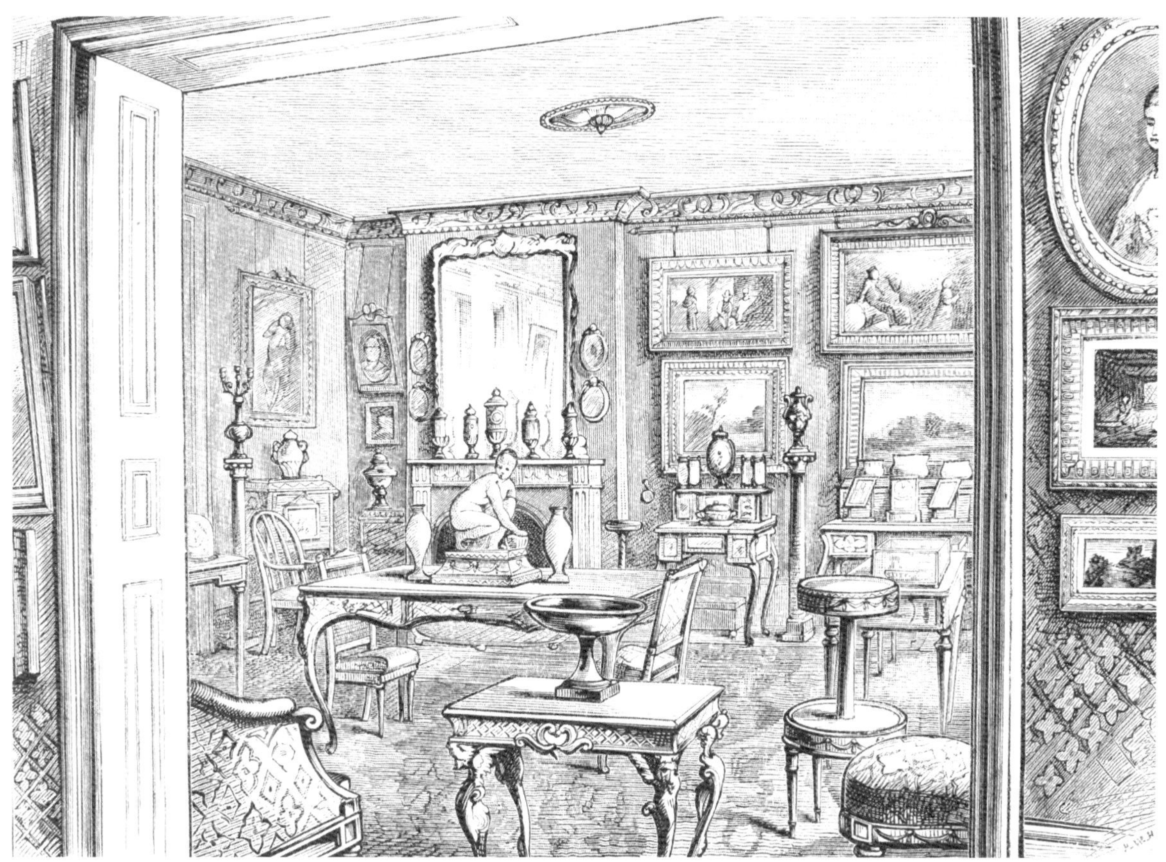

**90.** After A.W. Hogg, 'The Drawing Room at 95 Piccadilly, the Residence of John Jones', 1882, print, from *Handbook to the Jones Collection in the South Kensington Museum*, London, 1883. V&A: National Art Library.

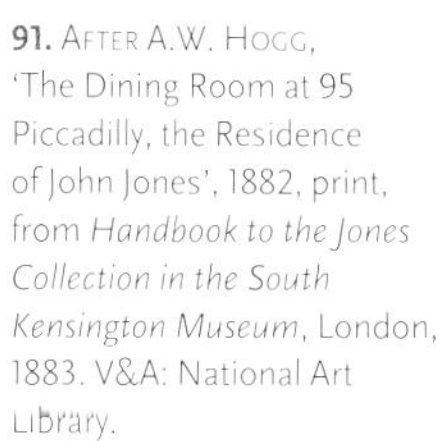

**91.** After A.W. Hogg, 'The Dining Room at 95 Piccadilly, the Residence of John Jones', 1882, print, from *Handbook to the Jones Collection in the South Kensington Museum*, London, 1883. V&A: National Art Library.

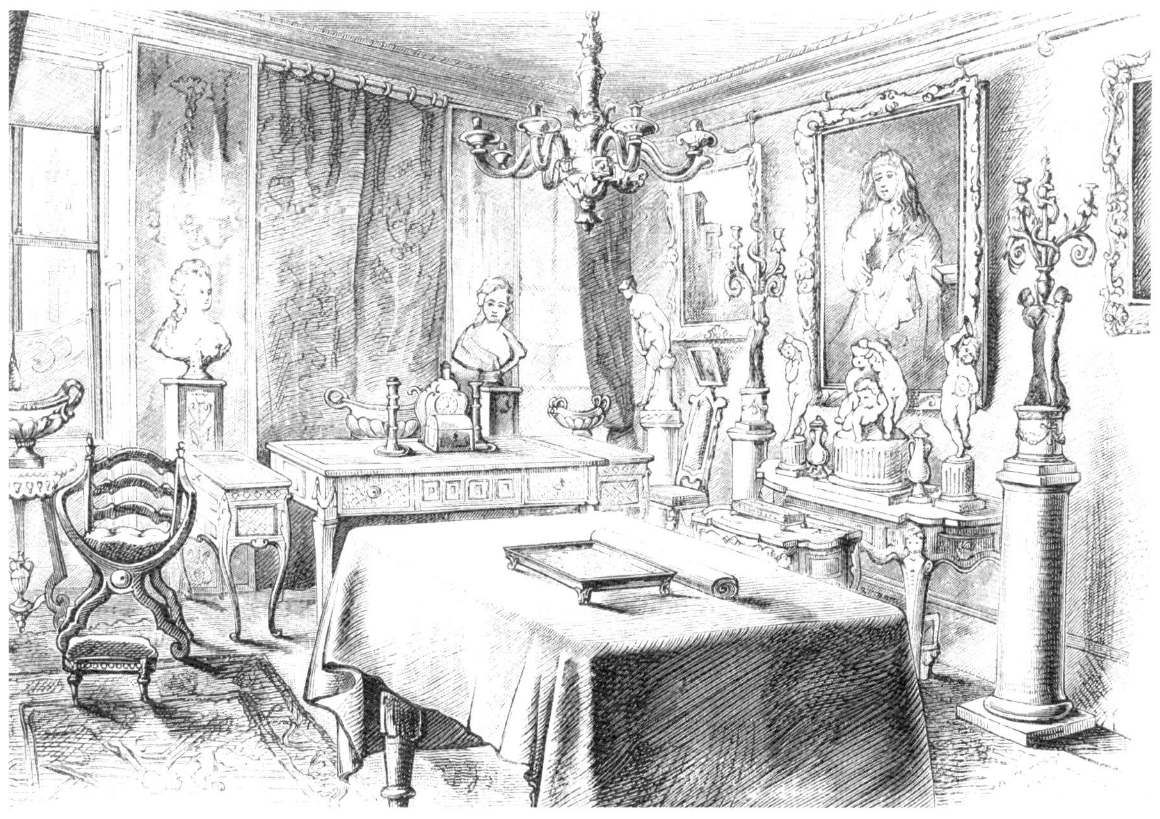

introduced the public to the Jones Collection in the *Art Journal*. He may be forgiven for some enthusiastic exaggeration when he described it as 'perhaps the noblest donation ever made by a private individual to any country in the world's history'.[6] The same year an article in the *Cabinet Maker and Art Furnisher* welcomed it as the latest in a series of named collections: 'No wonder that the South Kensington authorities can hardly find words to express their delight, for the Sheepshanks, Dyce, Forster, and Townshend legacies fall far short in value to the Jones Collection.'[7] But to *The Builder* it showed 'a most frivolous and false taste' and warned: 'it would be wrong for any who are aiming at guiding public taste to any degree to overlook the fact that this beautiful workmanship represents also a period of very corrupt taste'.[8] *The Athenaeum* called it 'voluptuous and unintellectual bric-a-brac'[9] while *The Times* felt 'nausea ensue from an over-seasoned richness'.[10] The *Saturday Review* concluded its long article: 'the ugliest objects are those rightly or wrongly attributed to the collection of Marie Antoinette'.[11]

Jones required that his bequest 'be kept separate as one collection and not distributed over various parts of the said Museum, or lent for exhibition'.[12] These terms echo the wishes of the art-dealer Alexander Barker (d.1873), the son of a London bootmaker who became Jones's near neighbour at 103 Piccadilly. After lending 55 objects to the Special Loan Exhibition in 1862 (see chapter 4), Barker served on several of the museum's exhibition committees. Between 1859 and 1867 he lent around 500 objects to the museum, ranging from maiolica, glass, crystal, bronzes and ivories to Russian wooden crosses. Some remained until he died in October 1873 when he bequeathed 34 examples of 'Furniture of a boudoir. Venetian. Early 18th century' to the museum 'upon condition they are all placed together in one apartment at South Kensington'.[13] Barker may have suggested the same stipulation to Jones. However, photographs of the Jones Collection when first on display in the V&A's galleries (rooms 100 and 101) show the practical and aesthetic challenges at that time of honouring Jones's wish. Once installed, secure within museum showcases, it all looked very different from 'Madame de Sérilly's Boudoir' and the carefully composed ensembles in the collector's home (fig.12).

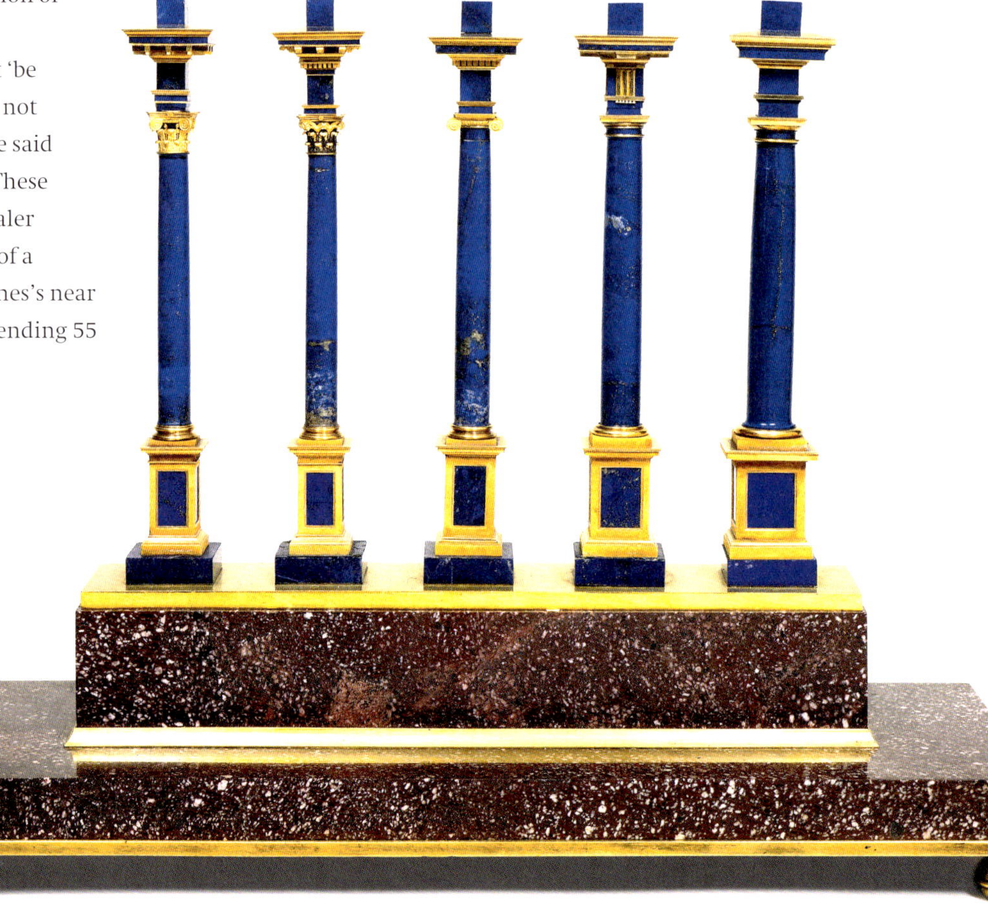

**92.** Robert Arnould Drais (attrib.), *The Five Orders of Architecture*, c.1780, lapis lazuli columns, mounted in gold; on a base of red porphyry mounted in ormolu. Bequeathed by John Jones. V&A: 853-1882. According to the first handbook to the Jones Collection (1883) this architectural model was 'made for Marie Antoinette, in order to teach her' the orders of classical architecture.

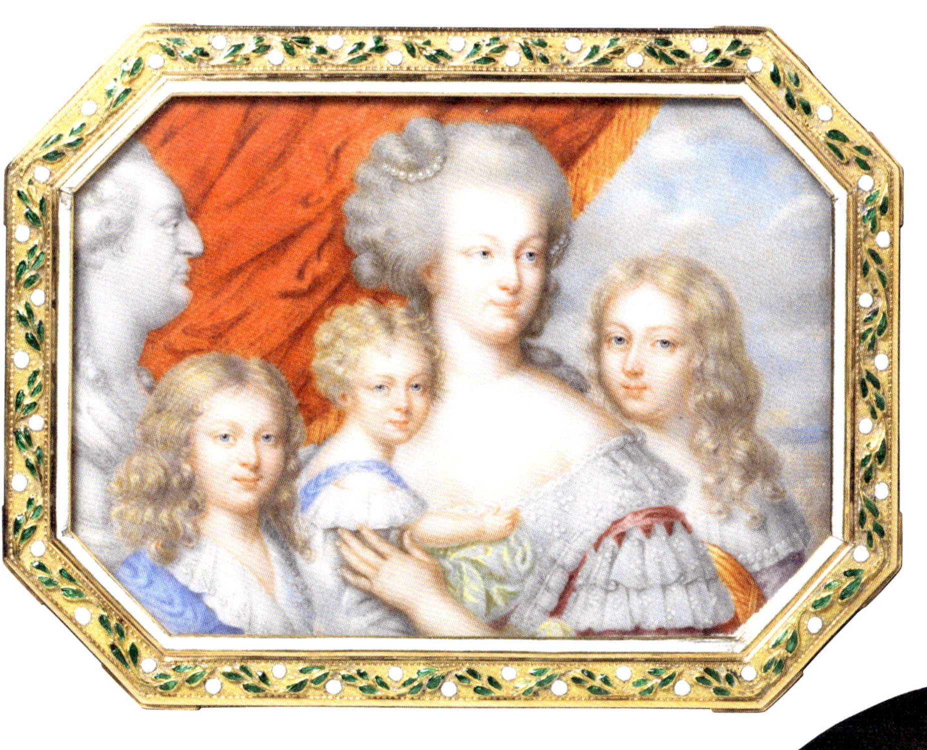

**93.** Pierre-François Drais, snuffbox, 1776–89, gold, enamel and lapis lazuli, mounted with later miniatures, the top showing Marie Antoinette and her children with a sculptured bust of Louis XVI, painted after the restoration of the French monarchy in 1814. Bequeathed by John Jones. V&A: 905-1882.

**94.** François-Hubert Drouais, *Marie Antoinette, Queen of France, while Dauphine, age Seventeen*, 1773, oil on canvas. Bequeathed by John Jones. V&A: 529-1882.

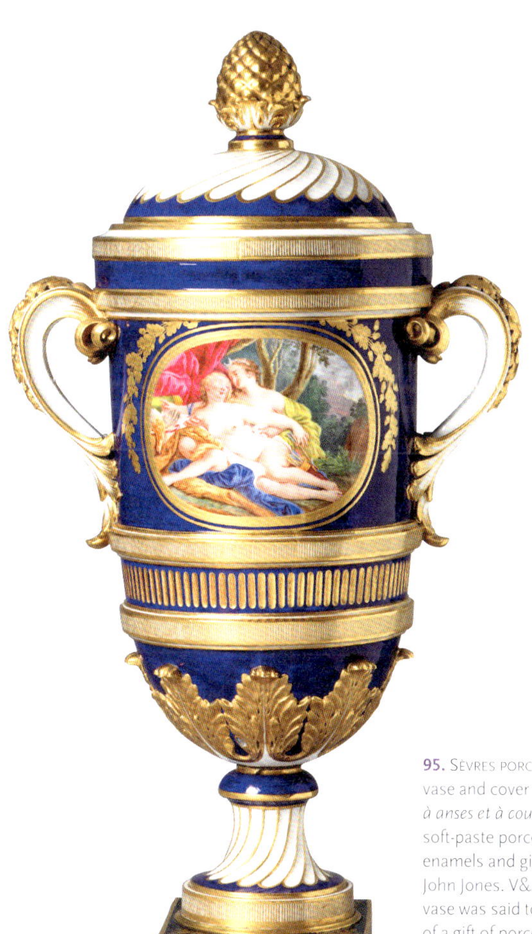

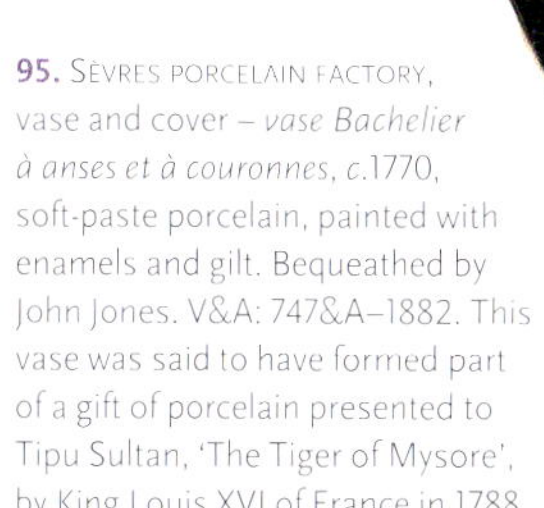

**95.** Sèvres porcelain factory, vase and cover – *vase Bachelier à anses et à couronnes*, c.1770, soft-paste porcelain, painted with enamels and gilt. Bequeathed by John Jones. V&A: 747&A–1882. This vase was said to have formed part of a gift of porcelain presented to Tipu Sultan, 'The Tiger of Mysore', by King Louis XVI of France in 1788.

**96.** JEAN-FRANÇOIS DE TROY, *The Alarm*, or *La Gouvernante Fidèle*, 1723, oil on canvas. Bequeathed by John Jones. V&A: 518-1882. A loyal governess warns a young couple of an approaching interruption. Acquired by Jones as by Watteau. Cleaning removed the false signature and revealed that of the artist and the date.

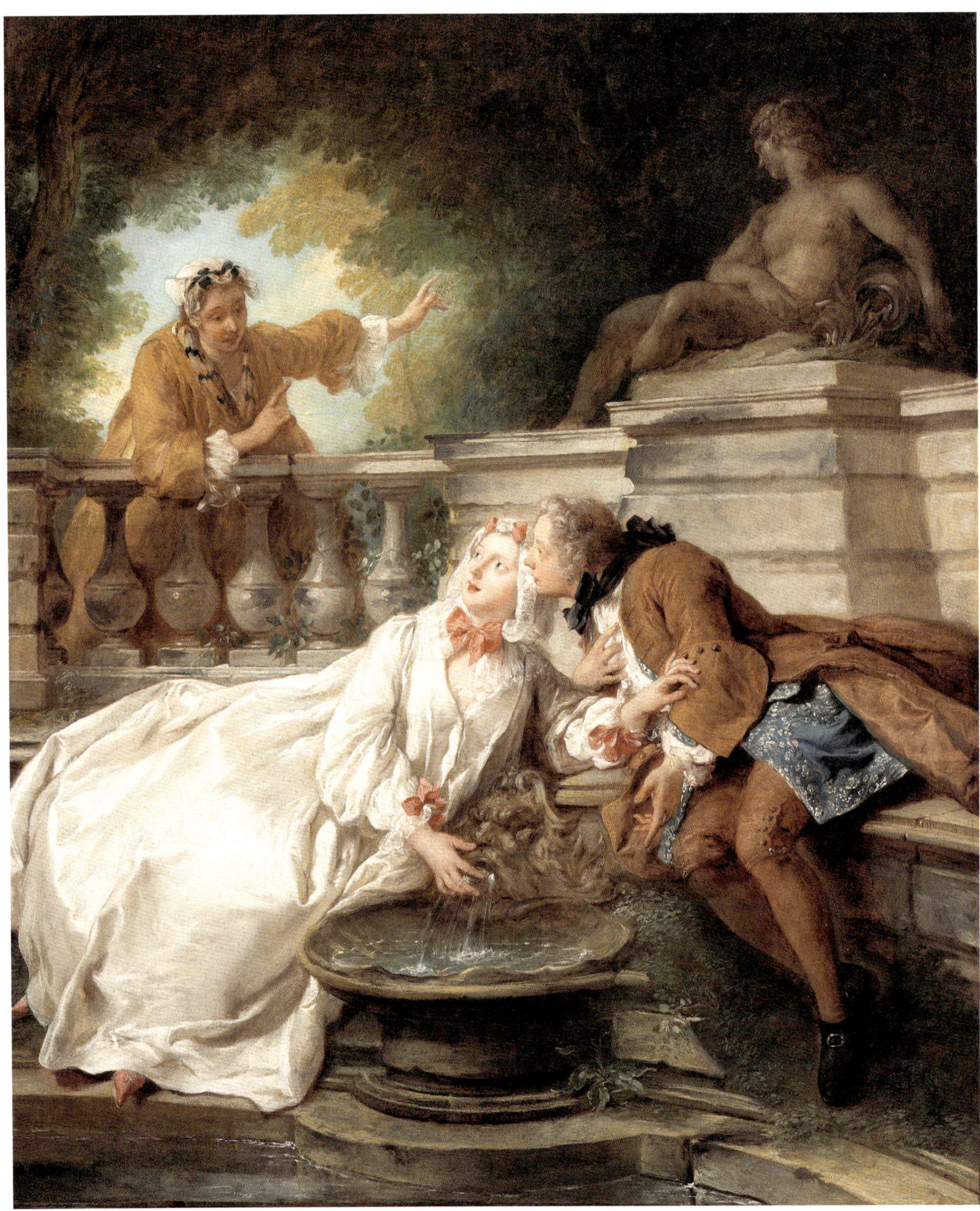

**97.** François Boucher, *Madame de Pompadour, Mistress of Louis XV*, 1758, oil on canvas. Bequeathed by John Jones. V&A: 487-1882.

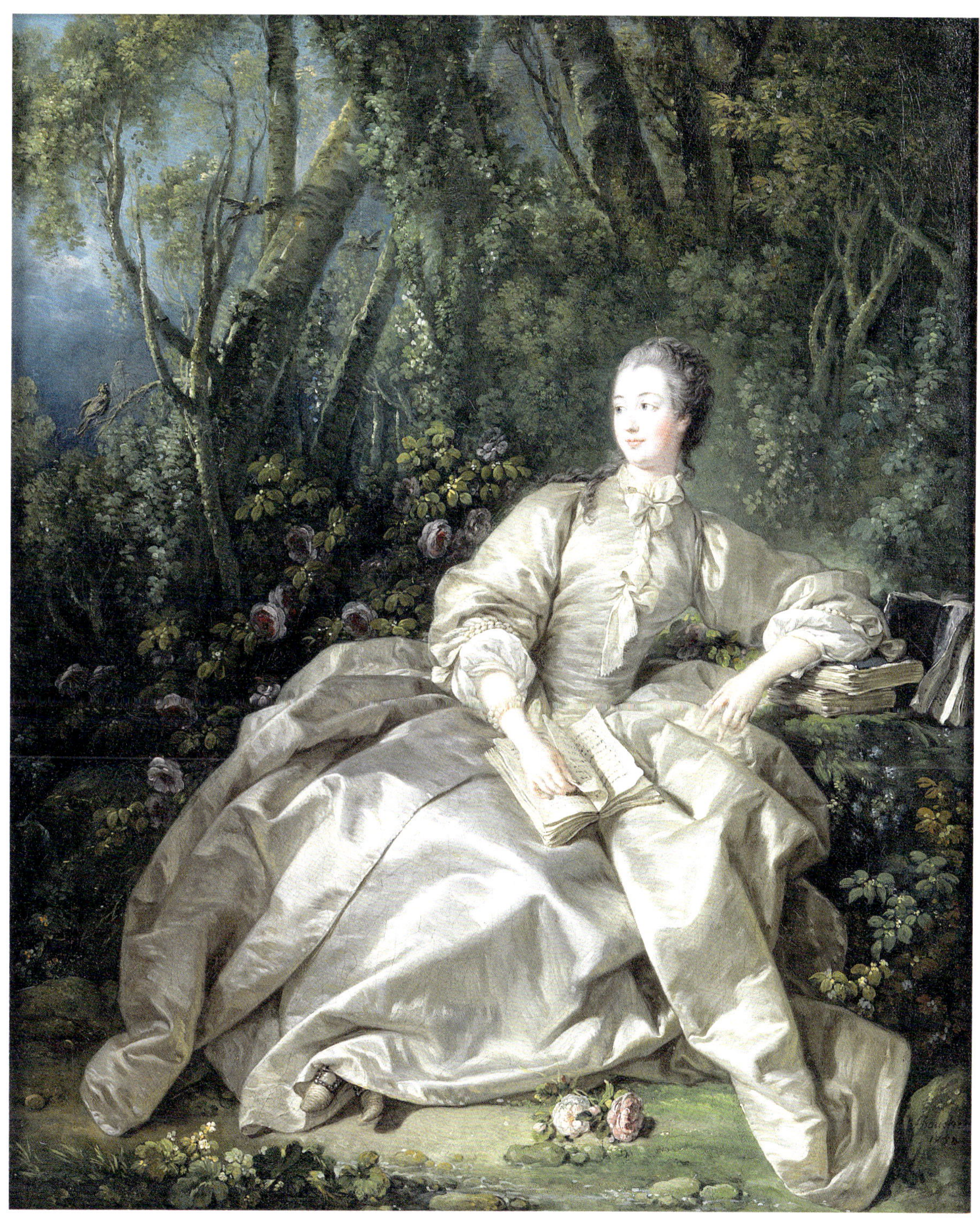

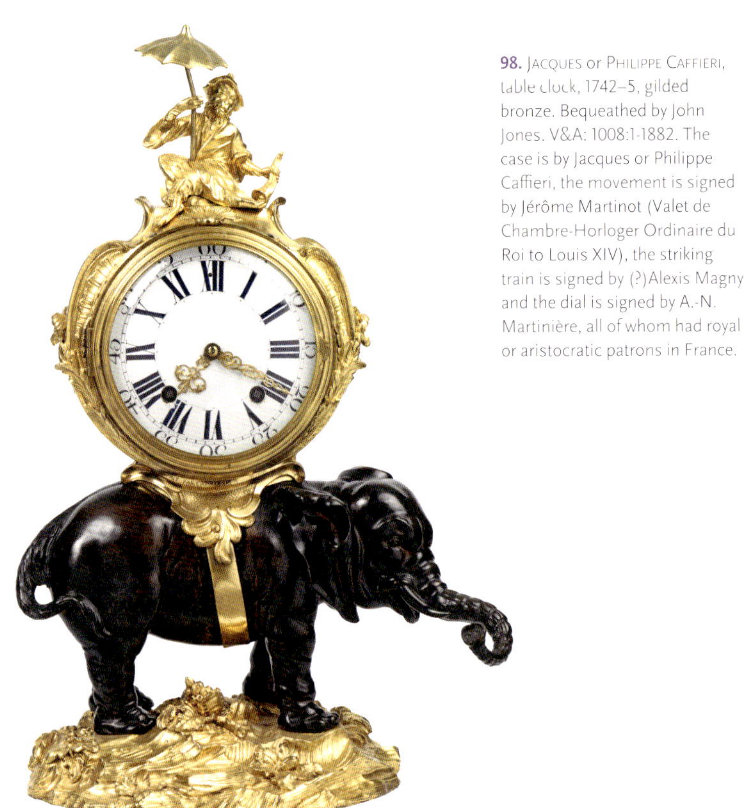

**98.** Jacques or Philippe Caffieri, table clock, 1742–5, gilded bronze. Bequeathed by John Jones. V&A: 1008:1-1882. The case is by Jacques or Philippe Caffieri, the movement is signed by Jérôme Martinot (Valet de Chambre-Horloger Ordinaire du Roi to Louis XIV), the striking train is signed by (?)Alexis Magny and the dial is signed by A.-N. Martinière, all of whom had royal or aristocratic patrons in France.

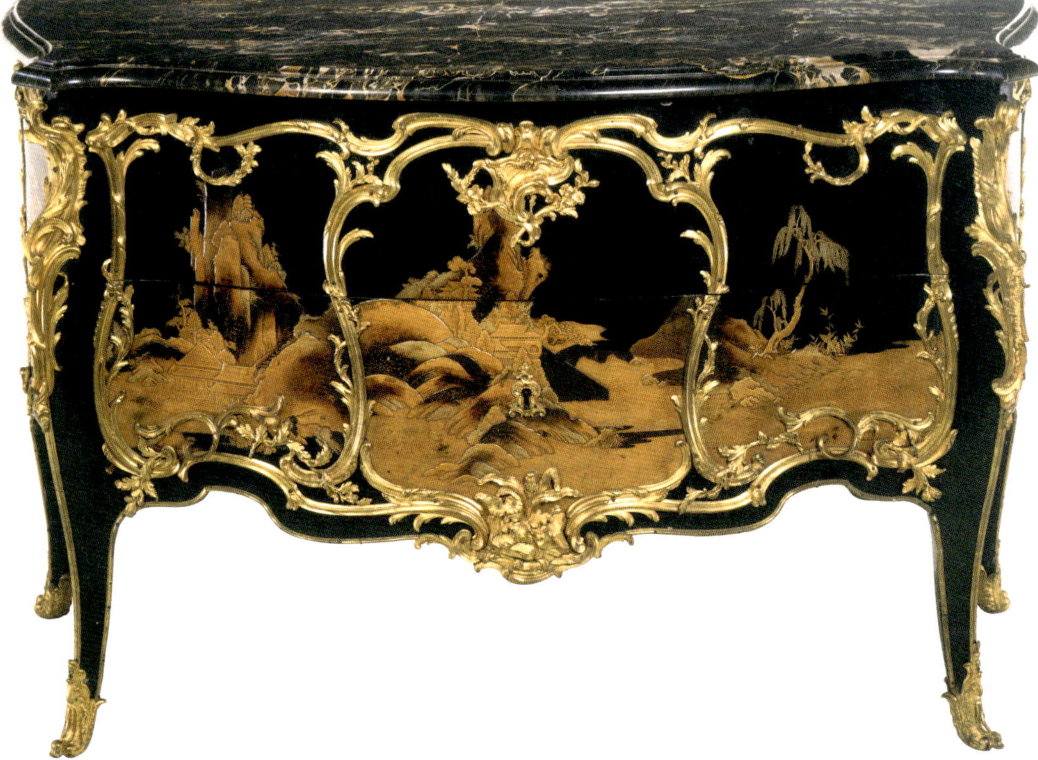

**99.** Bernard Vanrisamburgh II and workshop, commode, *c.*1760–65, mounted with Japanese lacquer and chased gilt bronze, with slab of Portoro Macchie Larga marble. Bequeathed by John Jones. V&A: 1105-1882.

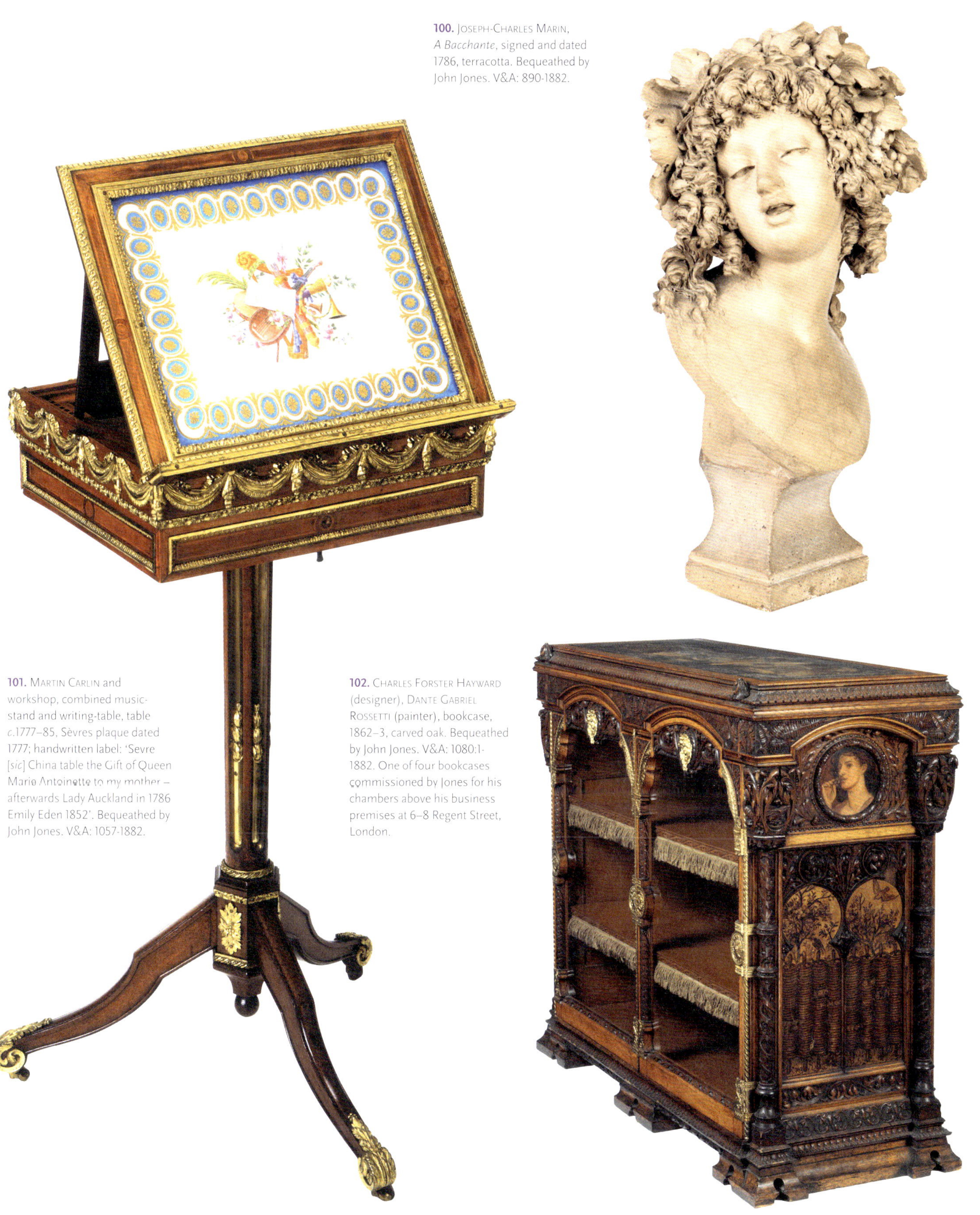

**100.** Joseph-Charles Marin, *A Bacchante*, signed and dated 1786, terracotta. Bequeathed by John Jones. V&A: 890-1882.

**101.** Martin Carlin and workshop, combined music-stand and writing-table, table *c.*1777–85. Sèvres plaque dated 1777; handwritten label: 'Sevre [*sic*] China table the Gift of Queen Marie Antoinette to my mother – afterwards Lady Auckland in 1786 Emily Eden 1852'. Bequeathed by John Jones. V&A: 1057-1882.

**102.** Charles Forster Hayward (designer), Dante Gabriel Rossetti (painter), bookcase, 1862–3, carved oak. Bequeathed by John Jones. V&A: 1080:1-1882. One of four bookcases commissioned by Jones for his chambers above his business premises at 6–8 Regent Street, London.

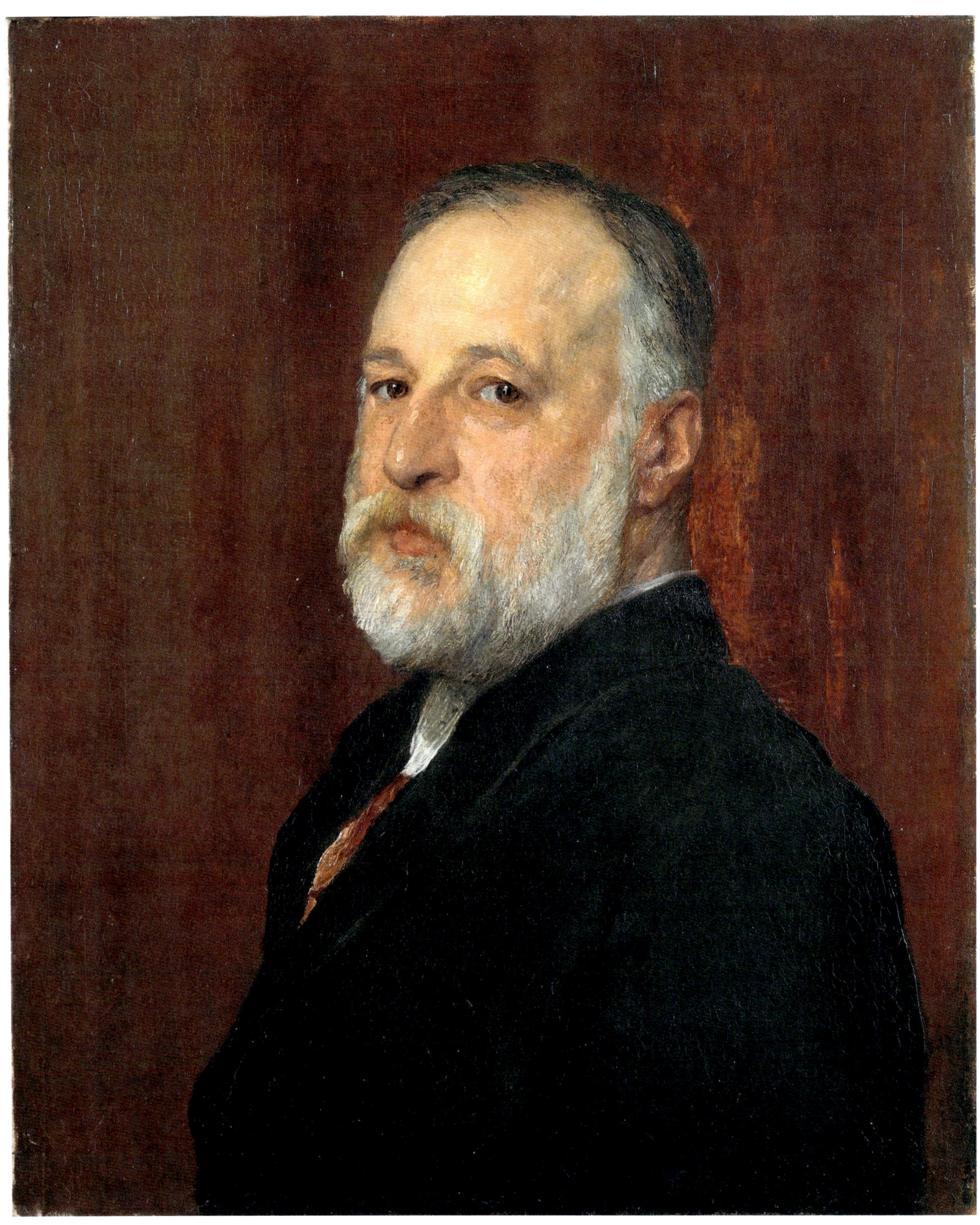

# 15 From Botticelli to Degas: Constantine Alexander Ionides

OPPOSITE:
**103.** George Frederic Watts, *Constantine Alexander Ionides*, 1880, oil on canvas. Bequeathed by Constantine Alexander Ionides. V&A: CAI.1141. Watts had been commissioned by Ionides's grandfather in 1840 to copy his portrait and went on to paint five generations of the family.

**104.** Edgar Degas, *The Ballet Scene from Meyerbeer's Opera 'Robert le Diable'*, 1876, signed, oil on canvas. Bequeathed by Constantine Alexander Ionides. V&A: CAI.19.

A successful stockbroker, Constantine Alexander Ionides (1833–1900) was the grandson of a Greek cloth merchant who had moved to England in 1825. Between 1864 and the early 1890s he formed a collection of around 90 oil paintings, 300 drawings and watercolours and 750 prints, including 123 etchings by Rembrandt and 78 by Piranesi.[1] His bequest includes masterpieces that span the Italian Renaissance, Pre-Raphaelitism, the Aesthetic Movement and the French avant-garde on the brink of Impressionism. Ionides purchased most of his paintings between 1878 and 1884, many direct from artists or from their agents or early patrons. Thanks to such short provenances, to high standards of curatorial care from the outset and to restrictions placed on lending from his bequest, his modern paintings are among the very best-preserved examples in the world. Many are in such 'mint' condition that they may be regarded, in museological terms, as type specimens. The significance of the collection also lies in its early display, for it made the V&A the leading public gallery in London for avant-garde French paintings, nearly two decades ahead of the National Gallery and the Tate Gallery.[2] For example, Ionides purchased his painting by Degas in Paris in 1881, only five years after it was painted; this masterpiece became the first Impressionist picture to enter a public collection in London (fig.104).

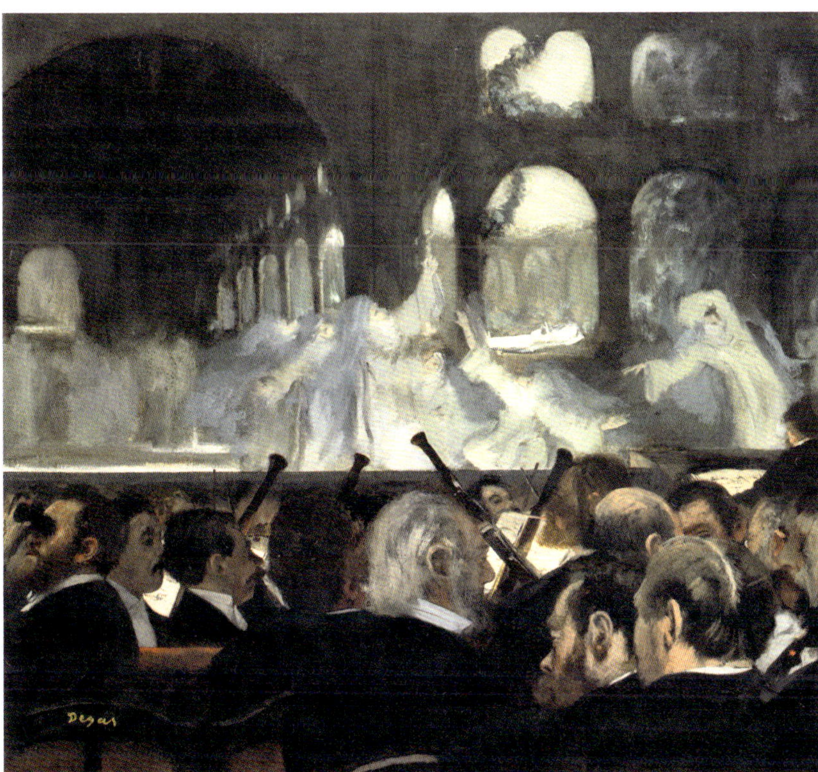


The Anglo-Greek Ionides family had settled among London's 'Holland Park circle' of artists and patrons. His parents' home there, from 1864, had been remodelled by Philip Webb and redecorated by Thomas Jeckyll, William Morris and Walter Crane. His collection reflects the taste of his father, of his brothers (who were friends of James Abbott McNeill Whistler, Dante Gabriel Rossetti and Edward Poynter) and the advice of the French artist Alphonse Legros (Professor of Fine Art at University College, London from 1876) with whom he travelled on the Continent. The 19th-century oil paintings include works by Ingres (fig.105), Delacroix (fig.106), Daumier (figs 2, 108), Millet (fig.107), Corot, Théodore Rousseau, Fantin-Latour, Courbet (fig.109), Legros, Rossetti (figs 110, 116), Burne-Jones (fig.114), Alma-Tadema and Watts (figs 103, 111), who painted

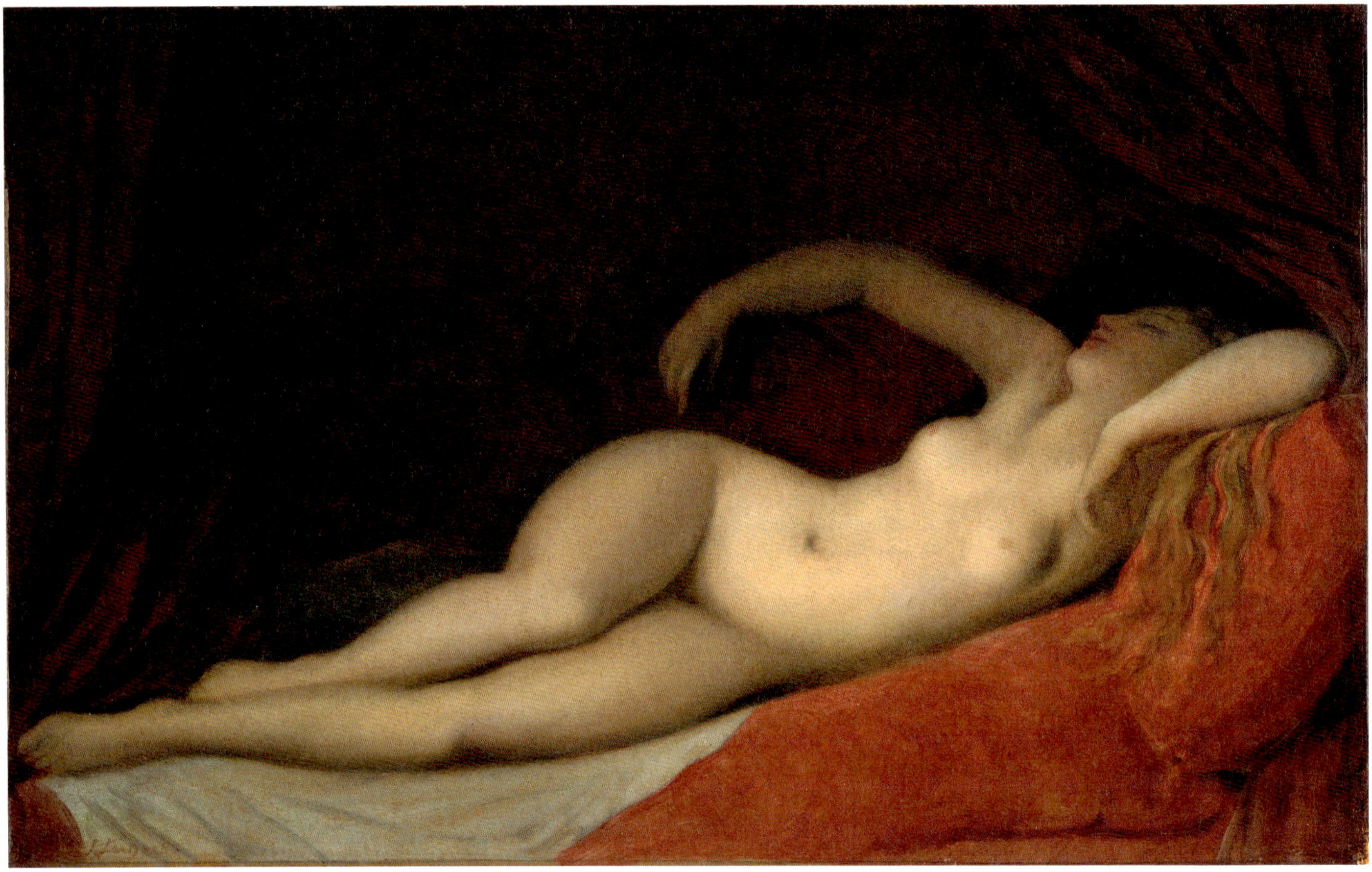

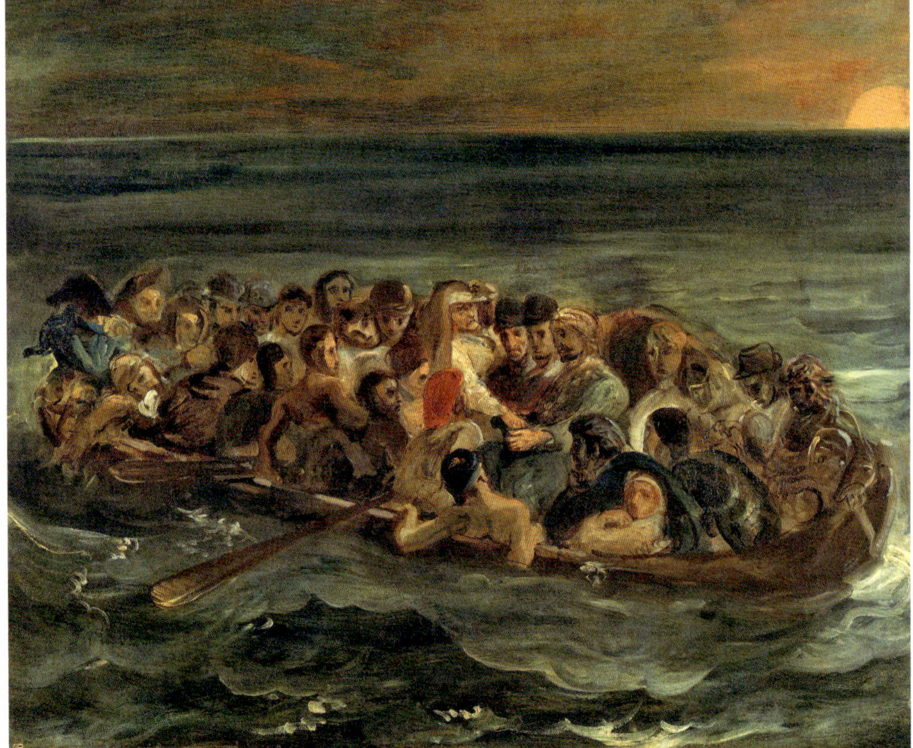

**105.** Jean-Auguste-Dominique Ingres, *A Sleeping Odalisque*, *c.*1810–30, oil on canvas. Bequeathed by Constantine Alexander Ionides. V&A: CAI.57.

**106.** Eugène Delacroix, *The Shipwreck of Don Juan: A Sketch*, *c.*1839–40, oil on canvas, sketch for the painting in the Louvre dated 1840. Bequeathed by Constantine Alexander Ionides. V&A: CAI.64.

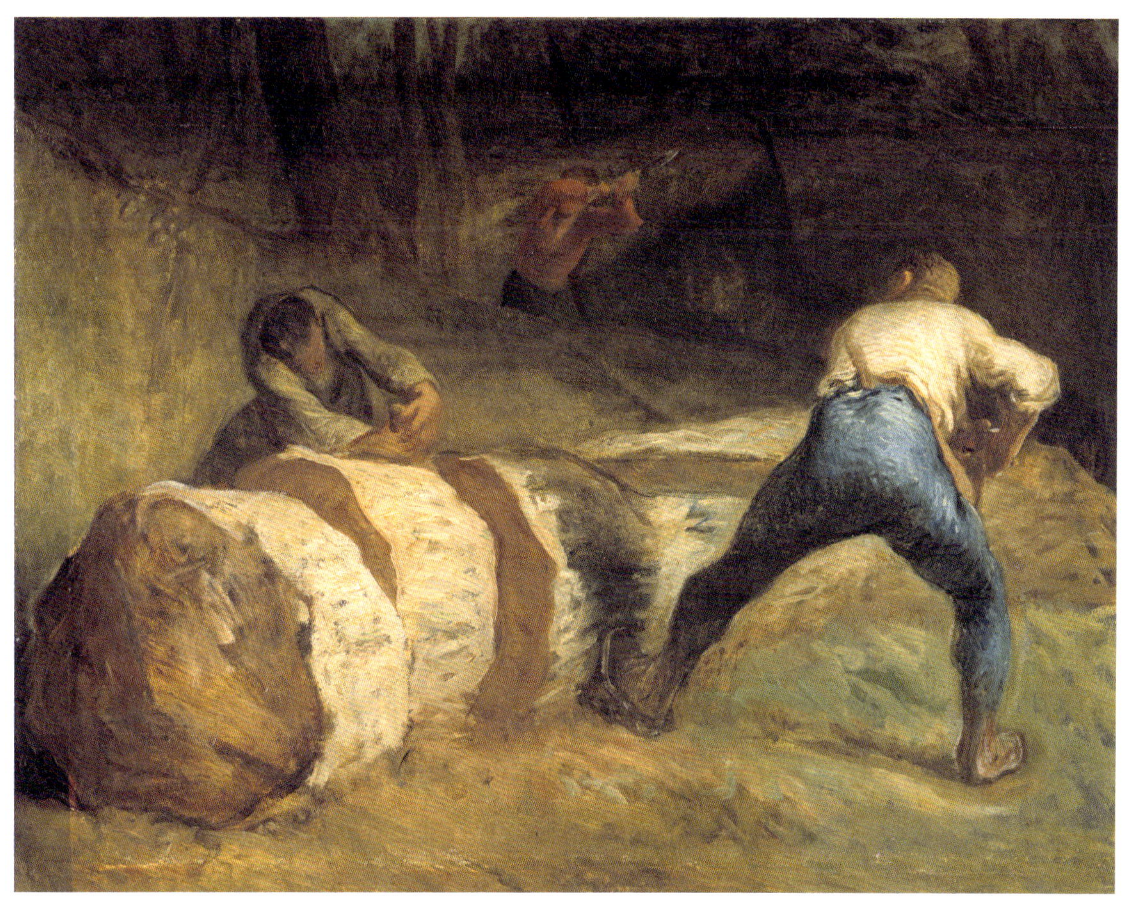

**107.** Jean-François Millet, *The Wood Sawyers*, 1850–52, oil on canvas. Bequeathed by Constantine Alexander Ionides. V&A: CAI.47.

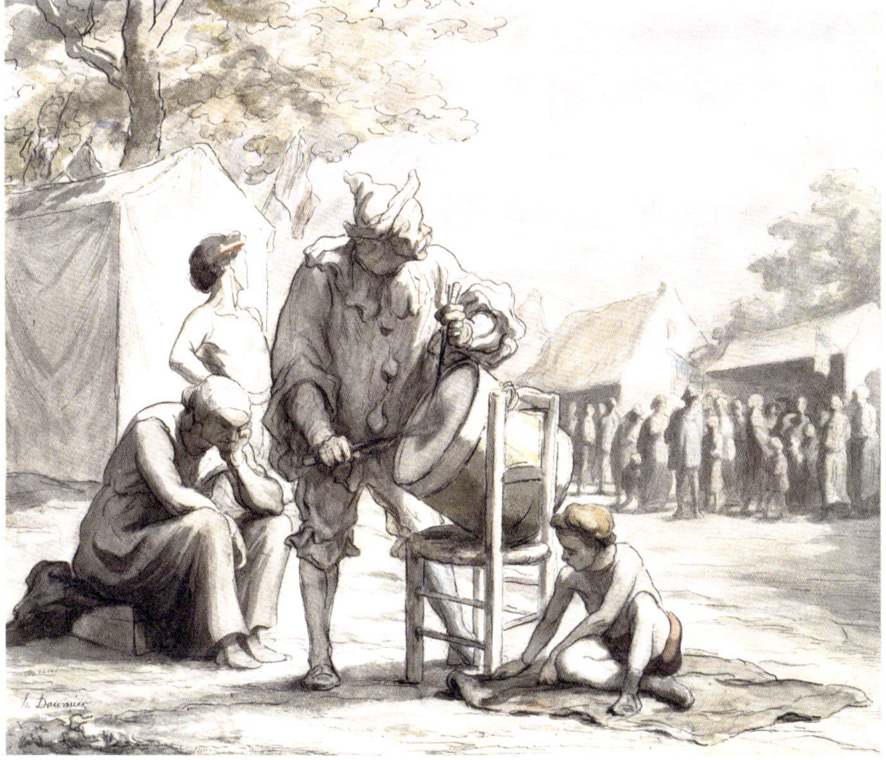


**108.** Honore Daumier, *Les Saltimbanques*, c.1866–7, watercolour. Bequeathed by Constantine Alexander Ionides. V&A: CAI.120.

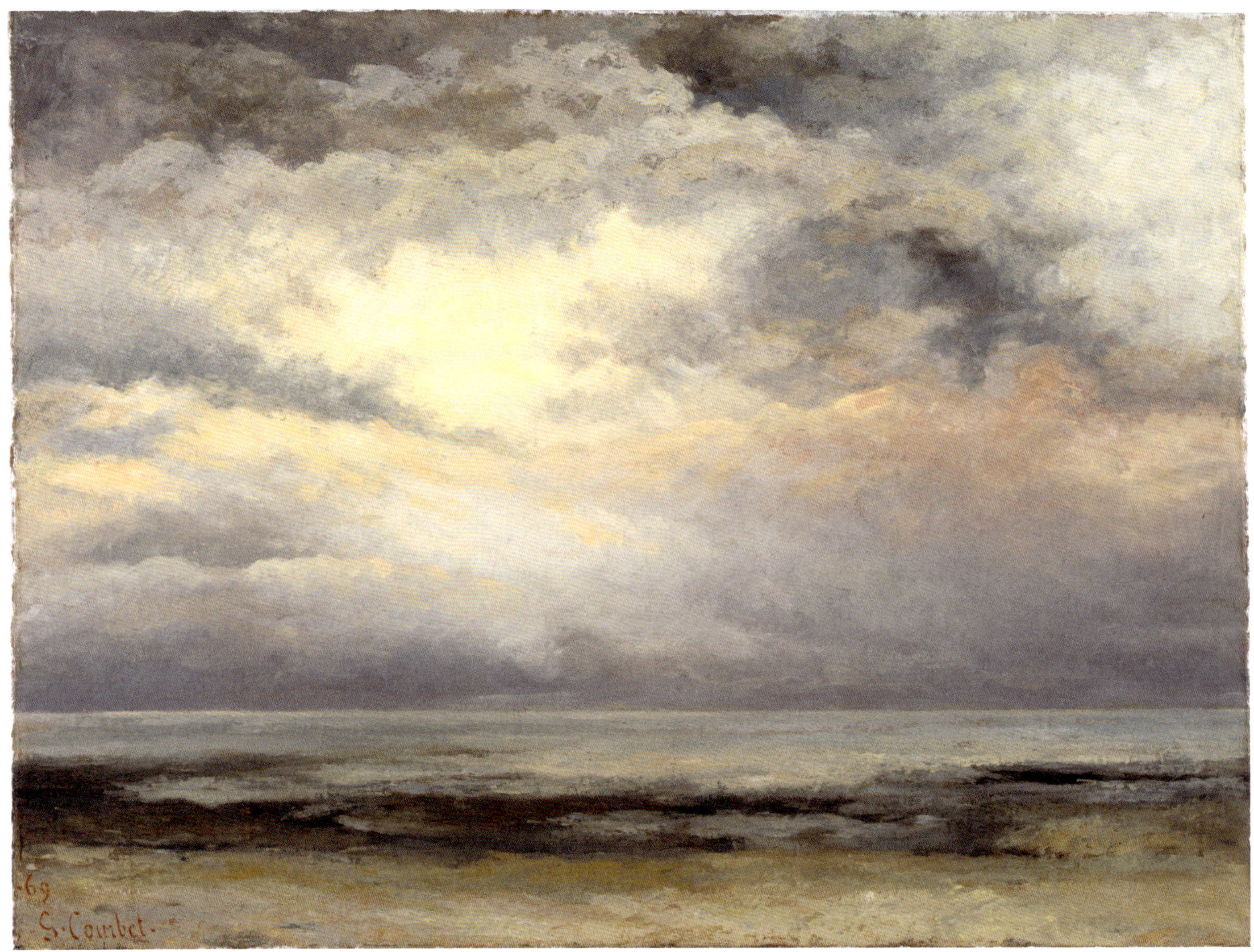


109. Gustave Courbet, *L'Immensité*, 1869, oil on canvas. Bequeathed by Constantine Alexander Ionides. V&A: CAI.59.

five generations of the family. Among the Old Master paintings are works by the Le Nain brothers, Poussin, Giandomenico Tiepolo and a self-portrait by Tintoretto (*c.*1548; fig.112).

Around 1880 Ionides bought from Rossetti his beguiling portrait of Smeralda Bandinelli by Sandro Botticelli (*c.*1473; fig.113). A few years earlier Ionides had seen in Rossetti's studio a chalk drawing of Jane Burden Morris, wife of William Morris, and commissioned a painting. The result was *The Day Dream* (1880; fig.116), Rossetti's fantasy portrait of her, for which he wrote an accompanying sonnet. From Burne-Jones, Ionides commissioned *The Mill* (begun 1870, completed 1882; fig.114) featuring his sister Aglaia and two other close members of the Anglo-Greek community, Marie Spartali and Maria Zambaco, known to their admirers as 'The Three Graces'.

Photographs record the collection in Constantine Ionides's home – 23 Second Avenue, Hove – in the late 1890s. The gallery extension, designed by Philip Webb (fig.115), took the form of a double octagon, for maximum wall space without corners, and was top-lit by daylight, as at Dulwich Picture Gallery and at the South Kensington Museum. The careful arrangement of the paintings, with sculptures by Rodin and Dalou (fig.117), set off by ceramics against panelling, reflects the influence of fashionable London galleries of the Aesthetic Movement era, such as the Grosvenor Gallery

**110.** Dante Gabriel Rossetti, *Maria Zambaco*, late 1860s, coloured chalks. Bequeathed by Constantine Alexander Ionides. V&A: CAI.1149.

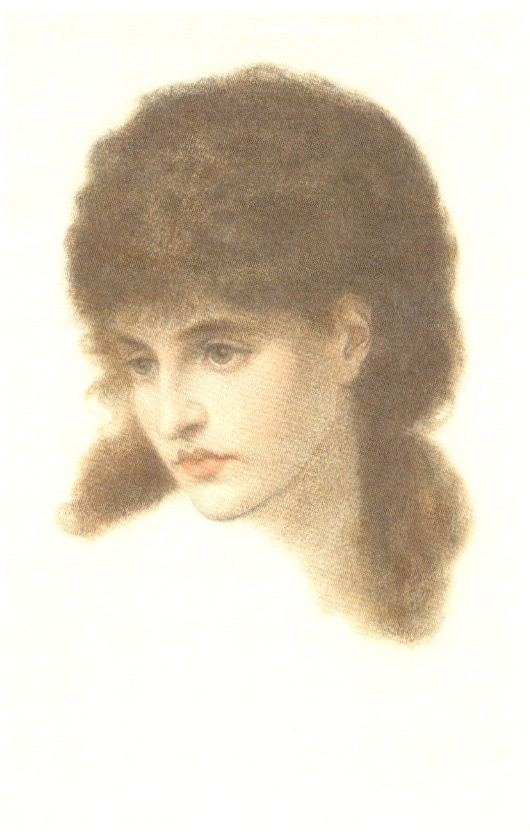

**111.** George Frederic Watts, *Zoe Ionides*, 1881, oil on canvas. Bequeathed by Constantine Alexander Ionides. V&A: CAI.1145.

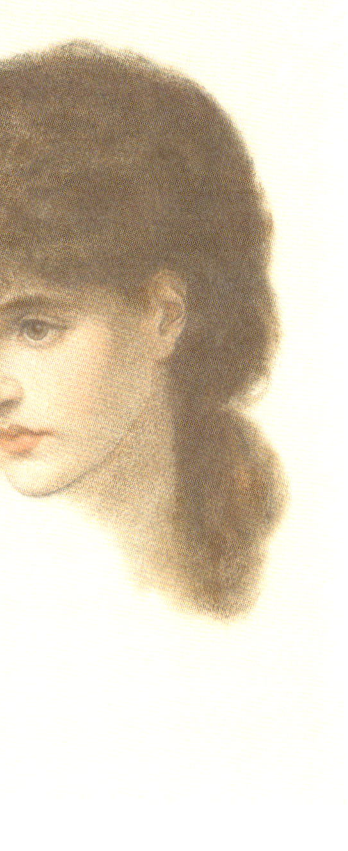

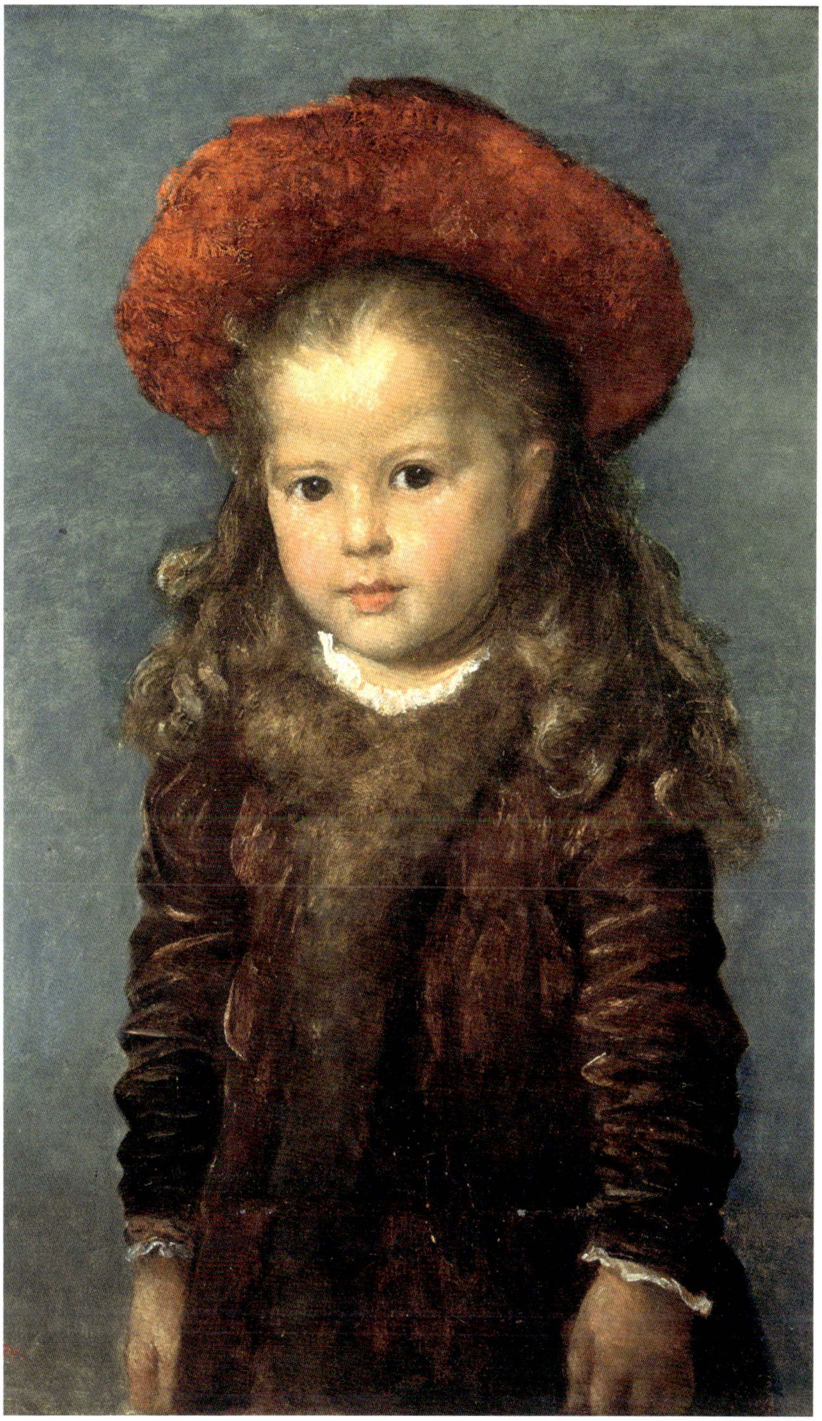

(opened in Bond Street in 1877), and of Rossetti's home in Chelsea, rather than the crowded walls of the Royal Academy and, indeed, of the South Kensington Museum's own paintings galleries.[3]

As with the terms of the Dyce, Jones, Schreiber and other bequests that each required their preservation as a named entity, Ionides's will specified that his was 'to be kept as one separate collection to be called "The Constantine Alexander Ionides Collection" and not distributed over the Museum or lent for exhibition'. The recurrence of such wording suggests that these conditions became a standard offer by museum directors when securing collections, despite the challenges to their successors in honouring them.

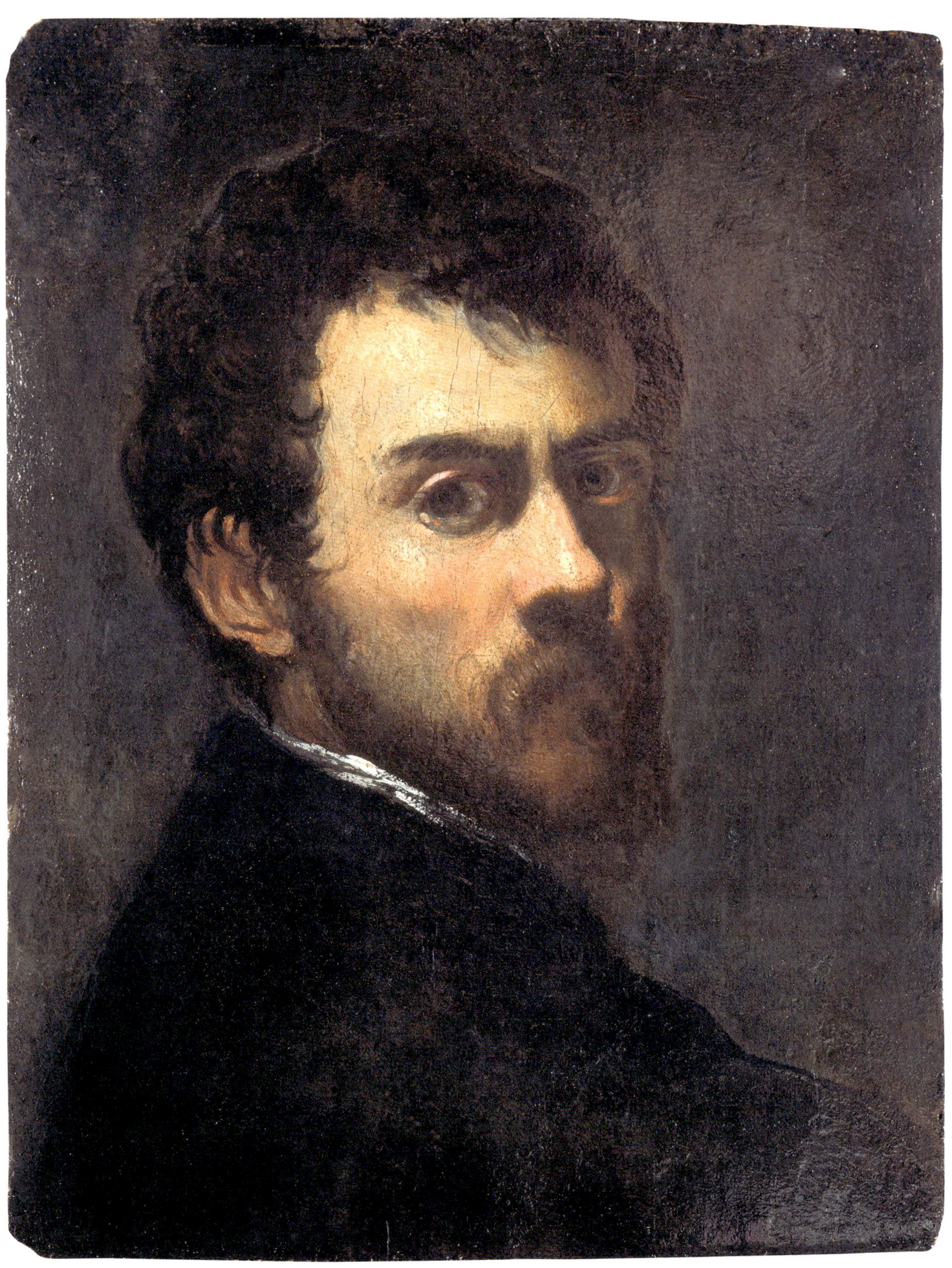

OPPOSITE:
**112.** JACOPO TINTORETTO, *Self-Portrait as a Young Man*, *c*.1548, oil on pine panel. Bequeathed by Constantine Alexander Ionides. V&A: CAI.103.

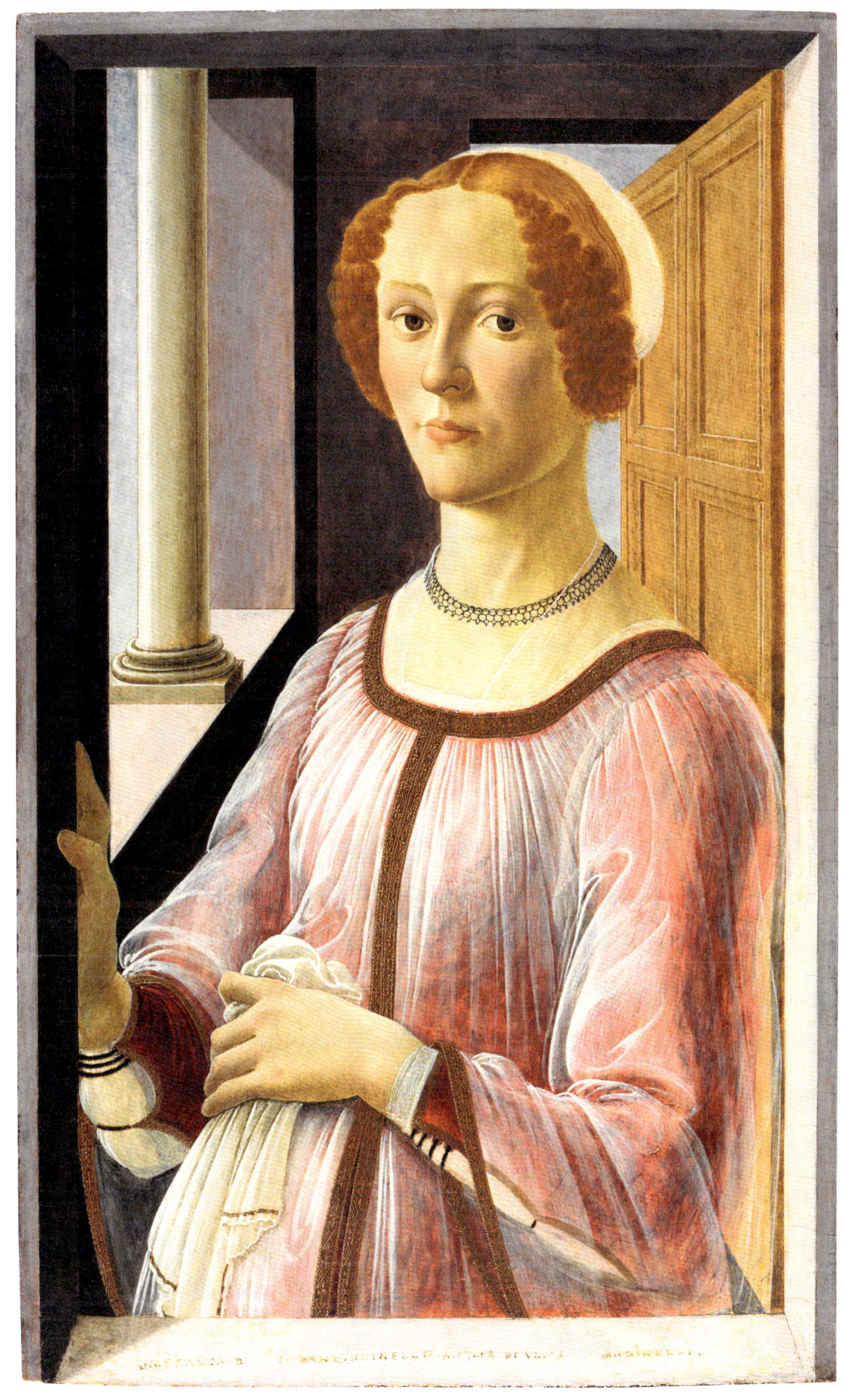

**113.** SANDRO BOTTICELLI, *Portrait of a Lady known as Smeralda Bandinelli*, *c*.1473, tempera on panel. Bequeathed by Constantine Alexander Ionides. V&A: CAI.100.

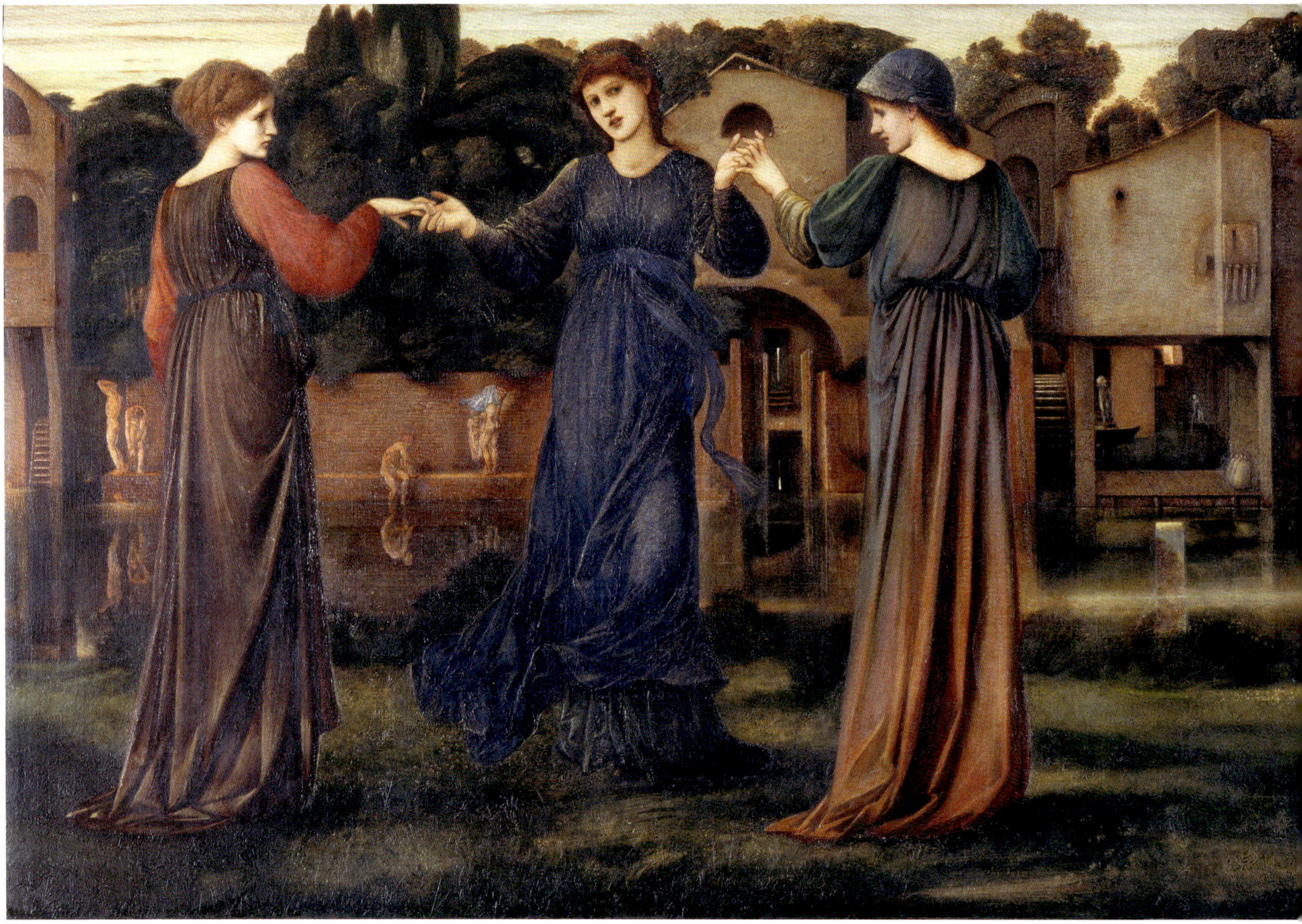

**114.** Edward Burne-Jones, *The Mill*, 1870 and 1882, oil on canvas. Bequeathed by Constantine Alexander Ionides. V&A: CAI.8.

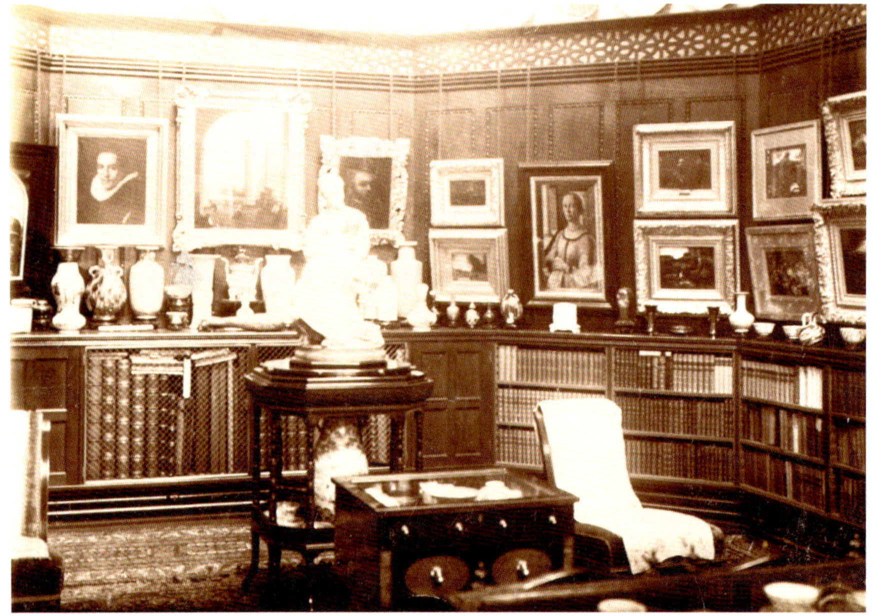

**115.** The Ionides family picture gallery at 23 Second Avenue, Hove, late 1890s, photograph from album bearing initials of Zoe Ionides. V&A: PH.2-1980.

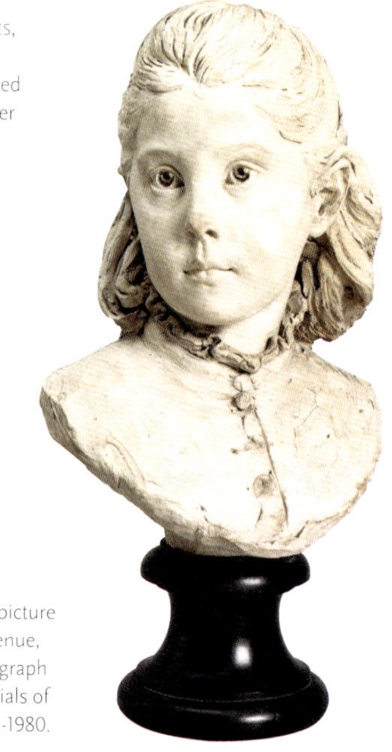

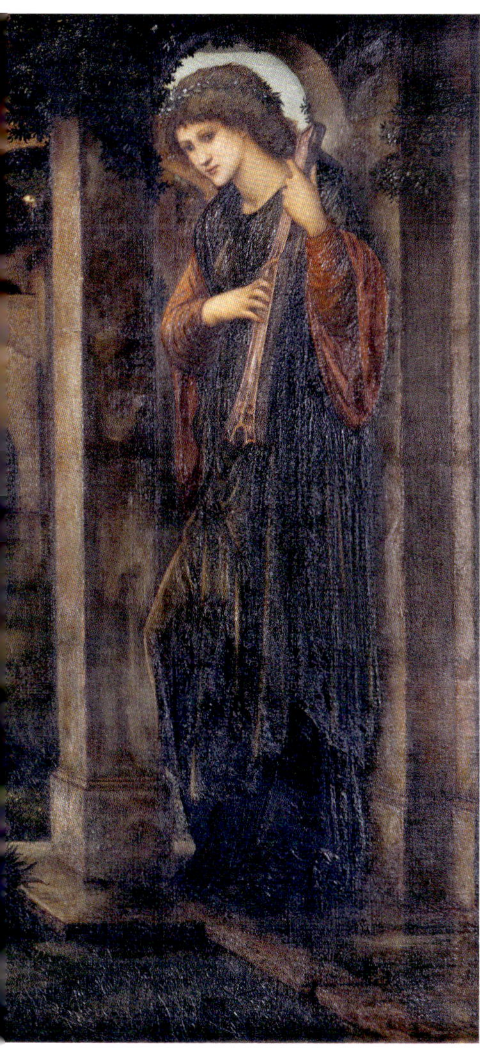

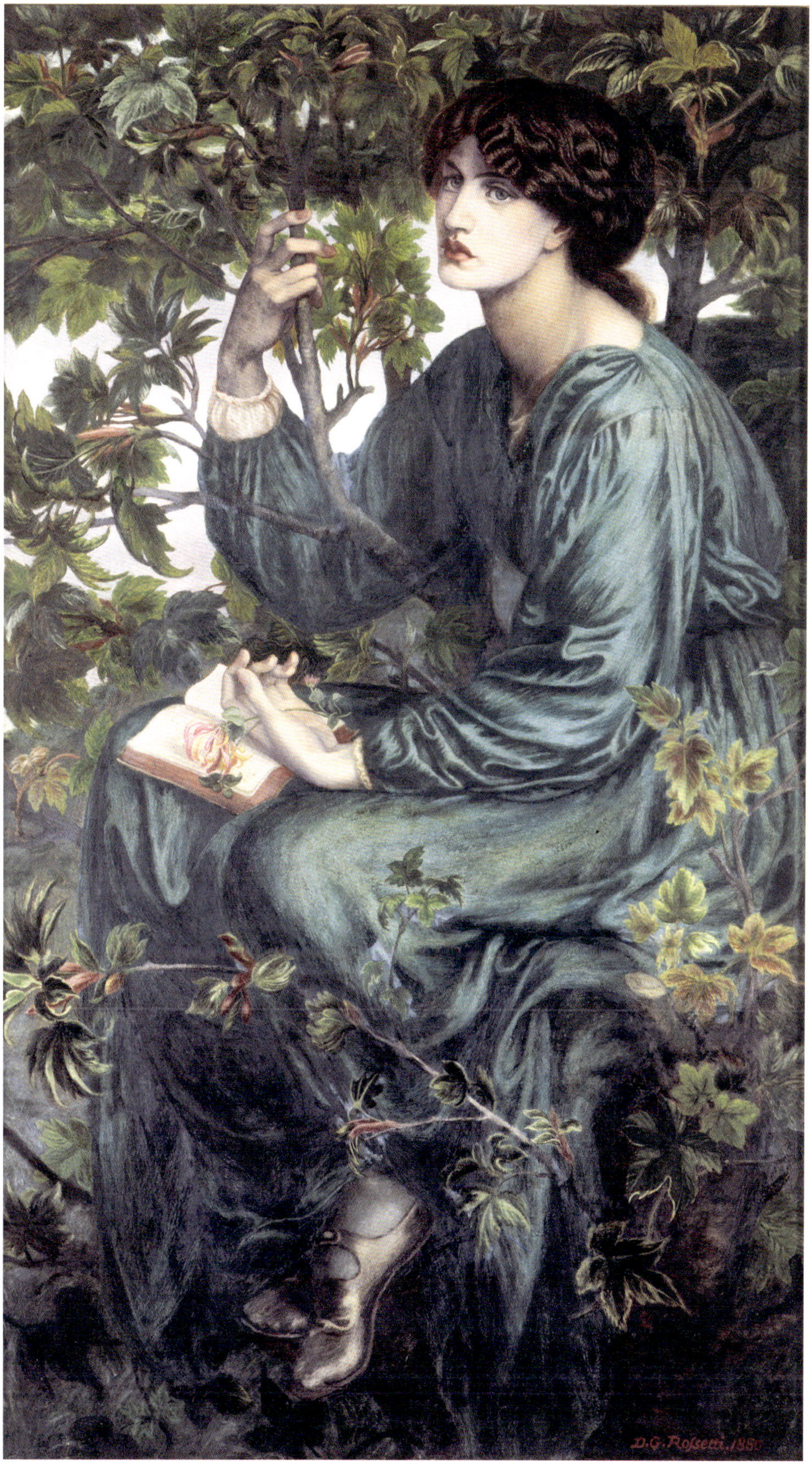

**116.** Dante Gabriel Rossetti, *The Day Dream*, 1880, oil on canvas. Bequeathed by Constantine Alexander Ionides. V&A: CAI.3.

**117.** Aime-Jules Dalou, *Miss Helen Ionides*, *c.*1879, terracotta. Given by the sitter, Miss Helen E. Ionides. V&A: A.10-1956.

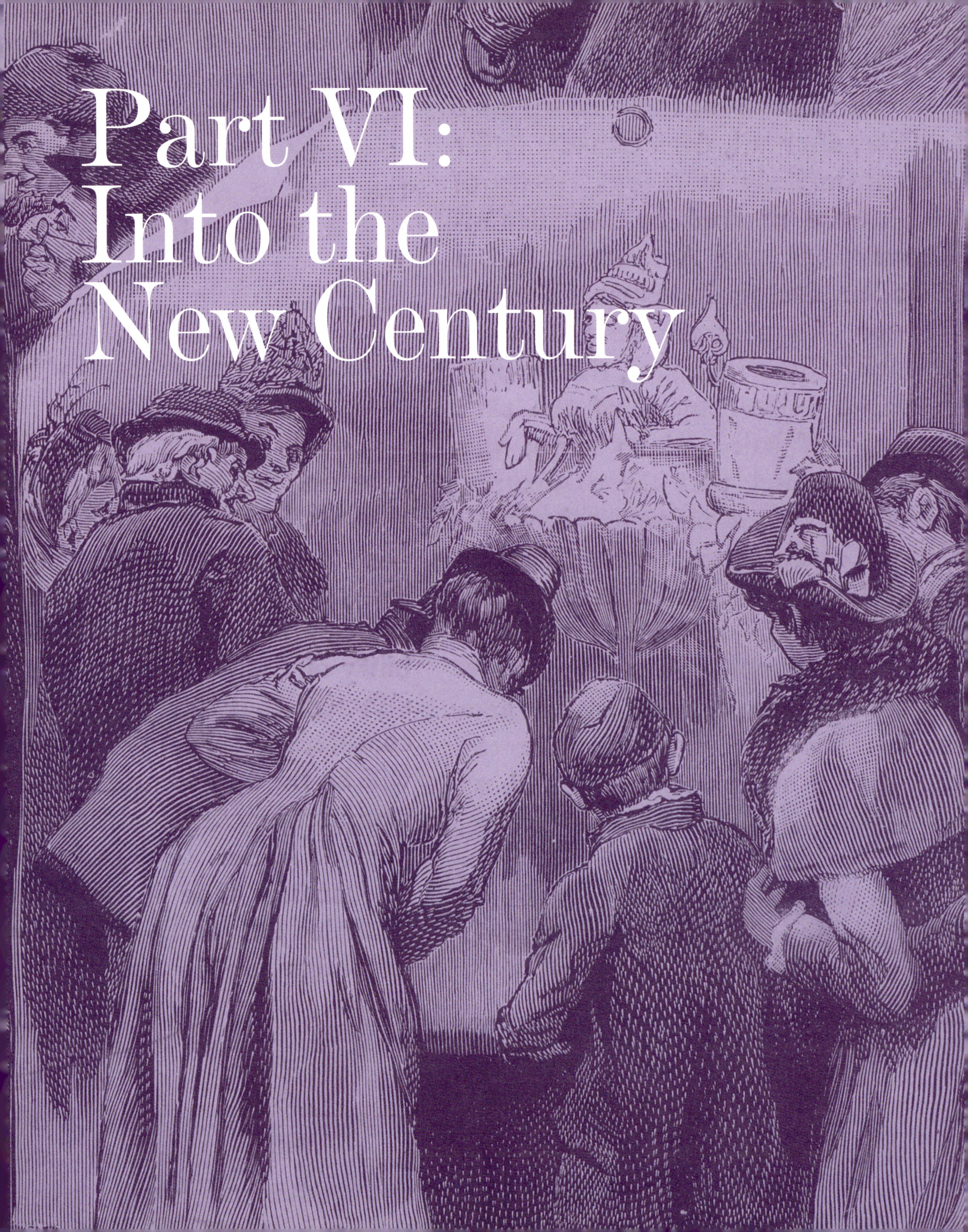

# Part VI: Into the New Century

In the first decade of the 20th century the V&A's civil-service masters subjected it to another fundamental review. Despite all the results of the Parliamentary Select Committee on Museums of the Science and Art Department (1897–8) it was found necessary to convene a 'Committee of Re-arrangement' (1908–9). This committee of independent outside experts was asked to advise on the best way to show collections in extensive new galleries that had doubled the size of the museum. Creative solutions were challenged by its brief: to return to the museum's initial aim of supporting the transformation of design in Britain. Its report led to the replacement of the director and to yet more controversy. The report did not, however, clarify the renewed commitment to contemporary art and design, which still wavered as a result of an outcry in 1900 over the acceptance of Art Nouveau furniture from Paris. Meanwhile the taste of collectors for Medieval and Renaissance decorative arts continued to be nourished through the largest ever bequest – from George Salting in 1909 – and through major long-term loans. However, in 1912 and 1913 the long-expected gifts of several thousand works of art already on loan from J.P. Morgan and from J.H. Fitzhenry disappeared. Their sudden departure left substantial gaps in the museum's representation of the history of art and design and prompted an internal review of the acquisitions to date. A more specific strategy was adopted in 1914 to set the V&A on a more secure path, one that would be less dependent on loans from private collectors.

# 16 Shock of the New: Art Nouveau and Rodin

THE MOST CONTROVERSIAL acquisition in the museum's history, the Donaldson Gift, in 1900, provides a fascinating case study for it raises questions as to the V&A's primary audience: students at the Royal College of Art and their teachers, competitive British manufacturers or the museum's multi-various visitors. The protests in *The Times* and the art press also reveal the key players in the world of art and design at that time, from academics to artists and the art trade (the V&A's director Caspar Purdon Clarke and his staff are conspicuous by their silence). The language of controversy also indicates the range of attitudes and values behind 'good taste', from British patriotism to xenophobia and from social paternalism to intellectual snobbery. Most significantly, the hostility towards the Donaldson Gift led to a policy against collecting the contemporary that lasted for decades.

From his gallery at 106 New Bond Street the antiques dealer George Donaldson (1845–1925) became, from 1884, a leading supplier to the museum of furniture, ceramics, tapestries, rugs and velvets. He also counted John Jones (see chapter 14) and George Salting (see chapter 17) among his regular clients.[1] At the Paris Expositions in 1899 and 1900, Donaldson served as the Vice President of the Jury of Awards for Furniture. Commissioned by the museum in 1900 to make a selection, with a limited budget, he became fascinated with the 'New Art', later known as Art Nouveau. Convinced that this must be the style of the future, he purchased for the V&A at his own expense his choice of 38 examples of furniture (figs 119–121), together with a vase designed by Georges Hoentschel. The museum also made its own purchases of glass, ceramics, textiles and metalwork. However, when shown at the V&A the following year his gift met with outrage. After initial display it was sent on tour, to museums in Birmingham, Edinburgh and Dublin, before the Donaldson Gift came to rest in the Bethnal Green Museum in 1909; there it remained into the late 1980s.[2]

Such was the controversy that for the first time a new donation carried a warning. When first installed in 1901 the collection had to carry a printed disclaimer, published by the Board of Education. Their *Public notice regarding 'New Art' furniture &c* pointed out that the furniture 'exhibits a style which is not consistent with the teaching at Art Schools in the United Kingdom'.[3] This followed a memorandum signed by the museum's Council for Advice for Art (forerunner of the trustees): Walter Crane, Sir William Blake Richmond, T.G. Jackson and Onslow Ford. All objected formally to the acquisition. The designer Lewis F. Day protested at these 'ill-mannered specimens of upstart art' which must not be 'endorsed by the educational authorities'.[4] The journal *The Artist* described it as 'this fungus kind of work' and the sculptor George Frampton warned 'it is made on the Continent and used by parents and others to frighten naughty children'.[5] An article in the *Architectural Review* dismissed Donaldson's collection as 'pretentious trash . . . wretched in design and construction', as evidence of 'design-disease', and recommended that examples of contemporary 'art ought to be

**118.** Auguste Rodin, *'The Age of Bronze'* (*L'Age d'Airain*), bronze, sand cast, Alexis Rudier, before July 1914 after a model of *c.*1876–77. The gift of Auguste Rodin. V&A: A.33-1914.

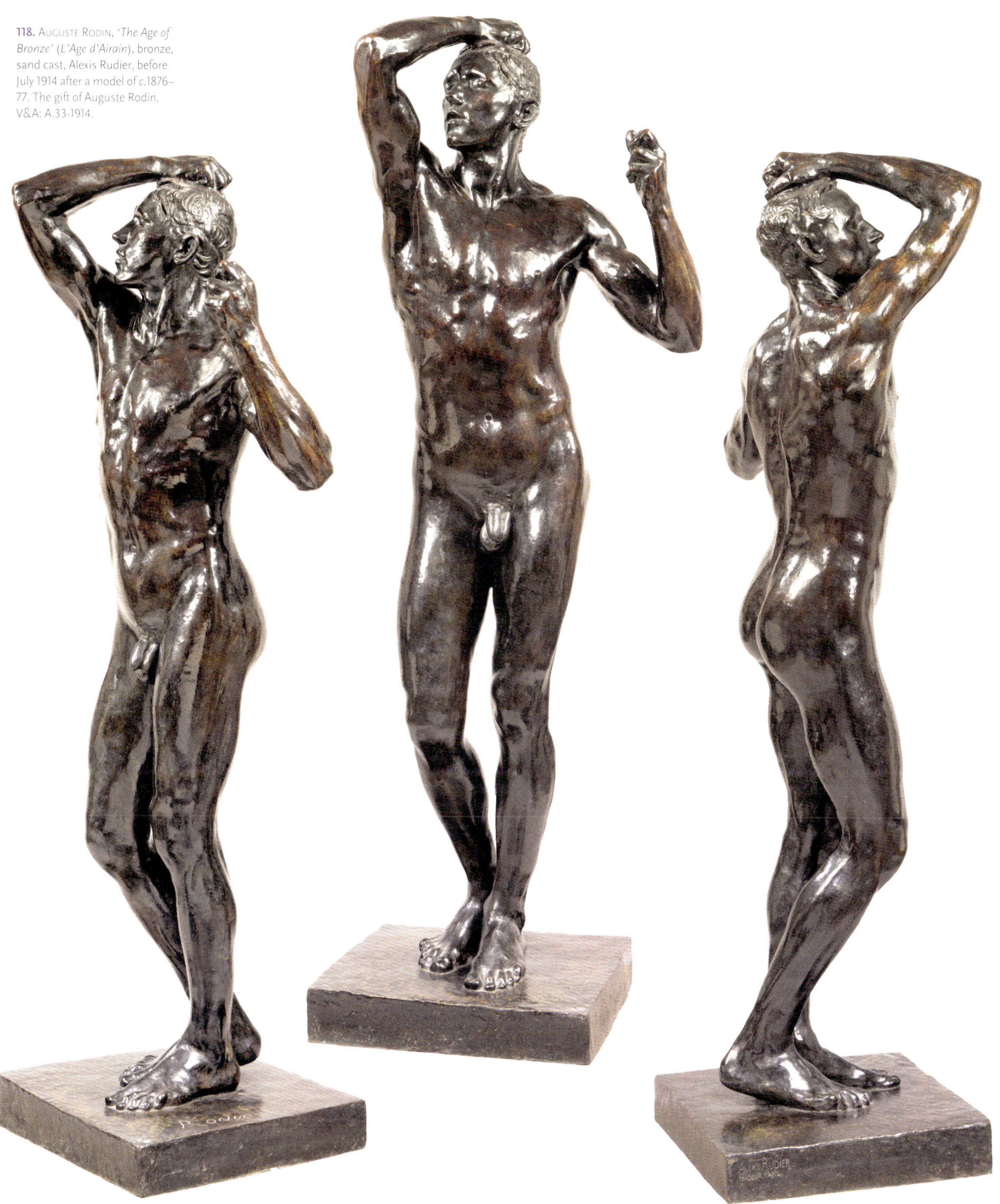

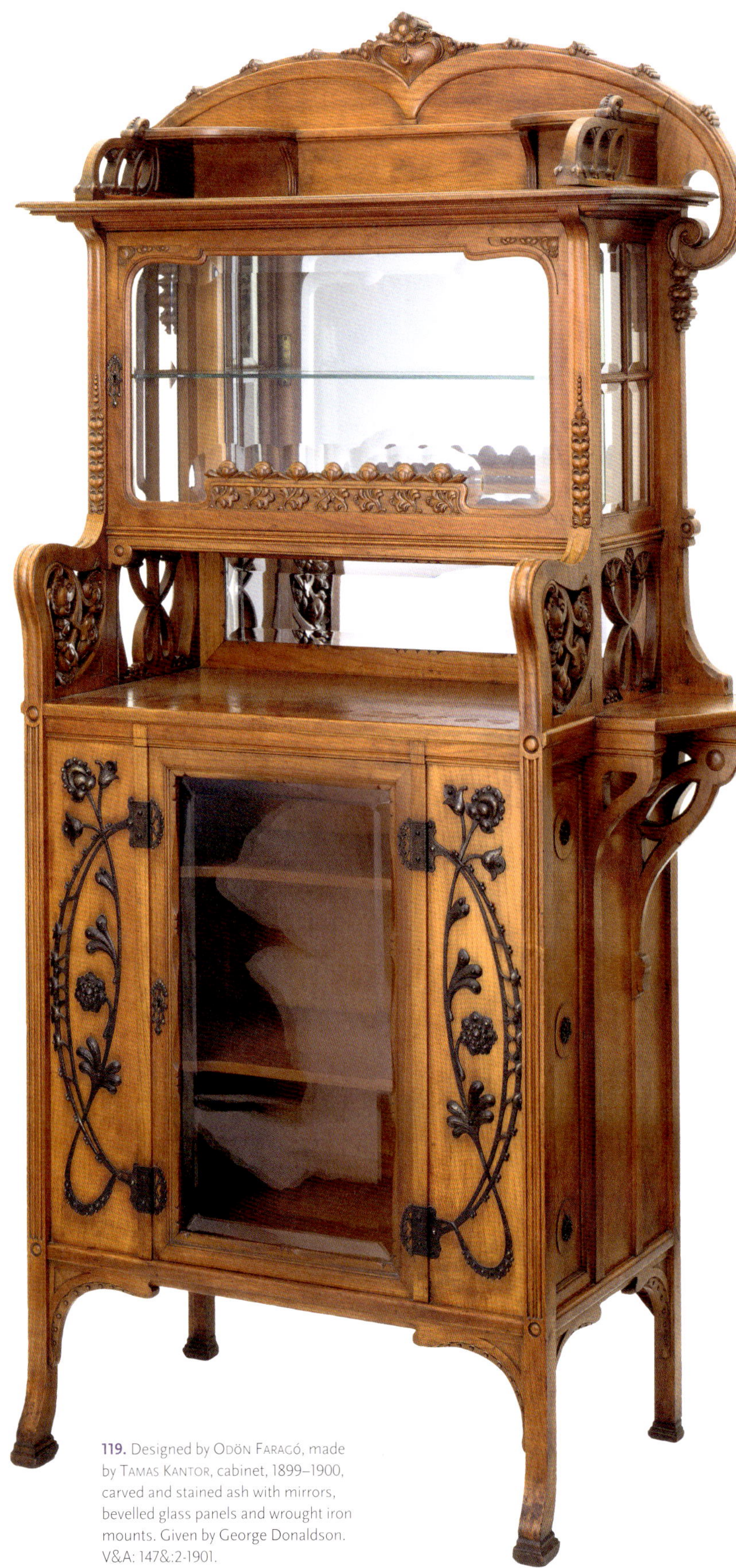

**119.** Designed by Odön Faragó, made by Tamas Kantor, cabinet, 1899–1900, carved and stained ash with mirrors, bevelled glass panels and wrought iron mounts. Given by George Donaldson. V&A: 147&:2-1901.

filtered through the appreciation of a generation at least before they are taken into our museums'.[6] Concerns included the use of expensive timbers as pictorial veneers and a sense of excessive virtuosity, as in the manipulation of wood through steam engineering. The basic issue was a patriotic urge to defend traditional values associated with British design, craft and materials against the influence of foreign rivals.

This controversy reinforced the museum's reluctance to collect works less than 50 years old, a policy that continued into the 1950s.[7] The Committee of Re-arrangement (1908–9; see chapter 19) observed 'the principle of admitting modern specimens presents grave difficulties; taste is apt to change with time; and the admission of the work of any one living manufacturer or craftsman would not improbably expose the administration to attack from others, and even to the charge of advertising for ulterior ends'.[8]

Despite this resolution, in 1914 the V&A agreed to accept on loan a group of sculptures by Auguste Rodin; the artist called it a collection 'he had been all his life forming'.[9] The sculptures had been stranded in London on the outbreak of war after an exhibition of modern French art at the Grosvenor Gallery closed. In November 1914 Rodin offered to turn the loan into a gift, the only one he made in his lifetime to a foreign country and the largest gift ever to the V&A from a living artist. Fortunately, the director, Sir Cecil Harcourt Smith (1859–1944), and the assistant keeper for sculpture, Eric Maclagan, could not resist. The V&A's overseers at the Board of Education objected that modern French art was beyond the museum's collecting field, but Harcourt Smith had chaired the Committee of Re-arrangement and pointed out that it allowed for exceptions to the rule, for the benefit of art students. At a stroke, a precedent was set; the new policy over collecting the contemporary could be overruled, at least by the brave.

120. Louis Majorelle, armchair, 1899–1900, carved walnut, stained; back and seat covered with embroidered and painted satin with a fringe (reproduction of the original upholstery). Given by George Donaldson. V&A: 2001-1900.

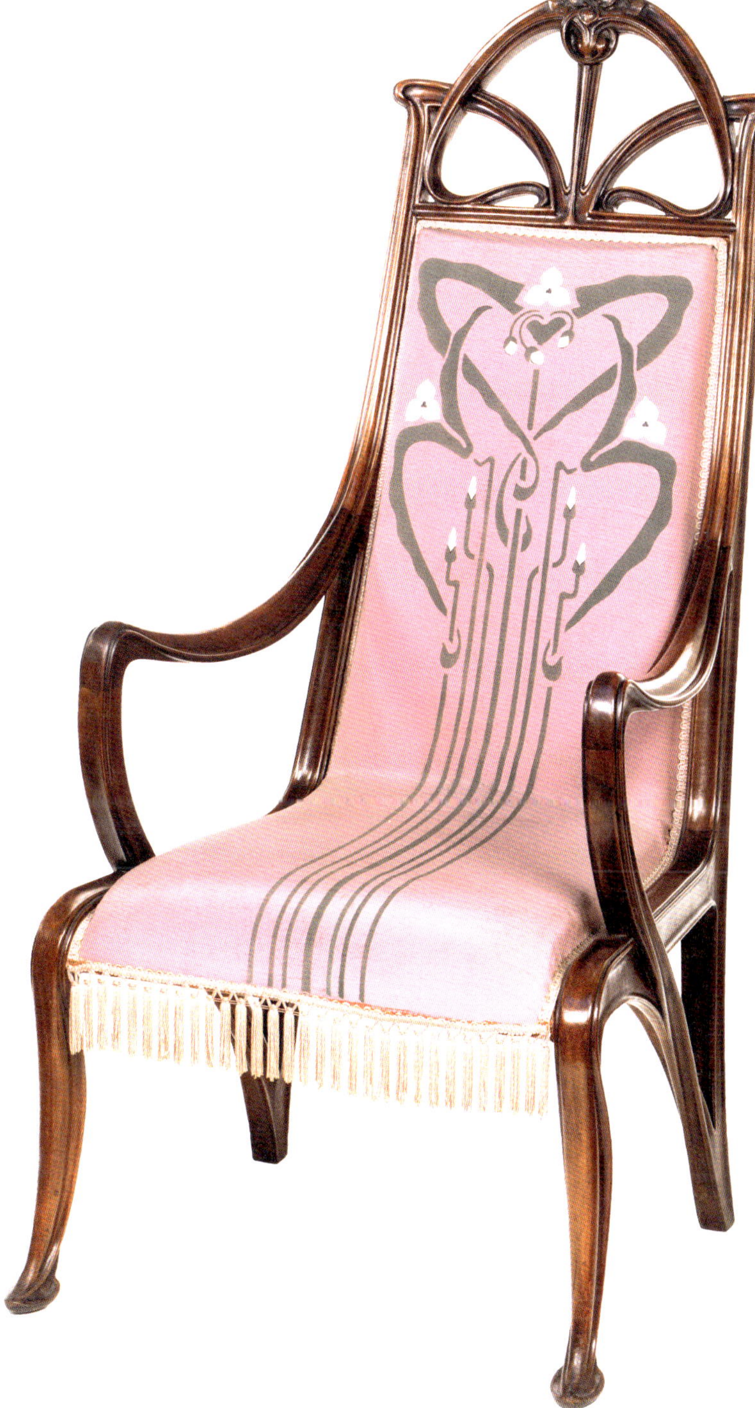

121. Louis Majorelle, cabinet, *c.*1900, solid purpleheart, and veneers of kingwood on a carcase of oak, beech and softwood. Given by George Donaldson. V&A: 1999:1 to 4-1900.

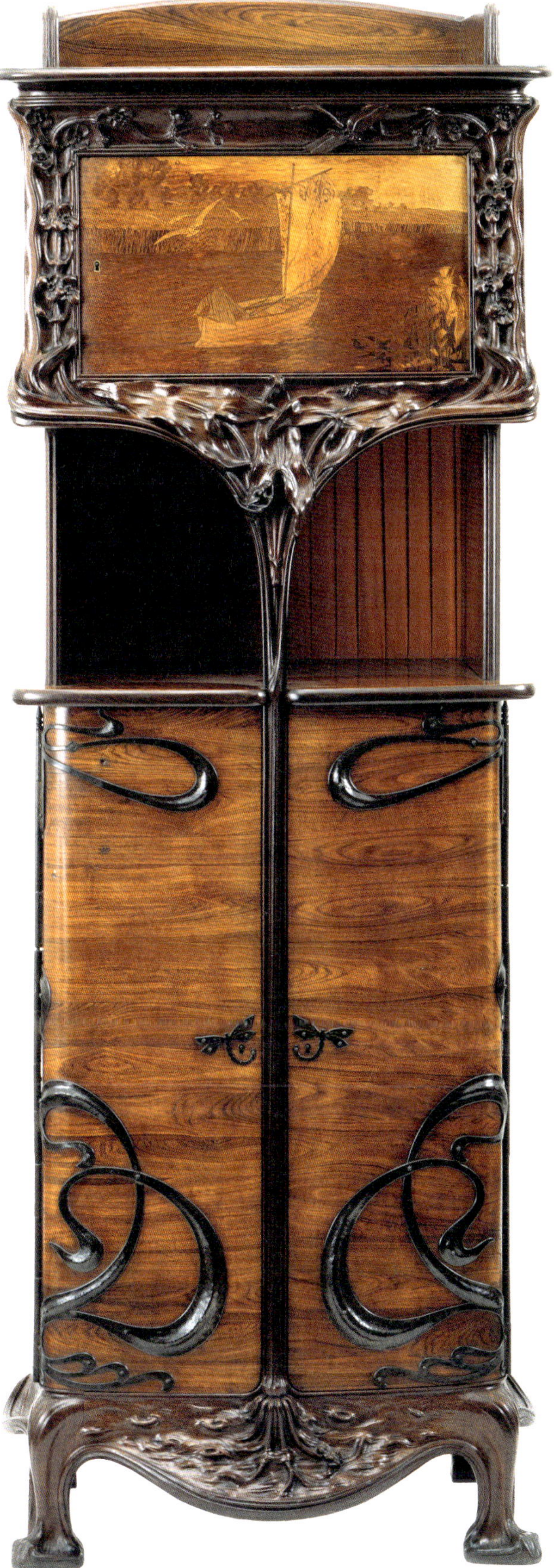

# 17 The V&A's Greatest Collector-Donor: George Salting

IN ITS OBITUARY for George Salting (1835–1909) *The Times* paid tribute to him as 'the greatest English art collector of this age, perhaps of any age'.[1] Salting's magnificent bequest of over 2,500 objects is still the largest single private gift to the V&A.[2] The quantity, quality and range is extraordinary, for there are key examples of Chinese and Japanese ceramics (1,405 items), Iranian carpets, medieval ivories, medieval and Renaissance manuscripts and cuttings, Renaissance bronzes, portrait miniatures and prints and drawings. Salting's collection evolved in the public eye, on loan to the museum for 35 years. Visitors never knew which pieces would stay on display as 'the prince of weeders'[3] refined his collection through sales, exchanges and new purchases. After his death five rooms were devoted to the Salting Collection in the V&A's new suites of galleries along Cromwell Road that opened in 1909. A picture postcard sent in March 1911 records in gallery 145 his first love (in 29 showcases): 'The Salting Collection of Chinese and Japanese Pottery' (fig.10).

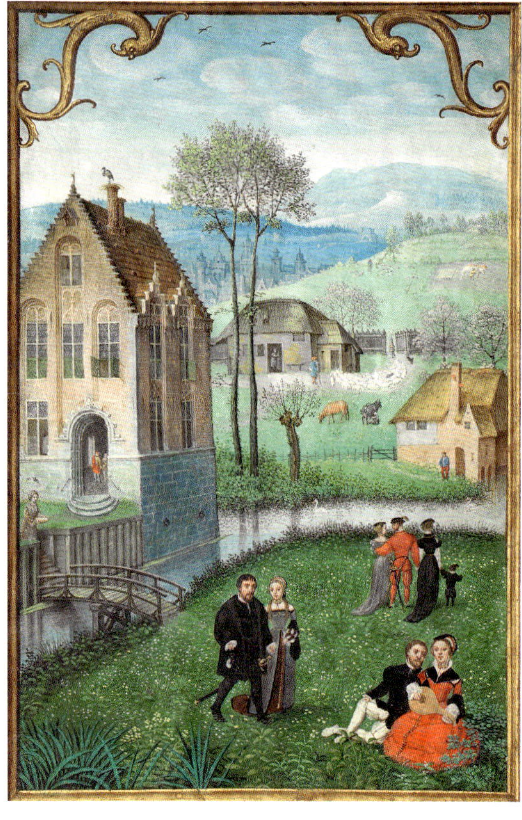

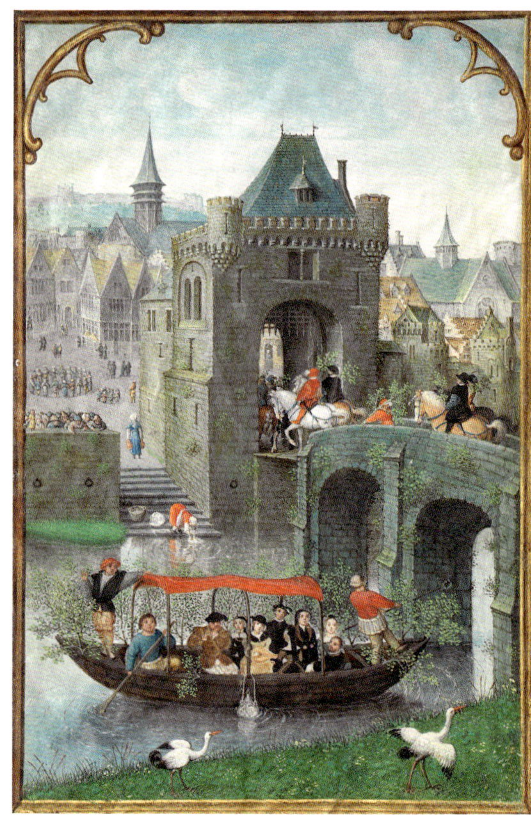

**122 a, b.** SIMON BENNINCK, *The Month of April; The Month of May*, leaf from a calendar of a book of hours, *c.*1540, bodycolour on vellum. Bequeathed by George Salting. V&A: E.4575-1910. One side of this page from a book shows courting couples in a field in April, the reverse shows a May Day boating party, floral procession and dancing.

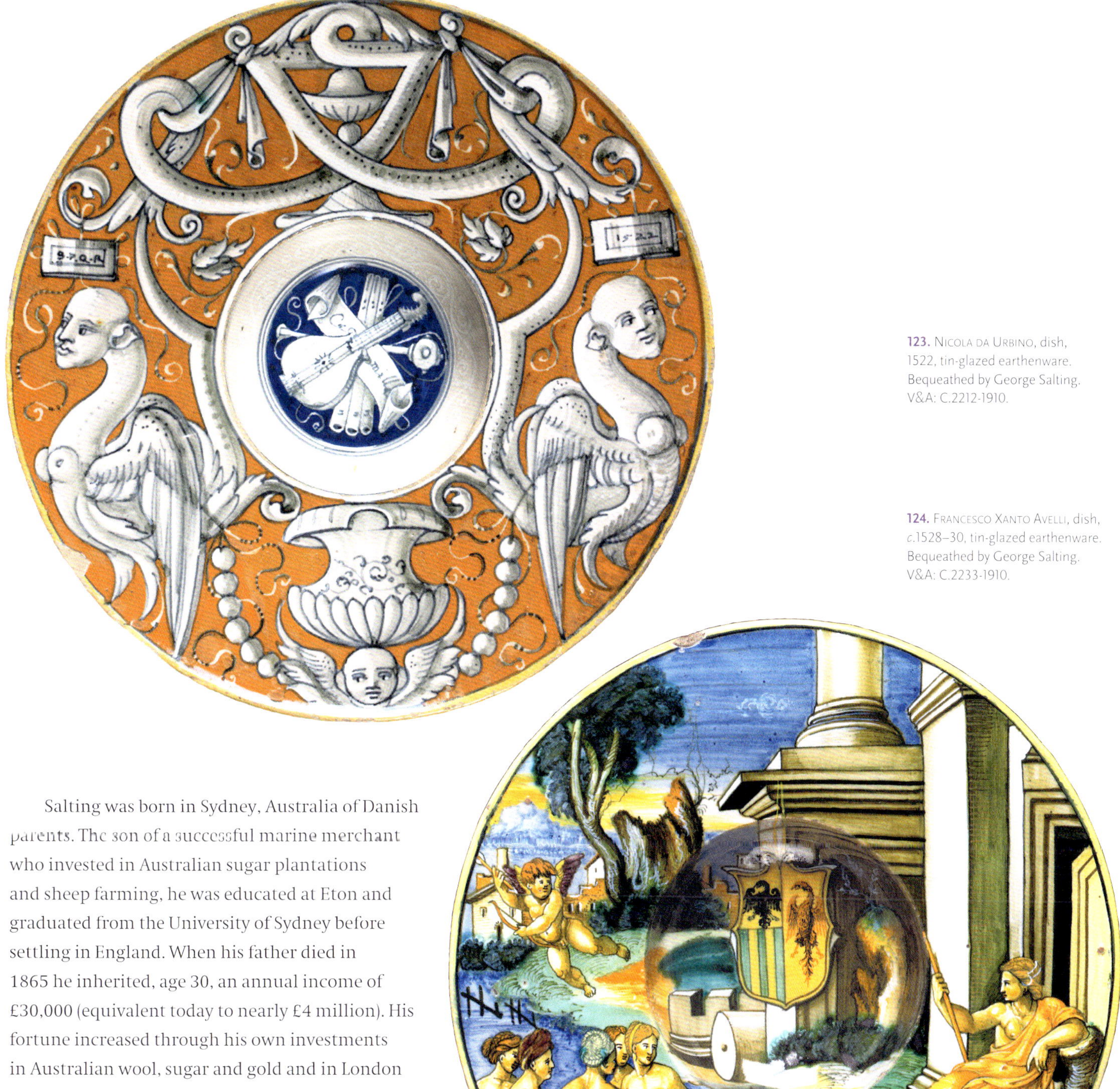

**123.** Nicola da Urbino, dish, 1522, tin-glazed earthenware. Bequeathed by George Salting. V&A: C.2212-1910.

**124.** Francesco Xanto Avelli, dish, *c.*1528–30, tin-glazed earthenware. Bequeathed by George Salting. V&A: C.2233-1910.

Salting was born in Sydney, Australia of Danish parents. The son of a successful marine merchant who invested in Australian sugar plantations and sheep farming, he was educated at Eton and graduated from the University of Sydney before settling in England. When his father died in 1865 he inherited, age 30, an annual income of £30,000 (equivalent today to nearly £4 million). His fortune increased through his own investments in Australian wool, sugar and gold and in London property developments. As a bachelor with no other commitments, he was happy spending his days in art dealers' galleries, auction houses and at his club. Salting was satisfied with his simple accommodation, two large, rented rooms above the Thatched House Club, 86 St James's Street, where

**125.** Hans Holbein, *Anne of Cleves*, 1539, watercolour on vellum. Bequeathed by George Salting. V&A: P.153:1, 2-1910.

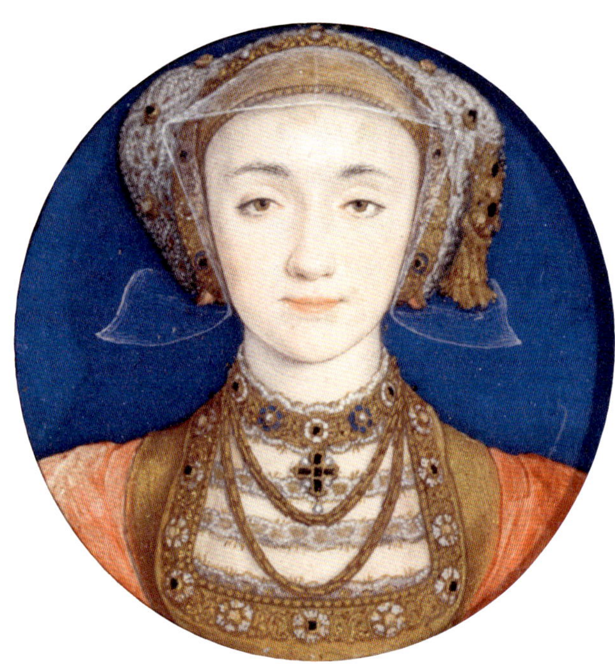

**126.** Isaac Oliver, *A Girl, aged Five, Holding a Carnation*, 1590, watercolour on vellum, inscribed: 'Ano Dm 1590/Aetatis Suae 5'. Bequeathed by George Salting. V&A: P.146-1910.

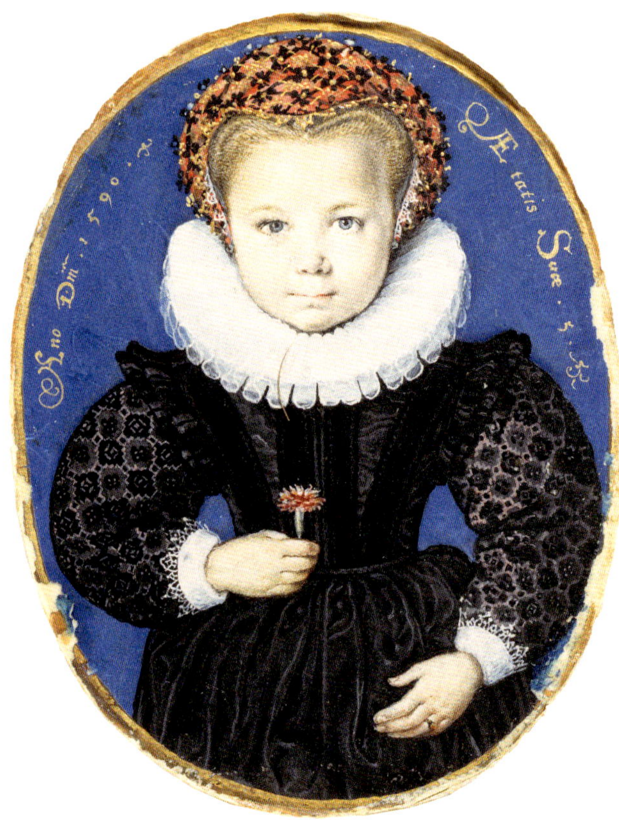

**127.** Nicholas Hilliard, *Young Man among Roses*, *c.*1587, watercolour on vellum. Bequeathed by George Salting. V&A: P.163-1910.

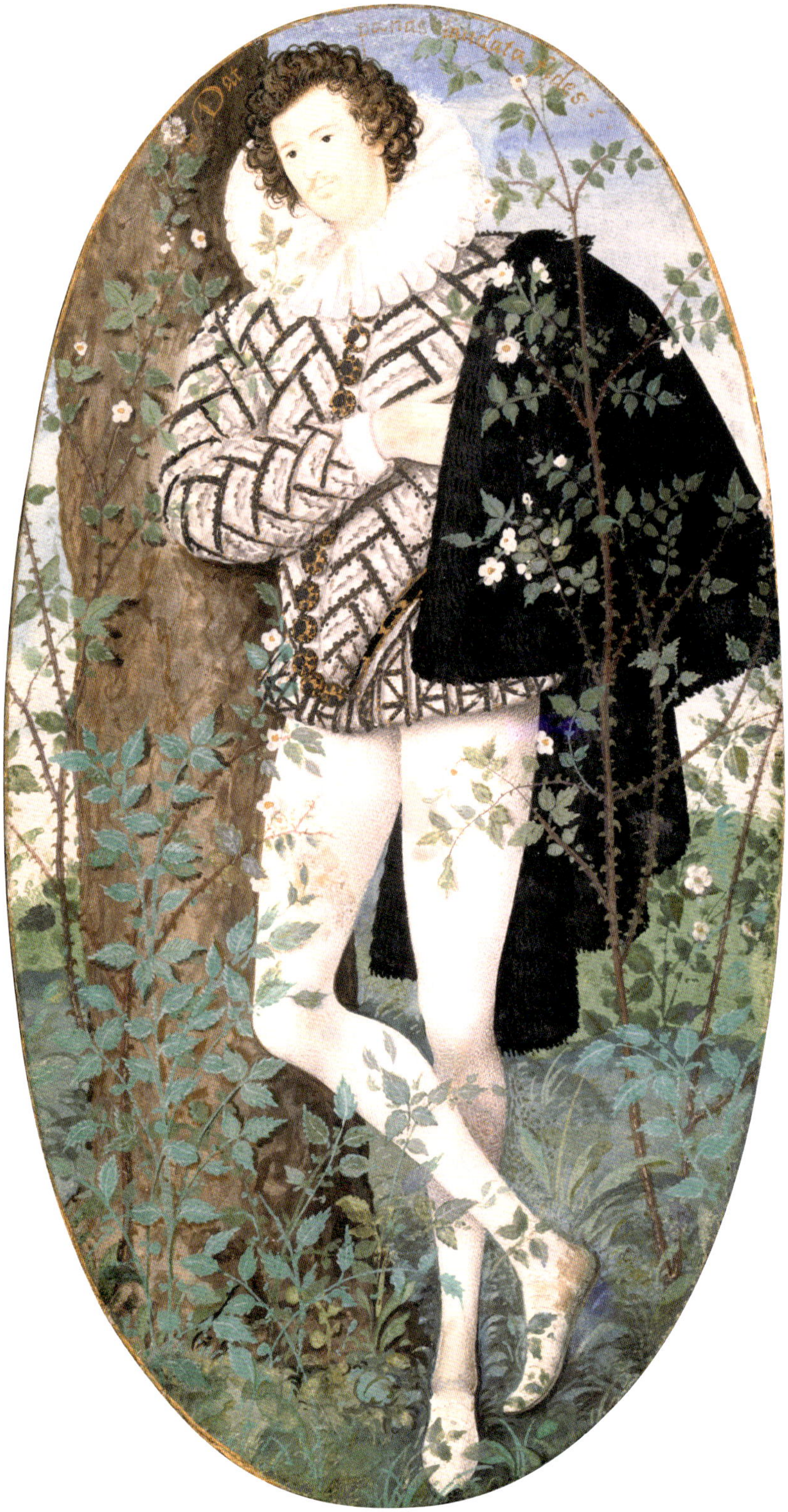

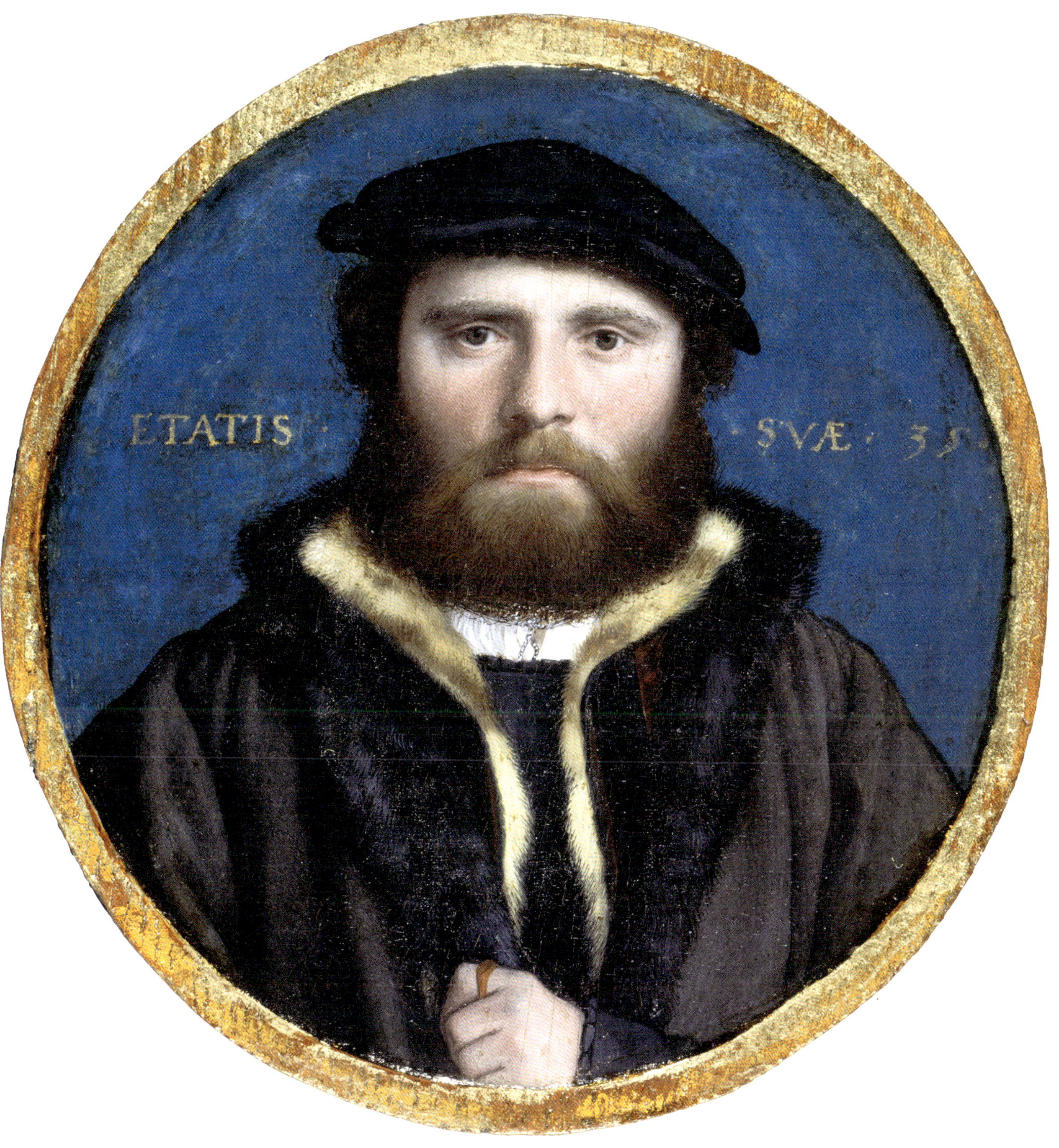


**128.** Hans Holbein, *Hans of Antwerp*, *c.*1532, oil on panel. Bequeathed by George Salting. V&A: P.158:2-1910.

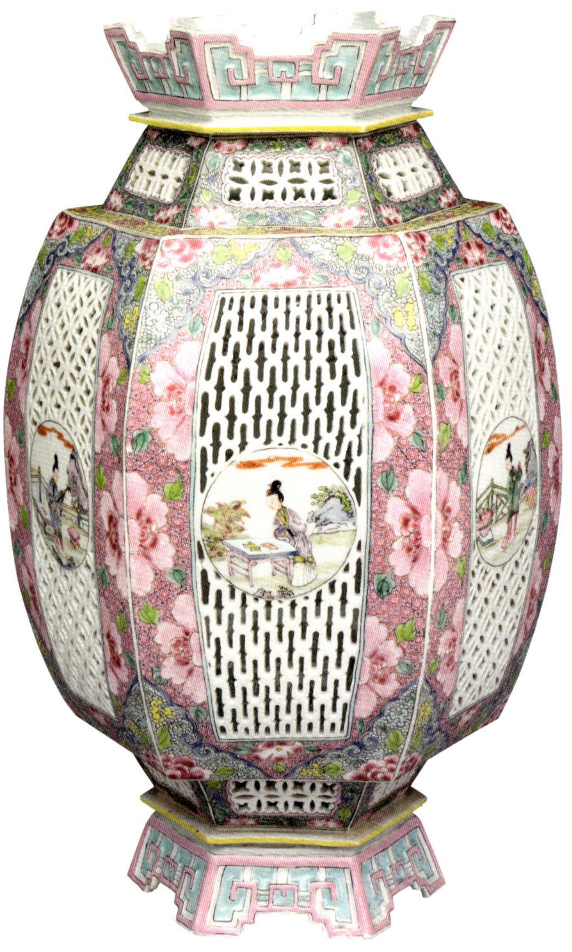

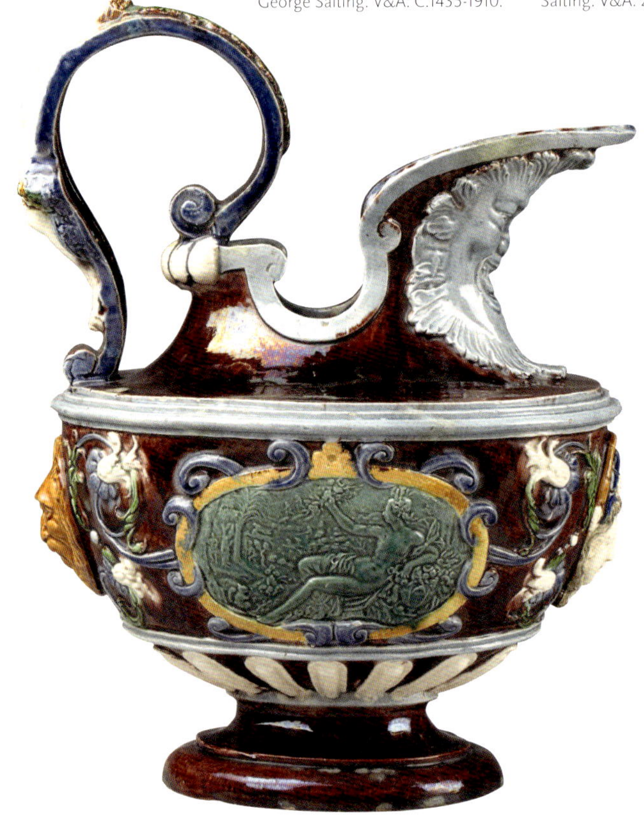

**129.** Unknown maker (China), lantern, *c.*1725–50, porcelain, pierced and painted with overglaze enamels. Bequeathed by George Salting. V&A: C.1435-1910.

**130.** Bernard Palissy (or close follower), ewer, *c.*1580–1600, earthenware with moulded decoration. Bequeathed by George Salting. V&A: 2305-1910.

he lived for the rest of his life. But he was not alone, for as *The Times* described, 'these rooms are like the apartments of Balzac's Cousin Pons for every corner is filled to congestion with masterpieces of the great artists of Italy, Holland and England stacked up in every available corner'.[4]

He found his other friends among experts. Salting formed his collection with the help of Arthur Skinner (1861–1911), who served as Keeper of the Art Museum and as Assistant Director of the V&A before succeeding Caspar Purdon Clarke as director in 1905. Salting also sought advice from A.W. Franks, Keeper of British and Medieval Antiquities at the British Museum, from his deputy and successor Charles Hercules Read, from the leading dealer Murray Marks, and from J.H. Fitzhenry, C.D.E. Fortnum and Wilhelm von Bode. He began with Chinese porcelain. As the collection outgrew his bachelor flat, he placed his ceramics on loan to the museum from 1874. In 1884 he was invited to join the museum's new committee of Art Referees. The auctions of the collections of Sir Andrew Fountaine (1884), Eugène Piot (1890; see chapter 8) and the dealer Frédéric Spitzer (1893) gave him opportunities to diversify. At Spitzer's sale in Paris, held over 70 days, he bid in person for nearly one-tenth of the 3,369 lots, spending £35,000 (today nearly £5 million) and sending his new acquisitions direct to the museum (figs 131–133). Salting also acquired master drawings at the sale of the museum's former curator, J.C. Robinson (1902). Other museums competed for his attention, but it was Skinner, according to *The Times*, 'who, above all others, had kept Mr Salting loyal to South Kensington'.[5]

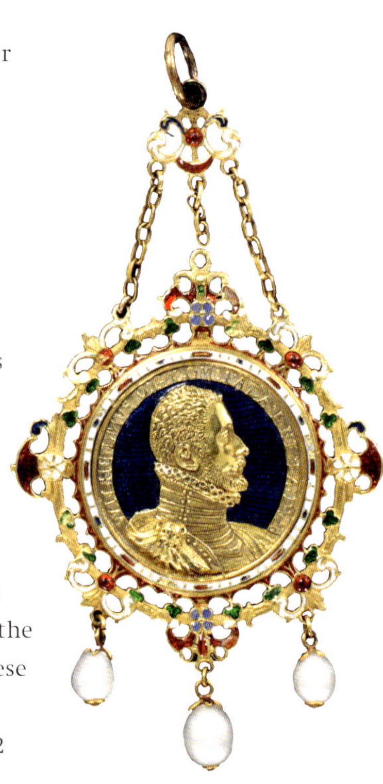

A map of the V&A published in 1905 entices visitors to the east side of the South Court with the promise of the 'Salting Loan Collection of Chinese Porcelain, Majolica, Enamels etc'.[6] On his death four years later, in accordance with his will, 192

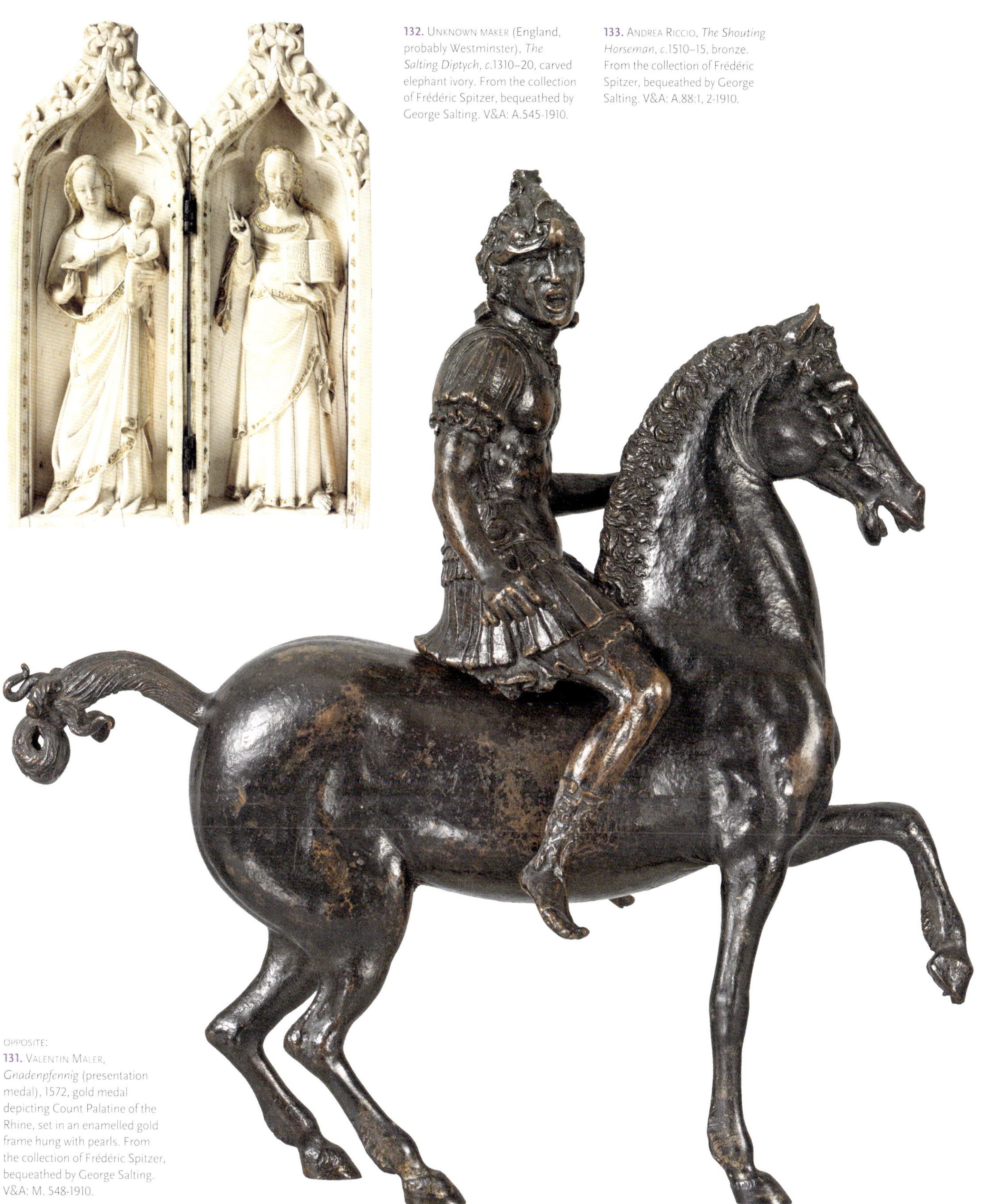

**132.** Unknown maker (England, probably Westminster), *The Salting Diptych*, *c.*1310–20, carved elephant ivory. From the collection of Frédéric Spitzer, bequeathed by George Salting. V&A: A.545-1910.

**133.** Andrea Riccio, *The Shouting Horseman*, *c.*1510–15, bronze. From the collection of Frédéric Spitzer, bequeathed by George Salting. V&A: A.88:1, 2-1910.

opposite:
**131.** Valentin Maler, *Gnadenpfennig* (presentation medal), 1572, gold medal depicting Count Palatine of the Rhine, set in an enamelled gold frame hung with pearls. From the collection of Frédéric Spitzer, bequeathed by George Salting. V&A: M. 548-1910.

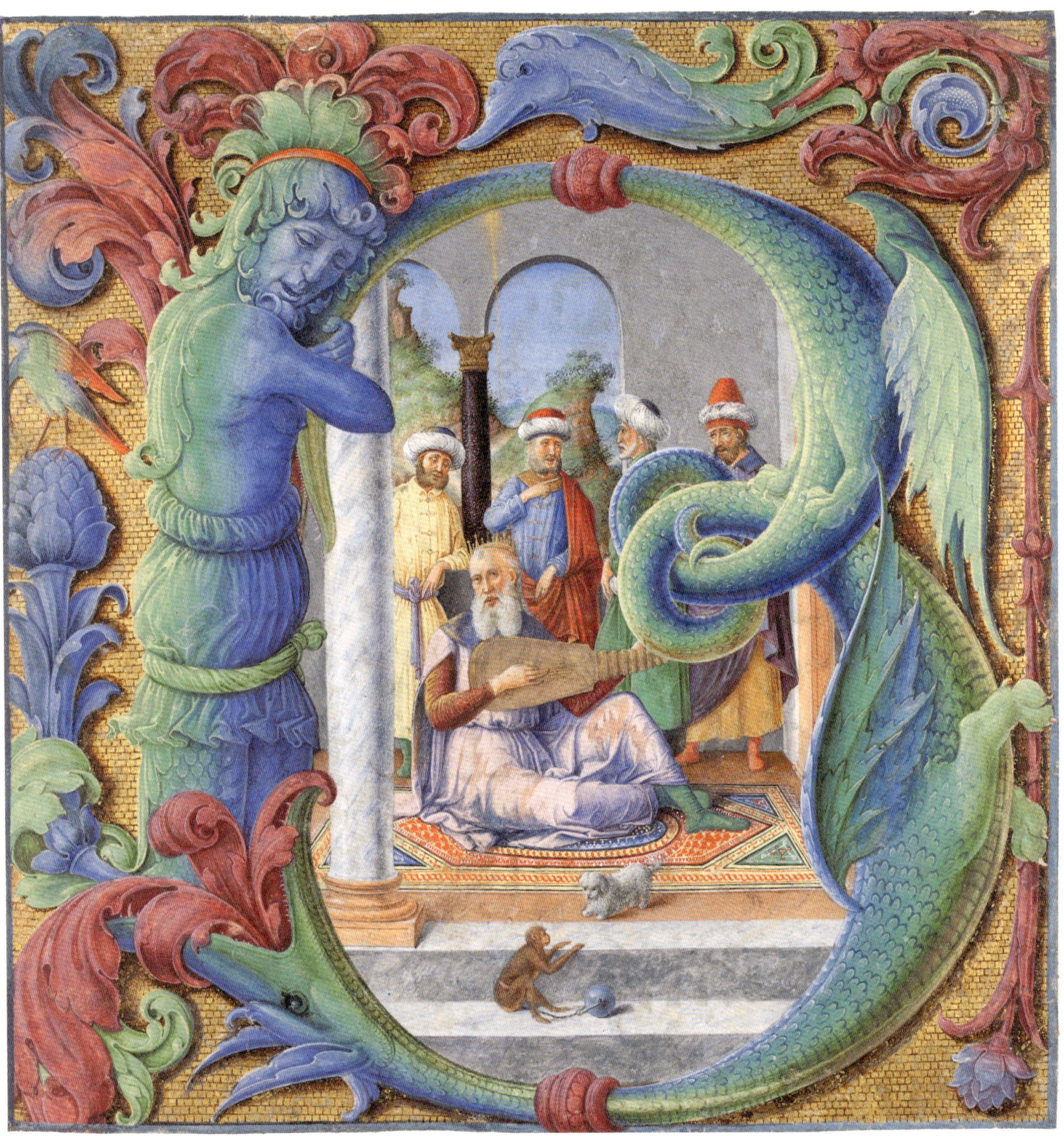

**134.** Girolamo and Francesco dai Libri (attrib.), historiated initial with King David playing the lute, illuminated *c.*1495–1505, manuscript cutting from a choir book, Verona. Bequeathed by David Martin Currie. V&A: E. 1168-1921.

paintings were selected by the National Gallery (in addition to three lent since 1900) including works by Constable, Memling, Verrocchio and Vermeer. The British Museum chose 151 prints and 291 drawings and watercolours. The V&A sought to acquire his portrait miniatures but they were not identified as such in his will and a rival claim from the British Museum for them as 'drawings' had to be resolved by the Law Officers of the Crown, who found in the V&A's favour. In his will he specified that his collection at the V&A should be 'kept at the said Museum, and not distributed over the various sections but kept all together according to the various specialities of my exhibits'.[7] The collector's death brought some stability to the displays, but the sheer range of his collection presented other challenges, both to the new policy of arranging the galleries by specific material, and to the museum's new materials-based curatorial structure (see chapter 5).

According to *The Times* Salting bought 'nothing but the best and rarest', with good condition and interesting provenance also guiding his choices.[8] Despite the years of advice from Skinner and other museums' staff, Salting did not aim, like a curator, to create a didactic

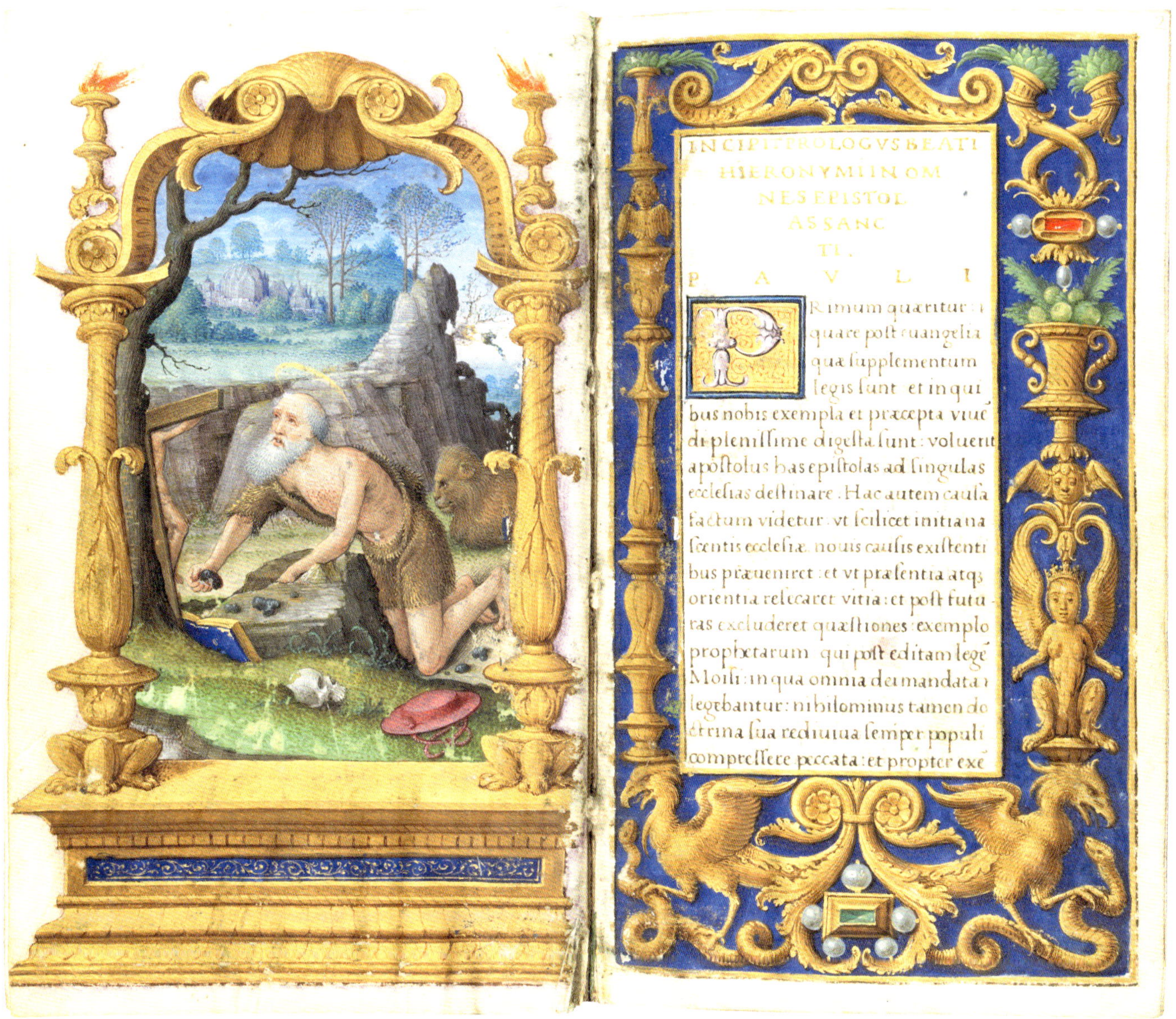

135. ANON. (France, Loire Valley), *The Leuville Epistles*, c.1520–30, manuscript. Bequeathed by David Martin Currie. V&A: MSL/1921/1721.

survey of materials, techniques and styles that could address historical narratives. Rather, he chose the most beautiful and rare according to his taste (reflecting the taste of his time and of his advisers) and refined his collection as he developed his connoisseur's eye and his growing knowledge. A tribute to Salting in the *Burlington Magazine* (February 1910), from the British Museum's Charles Hercules Read, points to a peculiarly British malaise that lies at the heart of the early history of the V&A, the antidote to which was seen as the social power of beauty, conveyed through collections in museums. Read writes:

> *It is often said that, in spite of our complicated racial composition, we are really not an artistic people; that we have not a reasoning love for beautiful things . . . bequests like Mr Salting's should go far to improve the position . . . A demand from the public for greater beauty in its daily life will assuredly have an effect in due time.*[9]

Several other collectors' long-term loans lay on display at the V&A, ready to turn into bequests in the traditional way. David Martin Currie (c.1837–1920) was a Scottish shipping magnate who, like Salting, had such a wide range of interests that he

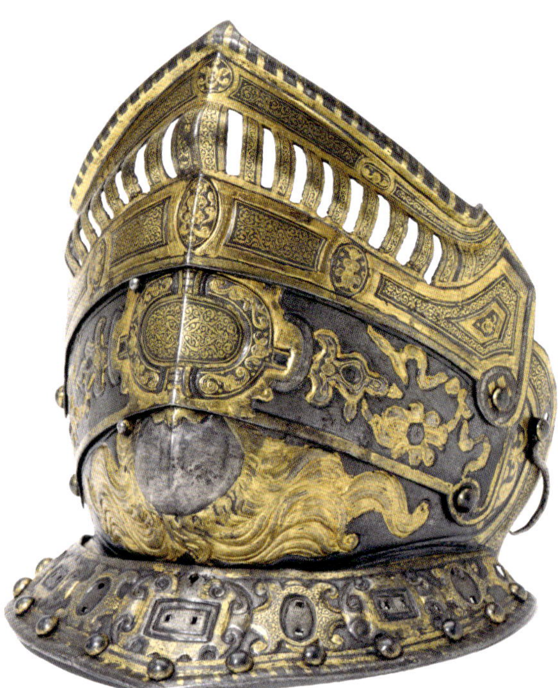

**136.** Lucio Piccinino (attrib.), *Buffe* (visor and neckguard), *c.*1585, steel, embossed, damascened with gold and silver, and rivetted, from an armour presented to Philip III in 1603. Bequeathed by David Martin Currie. V&A: M.111-1921.

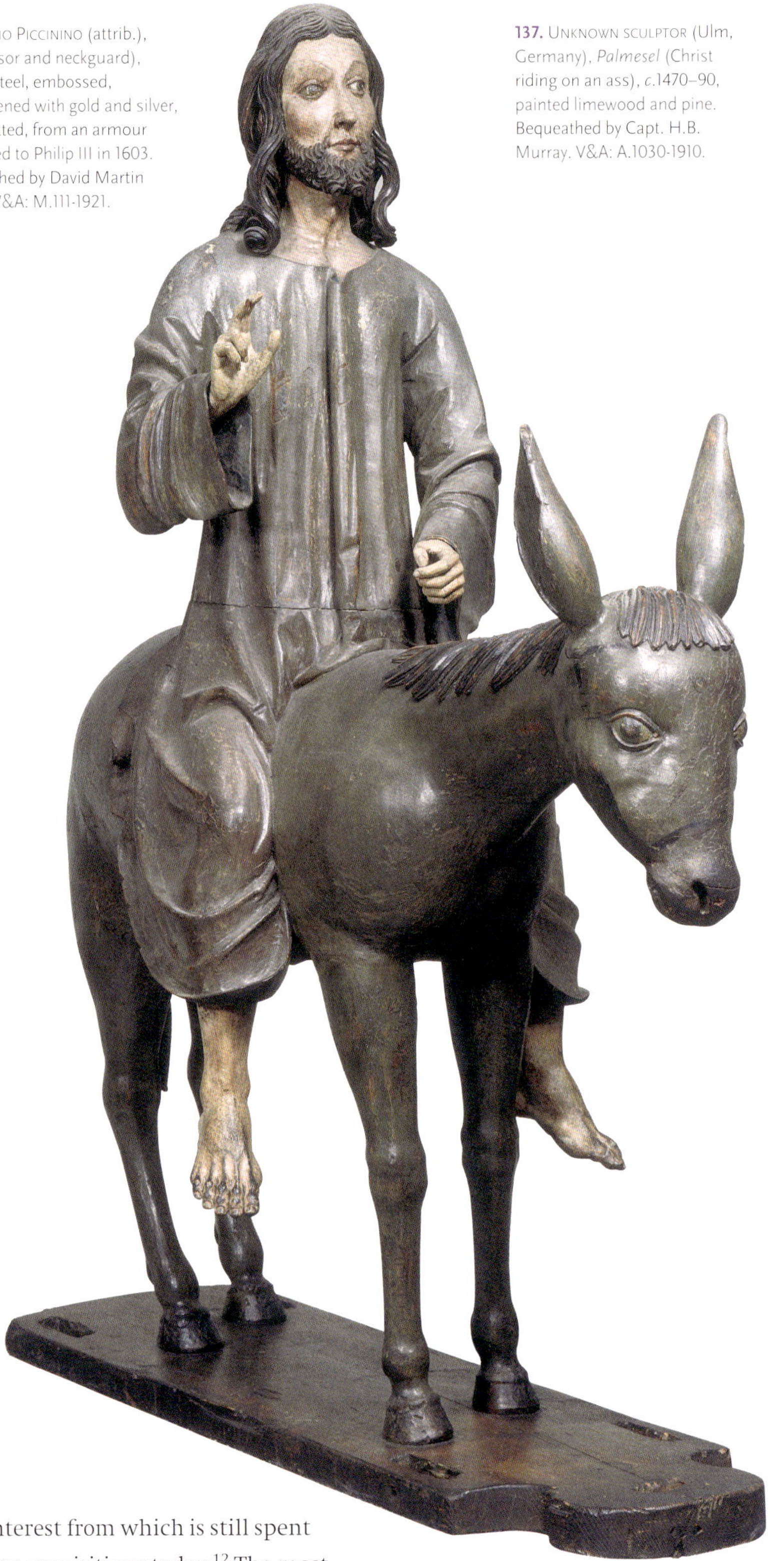

**137.** Unknown sculptor (Ulm, Germany), *Palmesel* (Christ riding on an ass), *c.*1470–90, painted limewood and pine. Bequeathed by Capt. H.B. Murray. V&A: A.1030-1910.

became well known as a collector in the salerooms of London and Europe. He first placed his collection on loan to the museum in 1887; there it grew over the next 33 years until it ranged from medieval manuscripts (fig.134) to historical arms and armour (fig.136). One benefit of lending was security: in 1904 Currie had the unusual experience of being offered 30 miniatures, a gold snuff box and other items to buy, until he recognised them as pieces stolen from his own office seven years before.[10] On his death he bequeathed to the V&A 'all the works belonging to him, including arms, armour, bronze, metalwork, enamel, Sèvres and other porcelain, majolica, missals, tapestry, and other things which may be on loan at the museum'.[11] One outstanding example from his collection is the *Leuville Epistles* (Loire Valley, 1520s) that had belonged to William Beckford and then to the 10th Duke of Hamilton (fig.135).

An even more ideal model for a collector-lender-donor is Captain Henry Boyles Murray (1843–1910). He kept his collection at home while he lived but it continues to grow, in effect forever. By the terms of his bequest the museum could not only choose what it wanted but also received £50,000 (equivalent today to around £2.3 million), the interest from which is still spent on new acquisitions today.[12] The most familiar object from Murray's original collection is the *Palmesel*, a large painted wooden figure of Christ riding an ass, made for carrying in Palm Sunday processions (fig.137).

# 18 The Ones that Got Away: J.P. Morgan; The Fitzhenry Gift

In May 1903 a Mrs Vincent in Deal received a picture postcard from her friend Pollie in Norfolk and kept it safe (fig.138). Beneath the photograph of a gallery filled with rows of well-laden showcases and a policeman, the succinct caption identifies 'Mr Pierpoint [*sic*] Morgan's Collection' in the 'Italian Court' (the North Court) of the 'South Kensington Museum'. The great American banker of America's 'Gilded Age', John Pierpont Morgan (1837–1913) began lending to the V&A in 1901. In November 1905 there were 934 objects; by 1912 the loan had swelled to 1,618 objects and had so overflowed that the Octagon Court was renamed the Loans Court, with half of it devoted to part of Morgan's collection.[1] The V&A fully expected his bronzes, ivories, jewellery, enamels, maiolica, portrait miniatures, illuminated manuscripts, arms, armour, metalwork and porcelain to form the museum donation *nonpareil*, surpassing even the recent arrivals of the Salting (1909) and Murray (1910) collections (see chapter 17). However, in 1913 Morgan shipped his collection to America. Most can be found in his home town, at the Wadsworth Atheneum in Hartford, Connecticut, in New York City at the Metropolitan Museum of Art, the Morgan Library and the Frick Collection, with more in museums in Boston, Washington and California.

Despite the banker's surprise withdrawals, some idea of Morgan's taste and standards can still be found at the V&A in the great collection of

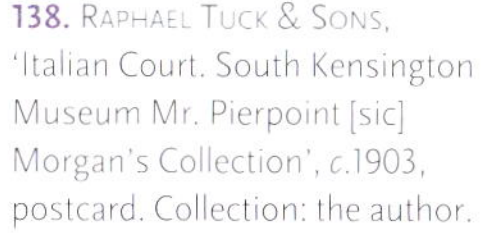

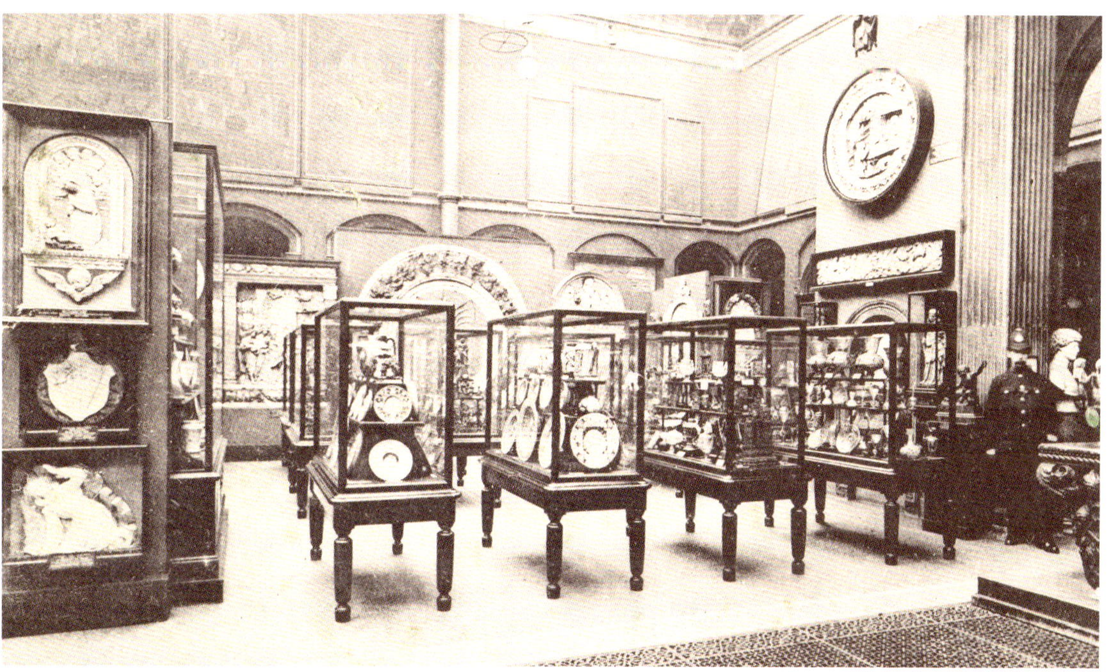

**138.** Raphael Tuck & Sons, 'Italian Court. South Kensington Museum Mr. Pierpoint [sic] Morgan's Collection', *c.*1903, postcard. Collection: the author.

stained glass that did not go to New York (figs 140, 141, 142). Morgan had purchased all 72 examples from the Paris dealer Georges Hoentschel, whose main source was the Prussian royal collection in Berlin. Morgan's son Jack (J. Pierpont Morgan Jr) donated the stained glass in 1919, 'prompted alike by the wish that the Museum should retain a worthy memorial of his father, and by his sense of the close friendship of the English-speaking nations which has been so greatly strengthened by the recent comradeship in arms' in the First World War.[2] The museum later acquired other works of art that had belonged to his father. But they are a tiny fraction of the greatest collection ever to escape from the V&A.[3]

Morgan formed his collection in London and Paris. He lived in London for six months each year and kept most of his growing collection there, close to the centre of the world's art market. His father, Junius S. Morgan, was the leading American banker in London where he had lived since 1854 and was also an art collector. He died in 1890, leaving his son his business, art collections, $15 million and two homes in England: 13 Princes Gate in Kensington and Dover House in Roehampton.[4] J.P. Morgan followed the example of George Salting in setting medieval and Renaissance art at the core of his

OPPOSITE:
**141.** Master of the Holy Kinship (Germany, Cologne School), window – *The Adoration of the Magi*, *c.*1500, clear and coloured glass with painted details and yellow (silver) stain. Given by J. Pierpont Morgan Jr, 1919, in memory of his recently deceased father and in acknowledgement of Anglo-American cooperation in the First Word War. V&A: C.74 & 75-1919.

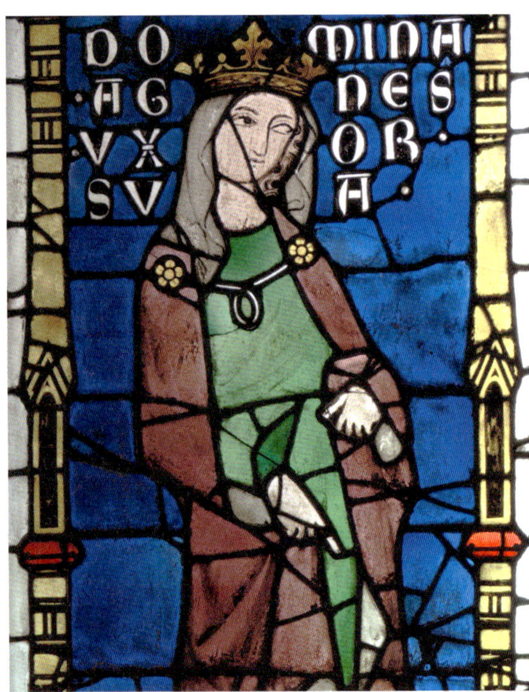


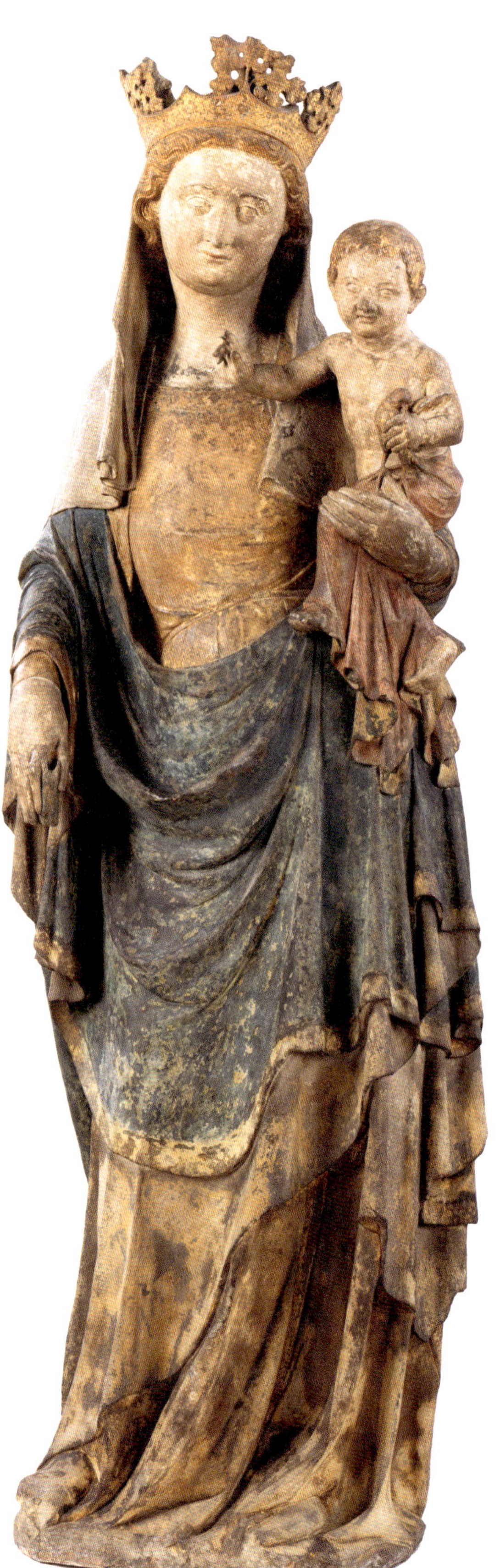

**139.** Unknown maker (Île-de-France), *Virgin and Child*, *c.*1340–50, limestone, painted and gilded. Given by J. Pierpont Morgan through Durlacher Brothers, London, 1911. V&A: A.98-1911.

**140.** Unknown maker (Bavaria), panel – *Agnes, Duchess of Lower Bavaria*, *c.*1309–14, clear and coloured glass with painted details, from the Cistercian convent of Seligenthal near Landshut, north of Munich; purchased by J.P. Morgan from a London dealer who had acquired it in Germany; on loan to the V&A from 1909. Given by J. Pierpont Morgan Jr, 1919, in memory of his recently deceased father and in acknowledgement of Anglo-American cooperation in the First Word War. V&A: C.83-1919.

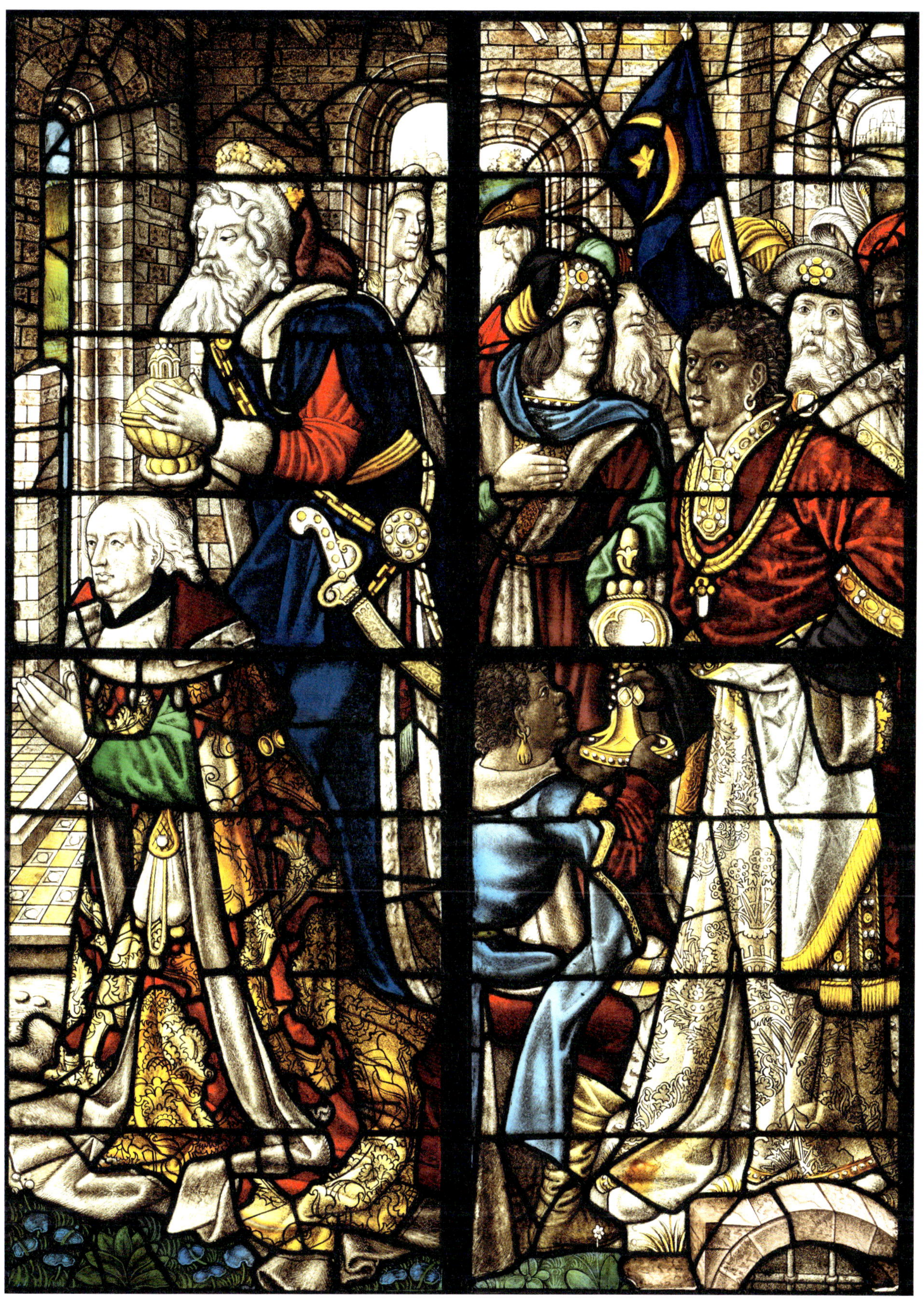

**142.** Unknown maker (Zurich), *The Personification of Justice*, 1586, clear glass panel painted with enamels and yellow (silver) stain. Given by J. Pierpont Morgan Jr. V&A: C.63-1919.

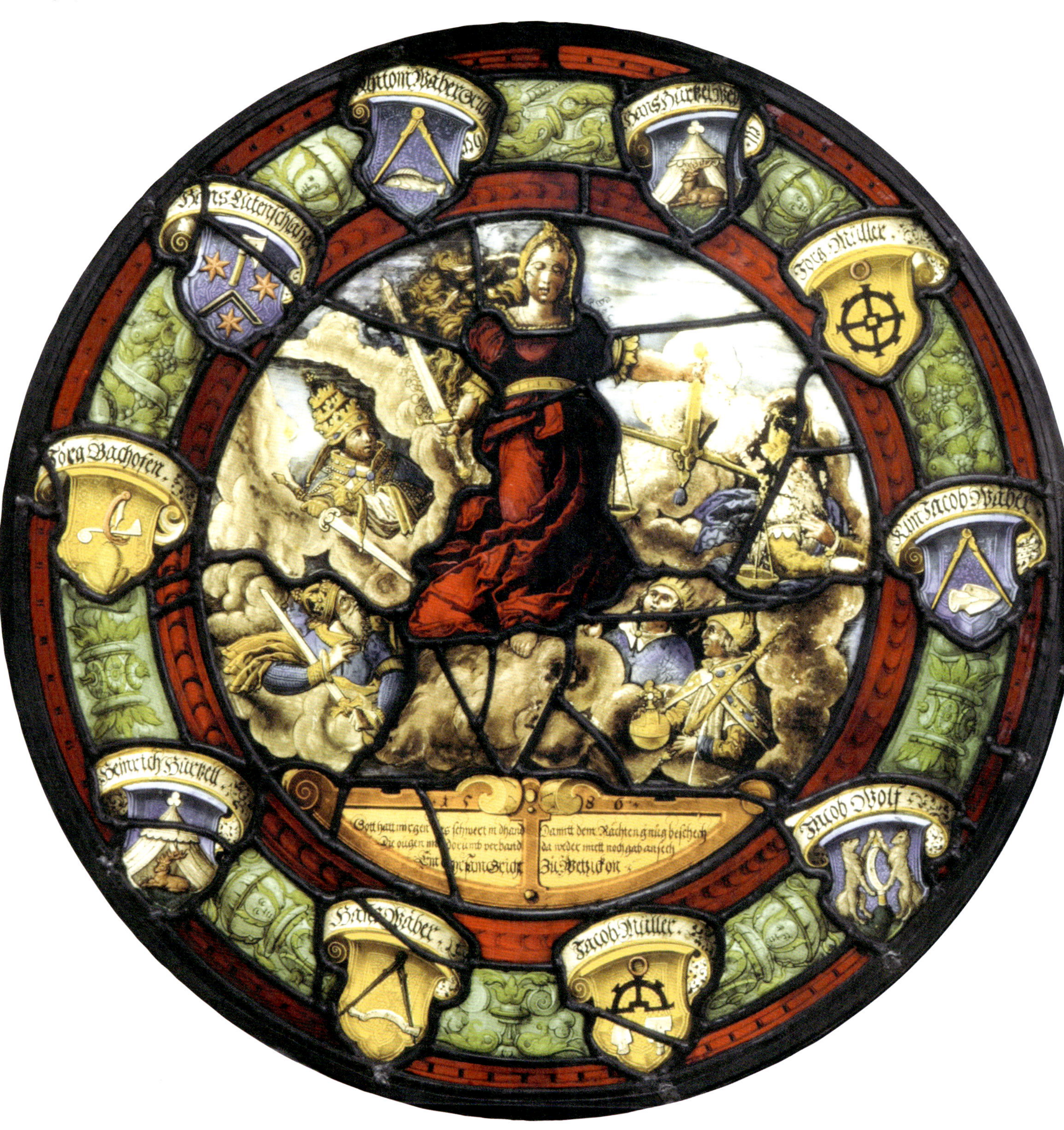

collection and in welcoming the advice of Salting's friend, the scholar-dealer Joseph Henry Fitzhenry (1836–1913). Morgan was also advised on his purchases by J.C. Robinson and by Murray Marks.

To his critics Morgan was a bulk buyer, for much of his collection was indeed an assembly of other collectors' endeavours. The banker took a businessman's approach to collecting, as if he were buying up companies. For example, in 1902 he purchased the library of William Bennett of Manchester; the 700 volumes included over 100 illuminated manuscripts, 29 of which had belonged to William Morris, as well as 32 incunabula printed by William Caxton.[5] In 1907 he purchased 30 paintings from the estate of the French collectors Maurice and Rodolphe Kann, including masterpieces by Gabriël Metsu and Rembrandt. Unlike his rival collectors, Morgan acted as a banker; through backing the purchase of the Kanns' collection by Duveen Brothers and Nathan Wildenstein he then had first choice.[6] In 1909 he bought the collection of 1,500 master drawings assembled by Charles Fairfax Murray.[7] But he also selected classic English portraits by Gainsborough, Reynolds, Raeburn, Romney, Lawrence and Hoppner, purchased through Agnew's, Wertheimer and other dealers.[8] Morgan also had the patience to form, over a decade, his own collection of around 800 portrait miniatures, including the *Heneage Jewel* (fig.144), the gold pendant setting for Hilliard's portrait of Queen Elizabeth I.

By 29 June 1909 Morgan needed more gallery space, partly due to the return of his long loans from museums in Glasgow. Fitzhenry wrote to reassure the V&A's director, Cecil Harcourt Smith:[9]

> *I had an interesting conversation with Pierpont Morgan today at his own house. He returns to N.Y. only on the 14th, so has very little time to see his own collections at the Museum. There is no question whatever of his sending any of the collections to New York for a long time, and besides the room he wants in the 'Octagon Court' for his present superb contributions, he 'wants' more so as to accommodate ulterior additions. That (at his age) means that any day he may decide to hand over to you 'selections' from his collections, and 'take example' by my 'late' and future acts towards the Museum. I must ask you to make an exception in his favour, and allow all he has bought to be on view amongst his collections . . . The Morgan collection would be one of the greatest attractions of our marvellous Museum.*[10]

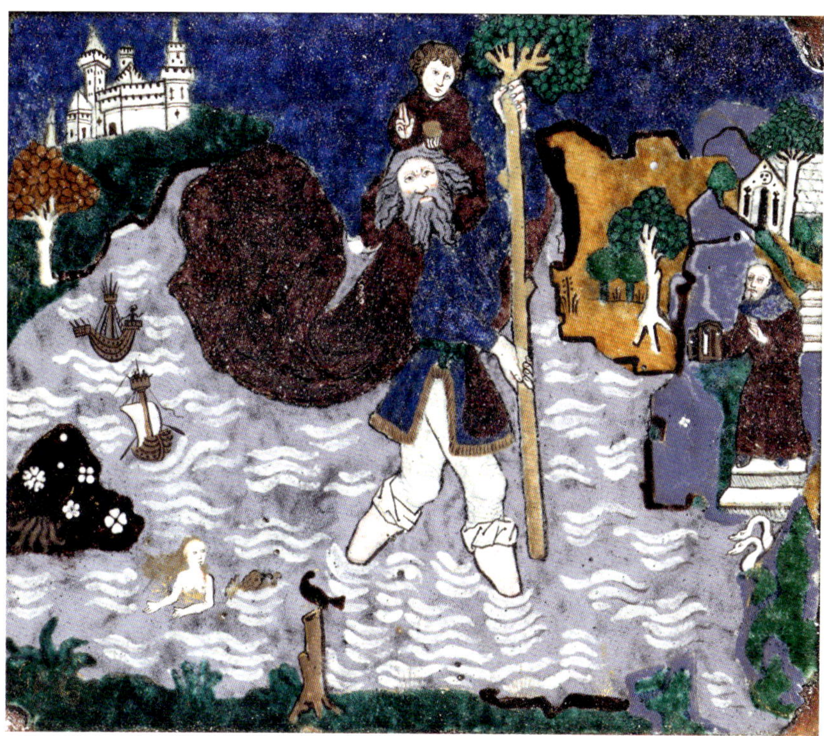

**143.** The 'Monvaerni' Master (France, Limoges), *St Christopher Carrying the Christ Child*, *c.*1480–90, copper plaque painted in polychrome enamels with some gilded detail. Donated by Mrs Bertha F. Skinner in memory of her late husband, Mr Arthur B. Skinner, sometime Director of the Museum, to whom given by J. Pierpont Morgan. V&A: C.143-1911.

However, Morgan's motives as a lender were not quite so predictable and public-spirited. The collection was linked to the assets of his bank, and he recognised the financial benefits of working with the V&A. Indeed, one could say he used the museum as an extension to his bank. Once on loan his objects increased in market value as endorsed by the museum, where they benefitted from expert opinions, sometimes even before he had decided to buy them. Morgan further increased their value by commissioning research for catalogues: Wilhelm von Bode of Berlin's museums produced a catalogue of his Renaissance bronzes and Bernard Rackham of the V&A catalogued his maiolica.[11] But there were risks to lending for display, as when in 1904 a bishop's cope among his loans at the V&A made front-page news in England, America and Italy when it was revealed to have been stolen from the cathedral in Ascoli Piceno. Morgan decided to present it to the Italian state.[12]

Fitzhenry liaised between Morgan and the museum for 12 years, after representing him in 1901 in the purchase of Charles Mannheim's collection of Renaissance objects and French medieval ivories. Fitzhenry had similarly liaised between the V&A and George Salting. But the V&A was not alone among museums in wooing Morgan. By 1908 his closest museum adviser was not a curator from the V&A but rather Charles Hercules Read, who started his career at the V&A but succeeded A.W. Franks in 1896 as the British Museum's Keeper of British and Medieval Antiquities.[13] Read had published in 1902 *The Waddesdon Bequest*, the catalogue of the works of art bequeathed to the British Museum by Baron Ferdinand de Rothschild in 1898. This collection went on display at the British Museum in 1900 and is still shown today, evoking a *Kunstkammer* of a Renaissance prince, with metalwork, jewellery, maiolica, enamels and glass; it set a standard for Salting, Morgan and other collectors.[14] Read wrote to *The Times* on 27 January 1913 (two months before Morgan's death) that 'his generosity to my department of the British Museum may truly be called princely', but if the British Museum hoped to benefit from Morgan's loans to South Kensington it too would be disappointed.[15]

At first, Morgan showed his evolving art collection both at the V&A and nearby at his home, 13 Princes Gate, which he opened for limited viewing in 1901. The five-storey Italianate terrace of houses, built 1846–53, still stands at the top of Exhibition Road, opposite Hyde Park (in 1851 it faced the Great Exhibition's Crystal Palace). A series of photographs taken around 1902 (fig.145) record Morgan's interiors already full of art. Two years later he purchased the house next door (number 14) and removed internal walls to convert the first two floors into show rooms, furnished in the French taste of Louis XV and Louis XVI, arranged by the dealer-decorators Duveen Brothers and by A.B. Daniell & Sons. On 18 June 1904 Morgan wrote to the V&A requesting the extension of his loan agreement for

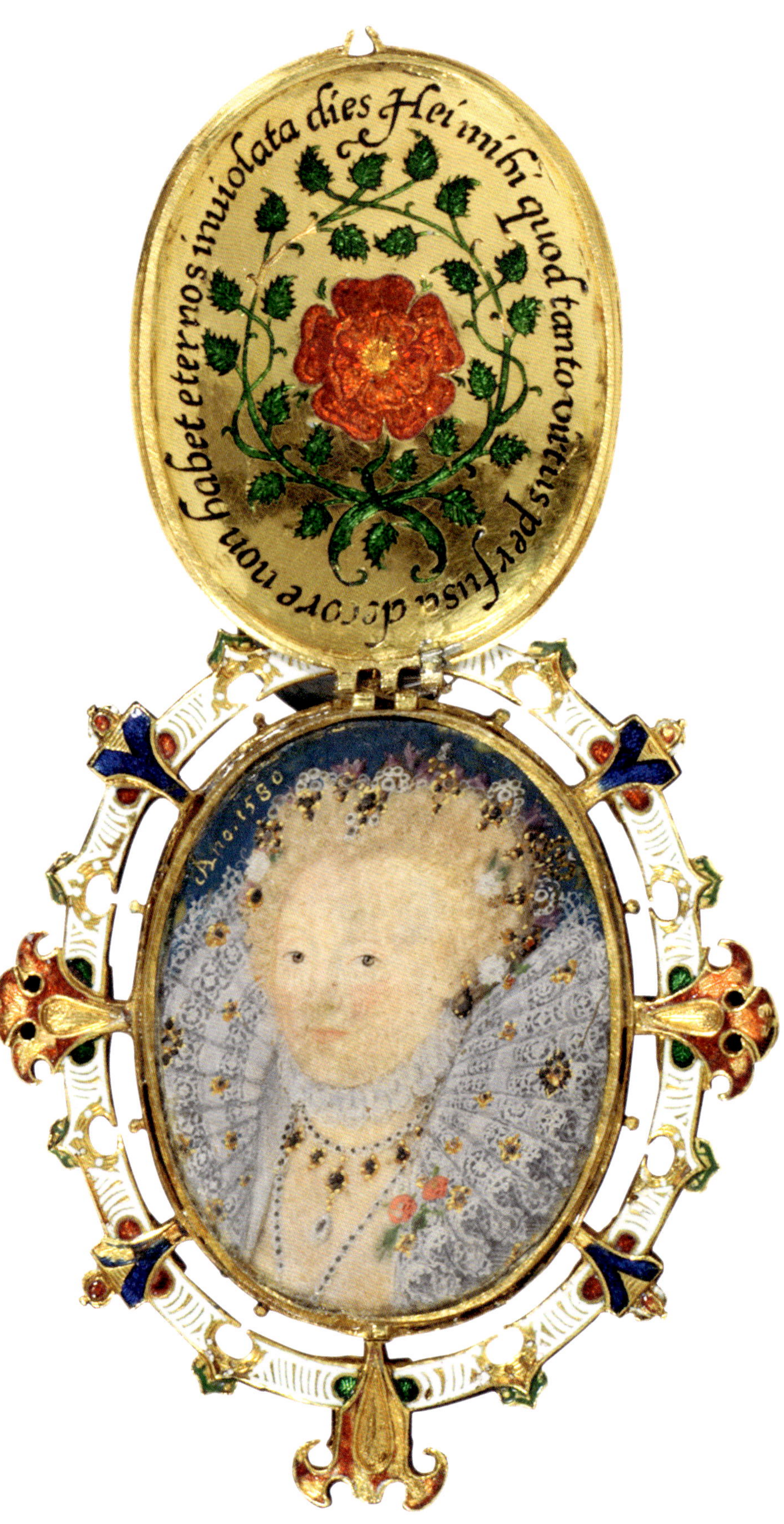

another year: 'I have recently acquired the premises adjoining my house in Princes Gate, and after considerable structural alterations have been made I hope to remove all my collections there and thus form a museum.'[16] He may have been inspired by the opening of the Wallace Collection in 1900, but he had rather more old-fashioned access arrangements. The writer of a detailed room-by-room account describes how it was 'open to hundreds of visitors who had requested the privilege of Mr Morgan and who presented his card' to his housekeeper or butler. When 'Queen Alexandra and her sister, the Empress of Russia, were being shown about the house' by Morgan they recognised family furniture that must have been sold by their brother.[17] In July 1906 Morgan showed King Edward VII around his palatial town house; later that same year the American art historian Bernard Berenson visited and dismissed it (writing to his client, Isabella Stewart Gardner) as 'like a pawnbroker's shop for Croesuses'.[18]

**144 a, b.** Unknown maker (England), *The Heneage Jewel*, c.1600, enamelled gold pendant set with cut diamonds and Burmese rubies enclosing a portrait miniature of Queen Elizabeth I by Nicholas Hilliard. Acquired by J. Pierpont Morgan in 1902; given by the Rt Hon. Viscount Wakefield CBE, through the Art Fund. V&A: M.81-1935.

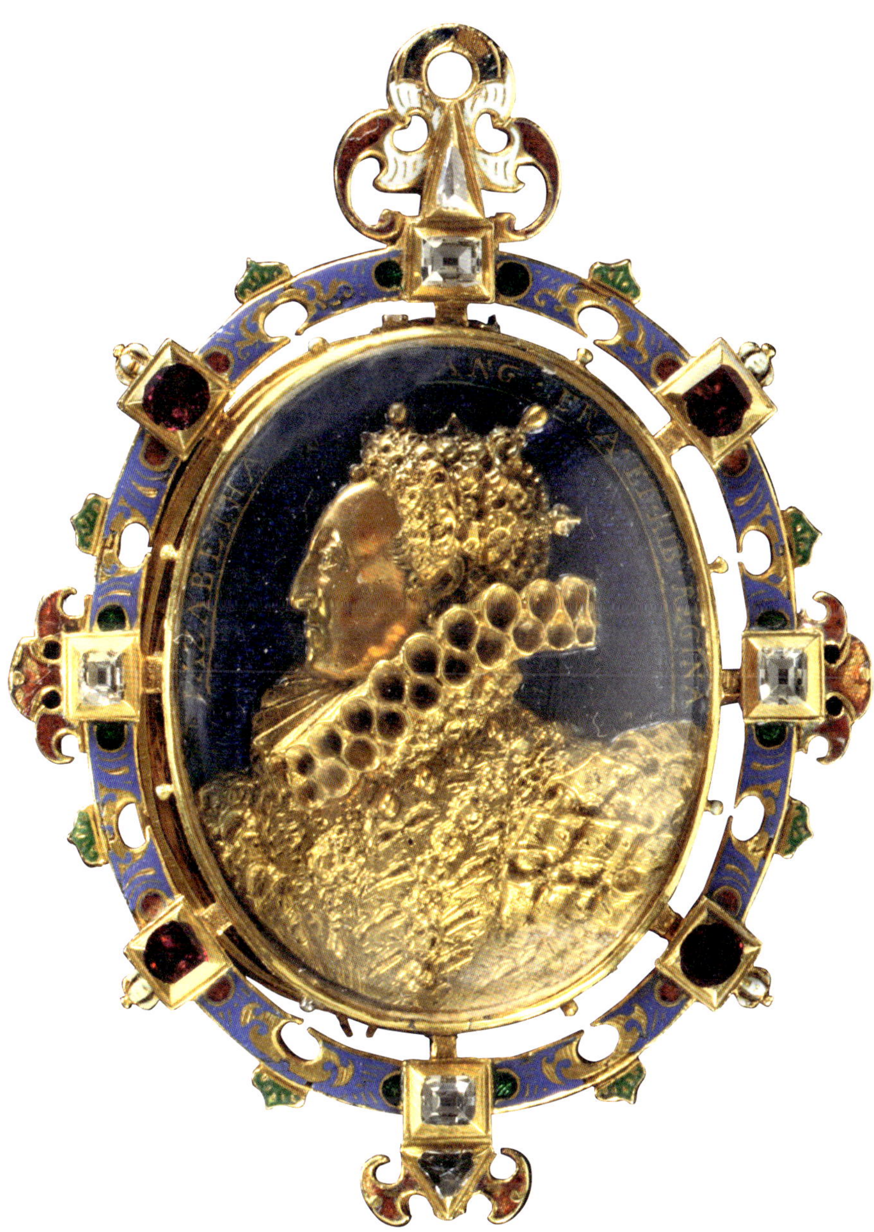

Several factors led Morgan to change his mind, against creating his own collector's house museum in London. He was still short of room, even after doubling his space by adding the house next door, as he told the V&A's director in 1905.[19] In 1904 he was appointed as the first vice-president of the Metropolitan Museum of Art in New York and became president later the same year. Months later, in 1905 he persuaded the V&A's director, Caspar Purdon Clarke (who had regularly agreed to extend his annual loans to the V&A), to run the museum in New York. Another factor behind abandoning his plans for Princes Gate would have been his success in 1905, after years of delays, in buying land for an extension to the museum in his home town, Hartford, Connecticut.

One reason for keeping his collection in South Kensington had been the US government's Revenue Act (1897) which set a 21 per cent tax on all imported works of art (other than books and manuscripts for educational and literary purposes). In 1909, after lobbying friends in the US Senate, Morgan convinced Congress to pass a bill that dropped import duty on works of art over a hundred years old. In 1910 David Lloyd George, as Britain's Chancellor of the Exchequer, introduced a budget that imposed crippling inheritance and income taxes. Conscious of ill-health and mortality, and wishing to consolidate his investments, in November 1911 Morgan confirmed his decision to move his collection to New York. The packing of 4,307 objects began in January 1912 and shipment to the Metropolitan Museum of Art was completed in December.[20]

At his death in 1913 Morgan left his art collection to his son, Jack, with the wish that it be put in the public domain. The works of art that went from the V&A to the Metropolitan Museum were only a fraction of Morgan's collection (today estimated at over 20,000 objects) and around half was sold. The National Gallery may also have hoped for a donation. The greatest painting to leave the V&A after a long loan was Raphael's *Colonna Altarpiece* (Metropolitan Museum of Art, New York). It had been lent to the South Kensington Museum for ten years, between 1886 and 1896, while the previous owner hoped to sell. Morgan must have seen it then but declined to buy the 'Madonna of a Million' as it was known, on account of its price. Morgan purchased it for 2 million francs ($400,000) in 1901 and placed it on loan to the National Gallery, but it too was finally shipped to New York.[21] In February 1914 *The Morgan Exhibition*, comprising around 4,100 objects from his collections in London and New York, opened at the Metropolitan Museum of Art. Two years later, soon after it closed in May 1916, Jack Morgan sold the Renaissance bronzes and maiolica. The following year he presented the rest of the loan exhibition to the Metropolitan, on condition that they build the Morgan Wing. Had the collection remained at the V&A the same condition may have applied.

The other great long-loan collection that eluded the V&A at this time belonged to J.H. Fitzhenry. A self-made art dealer in Paris, Fitzhenry was described by the *New York Times* as 'for years J. Pierpont Morgan's confidential adviser and art representative' in London.[22] A regular guest at Morgan's London home and on his yacht, *Corsair*, Fitzhenry had 'his private museum'[23] (presumably his showrooms) at 25 Queen Anne's Gate, close to Morgan, and lived opposite the V&A in Thurloe Place, where he died.[24] Acting on Morgan's behalf, in 1909 he supervised the installation of his Gobelins tapestries on loan to the V&A.[25] Fitzhenry's other friends who benefitted from his expert advice included Sir Richard Wallace, George Salting and two successive directors of the museum, Arthur Skinner and Cecil Harcourt Smith. The latter recalled that Fitzhenry and Salting visited the museum together almost every week and that 'Mr Salting almost invariably discussed his proposed purchases with Mr Fitzhenry'.[26]

Showcases dedicated to Fitzhenry's private loans were established in the museum by 1902. The 'Fitzhenry Gift', as it was known, ranged from early 16th-century French architectural carvings and Italian Renaissance sculpture to European portrait miniatures, snuff boxes, watches, Georgian silver punch ladles and caddie spoons. Not everything would be lost. In 1903 he donated six maiolica tiles from the pavement of Isabella d'Este's *studiolo* at the Castello di San Giorgio in Mantua, commissioned by the Gonzaga family in the 1490s (fig.146).[27] In 1905 he donated an elaborately carved dormer window from a French chateau built around 1523–35, one in a series of gifts of French architectural fragments and ironwork.[28] The same year the curator of ceramics, C.H. Wylde, published Fitzhenry's exceptional collection of French porcelain in the *Burlington Magazine*, praising it as 'probably the finest collection of French pâte-tendre [soft-paste porcelain] in the United Kingdom'.[29] Two years later the museum published some of his Delft.[30] However, in 1909 he sold part of the collection in Paris, in a four-day sale, to fund his recent purchases in other fields.

After Fitzhenry donated his French porcelain and his French and Dutch faience to the V&A in 1909, to mark the opening of the new building designed by Aston Webb, the director wrote in thanks: 'these two collections constitute what is probably the most valuable and generous gift which has ever been made to the Museum during the lifetime of the donor. They enable the Museum, which was hitherto lamentably deficient in objects of this character, to stand comparison with the collections of any Museum in Europe.'[31] One may need to allow for some exaggeration, given Harcourt Smith's hopes of translating the rest of the Fitzhenry Gift into gifts. When the V&A's new Advisory Council was set up in 1912–13 Fitzhenry was appointed as a founder member, to advise its overseers, the Board of Education, 'on questions of principle and policy'.[32]

Fitzhenry regularly lent and donated to the museum through a relationship stretching across more than 40 years, from 1870 until his death, by when he had over 3,150 objects on long-term loan to the V&A. According to *The Times* (29 August 1913), 'nearly every department of the South Kensington Museum contains loan exhibits

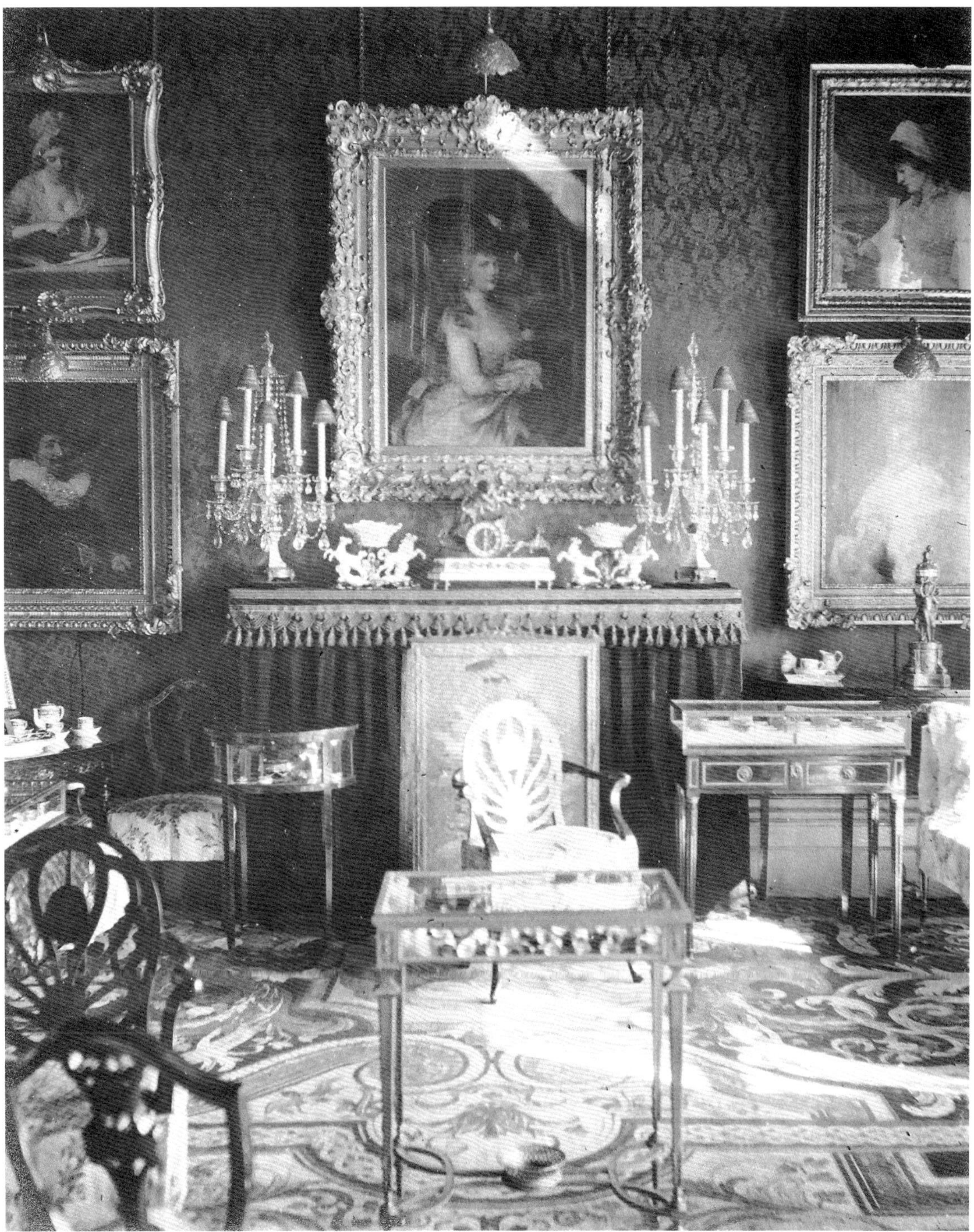

**145.** J.P. Morgan's London residence, 13 Princes Gate, photograph, 1902. Gainsborough's portrait of the Duchess of Devonshire, purchased by Morgan in 1901 from Agnew's, presides over the drawing room. From the Dover House and Princes Gate album, p.12. New York, The Morgan Library & Museum. ARC 1496.

from the Fitzhenry Gift'.[33] However, his death earlier that year did not lead to the long-expected confirmation of his bequest. Instead, to everyone's surprise, his executors sent most of his collection to Christie's. The auction spread over two weeks in November 1913 and even included his own portrait, by Sir William Orpen (1908, unlocated). Further sales were held later in Paris, of his book-covers and 18th-century porcelain. Once again, as with Morgan, great expectations led to surprise and disappointment. This time the explanation was more personal: Fitzhenry's doctor had insisted that the executors meet his client's medical expenses.

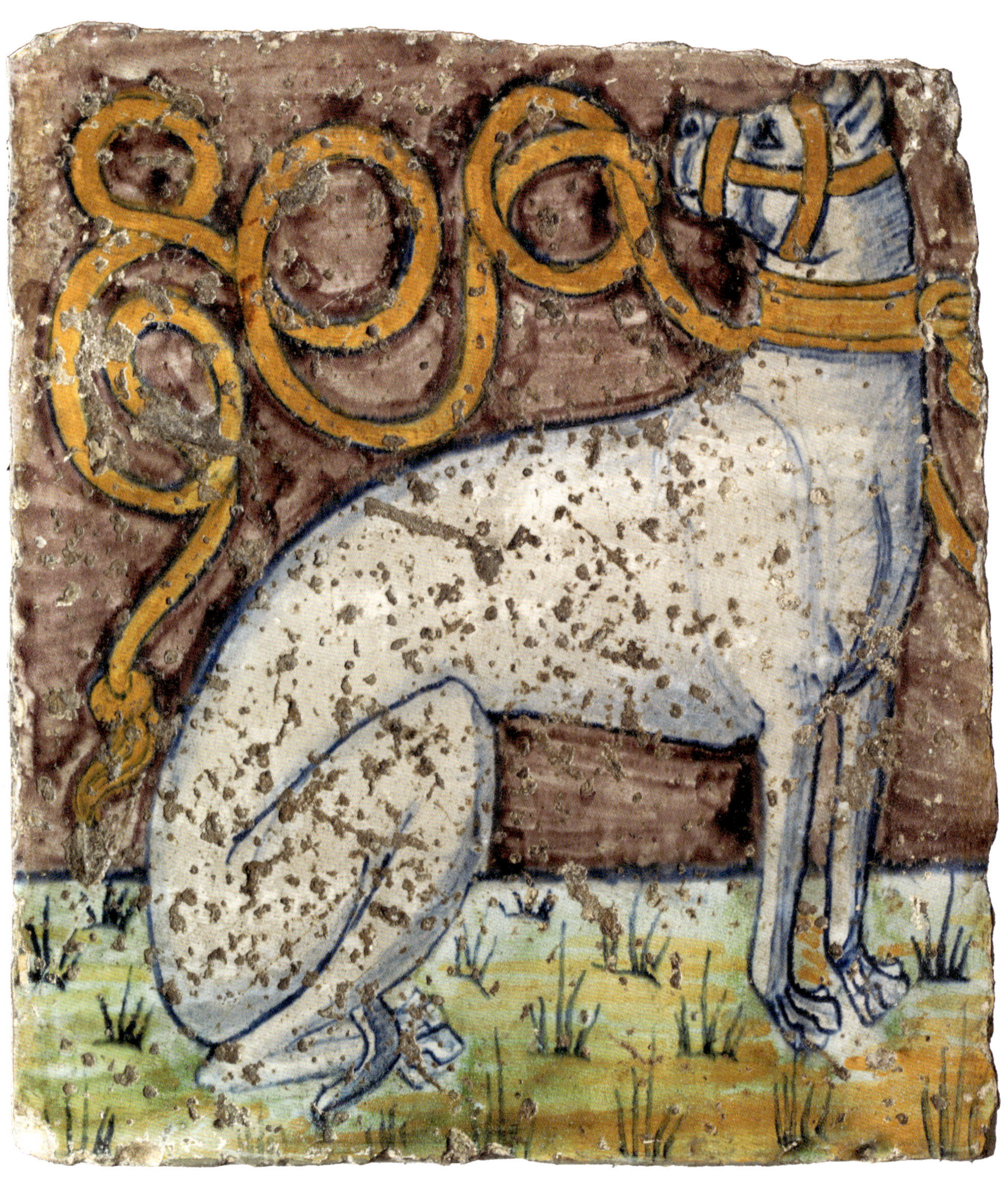

Before making any purchases for the V&A by using Captain Murray's financial bequest, Harcourt Smith wrote to one of its executors to explain that Fitzhenry

> *had on deposit here a large collection which it was always understood he was going to bequeath to the Museum . . . our policy of purchase was to some extent governed by the idea that certain gaps were already filled by the Fitzhenry exhibits. For some unknown reason, he changed his mind at the last moment, and the whole collection will . . . have to be sold by auction.*[34]

Such were the risks of relying on generous loans from collectors when developing a museum's collection. Fortunately, Fitzhenry's most visible donation to the museum was secure: a bronze replica of a fountain in Florence by Pietro Tacca, given as a memorial to George Salting, the museum's greatest benefactor. Standing in a central position in the V&A's garden from 1910 (fig.148), the Salting Fountain acknowledged the pivotal contribution, in effect, of all private collectors, at the heart of the museum, until it was dismantled and removed into storage in 1979.[35]

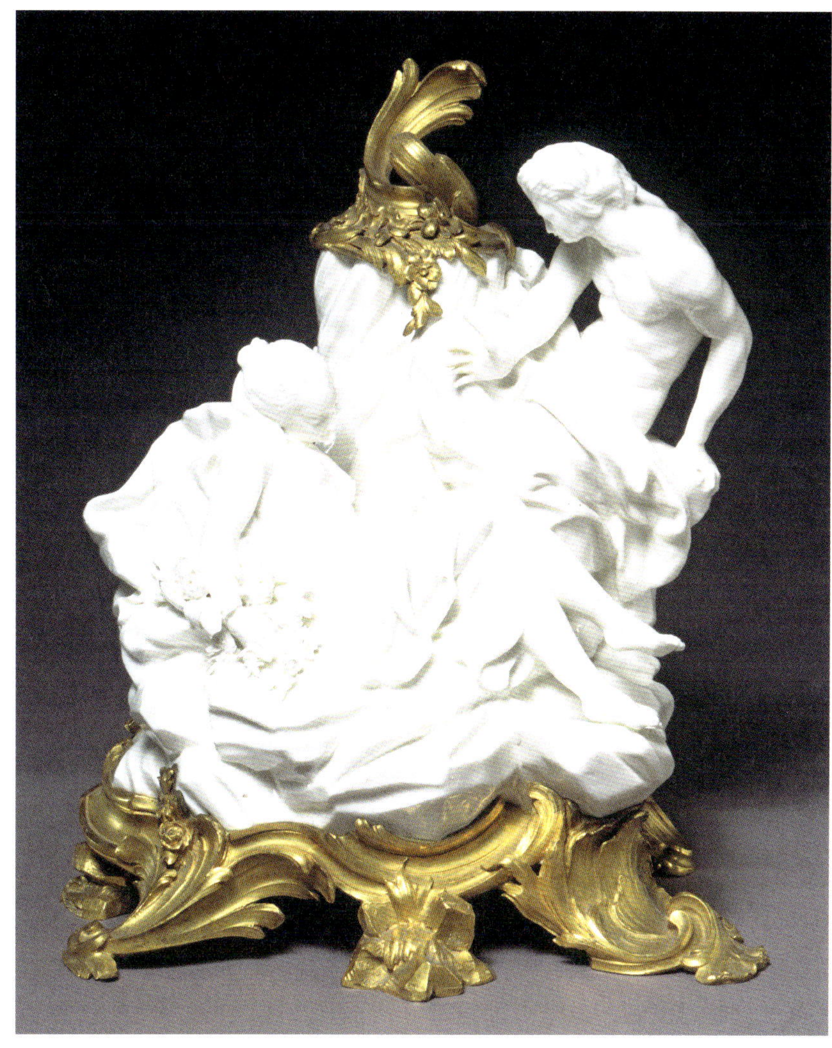

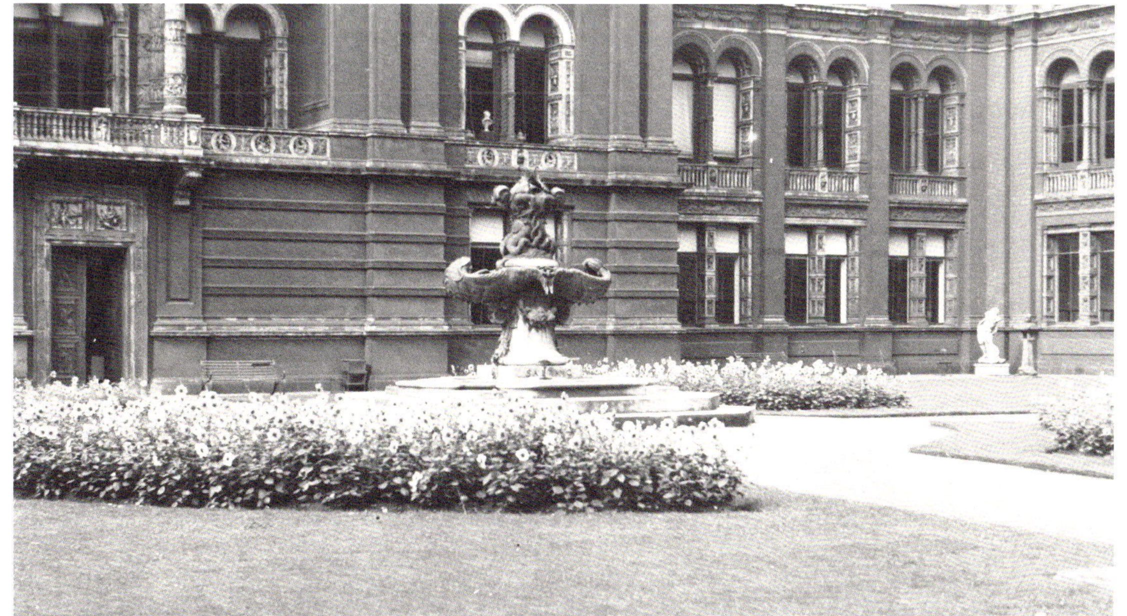

OPPOSITE:

**146.** Antonio de Fedeli, workshop (attrib.), floor tile, 1492–4, tin-glazed earthenware, painted, from a group of six in the V&A believed to be from the pavement of the *studiolo* of Isabella d'Este in the Gonzaga palace, Mantua. Fitzhenry Gift. V&A: 334:1-1903.

**147.** Vincennes porcelain factory (France), *L'Heure du Berger*, 1750–55, biscuit porcelain with gilt metal mount. Fitzhenry Gift. V&A: C.356-1909.

**148.** The George Salting Memorial Fountain, *c.*1890–1909, bronze replica made in Rome by Sangiorgi after a sculpture by Pietro Tacca, *c.*1629. Commissioned by J.H. Fitzhenry for the V&A's garden in memory of George Salting; removed to store 1979. V&A: A.2:1 to 33-2007.

# 19 'Re-arrangement': From Collectors to Designers

On a shelf of the National Art Library at the V&A sits a tall slim volume that provides a key with which to unlock a world of collecting through donors and benefactors in the museum's first half century. This vivid overview is modestly entitled: *List of the Bequests and Donations to the South Kensington Museum, now called The Victoria and Albert Museum, completed to 31st December 1900.*[1] Running to 270 pages of descriptions, many of which summarise large groups of objects, this is much more than a list. It reveals the extraordinary variety of donors and collections that succumbed to the omnivorous appetites of V&A directors and of tenacious staff. It also confirms the extent to which Victorian directors made acquisitions, despite reductions in their buying budgets, in the form of ready-made collections, through cultivating collectors, turning kind lenders into generous donors.

The 'list' documents the museum's scope in the second half of the 19th century as a global collector, with items allocated not only to the Art Museum, the Art Library and the Indian Section but also to other divisions of the South Kensington Museum as it was constituted at that time, including the Fish Collection, Animal Products, Food, Machinery and Inventions, Naval, Structural, Geological, Biological and the Science and Educational Library. This variety was evident on site, as John Ruskin had complained in the *Art Journal* in 1880: 'I lost myself in a Cretan labyrinth of military ironmongery, advertisements of spring blinds, model fish-farming, and plaster bathing nymphs with a year's smut on all the noses of them; and had to put myself in charge of a policeman to get out again.'[2]

The museum's complete list of donations and bequests to date is an extraordinary snapshot of a nation of collectors and reads like a meticulous inventory of Britain's official attic. Beginning with Victoria and Albert's own gifts, it records the Queen's support for the museum after Prince Albert's death through her continuing donations. Most royal donations relate to the royal family and to Prince Albert but there are also some that suggest diplomatic gifts in need of a better home.[3] In 1865, for example, Queen Victoria gave a 'collection of Japanese weapons, suit of armour in sixteen pieces, two sets of horse trappings, some domestic objects, and pieces of fabric'. The same year she placed on permanent loan Raphael's seven full-size designs ('cartoons') for tapestries in the Sistine Chapel, Rome (fig.149 and 150). After Queen Victoria's donations the list of gifts from 'Royal and Imperial Personages' continues with Napoleon III who gave a collection of 4,854 engravings in 1869. From Kaiser William I, Emperor of Germany came the works of Frederick the Great in 32 volumes (given 1871–5); from the Shah of Persia (1877) 'A collection of sixty-eight modern Persian carpets'; from the Khedive of Egypt came, in 1867, 'A collection of thirty Egyptian musical instruments'. The museum was also able to secure, for example, 30 modern Chinese musical instruments from the Alexandra Palace Company (1870), a 'collection of 102 pins, 1620–1800' and 2,175 sheets of drawings for Westminster Abbey by the architect Edmund Blore. The Egypt Exploration Fund kindly donated in 1897 a 'Collection of Roman antiquities found

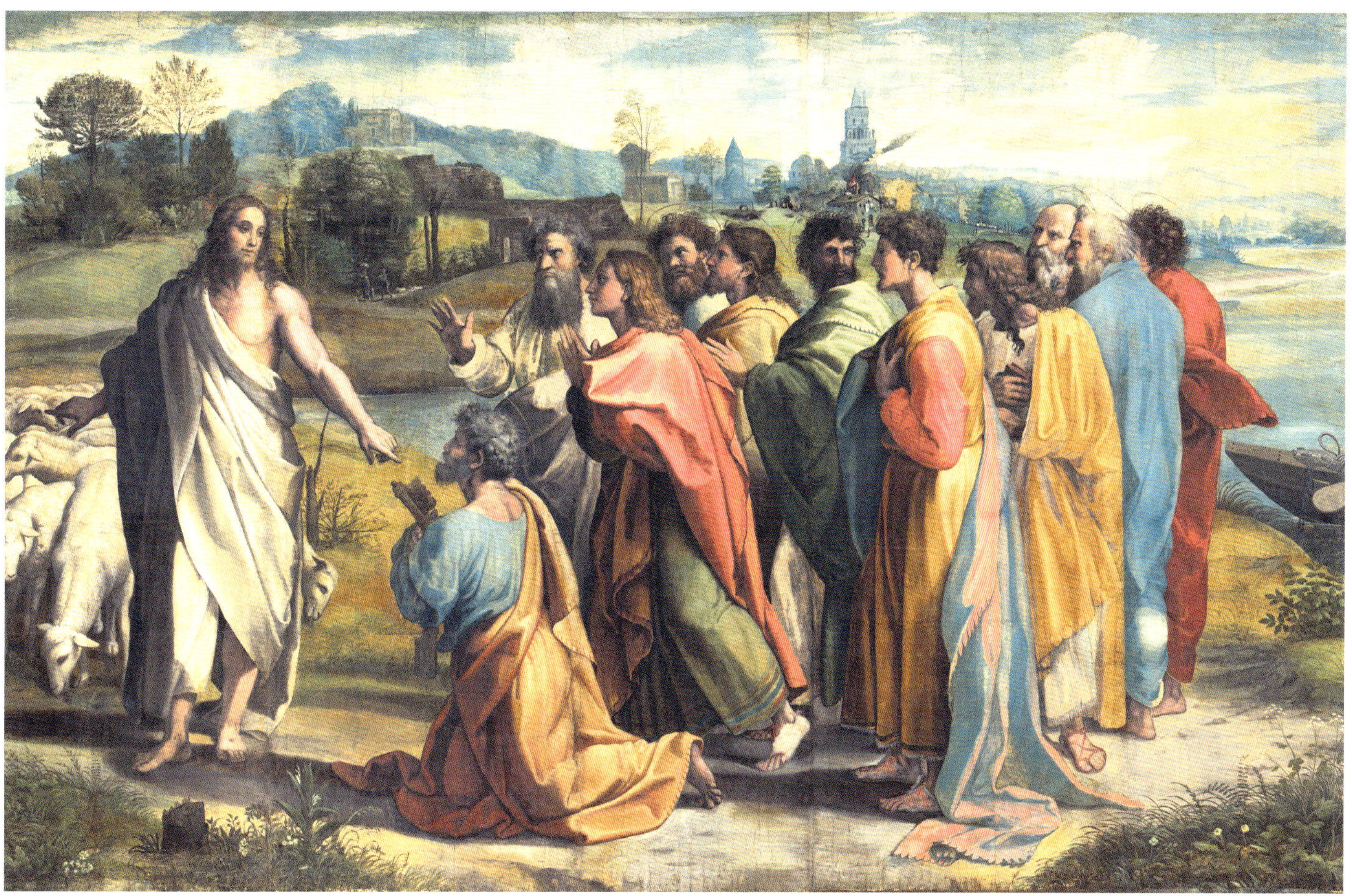

**149.** Raphael, *Christ's Charge to Peter*, *c.*1515–16, bodycolour over charcoal on paper, later mounted on canvas. On loan from Her Majesty The Queen, RCIN 912945. V&A. ROYAL LOANS. 3

at Behnesa (Oxyrhyncus) Upper Egypt'. Closer to home, from two years after Henry Cole's retirement, 1875 saw the arrival of 'Examples of the utilization of sewage', a legacy of his failed business speculation with the V&A's architect, Henry Scott, in recycling human waste as building cement. One could be forgiven for thinking that the Victorian V&A never refused a donation.

Another summary of the museum from the start of the 20th century is preserved in a map for visitors, published in 1908. The key to it identifies more than six galleries named after donors of collections (including Sheepshanks, Dyce, Forster, Jones, Ionides, plus 'Salting and others') as well as the Loans Court.[4] When Caspar Purdon Clarke moved to New York as director of the Metropolitan Museum of Art in 1905, Arthur Skinner had succeeded him as director of the V&A. By February 1908, with the grand new suites of galleries under construction along Cromwell Road nearing completion, concern spread that no one had decided how to fill them. The external Committee of Re-arrangement was convened by the museum's masters, the Board of Education. Chaired by Sir Charles Dilke, MP, it was dominated by Lewis F. Day who taught design at the South Kensington Schools and remained committed to the old idea of the museum as a technical 'storehouse'.[5] The four other committee members were W.A.S. Benson (the furniture maker who managed Morris & Co. after the death of William Morris), Harry Powell (from the glass-makers Powell's of Whitefriars), Josiah C. Wedgwood MP (from the pottery family) and Cecil Harcourt Smith, Keeper of Greek and Roman Antiquities at the British Museum.

Five months later, without any wider consultation, the Committee presented its report. It supported the recently formed curatorial structure of materials-based departments (see chapter 5) and created one more for graphic arts, called Engraving, Illustration and Design, drawn from the National Art Library. The Committee followed its brief in recommending that the museum return to its initial aims: rather than displaying collections of beauty and the best it should provide materials-based teaching displays to support the reform of British product design.[6] The Committee learnt how private loan collections had become a mixed blessing and observed that

> *at the present moment there are several important collections deposited on loan in the Museum. The Committee recognise the difficulties that may arise . . . the necessity of keeping together an assortment of specimens of different classes . . . gaps in the Museum series remain unfilled in consequence of reliance on a loan collection which may in time be withdrawn. At the same time, such loan collections may eventually become the property of the Museum by donation or bequest, and the Committee feel that it would be impolitic to discourage them.*[7]

The Committee's findings led to most galleries being devoted to different materials and techniques, in order to appeal primarily to students of design and crafts workers. This approach had been attempted for the museum in its first home, Marlborough House, in the 1850s under the intellectual guidance of Gottfried Semper.[8] After Semper returned to Germany in 1855 Robinson reinstalled the galleries in 1856 to suggest the period rooms of a collector's home.[9] The Committee's recommendation of reversion to materials-based displays was seen by many as a backward step. By 1908, the leading museums of applied art in Europe had moved on to reach a wider public. Museums in Vienna, Berlin, Munich, Nuremberg, Hamburg, Salzburg, Zurich and Oslo sought to display collections together by country and by successive period style within interiors (genuine, reconstructed or pastiche). Under the influence of the Viennese art historian Alois Riegl, leading European museums saw style driven not so much by the inherent properties of materials and techniques (as Semper had convinced Prince Albert and Cole in the 1850s) as by the 'artistic will' of makers fuelled by the spirit of their age. Europe's leading museum directors sought to evoke this *zeitgeist* through assembling collections in historical settings. In this way their museums could explore wider questions of aesthetic creativity and cultural identity.[10] Protests followed in the press that devoting galleries to specific materials ignored many of the museum's treasures that had been gathered over 50 years through collecting with different aims. In 1909 the director of the Wallace Collection, Claude Phillips, described the new V&A in the *Daily Telegraph* as like 'some immense, finely-appointed modern hospital for the analysis and dissection of applied art rather than that of a temple of the higher delight'.[11]

In 1909 Arthur Skinner was replaced as director by Cecil Harcourt Smith who had taken over from Dilke as chair of the Committee of Re-arrangement. Skinner was downgraded to Keeper of Architecture and Sculpture. His sudden death 15 months later, age 49, 'of a broken heart' was described at his funeral as an 'official murder'.[12] Despite the return to an 1850s display policy, two weeks after Skinner's death the V&A celebrated his greatest coup, with the opening of the Salting Collection (see chapter 17), shown as a single collection. Harcourt Smith faced another contradiction. For all his readiness to collect the contemporary he soon came up against the lingering 'general rule to acquire nothing that was less than fifty years old'.[13] This was due to controversy still lingering from 1900 over the donation by George Donaldson (chapter 16).

Another conspicuous commitment to collectors over contemporary designers was made in 1909 when one of the largest galleries in the new building, the Octagon Court (room 40, built to balance the Architectural ('Cast') Courts) was devoted to loans. Hitherto, for 45 years, loans had filled the even more spacious South Court, with J.P. Morgan's more recent loans in the North Court. This new 'Loans Court' would remain until 1933.[14] However, collectors' loans and bequests were at risk in unexpected ways. In 1912 the Loans Court, Salting Collection and the ceramics galleries (home to the Schreiber Collection) were all closed as a precaution against militant suffragettes, after two separate suffragette attacks on displays at the British Museum (it announced in May 1912 that women would only be admitted with a written assurance that they would be accompanied by a responsible adult).[15]

The loss of Morgan's collection and of the Fitzhenry Gift in 1912–13 left huge gaps in the galleries. In 1913 a new Advisory Council to the Board of Education was established to advise 'on questions of principle and policy, and on the conditions and needs of the museum'.[16] A summary was prepared of 'The Purposes and Functions of the Museum'.[17] Following an extensive review by Harcourt Smith, working with curators and sub-committees, in 1914 the Council adopted a *Report on the Principal Deficiencies in the Collections of the Victoria and Albert Museum.* Their report called for a new acquisitions policy and an increase in the museum's buying budget.[18] The strategic decision had been taken: in the 20th century the V&A's approach to collecting would be less dependent on private collectors as lenders.

In the same year the V&A published a *General Guide to the Collections*. This substantial (107-page) overview for the public describes eight curatorial departments, followed by chapters on the Salting Collection, the Jones Collection, the Murray Collection and 'The Octagon Court (loans)'. The *General Guide* reveals how these and other major donated collections had been given dedicated galleries in the new building, to meet the collectors' wishes, to retain the personal and period character of their collections, and to ensure their acknowledgement by name.[19] In his introduction, Harcourt Smith raised 'the question of the Loan Collections. It has been felt, for instance, that the interpolation of groups of assorted objects tends to confuse the general scheme, and that such loans by their liability to withdrawal are apt to disturb any ordered system. It has, therefore, been decided as a rule to confine collections deposited on loan to a special Court'.[20] After all this resolve to reduce dependence on private collections, it is surprising to read the section on the Octagon Court, which describes, through five pages, objects belonging to 55 living lenders, ranging from David Currie's Renaissance manuscripts, ceramics and metalwork to the coronation gifts received by His Majesty the King.

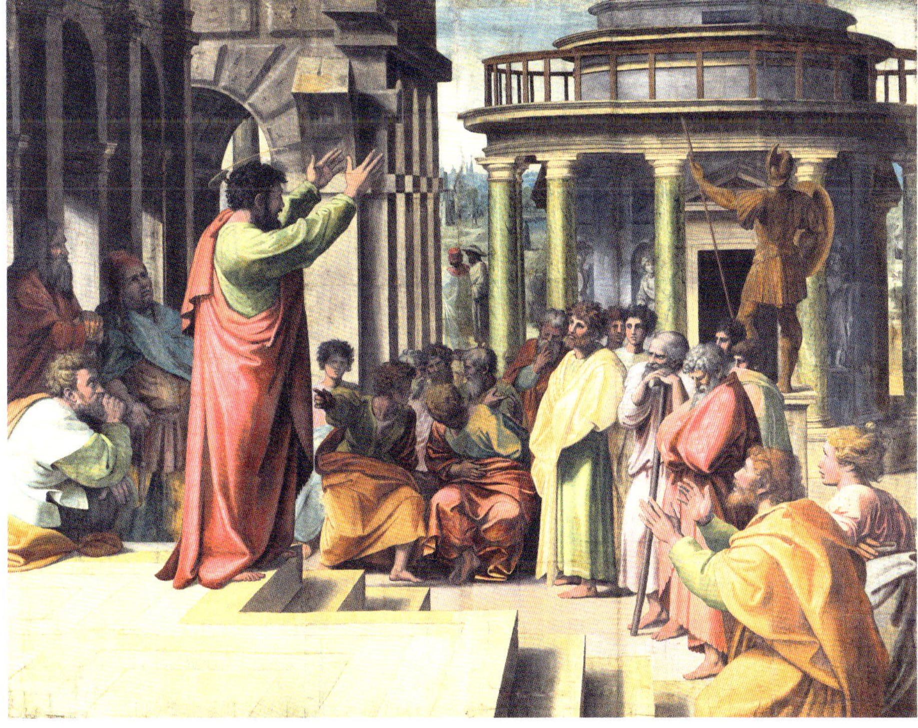

**150.** RAPHAEL, *Paul Preaching at Athens*, *c.*1515–16, bodycolour over charcoal on paper, later mounted on canvas. On loan from Her Majesty The Queen, RCIN 912945. V&A: ROYAL LOANS. 7

# 20 Postscript: After 1914

DESPITE THE NEW RESOLUTIONS, the love of collections continued. Harcourt Smith retired as director of the museum in 1924 and was succeeded by the former Keeper of Architecture and Sculpture, Eric Maclagan (1879–1951). When asked by a Royal Commission on National Museums and Galleries in 1928 to explain the purpose of the V&A, Maclagan replied: 'it satisfies communally a kind of collecting instinct of the nation'.[1] When the same royal commission asked him if the V&A had become 'a mere museum for connoisseurs and collectors' he replied that the observation was 'fair but for the insertion of the word "mere"'. In 1932 Maclagan wrote to the museum's Advisory Council suggesting that the time had come to find a new use for the Octagon Court, instead of devoting it to private loans. Maclagan had grown reluctant to accept private loans except as 'a preliminary stage to a gift or bequest' and told the Council 'I have always felt that the whole policy of extensive loans belongs rather to the earlier stages in a Museum's history'.[2] In 1936 the Octagon Court reopened; instead of a great variety of private loans it presented a chronological display of English furniture and art.

Maclagan recognised the need to find space to create new thematic galleries, where the collections could be arranged by country and period, to complement rather than replace the material-specific galleries, but the Second World War interrupted his plans. After the war the return of collections from safe storage brought the chance to rearrange the entire museum, so at last everything could change. In 1952 Maclagan's successor as director, Leigh Ashton (1897–1983), in a lecture given to the Royal Society of Arts, observed that under his predecessors 'the collector was considered at perhaps too high a value'.[3] Ashton implemented Maclagan's vision for reconciling the dual roles of the museum in the first comprehensive reinstallation since the building had been completed and reopened in 1909. He rearranged the V&A into two types of galleries and this brilliantly simple overall approach to display and interpretation still stands today. The galleries leading off from the main entrance on Cromwell Road present the cultural histories of the East (South Asia, Middle East, Korea, Japan and China), and of Europe and Great Britain. There, collections and displays can be explored in terms of the history of art and design, of patronage, taste and style. Most of the rest of the museum is arranged by grouping together specific materials and techniques.

To achieve this clear distinction the reinstallation divided up many of the collections that had traditionally been shown under the names of collectors and donors. Subject to new expert scrutiny and to the competing demands for gallery space, lesser items were withdrawn from display. Collecting and fashions in taste could still be studied in the period galleries in the context of historic collectors. In the 20th century the V&A was not alone among international museums in reducing the prominence of named collections and in renaming its dedicated galleries. In many museums, limitations of space and the obligations of fundraising meant that new names were given to old galleries, to recognise the generosity of new generations of supporters who contributed to refurbishment and redisplay projects, and to the collections themselves.

In recent years the history of collecting has achieved academic standing and wider interest, driven partly by high-profile legal cases for the restitution of art objects to families of former owners and by appeals from countries seeking their cultural heritage. International concerns about imperial loot and restitution claims have generated political debates and greater investment in provenance research. For V&A visitors curious about how and why objects came together and into the galleries, understanding the museum's relationships with collectors and donors can be a first step; many accounts can be found in catalogues, online and in specialist displays and journals (see Further Reading).

In the 21st century the V&A still collects and displays collections, as space permits. One great example is the Rosalinde and Arthur Gilbert Collection of around 1,200 items, on loan to the V&A since 2008. Shown as a collection, ranging from portrait miniatures and furniture decorated with micromosaics to goldsmiths' masterpieces worthy of a princely *Kunstkammer*, the Gilbert Collection leads the museum in researching provenance, to identify past owners of objects to whom they could rightfully belong. In 2014 the Wedgwood Collection of 3,000 items was saved from dispersal through sale by the Art Fund and donated to the V&A, for display in its own museum in Barlaston. The Royal Photographic Society's collection of around 300,000 objects transferred from the Science Museum to the V&A in 2017; as well as key early works and equipment from the history of photography there is the RPS Library of over 26,000 items that includes the world's best collection of 19th- and early 20th-century photographic publications. Another recent arrival, in 2020, is Leslie Linder's collection of some 8,000 sketches and books by Beatrix Potter that joins the earlier donation of the Linder Bequest. Gifts can also establish new national collection fields at the museum, as with the donation of the Computer Art Society's archive of pioneering digital art, begun in the 1950s (2008). With the opening of V&A East Storehouse, the collections research centre in Stratford, east London, the work of artists and designers can be more visible in the Archive of Art and Design. Examples include Eduardo Paolozzi's Krazy Kat Arkive of 20th-century popular visual culture (donated in 1985) and the career archives of designers such as Alec Cobbe (2013) and Kenneth Grange (2021).

Edmund de Waal has stimulated appreciation of collectors and collecting through his best-selling memoir of the Ephrussi family collection, *The Hare with Amber Eyes. A Hidden Inheritance* (2010) and through his art as a ceramicist. In 2015 he donated to the V&A *The Collector (for Paul)*, a new installation comprising seventeen porcelain vessels arranged in a cabinet, given in honour of Sir Paul Ruddock, chairman of the V&A's trustees at the time and creator of The Wyvern Collection of medieval, renaissance and later art. [4]

When museum collections are understood as the legacies of collectors, they can offer rich levels of meaning and interpretation, as evidence of the taste and ambitions of a historical period, and as keys to fascinating characters, some of whom were pioneers in the history of scholarship in their chosen fields. As more and more questions are asked about the sources of collections, some bring uncomfortable answers and issues to address around exploitation and appropriation. Thanks to investment by museums in online catalogues, today anyone can begin to research and reassemble on screen historical collections that may now be dispersed through galleries, stores, in multiple museums and the art market.

This book has sought to reintroduce the V&A's leading Victorian and Edwardian collectors through exploring their motivations for forming their collections, together with their impact on museum policies and displays. This great tradition continues today, as generous lenders and donors to the V&A play a vital role in the appreciation of historic collections, and in our understanding of the irrepressible human impulse to collect.

# Notes

## Part I

### Chapter 1

1. Barry E. O'Meara, *Napoleon in Exile*, London, 1822, vol.1, p.81.
2. Quoted in Elsner and Cardinal, 1994, p.9.
3. Bryant, 2019, pp 47–50, 60–66.
4. Bryant, 2019, pp 44–9.
5. *List of Objects in the Art Division, South Kensington Museum, Lent during the year 1879*, London, 1880. See also, Eatwell, 2000, pp 21, 25, 26.

### Chapter 2

1. Conforti, 1997, pp 23–4.
2. Reitlinger, 1963, pp 112–23.
3. Hobsbawn, 1975, pp 307–8; Hobsbawn, 1987, pp 35–46.
4. *Seventeenth Report of the Science and Art Department of the Committee of Council on Education*, London, 1870, p.xviii.
5. Anon., 'Earl Spencer's pictures at South Kensington', *Architect*, 30 September 1876, p.194.
6. David A. Traill, *Schliemann of Troy*, London, 1995, pp 205–6. Abigail Baker, *Troy on Display: Scepticism and Wonder at Schliemann's First Exhibition*, London and New York, 2020, pp 131–7. From South Kensington the exhibition moved to the Royal Museum in Berlin for another three-year display.
7. Conway, 1882, p.81.
8. *Truth*, 20 September 1883, p.397, V&A Press Cuttings, MA/49/2/59 (July 1883–August 1884), p.1.
9. *Twenty-eighth Report of the Science and Art Department of the Committee of Council on Education*, London, 1881, p.xxi.

### Chapter 3

1. J.C. Robinson, *Department of Science and Art: Catalogue of a Collection of Works of Decorative Art . . . Circulated for Exhibition in Provincial Schools of Art*, London, 1855, p.3.
2. J.C. Robinson, *Catalogue of the Soulages Collection, Compiled by J.C. Robinson*, London, 1856, pp iv–v.
3. Neiswander, 2008, pp 11–31.
4. Eastlake, 1969, pp 135–6.
5. Kerr, 1864, p.358.
6. Loftie, 1876, p.89, cited in Black, 2000, pp 75–6.
7. Loftie, 1876, p.89, cited in Black, 2000, pp 75–6.
8. Eastlake, 1969, p.281.
9. Conway, 1882, p.15.

### Chapter 4

1. Bryant, 2014, pp 58–81.
2. *Tenth Report of the Science and Art Department of the Committee of Council on Education*, London, 1863, pp x–xi.
3. Anon., *The Art Wealth of England: A Series of Photographs, Representing Fifty of the Most Valuable Works of Art Contributed on Loan to the Special Exhibition of the South Kensington Museum*, London, 1862.
4. *Tenth Report of the Science and Art Department . . .*, 1863, p.xxi; see also pp 135, 141, 185.
5. J.C. Robinson, 'Our public art museums: A retrospect', *The Nineteenth Century*, vol.42, no.250, December 1897, pp 940–64, p.959.
6. J.C. Robinson (ed.), *Catalogue of the Special Exhibition of Works of Art of the Medieval, Renaissance, and More Modern Periods on Loan at the South Kensington Museum, June 1862*, 5 parts, London, 1863. Robinson lists all the contributors in his annual report in *Tenth Report of the Science and Art Department . . .*, 1863, p.135.
7. A.W. Franks, 'The Apology of My Life', in Caygill and Cherry, 1997, pp 318–31, p.322.
8. Eatwell, 1994.
9. For Layard's books, prints, drawings and photographs donated by Lady Layard's niece, see Rebecca Coombes, 'Sir Austen Henry Layard 1817–1894', in National Art Library, 1995, pp 11–17.
10. *Tenth Report of the Science and Art Department . . .*, 1863, p.135.
11. *Tenth Report of the Science and Art Department . . .*, 1863, p.134.
   For purchases in 1851 and the Soltykoff Collection sale in 1861, see Bryant, 2019, pp 28–33, 67–8, 94–101.
12. *Tenth Report of the Science and Art Department . . .*, 1863, p.132.
13. *Eighteenth Report of the Science and Art Department of the Committee of Council on Education*, London, 1871, p.401.

### Chapter 5

1. *Eleventh Report of the Science and Art Department of the Committee of Council on Education*, London, 1864, pp 7–8.
2. For Webb see Wainwright, 1989, pp 45–6, 292–3 and Wainwright, 2002, IV.
3. Clive Wainwright, '"A gatherer and disposer of other men's stuffe": Murray Marks, connoisseur and curiosity dealer', *Journal of the History of Collections*, vol.14, no.1, 2002, pp 161–7, pp167–8.
4. *Second Report from the Select Committee on the Museums of the Science and Art Department; with the Proceedings of the Committee, Minutes of Evidence, and Appendix*, London, 1898, pp xiii–xiv. Appendix 9 records payments for advice. For the Art Referees' duties, see V&A Archive ED 84/33.
5. Jane Dyson and Timothy Wilson, 'Draft letter from C.D.E. Fortnum to Sir Charles Robinson, 1897, commenting on the management of the South Kensington Museum and Robinson's treatment by the authorities', *Journal of the History of Collections*, vol.11, no.2, 1999, pp 271–3. See also: Wainwright, 1999 and Wilson, 2004.
6. Bryant, 2015, pp 16–17.
7. Elizabeth James, 'Publishing the museum collection', in Bryant, 2011, pp 186–7; and James, 1998, pp 31–53.
8. Science and Art Department, *Dyce Collection: A Catalogue of the Paintings, Miniatures, Drawings, Engravings, Rings and Miscellaneous Objects Bequeathed by the Reverend Alexander Dyce*, London, 1874, p.1.
9. Simon Spier, 'Between the museum and the market: John Hungerford Pollen (1820–1902) and antique furniture, with special reference to his work at the South Kensington Museum', *Furniture History*, vol.57, 2021, pp 191–208.
10. *Précis of the Minutes of the Science and Art Department, 16th Feb. 1852 to 1st July 1863*, London, 1864, p.250.
11. Anon., 'Minor topics of the month', *The Art Journal*, 1863, p.230, describes Wallis as 'assistant keeper of the Museum' under the newly promoted keeper, R.H. Soden Smith.
12. George Wallis, 'The economical formation of art museums for the people', *Transactions of the National Association for the Advancement of Art and its Application to Industry, Liverpool Meeting, 1888*, London, 1888, pp 288–90, quoted in Burton, 1999, p.79.
13. Grant and Patterson, 2018; Bryant, 2011, pp 196–205. For the Cast Courts see Patterson and Trusted, 2018; also Bryant, 2017, pp 141–45 and Physick, 1982, pp 156–60.
14. Peter H. Hoffenberg, *An Empire on Display: English, Indian and Australian Exhibitions from the Crystal Palace to the Great War*, Berkeley, 2001, p.1; Bryant and Weber, 2017, pp 27–8, 251–8; Burton, 1999, pp 116–17.
15. Baker and Richardson pp 232–3, 269–72. See also: Faulkner and Jackson, pp 152–95.
16. William Morris to Henry Wallis, 11 March 1882, Bodleian Library, Oxford, quoted in Wilson, 2002, part 1, p.154.
17. *Morning Post*, February 1883, V&A Cuttings Book, April 1882–June 1883, p.48.
18. Emilia Dilke, 'Art-teaching and technical schools', *Fortnightly Review*, February 1890, p.234, quoted in Burton, 1999, p.129. See also Robson, 1995 and Israel, 1999.

19. Fiona MacCarthy, *William Morris*, London, 1994, pp 332, 662.
20. Norman Kelvin (ed.), *The Collected Letters of William Morris*, 2 vols, New Jersey, 1987, vol.2, p.403n.
21. Quoted in Yallop, 2011, p.116.
22. *Forty-fourth Report from the Department of Science and Art . . .*, 1896, para 49.
23. House of Commons, *First Report . . .*, 1897; *Second Report . . .*, 1898.
24. House of Commons, *Second Report . . .*, 1898, p.xxi.
25. House of Commons, *Second Report . . .*, 1898, p.xxii.
26. House of Commons, *Second Report . . .*, 1898, pp xxi–xxii.
27. Burton, 1999, pp 145–151; Hobhouse, 2002, pp 254–6.
28. Board of Education, *Report of the Board of Education for the Year 1913–1914*, London, 1915, p.185.
29. V. & A. M. Advisory Council, Reports no.4, *Report on the Principal Deficiencies in the Collections of the Victoria and Albert Museum &c., Adopted by the Advisory Council at a Meeting Held on 13th February 1914*, V&A Archive, Ed.84/106.

# Part II

## Chapter 6

1. For Sheepshanks's Deed of Gift, see Department of Science and Art, 1889, pp 6–7. See also: Sheepshanks Collection nominal file MA/2/S10, V&A Archive; Redgrave, 1857; Heleniak, 2000, pp 91–107; Heleniak, 2012/13, pp 69–80; Bryant, 2019, pp 111–15; Whitehead, 2005, pp 164–76.
2. Department of Science and Art, 1889, pp 6–7.
3. Department of Science and Art, 1889, p.8.
4. Graham Reynolds, *Catalogue of the Constable Collection*, London, 1973, p.3.
5. Turner, White and Evans, 2014, p.xxi.
6. Bryant, 2017, p.80; Bryant, 2019, pp 122–4.

## Chapter 7

1. C.H. Townshend nominal file MA/1/T1191, V&A Archive. Department of Science and Art, 1889, pp 11–12. See also Shalloo, 1995, pp 2–9.
2. G. Hogarth and M. Dickens (eds), *The Letters of Charles Dickens*, 3 vols, London, 1880–82, vol.2, p.372.
3. Parke Godwin, *A Biography of William Cullen Bryant*, New York, 1883, vol.1, pp 392–3. See also Haworth-Booth, 1984, pp 11–21.
4. Quoted in Kauffmann, 1973, vol.2, p.9.
5. Gustav Waagen, *Galleries and Cabinets of Art in Great Britain*, London, 1857, pp 176–81.
6. Robert Rosenblum, *Modern Painting and the Northern Romantic Tradition: From Friedrich to Rothko*, New York, 1975.
7. Rev. Chauncy Hare Townshend, post-mortem register of the contents of his London house, 1868, in nominal file MA/1/T1191, V&A Archive. For inventories see *Seventeenth Report of the Science and Art Department . . .*, 1870, pp xviii, 383.
8. George Barrington, *A Voyage to New South Wales*, London, 1795 and 1801, and *The History of New South Wales*, London, 1802 and 1810.
9. *Guide to the Art Collections*, London, 1869, passim. For the Meyrick Collection, see Wainwright, 1989, pp 241–68.
10. Rev. Alexander Dyce and John Forster, Esq (bequests) nominal file MA/1/D2023/1–8, V&A Archive. See also: Department of Science and Art, 1889, pp 13–14.
11. William Carew Hazlitt, *Four Generations of a Literary Family: The Hazlitts in England, Ireland, and America*, 2 vols, London, 1897, vol.2, p.262.
12. Anon., *Handbook of the Dyce and Forster Collections in the South Kensington Museum*, London, 1880, p.12.
13. Samuel Redgrave, George William Reid and Charles C. Black, *Dyce Collection: A Catalogue of the Paintings, Miniatures, Drawings, Engravings, Rings and Miscellaneous Objects Bequeathed by the Reverend Alexander Dyce*, London, 1874, pp v–vi.
14. South Kensington Museum, *A Series of Twelve Plates of Views and Decorative Details of the Museum from Drawings by John Watkins*, London, 1889, plate 12.
15. *Seventeenth Report of the Science and Art Department . . .*, 1870, pp xvii–xviii.
16. Department of Science and Art, 1889, p.12.

## Chapter 8

1. James A. Davies, *John Forster: A Literary Life*, Leicester, 1983, p.166. See also pp 260–61.
2. The British Library has the manuscript of *Nicholas Nickleby* and some fragments of *Oliver Twist*. The manuscript for *Great Expectations* is in Wisbech and Fenland Museum, Wisbech, Cambridgeshire; *A Christmas Carol* and *Our Mutual Friend* are in the Morgan Library, New York.
3. V&A: F.74.
4. Christopher Frayling, *Henry Cole and the Chamber of Horrors: The Curious Origins of the Victoria and Albert Museum*, London, 2010, pp 18–21; Bonython and Burton p.155.
5. Department of Science and Art, 1889, pp 17–19: 'The Will of John Forster'. See also: Anon., *Handbook of the Dyce and Forster Collections . . .*, 1880, pp 74–94.
6. Redgrave, Reid and Black, 1874, pp v–vi. For the new museum building in 1848 see Lucilla Burn, *The Fitzwilliam Museum: A History*, London and New York, 2016, pp 61, 67, 75, 77.
7. Anon., *Handbook of the Dyce and Forster Collections . . .*, 1880, p.2.
8. Piot bequeathed his fortune to the Académie des Inscriptions et Belles-Lettres in Paris, which sponsored the publication of art and archaeology studies, for which he is best known. See: Fondation Piot, *Monuments et mémoires de la fondation Eugène Piot*, Paris, 1894–2005, vol.1, pp vii–xxiii.
9. Rowan Watson, *Western Illuminated Manuscripts: A Catalogue of Works in the National Art Library . . . with a Complete Account of the George Reid Collection*, 3 vols, London, 2011, vol.2, pp 8–11.
10. Robson, 1995, pp 18–25. See also: Colin Eisler, 'Lady Dilke (1840–1904): the six lives of an art historian', in Claire Richter Sherman with Adele M. Holcomb (eds), *Women as Interpreters of the Visual Arts, 1820–1979*, Westport, Connecticut, and London, 1981, pp 147–80.
11. Bettley, 2001. See also Watson, James and Bryant, 2015.

# Part III

## Chapter 9

1. Bryant, 2019, p.58.
2. Lady C. Schreiber nominal file MA/1/S793, V&A Archive; Anon., *Catalogue of English Porcelain, Earthenware, Enamels &c: Collected by Charles Schreiber and Lady Charlotte Elizabeth Schreiber and Presented to the South Kensington Museum in 1884*, London, 1885.
3. John Malcolm Russell, *From Nineveh to New York*, New Haven and London, 1997.
4. Guest, 1911, vol.2. p.433 (1 September 1884).
5. Guest, 1911, vol.1, p.6 (21 May 1869). See also: Somers Cocks, 1980, pp 48–52; Eatwell, 1994, pp 125–45.
6. As Eatwell noted (1994, p.127), one influence was probably Lady Schreiber's son Monty Guest who began collecting ceramics in 1860, about five years before his mother.
7. Guest, 1911, vol.1, p.xxvi.
8. For Spence's contribution to the V&A's collections, see Bryant, 2019, pp 59, 68–9,77, 85, 99.
9. Guest, 1911, vol.1, p.9 (3 June 1869).
10. Guest, 1911, vol.1, pp 6–7 (22 May 1869).
11. Guest, 1911, vol.2, p.435 (1 September 1884).
12. Eatwell, 1994.
13. Guest, 1911, vol 2, p.433 (30 August 1884).
14. Guest, 1911, vol.2, p.450 (24 October 1884). The portraits by G.F. Watts are reproduced in Guest, 1911, vol.2, pp 432, 436.
15. Deed of Gift, Lady C. Schreiber nominal file MA/1/S793, V&A Archive.
16. Guest, 1911, vol.2, p.471 (18 March 1885). Her son Ivor suggested mosaic; the idea may have come from the mosaic memorial to Henry Cole on the museum's main staircase, installed 1878, or from the mosaic portraits in the South Court (Bryant, 2017, pp 68, 95–108).
17. Read found great prominence as an art critic and historian after leaving the V&A in 1931 to become Professor of Fine Arts at the University of Edinburgh.
18. Herrmann, 1999, pp 329–30.

19. Bernhard Rackham, *Catalogue of the Schreiber Collection of English Porcelain, Earthenware, Enamels etc*, 2 vols, London, 1915, rev. 1928–30.

## Chapter 10

1. Bryant, 2019, pp 26–8, 33, 37, 40.
2. Wainwright, 2002, III, p.55.
3. Quoted in Wainwright, 2002, III, pp 56–7.
4. *Précis of the Board Minutes of the Science and Art Department, from 23rd December 1869 to 31st December 1877*, London, 1878, pp 400–401.
5. J.F. Riaño nominal file MA/1/R741/1–8 (Art Referee reports); Thompson, Mr and Mrs Yates (Riaño Collection) nominal file MA/1/T650/1–2; Juan F. Riaño, *Classified and Descriptive Catalogue of the Art Objects of Spanish Production in the South Kensington Museum*, London, 1872; Juan F. Riaño, *The Industrial Arts in Spain*, London, 1879. See also: Trusted, 2006; Wainwright, 2002, III, pp 46–7, 58–9.
6. Conway, 1882, pp 78–9.
7. *Précis of the Board Minutes of the Science and Art Department, 1st January 1878 to 31 December 1880*, London, 1881, p.380.
8. Quoted in Davies, 1992, p.320.
9. Tucker, 2002.
10. Dr & Mrs S.W. Bushell nominal file MA/1/B3676, V&A Archive; S.W. Bushell. 'Notes on the old Mongolian capital of Shangtu', *Journal of the Royal Asiatic Society of Great Britain and Ireland*, vol.7, 1875, pp 329–38. See also: Pearce, 2005–6. Bushell's other major projects included *Oriental Ceramic Art* in ten volumes (1896), the catalogue of the collection of W.T. Walters of Baltimore.
11. Rebecca Naylor, 'Major General Sir Robert Murdoch Smith', in Stanley, 2004, pp 136–7. See also: Scarce, 1981; Burton, 1999, p.120; and Thomas, 2011.
12. Quoted in Michael Leonard Helfgott, *Ties that Bind: A Social History of the Iranian Carpet*, Washington D.C., 1994, p.126.
13. For a first-hand description of the museum's display of Persian art collected by Murdoch Smith, see Conway, 1882, pp 94–8.
14. Helfgott, 1994, pp 131–3; Carey, 2017, pp 100–107.
15. For Clarke in India, where he was guided as a collector by J.L. Kipling, see Bryant and Weber, 2017, pp 25–29.
16. Stanley, 2004; Carey, 2017, pp 41–69, 87–108.
17. Rev. Greville John Chester nominal file MA/1/C1212, V&A Archive. Hinson, 2021.
18. Mercedes Volait, *Antique Dealing and Creative Reuse in Cairo and Damascus 1850–1890*, Leiden and Boston, 2021, pp 44–9, 62–5, 134, 137.
19. V&A: 7004 to 7095-1860.
20. V&A: 8553 to 8713-1863.
21. Dr Franz Johann Joseph Bock nominal file MA/1/B1764, V&A Archive; Wainwright, 2002, III, p.55.
22. Norbert Jopek, 'Kanonikus Dr. Franz Bock und das South Kensington Museum', in Michael Embach (ed.), *Sancta Treveris: Festscrift für Franz Ronig zum 70. Geburtstag*, Trier, 1999.
23. George Wingfield Digby, *Victoria and Albert Museum: The Tapestry Collection, Medieval and Renaissance*, London, 1980, cat.10: V&A: 8241-1863.
24. Henry Wallis nominal file MA/1/W330 Part I–VI, V&A Archive. See also Wilson, 2002.
25. Flinders W. Petrie nominal file MA/1/P1061, V&A Archive. See also: Persson, 2012.
26. Major W.J. Myers and Mr D.B. Myers nominal file MA/1/M3321 Part I–V, V&A Archive.

## Chapter 11

1. Barringer, 1998; Mitter and Clunas, 1997, pp 221–273; Bryant and Weber, 2017, pp 1–35; Schuhmacher, 2022.
2. Schuhmacher, 2022.
3. Edward M. Spiers, 'Spoils of war: Custom and practice', in Lidchi and Allan, 2020, pp 19–38. See also: Richard H. Davis, 'Three styles in looting India', *History and Anthropology*, vol.6, no.4, 1994, pp 293–317.
4. Bryant and Weber, 2017, pp 14–15, 20.
5. Stronge, 1999, p.82.
6. Robert Skelton, 'The Shah Jahan Cup', *Bulletin of the Victoria and Albert Museum*, vol.2, no.3, 1966, pp 104–11; Stronge, 1993–4. See also: catalogue entries by Susan Stronge in Bryant, 2011, pp 240–41.
7. For Henry Hardy Cole, see Bryant and Weber, 2017, pp 20–25.
8. Science and Art Department, *A Guide to the Collections of the South Kensington Museum, Illustrated with Plans and Wood Engravings*, London, 1894, p.25.
9. Victoria and Albert Museum, 1901, p.85.
10. Volker Matthies, *The Siege of Magdala: The British Empire Against the Emperor of Ethiopia*, Princeton, New Jersey, 2011.
11. *Seventeenth Report of the Science and Art Department . . .* , 1870, p.xvii.
12. William Gladstone, 'Motion for an Address' (30 June 1871), *House of Commons Hansard Archive*, vol.207, 1871, cols 939–52, 949. See also: Anon., 'The expedition to Abyssinia', *Illustrated London News*, vol.52, no.1488, 20 June 1868, p.609, and Jacques Mercier, 'The gold crown of Magdala', *Apollo*, vol.164, December 2006, no.538, pp 46–53.
13. For other Ethiopian objects relating to Maqdala in the V&A, including jewellery, arms and armour, drawings, sacred texts and documentary photographs, and the V&A display, see Jones, 2019.
14. Martin Bailey, 'UK museums face controversial Ethiopian legacy', *Art Newspaper*, no.151, October 2004, pp 15, 18–19.
15. For the Maqdala and Asante campaigns and the V&A display in 2018, see Jones, 2019; also Lidchi and Allan, 2020, pp 23–30, 277–8.
16. Garrard's records of the auction were destroyed in the Second World War.
17. *Twenty-second Report of the Department of Science and Art*, London, 1875, p.xiv.
18. Anon., 'From Cape Coast to Coomassie: An illustrated narrative of the Ashanti War', *Illustrated London News*, vol.64, no.1801, 28 February 1874, pp 189; no.1802, 7 March 1874, pp 213, 216–17; no.1803, 14 March 1874, pp 240–42, 244–5; no.1804, 21 March 1874, pp 264–6, 278; no.1805, 28 March 1874, pp 290, 292–3; no.1806, 4 April 1874, pp 314–16.
19. Anon., 'King Coffee Calcalli's Umbrella at the South Kensington Museum', *The Graphic*, vol.10, no.243, 25 July 1874, pp 78, 89. See also: 'Coffee Calcallee's umbrella', *Illustrated London News*, vol.64, no.1799, 14 February 1874, pp 141, 143–5.
20. Conway, 1875, p.72.
21. William Fagg, 'Ashanti gold', *The Connoisseur*, vol.185, January 1974, pp 41–8; Angus Patterson, 'Asante goldweights', *Journal of the Antique Metalware Society*, vol.15, June 2007, p.38.
22. Spiers, 2020, p.22 and in the same volume: Louise Tythacott, 'Military histories of "Summer Palace" objects from China in military museums in the United Kingdom', pp 187–204; see also Hill, 2013.
23. James L. Hevia, 'Loot's fate: The economy of plunder and the moral life of objects "from the Summer Palace of the Emperor of China"', *History and Anthropology*, vol.6, no.4, 1994, pp 319–45.
24. Viscount Garnet Wolseley, *Narrative of the War with China in 1860*, London, 1862, p.236. Cushion covers donated by Wolseley's widow are V&A: T.134-5-1917 and T.138-140-1917.
25. Craig Clunas, 'The Imperial Collections: East Asian art', in Baker and Richardson, 1997, pp 230–37, 259 cat.105; and Clunas, 1998.
26. Grant and Patterson, 2018, chapter 8 (pp 128–35): 'Expressions of imperial power: Electrotypes of the Perak Royal Regalia at the Colonial and Indian Exhibition (1886)'. Electrotypes were also produced after Asante gold ornaments: Grant and Patterson, 2018, p.134.
27. John Clarke, 'On the road back to Mandalay: The Burmese Regalia – seizure, display and return to Myanmar in 1964', in Louise Tythacott and Panggah Ardiyansyah (eds), *Returning Southeast Asia's Past: Objects, Museums and Restitution*, Singapore, 2021, pp 111–38.
28. See for example the book accompanying a V&A display: Gill Saunders and Zoe Whitley, *In Black and White: Prints from Africa and the Diaspora*, London, 2013.
29. Jones, 2019.

# Part IV

## Chapter 12

1. E.T. Cook and Alexander Wedderburn (eds), *The Works of John Ruskin*, 39 vols, London, 1903–12, vol 33, p.307 (first published in *The Art of England*, 1883–4).
2. *Second Report of the Commissioners for the 1851 Exhibition*, London, 1852, p.11.
3. Gottfried Semper, 'Practical art in metals', 1854, no.2, manuscript, National Art Library; Bryant, 2011, p.153.
4. Bud, 2010, p.14: 'as a consequence of conflating the history of the South Kensington Museum with that of the V&A Museum the [Science] Museum has been portrayed as the . . . remnant left behind.'
5. For a summary of Prince Albert's intellectual training, see Bryant, 2011, pp 24–39.
6. In its responsibility for the museum the Department of Science and Art replaced the Board of Trade's Department of Practical Art, established in 1852.
7. Physick, 1982, p.127. For the windows, made in 1866 by J. Powell & Sons, removed in 1912, see Bryant, 2017, pp 64–7.
8. Conway, 1882, p.49. This text is expanded from articles first published in *Harper's New Monthly Magazine*, vol.51, 1875, pp 486–503, 649–66. See also Bryant, 2017, p.163 fig.206.
9. John Hewish, *The Indefatigable Mr Woodcroft*, London, 1979; Burton, 1999, pp 44, 51; Taylor, 1975, pp 248–56.
10. Bryant, 2011, pp 208–13; Bryant, 2019, pp 127–9.
11. Quoted by Susan Owens in Bryant, 2011, p.210, cat.238.
12. Dale Dishon, 'South Kensington's forgotten palace', *The Decorative Arts Society Journal*, vol.38, 2014, pp 21–43.
13. The importance of ship models to the South Kensington Museum is evident from the *Catalogue of the Naval Models in the South Kensington Museum*, London, 1865, revised editions of which were published in 1869, 1874, 1878 and 1889.
14. Science and Art Department, *Catalogue of the Special Loan Collection of Scientific Apparatus at the South Kensington Museum, 1876*, third edition, London, 1877.
15. Quoted in Bud, 2010, p.23. See also: Hobhouse, 2002, p.204.
16. Bryant, 2011, pp 209, 211.
17. Anon., 'The Science Collections at South Kensington', *Nature*, vol.XLI, no.1062, 6 March 1890, p.409. The journal's founder-editor, Norman Lockyer, had been lobbying for a separate museum since the loan exhibition in 1876.
18. David Follett, *The Rise of the Science Museum under Henry Lyons*, London, 1978, p.5.
19. Hobhouse, 2002, p.255.
20. Anon., *The Guide to the Victoria and Albert Museum*, London, 1908, pp 53–65.
21. https://www.discoversouthkensington.com.

## Chapter 13

1. Physick, 1982, pp 143–6.
2. Bryant, 2021.
3. For the Food Museum and Animal Products Collection, see Burton, 1999, pp 45, 51–3, 56, 81.
4. Charles Dickens Jr, *Dickens's Dictionary of London*, London, 1879, p 25. See also: Anon., 'Royalty at Bethnal-Green', *Illustrated London News*, 29 June 1872, p.614.
5. Barbara Lasic, '"Splendid patriotism": Richard Wallace and the construction of the Wallace Collection', *Journal of the History of Collections*, vol.21, no.2, 2009, pp 173–82; Suzanne Higgott, *The Most Fortunate Man of his Day: Sir Richard Wallace, Connoisseur, Collector & Philanthropist*, London, 2018.
6. Donald Mallett, *The Greatest Collector: Lord Hertford and the Founding of the Wallace Collection*, London, 1979, p.148.
7. *Catalogue of the Anthropological Collection Lent by Colonel Lane Fox for Exhibition in the Bethnal Green Branch of the South Kensington Museum June 1874: Parts I and II*, London, 1874, p.xvi.
8. Alison Petch, '"Man as he was and Man as he is": General Pitt Rivers's collection', *Journal of the History of Collections*, vol.10, 1998, pp 75–85; Alison Petch, 'Chance and certitude: Pitt Rivers and his first collection', *Journal of the History of Collections*, vol.18, 2006, pp 256–66. Lane Fox assumed the name of his great uncle, Pitt Rivers, when he inherited his estate in 1880.
9. *Twenty-eighth Report of the Department of Science and Art*, London, 1880, p.xxi.
10. Joseph Bond nominal file MA/1/B1844, V&A Archive. The Bond collection inventory numbers are 803 to 845-1890, plus the earlier purchases: 549 to 578-1874; 481 to 528-1875; 751 to 781-1877.
11. Gladstone had lent ceramics (in 1867), jewellery (1871) and ivories (1875).
12. Charles H. Derby, *A Brief Guide to the Various Collections in the Bethnal Green Branch of the South Kensington Museum*, London, 1890, p.4. See also: Anthony Burton, *The Bethnal Green Museum of Childhood*, London, 1997; Burton, 1999, pp 106–7, 120–22; and Anthony Burton, 'Design history and the history of toys: Defining a discipline for the Bethnal Green Museum of Childhood', *Journal of Design History*, vol.10, no.1, 1997, pp 1–21.
13. 'Exhibition of Her Majesty's Jubilee Presents at the Bethnal Green Museum', *The Graphic*, vol.37, no.952, 25 February 1888, p.1. For the later display of the Indian gifts, see Julius Bryant, 'Royal gifts from Victorian India: The new display in the Durbar Room at Osborne House', *Collections Review, English Heritage*, vol.4, 2003, pp 116–124.
14. *Forty-third Report of the Department of Science and Art*, London, 1896, p.xlviii.
15. Wilk, 1996, pp 14–15.
16. *Précis of the Board Minutes of the Department of Science and Art, 1 January 1884 to 31st December 1887*, London, 1892, p.95; Joshua Dixon nominal file MA/1/D1240/1–2, V&A Archive.
17. W. Shaw Sparrow, 'The Dixon Bequest at Bethnal Green, I: The foreign oil paintings', *The Magazine of Art*, vol.15, 1892, pp 158–64; R. Jope-Slade, 'The Dixon Bequest at Bethnal Green, II: The water-colours', *The Magazine of Art*, vol.15, 1892, pp 243–8.
18. 'Editorial', *Modern Society*, 8 September 1906, pp 11–12, quoted in Black, 2000, p.33.
19. Anon., 'Art connoisseurs at the East-End, and the portrait of Sir Richard Wallace', *The Graphic*, vol.7, no.117, 19 April 1873, pp 362, 368–9.
20. Octavia Hill, *Homes of the London Poor*, London, 1875, p.45.
21. Anon., 'Bethnal Green Museum', *Eastern Argus*, 24 March 1883, quoted in Black, 2000, p.76.
22. Burton, 1999, p.227.

# Part V

## Chapter 14

1. The marble bust of Marie Antoinette in the Jones Collection (1126-1882) was acquired as dating from around 1785 but is now 19th century and unattributed. See Victoria and Albert Museum, *Catalogue of the Jones Collection*, 3 vols, London 1922–4, vol.2, no.404.
2. *Handbook of the Jones Collection in the South Kensington Museum*, London, 1884, pp vii–viii. The handbook is based on recollections by Jones's manservant. For Jones's will, see Department of Science and Art, 1889, pp 20–21. See also: John Jones nominal file MA/1/J721, V&A Archive; Denys Sutton (ed.), *The Jones Collection, Victoria and Albert Museum*, reprint of *Apollo* special issue, vol.95, no.121, March 1972.
3. Jones's finest Italian Renaissance painting is the *Virgin and Child* by Carlo Crivelli, V&A: 492-1882.
4. *Thirtieth Report of the Department of Science and Art*, London, 1882, p.504.
5. The room is V&A: 1736 to E-1869; the harp V&A: 8531-1863. M.D. Wyatt, Art Referee report RF 8475/69. See also: Emilia, Lady Dilke, *French Furniture and Decoration in the Eighteenth Century*, London, 1901, chapter 4 (pp 55–71): 'Rousseau de la Rottière and the boudoirs of the marquise de Sérilly and of the Queen'. Photograph by Isabel Agnes Cowper, V&A: 72372.
6. Gilbert R. Redgrave, 'The Jones Bequest to the South Kensington Museum', *The Art Journal*, 1883, pp 124–8.
7. Quoted in Baker and Richardson, 1997, p.66.
8. Anon., 'The Jones Collection at the South Kensington Museum', *The Builder*, vol.43, no.2081, 23 December 1882, pp 799–800.
9. Quoted in Somers Cocks, 1980, p.83.
10. *The Times*, 12 December 1882, V&A Press Cuttings, MA/49/2/57 (April 1882–June 1883), p.47.
11. Anon., 'The Jones Collection', *The Saturday Review*, 23 December 1882, pp 823–4, V&A Press Cuttings, MA/49/2/57 (April 1882–June 1883), p.47.
12. Department of Science and Art, *List of the Bequests and Donations*

*... for the South Kensington Museum ...*, London, 1889, p.20. See also: Anon., *Handbook of the Jones Collection in the South Kensington Museum*, London, 1884, p.12.

13. *Twenty-second Report of the Department of Science and Art*, London, 1875, p.413. The suite was deaccessioned by the V&A in 1952. Most of Barker's collection was sold at Christie's, 6–11 June 1874, where the museum's acquisitions included a table (381-1874; the first piece by David Roentgen to be purchased by a public collection), a Sèvres plaque (397-1874) and a copy by Sèvres of the Medici vase (396-1874). At the same sales the National Gallery purchased several of its 20 paintings from Barker's collection, including major works by Botticelli and by Piero della Francesca. In 1855 Barker had sold to Baron Meyer de Rothschild for Mentmore Towers the 'Marie de Medici Cabinet' (W.64-1977). See Harry Dougall, 'Guest blog: Alexander Barker and the South Kensington Museum', 2017, V&A website: www.vam.ac.uk/blog/network/guest-post-alexander-barker-and-the-south-kensington-museum.

## Chapter 15

1. C.M. Kauffmann, 'Ionides, Constantine Alexander', *Oxford Dictionary of National Biography*, 2004, https://doi.org/10.1093/ref:odnb/14441.
2. Edward Morris, *French Art in Nineteenth-Century Britain*, New Haven and London, 2005, pp 142–3 notes mid-century French paintings in the Townshend and Dixon bequests to the South Kensington Museum (1868, 1886) and in the loan of the Wallace Collection at Bethnal Green Museum (1872–5), and that regional museums already had some contemporary foreign paintings. The display of Hugh Lane's collection at the National Gallery in 1917 was the turning point for London.
3. Constantine A. Ionides nominal file MA/1/1246, V&A Archive. Basil S. Long, *Catalogue of the Constantine Alexander Ionides Collection, vol.I: Paintings in Oil, Tempera and Water-Colour Together with Certain of the Drawings*, London, 1925. See also: Mark Evans and Melanie Vandenbrouck, '"A Collection as a man of taste would wish to live with it": Constantine Ionides at home', *Decorative Arts Society Journal*, vol.36, no.2, 2012, pp 22–45; Charles Harvey and Jon Press, 'The Ionides family and 1 Holland Park', *Decorative Arts Society Journal*, vol.18, 1994, pp 2–14. For views of the galleries of paintings at the South Kensington Museum, see Bryant, 2017, p.83.

# Part VI

## Chapter 16

1. Sir George Donaldson nominal file MA/1/D1359/1–2, V&A Archive; New Art Furniture Collection MA/2/N3, V&A Archive. See also: Aslin, 1983 and Neiswander, 1988.
2. Baker and Richardson, 1997, pp 354–7. The present writer recalls the Art Nouveau furniture still there, with the Rodin sculptures, *c*.1978, after the Bethnal Green Museum had been relaunched as the V&A Museum of Childhood in 1974.
3. Quoted by Christopher Marsden in Bryant, 2011, p.256, cats 338, 339.
4. Lewis F. Day, 'The "New Art" at South Kensington', *Manchester Guardian*, June 1901, V&A Press Cuttings, MA/49/2 (June 1901–June 1903), p.1.
5. Both quoted in Neiswander, 1988, pp 311–12. See also Somers Cocks, 1980, pp 88–9 and Burton, 1999, p.169.
6. Anon., 'L'Art Nouveau at South Kensington', *The Architectural Review*, vol.10, no.58, September 1901, pp 104–5.
7. Burton, 1999, p.168 quotes Cecil Harcourt Smith: 'it was a general rule to acquire nothing that was less than fifty years old'. Neiswander, 1988, p.313 notes 'acquiring modern furniture ... was not resumed until the 1950s'.
8. 'The Victoria and Albert Museum, Art Division: Report of the Committee on Re-arrangement', 1908, pp 19–20, quoted in Christopher Wilk, 'Collecting the twentieth century', in Baker and Richardson, 1997, p.346.
9. Quoted in Catherine Lampert, 'The Rodin Donation of 1914', in *Rodin*, exh.cat., Royal Academy of Arts, London, 2007, p.287; Claudine Mitchell, 'The gift to the nation: Rodin at the V&A', in Claudine Mitchell (ed.), *Rodin: The Zola of Sculpture*, Leeds, 2003, pp 183–200. See also: Jennifer Hawkins, *Rodin Sculptures*, London, 1975: and Alicia Robinson, 'The Rodin Gift', in Hunt, 2020 pp 112–25.

## Chapter 17

1. 'Mr George Salting', *The Times*, 14 December 1909, p.10. See also: 'The Salting Collection', *The Times*, 25 December 1909, p.6.
2. George Salting nominal file MA/1/S293, V&A Archive; *Victoria & Albert Museum Guides: The Salting Collection*, London, 1911; C.H. Read, 'George Salting', *The Burlington Magazine*, vol.16, no.83, February 1910, pp 250–51; Stephen Coppel, 'George Salting (1835–1909)', in Antony Griffiths (ed.), *Landmarks in Print Collecting: Connoisseurs and Donors at the British Museum since 1753*, London, 1996, pp 189–210; Motture, 2001.
3. R.H. Benson in 1914, quoted in Stephen Coppel, 'George Salting', *Oxford Dictionary of National Biography*, 2006, https://doi.org/10.1093/ref:odnb/35920.
4. 'The Salting Collection', *The Times*, 15 December 1909, p.10.
5. 'The Salting Bequest: The display at South Kensington', *The Times*, 23 March 1911, p.7.
6. Anon., [Hugh Parker Mitchell], *The Red Line Guide to the Victoria and Albert Museum, South Kensington, (Art Collections, Main Building)*, London, 1905.
7. Deed of Gift, George Salting nominal file MA/1/S293, V&A Archive.
8. 'Mr Salting's Spitzer purchases', *The Times*, 14 July 1893, p.15.
9. C.H. Read, 'George Salting', *The Burlington Magazine*, vol.16, no.83, February 1910, pp 249–50.
10. 'The charge of stealing curios', *The Times*, 25 February 1904; 'Central Criminal Court', *The Times*, 2 March 1904, V&A Press Cuttings MA/49/2/101.
11. David M. Currie nominal file MA/1/C3543/1–2, V&A Archive.
12. Captain H.B. Murray nominal file MA/1/M3230, V&A Archive. Murray specified that his bequest should be kept 'as one collection, and to be known as Capt. H.B. Murray's Bequest'.

## Chapter 18

1. J.P. Morgan nominal file MA/1/M2725/1–14 Parts 3 and 4: 'Loans and Gifts, Inventory of Objects' dated 11 November 1905; Part 8 (1912–36): full lists of loans for withdrawal, V&A Archive.
2. B. Rackham, 'The Pierpont Morgan Gift of ancient stained glass to the British nation', *The Landmark*, vol.2, July 1922, pp.461–5. See also: Paul Williamson, *Medieval and Renaissance Stained Glass in the Victoria and Albert Museum*, London, 2003, pp 11–12. Morgan's stained-glass collection is V&A: C.37-108-1919.
3. See also: Linda Horvitz Roth (ed.), *J.P. Morgan, Collector: European Decorative Arts from the Wadsworth Atheneum*, exh.cat., Wadsworth Atheneum, Hartford, Connecticut, 1987; Flaminia Gennari-Santori, 'Medieval art for America: The arrival of the J. Pierpont Morgan collection at the Metropolitan Museum of Art', *Journal of the History of Collections*, vol.22, no.1, 2010, pp 81–98; Flaminia Gennari-Santori, 'An art collector and his friends: John Pierpont Morgan and the globalization of medieval art', *Journal of the History of Collections*, vol.27, no.3, 2015, pp 401–11.
4. Dover House, Roehampton, was purchased by the London County Council in 1920 and demolished in 1921 to create a housing estate.
5. Jean Strouse, *Morgan: American Financier*, New York, 1999, p.490.
6. Colin Simpson, *The Partnership: The Secret Association of Bernard Berenson and Joseph Duveen*, London, 1987, pp 108–9.
7. Charles E. Pierce Jr and Jean Strouse, *The Morgan Library: An American Masterpiece*, New York and London, 2000, p.26.
8. Julius Bryant, *Kenwood: Paintings in the Iveagh Bequest*, London, 2003, pp 12, 15, 16, 94, 290, 371.
9. Cecil Smith became Cecil Harcourt Smith by the time of his knighthood in 1909 and added a hyphen in 1928 when he was appointed Surveyor of the King's Works of Art.
10. J.H. Fitzhenry to Cecil Harcourt Smith, 29 June 1909, typescript copy of letter, J.P. Morgan nominal file MA/1/M2725 Part 7 (January to October 1909), V&A Archive.

11. Wilhelm von Bode, *Collection of J. Pierpont Morgan: Bronzes of the Renaissance and Subsequent Periods*, Paris, 1910. Rackham succeeded the French dealer Alexandre Imbert (who had sold Morgan hundreds of works of art) but the maiolica project was stopped by Jack Morgan before publication.
12. Clare Browne, Glyn Davies and M.A. Michael (eds), *English Medieval Embroidery: Opus Anglicanum*, New Haven and London, 2016, p.146; Flaminia Gennari Santori, *The Melancholy of Masterpieces: Old Master Paintings in America 1900–1914*, Milan, 2005, p.112.
13. Read began work at the South Kensington Museum under the Keeper of the National Art Library, Robert Soden Smith. There he met A.W. Franks who hired him as a private assistant, age 17.
14. Dora Thornton, *A Rothschild Renaissance: Treasures from the Waddesdon Bequest*, London, 2015. For a comparable collection from the Gilded Age, on public display today, see Bryant and Ekserdjian, 2002.
15. V&A Press Cuttings, MA/49/2/88 (October 1912–May 1913), p.125. Strouse, 1999, p.642 notes Read and Fitzhenry both wrote letters to *The Times* defending Morgan's decision to take his collections to New York.
16. J.P. Morgan to the Director of Education, South Kensington, 18 June 1904, J.P. Morgan nominal file MA/1/M2725 Part 4 (1903–4), V&A Archive.
17. Bishop William Lawrence, writing in 1914, quoted in Francis Henry Taylor, *Pierpont Morgan as Collector and Patron, 1837–1913*, New York, 1957, pp 24–5.
18. Quoted in Strouse, 1999, p.504.
19. C.P. Clarke to Mr Ogilvy, 21 June 1905, J.P. Morgan nominal file MA/1/M2725 Part 5 (1905–May 1906), V&A Archive. For 13 Princes Gate, see: Taylor, 1975, pp 21–28; Horvitz Roth, 1987, pp 31–33; and Strouse, 1999, pp 502–50.
20. Horvitz Roth, 1987, p.41 n.5.
21. Jean Strouse, 'J. Pierpont Morgan, financier and collector', reprint of *The Metropolitan Museum of Art Bulletin*, Winter 2000, pp 33–5.
22. Quoted in Baudis, 2009, p.4.
23. C.H. Wylde, 'Mr J.H. Fitzhenry's collection of early French pâte-tendre', *The Burlington Magazine*, vol.7, no.27, June 1905, pp 188–97.
24. Obituary, *The Times*, 18 March 1913.
25. J.H. Fitzhenry nominal file MA/1/F677/1–22, V&A Archive.
26. Memorandum, Cecil Harcourt Smith to the Secretary of the Board of Education, 20 July 1910, quoted in Motture, 2001, p.42.
27. V&A: 334:1-6-1903.
28. V&A: 531-1905. See Williamson, 1996, pp 19, 114–15.
29. Wylde, 1905.
30. *A Series of Twelve Delft Plates Illustrating the Tobacco Industry: Presented by J.H. Fitzhenry, Esq. to the Victoria and Albert Museum*, London, 1907.
31. Cecil Harcourt Smith to J.H. Fitzhenry, 7 June 1910, J.H. Fitzhenry nominal file MA/1/F677/13, V&A Archive.
32. Anon., 'Victoria and Albert Museum', *Museums Journal*, vol.12, February 1913, pp 252–3.
33. *The Times*, 29 August 1913, V&A Press Cuttings, MA/49/2. For obituary see *The Times*, 18 March 1913, MA/49/2/88, p.123.
34. Cecil Harcourt Smith to Sir Wyndham Murray, 3 October 1913, transcript of letter, J.H. Fitzhenry nominal file MA/1/F677/21, V&A Archive.
35. V&A: A.2:1 to 33-2007, made around 1890–1909 by Sangiorgi after the original, *c.*1629, in the Piazza della Santissima Annunziata, Florence.

## Chapter 19

1. Victoria and Albert Museum, 1901.
2. Cook and Wedderburn, 1903–12, vol.34, p.249.
3. The armour (V&A: 362 to R-1865) was part of a diplomatic gift from Shogun Tokugawa Iemochi to Queen Victoria in 1860.
4. Board of Education, *Victoria and Albert Museum*, London, 1908, pp 4–5.
5. Lewis Foreman Day, 'How to make the most of a museum', *Journal of the Society of Arts*, vol.56, 1908, pp 146–60.
6. Burton, 1999, pp 162–3.
7. Board of Education, *The Victoria and Albert Museum (Art Division), Report of the Committee of Re-arrangement*, London, 1908, p.22.
8. Bryant, 2011, pp 151–3, 284.
9. Bryant, 2019, pp 41–3.
10. For a concise discussion of the influence of Riegl's book *Stilfragen* (1893) on European museums, see Burton, 1999, pp 158–62.
11. Claude Phillips, 'Art notes: More about South Kensington', *The Daily Telegraph*, 31 July 1909, in V&A Press Cuttings, MA/49/2 (November 1908–March 1910), pp 13–14.
12. Quoted in Physick, 1982, p.244.
13. Anon., 'The Wembley Conference, 1924', *Museums Journal*, vol.24, no.3, 1924–5, pp 54–60, 59.
14. V&A Archive, MA/47/1/1 for discussion in 1924 over the future use of the court for loans, and MA/49/1/3 for discussion at the museum's Advisory Council, 25 January 1934.
15. Andrew Rosen, *Rise Up, Women!*, London, 1973, p.234, cited in Timothy Wilson, 'A Victorian artist as ceramic-collector: The letters of Henry Wallis, Part 2', *Journal of the History of Collections*, vol.14, no.2, 2002, pp 231–69.
16. Anon., 'Notes and news', *Museums Journal*, vol.12, no.8, 1912–13, pp 252–3. See also: Burton, 1999, pp 166–7, 170.
17. V&A Archive, Ed.84/107.
18. V&A Archive, V. & A. M. Advisory Council, Reports no.4, *Report on the Principal Deficiencies in the Collections of the Victoria and Albert Museum &c., adopted by the Advisory Council at a meeting held on 13th February 1914*, V&A Archive, Ed.84/106.
19. The Salting Collection filled rooms 128–131 and 144–145; Jones, 66–69; Sheepshanks, 96–98; Ionides, 92–93; Dyce and Forster, 84; Schreiber, 139; and Murray, 100.
20. Victoria and Albert Museum, *General Guide to the Collections*, London, 1914, p.4. Cecil Harcourt Smith's introduction is reprinted from *Guide to the Victoria and Albert Museum, South Kensington*, London, 1909, pp 3–4.

## Chapter 20

1. *Royal Commission on National Museums and Galleries: Oral Evidence, Memoranda and Appendices to the Interim Report*, London, 1928, para.2879.
2. Eric Maclagan, memorandum, January 1932, PRO, Ed.84/114, *Minutes of the Advisory Council*, quoted in Physick, 1982, p.268.
3. Leigh Ashton, '100 years of the Victoria & Albert Museum', *Museums Journal*, vol.53, 1953, p.47.
4. Edmund de Waal's *Signs and Wonders* (2009) comprising 425 porcelain pots on a red circular shelf, is a permanent installation high above the grand entrance beneath the dome (gallery 141).

# Further Reading

Aslin, Elizabeth, 'Sir George Donaldson and "Art Nouveau" at South Kensington', *The Decorative Arts Society Journal*, vol.7, 1983, pp 9–14.

Baker, Malcolm and Richardson, Brenda (eds), *A Grand Design: The Art of the Victoria and Albert Museum*, London, Baltimore and New York, 1997.

Barringer, Tim, 'The South Kensington Museum and the Colonial Project', in Barringer and Flynn, 1998, pp 11–27.

--- and Flynn, Tom (eds), *Colonialism and the Object: Empire, Material Culture and the Museum*, London and New York, 1998.

Baudis, Macushla, 'Tea parties at the Museum: The collector J.H. Fitzhenry and his relationship with the V&A', *V&A Online Journal*, no.2, Autumn 2009, pp 1–16.

Bettley, James (ed.), *The Art of the Book*, London, 2001.

Black, Barbara J., *On Exhibit: Victorians and Their Museums*, Charlottesville and London, 2000.

Bonython, Elizabeth and Burton, Anthony, *The Great Exhibitor: The Life and Work of Henry Cole*, London, 2003.

Bryant, Julius (ed.), *Art and Design for All: The Victoria and Albert Museum*, London and Munich, 2011.

Bryant, Julius, '"The progress and present condition of Modern Art": Fine art at the 1862 Exhibition', in *The Decorative Arts Society Journal*, vol.38: *Almost Forgotten – The International Exhibition of 1862*, 2014, pp 58–81.

---, 'Word and image: The evolution of the Victoria and Albert Museum's library', in Watson, James and Bryant, 2015, pp 10–25.

---, *Designing the V&A: The Museum as a Work of Art (1857–1909)*, London, 2017.

---, *Creating the V&A: Victoria and Albert's Museum (1851–61)*, London, 2019.

---, 'Prince Albert, South Kensington, and the Victorian taste for Renaissance Revival ceramic architectural decoration', in Susan Weber et al (eds), *Majolica Mania: Transatlantic Pottery in England and the United States 1850–1915*, 3 vols, New York and London, 2021, vol.1, pp 70–95.

--- and Ekserdjian, David (eds), *Decorative Arts from the Wernher Collection*, London, 2002, reprint of *Apollo* special issue, vol.155, no.483, May 2002, pp 3–54.

--- and Weber, Susan (eds), *John Lockwood Kipling: Arts & Crafts in the Punjab and London*, New Haven and London, 2017.

Bud, Robert, 'Infected by the bacillus of science: The explosion of South Kensington', in Morris, 2010, pp 11–39.

Burton, Anthony, *Vision and Accident: The Story of the Victoria and Albert Museum*, London, 1999.

---, 'Cultivating the first generation of scholars at the Victoria and Albert Museum', *Nineteenth-Century Art Worldwide*, vol.14, no.2, summer 2015: http://www.19thc-artworldwide.org/summer15/burton-on-first-generation-of-scholars-at-victoria-and-albert-museum.

Carey, Moya, *Persian Art: Collecting the Arts of Iran for the V&A*, London, 2017.

Caygill, Marjorie and Cherry, John (eds), *A.W. Franks: Nineteenth-Century Collecting and the British Museum*, London, 1997.

Clunas, Craig, 'China in Britain: The Imperial Collections', in Barringer and Flynn, 1998, pp 41–51.

Conforti, Michael, 'The idealist enterprise and the applied arts', in Baker and Richardson, 1997, pp 23–47.

Conway, Moncure Daniel, *Travels in South Kensington*, London, 1882, revised version of 'The South Kensington Museum', *Harper's New Monthly Magazine*, vol.51, 1875, pp 486–503; 649–66.

Coombes, Annie, *Reinventing Africa: Museums, Material Culture and Popular Imagination in Late Victorian and Edwardian England*, New Haven and London, 1994.

Davies, Helen, *Sir John Charles Robinson, (1824–1913): His Life as a Connoisseur and Creator of Public and Private Collections*, PhD thesis, University of Oxford, 1992.

---, 'John Charles Robinson's work at the South Kensington Museum Part I . . . 1853–62', *Journal of the History of Collections*, vol.10, no.2, 1998, pp 169–88; 'Part II. From 1863 to 1867: consolidation and conflict', vol.11, no.1, 1999, pp 95–115.

Eastlake, Charles Locke, *Hints on Household Taste in Furniture, Upholstery and Other Details*, London, 1868, fourth edition, London, 1878, republished London, 1969.

Eatwell, Ann, 'The Collector's or Fine Arts Club 1857–1874: The first society for collectors of the decorative arts', *The Decorative Arts Society Journal*, vol.18, 1994, pp 25–30.

---, 'Private pleasure, public beneficence: Lady Charlotte Schreiber and ceramic collecting', in Clarissa Campbell Orr (ed.), *Women in the Victorian Art World*, Manchester, 1995, pp 125–45.

---, 'Borrowing from collectors: The role of the loan in the formation of the Victoria and Albert Museum and its collection (1852–1932)', *The Decorative Arts Society Journal*, vol.24, 2000, pp 21–8.

Elsner, John and Cardinal, Roger (eds), *The Cultures of Collecting*, London, 1994.

Faulkner, Rupert and Jackson, Anna, 'The Meiji period in South Kensington: The representation of Japan in the Victoria and Albert Museum, 1852–1912', in O.R. Impey and M. Fairley (eds), *Meiji No Takara: Treasures of Imperial Japan*, London, 1995, pp 152–95.

Grant, Alistair and Patterson, Angus, *The Museum and the Factory: The V&A, Elkington and the Electrical Revolution*, London, 2018.

Guest, Montague John (ed.), *Lady Schreiber's Journals; Confidences of a Collector . . . 1869 to 1885*, 2 vols, London and New York, 1911.

Haskell, Francis, 'The British as collectors', in Gervase Jackson-Stops (ed.), *The Treasure Houses of Britain: Five Hundred Years of Private Patronage and Art Collecting*, exh.cat., National Gallery, Washington D.C., 1985, pp 50–59.

Haworth-Booth, Mark, 'The dawning of an age: Chauncy Hare Townshend – eyewitness', in Mark Haworth-Booth (ed.), *The Golden Age of British Photography, 1839–1900*, New York, 1984, pp 11–21.

Heleniak, Kathryn Moore, 'Victorian collections and British nationalism: Vernon, Sheepshanks and the National Gallery of British Art', *Journal of the History of Collections*, vol.12, no.1, 2000, pp 91–107.

———, 'An art patron and his housemaid: William Mulready's portrait of John Sheepshanks', *The British Art Journal*, vol.13, no.3, 2012/13, pp 69–80.

Herrmann, Frank, *The English as Collectors*, London and New York, 1972, revised edition, London and New Castle, Delaware, 1999.

Hill, Katrina, 'Collecting on campaign: British soldiers in China during the Opium Wars', *Journal of the History of Collections*, vol.25, no.2, 2013, pp 227–52.

Hinson, Benjamin, 'A very Victorian tourist: The Reverend Greville John Chester and 19th-century textile collecting at the Victoria and Albert Museum', in Antoine De Moor, Cäcilia Fluck and Petra Linscheid (eds), *Explorers, First Collectors and Traders of Textiles from Egypt of the 1st millennium AD*, Veurne, 2021, pp 12–21.

Hobhouse, Hermione, *The Crystal Palace and the Great Exhibition: Art, Science and Productive Industry – A History of the Royal Commission for the Exhibition of 1851*, London, 2002.

Hobsbawm, E.J., *The Age of Capital 1848–1875*, London, 1975.

———, *The Age of Empire 1875–1914*, London, 1987.

House of Commons, *First Report from the Select Committee on Museums of the Science and Art Department, with the Proceedings of the Committee*, London, 1897; *Second Report . . .* , London, 1898.

Hunt, Tristram (ed.), *The Lives of the Objects: Collecting Design*, London, 2020.

Israel, Kali, *Names and Stories: Emilia Dilke and Victorian Culture*, Oxford and New York, 1999.

Jackson, Anna, 'Art and design: East Asia', in John M. Mackenzie (ed.), *The Victorian Vision: Inventing New Britain*, exh.cat., Victoria and Albert Museum, London, 2001, pp 297–313.

James, Elizabeth, *The Victoria & Albert Museum: A Bibliography and Exhibition Chronology, 1852–1996*, London, 1998.

Jones, Alexandra, 'Ethiopian objects at the Victoria and Albert Museum', *African Research & Documentation*, no.135, 2019, pp 8–24: https://research-repository.st-andrews.ac.uk/bitstream/handle/10023/19933/A_Jones_Ethiopian_Collections_at_the_VA_2019_SCOLMA_African_Research_No.135_1.pdf?sequence=1&isAllowed=y.

Kauffmann, C.M., *Victoria and Albert Museum, Catalogue of Foreign Paintings, Vol.I: Before 1800*, London, 1973; *Vol.II: 1800–1900*, London, 1973.

Kerr, Robert, *The Gentleman's House; or, How to Plan English Residences, from the Parsonage to the Palace*, London, 1864.

Lidchi, Henrietta and Allan, Stuart (eds), *Dividing the Spoils: Perspectives on Military Collections and the British Empire*, Manchester, 2020.

Loftie, W.J., *A Plea for Art in the House*, London, 1876.

MacGregor, Arthur, 'Collectors, connoisseurs and curators in the Victorian age', in Caygill and Cherry, 1997, pp 6–33.

Maniz, Vera, 'From Portugal to England: John Charles Robinson in the Portuguese art market', *Journal of the History of Collections*, vol.32, no.1, March 2020, pp 91–102.

Minter, Alice, 'Jewish collectors made an important contribution to the fledgling museum', *Apollo*, vol.191, no.687, June 2020, pp 17–18.

Mitter, Partha and Clunas, Craig, 'The Empire of Things: The engagement with the Orient', in Baker and Richardson, 1997, pp 221–73.

Morris, Peter J.T. (ed.), *Science for the Nation: Perspectives on the History of the Science Museum*, London, 2010.

Motture, Peta, '"None but the finest things": George Salting as a collector of bronzes', *The Sculpture Journal*, vol.5, 2001, pp 42–61.

National Art Library, *A Diversity of Gifts: Four Benefactors of the National Art Library*, London, 1995.

Neiswander, Judith A., '"Fantastic malady" or competitive edge? English outrage at Art Nouveau in 1901', *Apollo*, vol.128, no.321, November 1988, pp 310–13.

———, *The Cosmopolitan Interior: Liberalism and the British Home, 1870–1914*, New Haven and London, 2008.

Owens, Susan, '"Straight lines are a national want": South Kensington and art education reform', in Bryant, 2011, pp 74–81.

Patterson, Angus and Trusted, Marjorie, *The Cast Courts*, London, 2018.

Pearce, Nick, 'Collecting, connoisseurship and commerce: An examination of the life and career of Stephen Wootton Bushell (1844–1908)', *Transactions of the Oriental Ceramic Society*, vol.70, 2005–6, pp 17–25.

Persson, Helen, 'Collecting Egypt: The textile collection of the Victoria and Albert Museum', *Journal of the History of Collections*, vol.24, no.1, March 2012, pp 3–13.

Physick, John, *The Victoria and Albert Museum: The History of Its Building*, London, 1982.

Redgrave, Richard, *A Catalogue of the Pictures, Drawings, & Etchings in the British Fine Art Collections Deposited in the New Gallery, at South Kensington; Being for the Most Part the Gift of John Sheepshanks, Esq.*, London, 1857.

Reitlinger, Gerald, *The Economics of Taste, Volume II: The Rise and Fall of Objets d'Art Prices Since 1750*, London, 1963.

Robson, Susanna, 'Emilia Francis Strong Pattison, Lady Dilke (1840–1904)', in National Art Library, 1995, pp 18–25.

Scarce, Jennifer M., 'Persian art through the eyes of nineteenth-century British travellers', *Bulletin (British Society for Middle Eastern Studies)*, vol.8, no.1, 1981, pp 38–50.

Schuhmacher, Jacques, 'Museums and restitution', in Tim Clack and Mark Dunkley (eds), *Cultural Heritage in Contemporary Conflict*, London, 2022.

Shalloo, Eoin, 'Chauncy Hare Townshend (1798–1868)', in National Art Library, 1995, pp 2–9.

Somers Cocks, Anna, *The Victoria and Albert Museum: The Making of the Collection*, Leicester, 1980.

Stanley, Tim (ed.), with Mariam Rosser-Owen and Stephen Vernoit, *Palace and Mosque: Islamic Art from the Middle East*, London, 2004.

Stourton, James and Sebag-Montefiore, Charles, *The British as Art Collectors: From the Tudors to the Present*, London, 2012.

Stronge, Susan, 'Colonel Guthrie's collection: Jades of the Mughal era', *Oriental Art*, vol.39, no.4, Winter 1993–4, pp 4–13.

––– (ed.), *The Art of the Sikh Kingdoms*, London, 1999.

–––, *Tipu's Tigers*, London, 2009.

Taylor, Nicholas, 'South Kensington and the Science and Art Department', in F.H.W. Sheppard, (ed.), *Survey of London*, vol.38, *The Museums Area of South Kensington and Westminster*, London, 1975.

Thomas, Abraham, 'The Orient and ornament at the South Kensington Museum', in Bryant, 2011, pp 91–7.

Trusted, Marjorie, 'In all cases of difference adopt Signor Riaño's view: Collecting Spanish decorative arts at South Kensington in the late nineteenth century', *Journal of the History of Collections*, vol.18, no.2, 2006, pp 225–36.

Tucker, Paul, '"Responsible outsider"': Charles Fairfax Murray and the South Kensington Museum', *Journal of the History of Collections*, vol.14, no.1, 2002, pp 115–37.

Turner, Jane and White, Christopher, edited by Mark Evans, *Dutch & Flemish Drawings in the Victoria and Albert Museum*, 2 vols, London, 2014.

*V&A Archive Research Guide*: *Donors, Collectors and Dealers Associated with the Museum and the History of its Collections*: https://www.vam.ac.uk/info/archives.

Victoria and Albert Museum, *List of the Bequests and Donations to the South Kensington Museum, now called The Victoria and Albert Museum, completed to 31st December 1900*, London, 1901.

Victoria and Albert Museum (Art Division), *Report of the Committee of Re-arrangement . . . presented to Parliament by Command of His Majesty*, London, 1908.

Wainwright, Clive, *The Romantic Interior: The British Collector at Home, 1750–1850*, New Haven and London, 1989.

–––, 'Shopping for South Kensington: Fortnum and Cole in Florence 1858–1859', *Journal of the History of Collections*, vol.11, no.2, 1999, pp 171–85.

–––, Gere, Charlotte and Sargentson, Carolyn (eds), 'The making of the South Kensington Museum: III, Collecting abroad; IV, Relations with the trade: Webb and Bardini', *Journal of the History of Collections*, vol.14, no.1, 2002, pp 45–61, 63–78.

Watson, Rowan, James, Elizabeth and Bryant, Julius (eds), *Word & Image: Art, Books and Design from the National Art Library*, London, 2015.

Whitehead, Christopher, *The Public Art Museum in Nineteenth Century Britain: The Development of the National Gallery*, Aldershot, 2005.

Wilk, Christopher (ed.), *Western Furniture 1350 to the Present Day in the Victoria and Albert Museum*, London and New York, 1996.

–––, 'Collecting the twentieth century', in Baker and Richardson, 1997, pp 345–53.

Williamson, Paul (ed.), *European Sculpture at the Victoria and Albert Museum*, London, 1996.

Wilson, Timothy, 'A Victorian artist as ceramic-collector: The letters of Henry Wallis', *Journal of the History of Collections*, part 1: vol.14, no.1, 2002, pp 139–59; part 2: vol.14, no.2, 2002, pp 231–69.

–––, 'Charles Drury Edward Fortnum', *Oxford Dictionary of National Biography*, 2004, online: https://doi.org/10.1093/ref:odnb/9951.

Yallop, Jacqueline, *Magpies, Squirrels & Thieves: How the Victorians Collected the World*, London, 2011.

# Acknowledgements

THIS LATEST VOLUME in the V&A Nineteenth Century series is made possible thanks to the support of the V&A Americas Foundation through the generosity of the Dr Lee MacCormick Edwards Charitable Foundation. The V&A is greatly indebted to the family and estate of the art historian, the late Dr Lee MacCormick Edwards, represented by Tina Albright, and to Lucy Myers, managing director of Lund Humphries, whose enterprise brought the idea of the series to the museum. For encouragement, editorial counsel and project management I am most grateful to Lucy Myers and at the V&A to Tom Windross, Head of Content, supported by Coralie Hepburn and Karen Fick. At Lund Humphries the expertise and understanding of Sarah Thorowgood, Abigail Grater and Alex Batten was much appreciated.

Clive Wainwright, the V&A's former curator of Victorian art and design, worked as a senior research fellow on a book, to be entitled *The Making of the Collections of the South Kensington Museum*. After his sudden death, aged 57, in 1999 four chapters were edited by Charlotte Gere and Carolyn Sargentson and published posthumously in a special issue of the *Journal of the History of Collections* (2002). Dr Wainwright's torch as historian of the V&A was not the only one burning brightly. In *The Victoria and Albert Museum: The Making of the Collection* (1980) Anna Somers Cocks covered the formation of the collections in the curatorial departments. John Physick, the V&A's deputy director, published his PhD thesis on the history of the building in 1982. Anthony Burton's *Vision and Accident: The Story of the Victoria and Albert Museum* (1999) and biography of Henry Cole, written with Elizabeth Bonython, *The Great Exhibitor* (2003) introduced many colourful and intriguing characters and raised key issues of museum management and collections development. Burton's whimsical but telling title for his wide-ranging account of the V&A may have been intended as a reply to the landmark exhibition catalogue, *A Grand Design* (1997) edited by Malcolm Baker and Brenda Richardson. Since then, several V&A curators, especially Ann Eatwell, and others beyond the V&A, have published important studies on the collectors (see Further Reading). For a more comprehensive history of the museum the reader is referred to these books and articles, none of which is superseded by this volume.

The origins of this book date back to my first publication on the V&A, begun in 1982, when I was most fortunate in being able to discuss my draft texts with Clive Wainwright, John Physick, Michael Kauffmann, Peter Thornton, Simon Jervis, Robert Skelton, Malcolm Baker, Deborah Swallow, Paul Williamson and other (now legendary) keepers and curators at that time. Within the Word and Image Department, since 2005, I have enjoyed working with Nazek Ghaddar and with many curators, librarians and archivists, especially my brilliant management team over 16 years, now dispersed: Bernadette Archer, Martin Barnes, Ana Debenedetti, Douglas Dodds, Mark Evans, Martin Flynn, Olivia Horsfall Turner, Elizabeth James, Christopher Marsden, John Meriton, Keith Percival, Gill Saunders, Rowan Watson, Gerry White and Vicky Worsfold. Elsewhere in the museum I am especially grateful to my colleagues in the Asia Department, to Angus Patterson, to Jacques Schuhmacher and to Andrew Mellon Professorial Fellow Arthur MacGregor, for reading and commenting on my draft chapter on imperial collecting. Their own publications will be found in Notes and Further Reading. Sir Ian Blatchford, director of the Science Museum Group, kindly read chapter 12 in draft. Any errors that remain are mine alone. For welcoming the book proposal and for their more recent support I am grateful to Antonia Boström and Joanna Norman. Peter Kelleher and Sarah Duncan kindly undertook new photography. All the staff of the National Art Library and of the V&A Archive could not have been more helpful. At home, once again I thank Dr Barbara Bryant for understanding why I had to write it all in my own time. I am grateful to Dr Max Bryant and Dr Sophie Pitman for their encouragement, and I would like to dedicate this book to their beautiful daughter, Stella who, like all new babies, will someday inherit the V&A.

J.B.

# Index

NOTE: *italic page numbers* indicate figures;
page numbers followed by n refer to notes.

First published in 2022 by Lund Humphries
in association with V&A Publishing

Lund Humphries
Huckletree Shoreditch
Alphabeta Building
18 Finsbury Square
London, EC2A 1AH
UK
www.lundhumphries.com



ISBN: 978-1-84822-618-0

Supported by the V&A Americas Foundation through the generosity of the Dr Lee MacCormick Edwards Charitable Foundation.

A Cataloguing-in-Publication record for this book is available from the British Library.



Editor Abigail Grater
Designed by Nigel Soper
Set in SwiftEF and Scala Sans
Printed in Belgium

**Front cover:**
CHARLES E. EMERY, *The Entrance to the South Kensington Museum*, 1872, watercolour (detail). V&A: 7927:1.

**Back cover:**
[also fig.58] CHARLES FAIRFAX MURRAY, *Maiolica from the Collection of Charles Fairfax Murray*, *c.*1886, watercolour. V&A: D.287-1890.